A Handbook of Literary and Critical Terms

I. H-Shihan

ATLANTIC
PUBLISHERS & DISTRIBUTORS (P) LTD

Published by
ATLANTIC
PUBLISHERS & DISTRIBUTORS (P) LTD
7/22, Ansari Road, Darya Ganj, New Delhi-110002
Phones : +91-11-40775252, 40775214, 23273880, 23275880
Fax : +91-11-23285873
Web : www.atlanticbooks.com
E-mail : orders@atlanticbooks.com

Branch Office
5, Nallathambi Street, Wallajah Road, Chennai-600002
Phones : +91-44-48531784, 28411383
E-mail : chennai@atlanticbooks.com

Printed in India at Nice Printing Press, A-33/3A, Site-IV, Industrial Area, Sahibabad, Ghaziabad, U.P.

To My
Students and Readers

Preface to the Second Edition

The first edition of the book came into existence in 2005 and, in spite of many shortcomings and typographical errors, the book was received well among students and teachers. The very next year Imprint Publishers found it commercially lucrative and also ethically appropriate to issue a secret edition/ reprint of the same book (2006). However, in this new and revised edition published by the Atlantic Publishers and Distributors (P.) Ltd., as usual, some new entries, including a few from the Indian critical school, are included and some old entries have been given fresh attention. For this, the consulted sources are the old books referred to in the Preface of the first edition and also several websites, such as Wikipedia, etc. I tried my best to eliminate all types of error. At the end of the entries, wherever possible, a short bibliography is included for further reference. I gratefully thank the Atlantic Publishers and Distributors (P.) Ltd., New Delhi, for showing interest and publishing the book. Since the change of publisher was a requirement, the slight change in the name of the book too was found inevitable. In place of *An Imprint Handbook of Select Literary and Critical Terms*, now it is simply *A Handbook of Literary and Critical Terms*. I am aware that some of the terms may look foreign in a book of literary terms, but they are relevant; literature has enough flexibility to incorporate such terms from other subjects every now and then, however, any suggestion and/or complaint regarding the book, its merits or demerits, will be highly appreciated and they can be mailed to: <ihshihan@gmail.com>. Hope, the book will satisfy the needs of the reader will.

I. H-Shihan

Preface to the First Edition

While discussing some of the university prescribed literary terms with my undergraduate students, I felt that a book, specially designed for them, was much needed. It was not that there were no good books on the subject; but seen from the students' point of view, I supposed, there were some troublesome areas that needed special address: lack of uniformity was one such problems—the terms they had to look at carefully were often either too briefly or too elaborately discussed to serve their purpose; and high price of good books was another worrying concern for many of them.

These factors primarily motivated me to take up the project. First, I asked my students to join hands in making it a kind of departmental exercise. But it appeared, as preoccupied they had been with so many curricular and extra-curricular things, it was outside their priority. I, therefore, had to invest time myself alone for the job. Initially, I began with only the prescribed literary and critical terms, and later thought it would be unwise to keep myself limited to those small numbers in case I really wanted to make it a book. The main poser at the time was to decide what to put in and what not. The theory of the golden mean solved the problem—I decided in favour of the essential needs of students, scholars, even teachers to some extent, and excluded many items for the orismologist. I have tried to be more relevant than scholarly here and included those items—new and old, English, a few French, German, and American—that students of literature, English Literature specially, would frequently come across or habitually need to refer back to.

As usual with the kind of compilation no questions of originality generally arise. I have liberally borrowed from encyclopaedias, including Encyclopaedia

Britannica, books of MH Abrams, JT Shipley, Chris Baldick, Ross Murfin and Supriya M Ray, Peter Barry, Wilfred L Guerin & others, Julian Wolfreys and Baker, CW Watson, Robert JC Young and other known as well as not-so-known authors and editors. Any inadequacy in the content of the book that may appear to the reader is wholly mine.

I. H-Shihan

Contents

A

Accent A tonal emphasis placed upon a syllable in pronunciation, a particular stress or effort of the voice on certain syllables of words. The English language customarily follows a pattern of *accented* (stressed) and *unaccented* (unstressed) syllables associated with each word. There are three main types of accent: [1] *word accent* or *etymological accent*, emphasis or lack thereof on syllables of words in ordinary speech; [2] *rhetorical accent* or *sense accent/stress*, weight placed on syllables or words according to their locations and importance in a sentence; and [3] *metrical accent/stress*, placed on syllables as metrical requirement in a verse line. Words consisting of two or three syllables have, as a rule, only one accent. Longer words often may contain two accented syllables, e.g. *accidental* (the first and the third syllables accented: *ác*-ci-*dén*-tal). In such cases, the first accent is normally weaker than the second. The more prominent accent of the two (the second one here) is therefore called the *primary accent/stress* and the less prominent (the first one) is the *secondary accent/stress*. Normally, there is a constant tendency in the English language to throw the *primary accent* backward as far as possible. The meter of a poem either strengthens this natural pattern or varies it by operating its own stress pattern. If metrical stress works against the normal accent, it is called *wrenched* or *forced accent*, a feature very common in ballads. [Cf. foot, scansion]

Ref: D Crystal & R Quirk, *Systems of Prosodic and Paralinguistic Features in English* (1964). John Hollander, *Rhymes Reason: A Guide to English Verse* (1981). ME Beckman, *Stress and Non-Stress Accent* (1986).

Acronym <Greek *acron*, tip, end + *nyma*, name> An abbreviation by which a word is formed from the initial letters in a phrase or expanded terminology, usually long or difficult one. For instance, AIDS is an acronym for 'Acquired Immune Deficiency Syndrome' in which only the initial letters of the four words have been taken to form the new coinage. Acronyms are quite common in bureaucracy, in business, in politics and in areas of high-tech and specialized fields. Other examples include OPEC (Organization of Petroleum Exporting Countries), Radar > RADAR (Radio Detection And Ranging), and Laser > LASER (Light Amplification by Stimulated Emission of Radiation), etc. Generally, acronyms first appear with periods to indicate the abbreviations and later as the new formation becomes widespread, the periods vanish and eventually the capitalization also falls away as the word enters common usage: e.g. L.A.S.E.R.> LASER> laser. [Cf. anagram, jargon]

Acrostic <French *Acrostiche*, topmost, at the tip of the verse> A mediaeval model of composing a poem or a stanza in a particular fashion. The word *acrostic* is both noun and adjective. It refers to the style and the result is known as *acrostich*. In an acrostic pattern the first letters of a few successive lines spell out the title of the poem or the motif or even a high value message involved in the work. Normally the pattern involves the first stanza of the poem or a minor part of a dramatic work. It also may be just an *alphabetical acrostic* in which the first letters of the lines give all the letters of a language alphabetically. The practice may not be very artistic; but often used as a mnemonic device to aid memory retrieval. Examples of such practice abound in old texts like *The Book of Lamentations* and in some of the Psalms in the Hebrew language. In mediaeval literature the practice was common where they usually served to highlight the name of the poem, the poet or his patron or a prayer to a saint, etc. In the English language, Ben Jonson, Edgar Allan Poe and Lewis Carroll are among the best known writers who have often tried this trick. Here is an example from Ben Jonson's *Volpone*:

V*olpone, childlesse, rich, faines sicke, despaires,*
O*ffers his state to hopes of several heirs,*
L*ies languishing; His Parasite receives*
P*resents of all, assures, deludes: Then weaves*
O*ther cross-plots, which ope' themselves, are told.*
N*ew tricks for safety, are sought; they thrive: When, bold,*
E*ach tempts th' other againe, and all are sold.*

Jonson, thus, in the "Argument" section, at the very outset, gives a short summary and also the name of the play in a seven line *acrostich*—Volpone. The device of acrostic pattern Ben Jonson probably borrowed from the classical poet Plautus. Similarly when the significant word or phrase is spelt out by the last letters of each line, it is known as *telestich*. However, acrostic can be complex or double also in which the first letters and the last letters of lines vertically form two meaningful words on both the sides. Paul Hansford's poem "Stroud" is an interesting example of a complex acrostic poem in which both the acrostich and the telestich spell out the name of a market—Stroud.

Act A major division of dramatic action of a play. Classical plays are normally divided into five major divisions or acts (and again *act* into several *scenes*). A new act coincides with a fresh development of the action of a play. Elizabethan dramatists, including Shakespeare, have faithfully followed this Roman tradition. In the influential pyramidal outline of dramatic structure, as advanced by the German playwright Gustav Freytag (1816-1895) in *Die Technik des Dramas* (1863), the five divisions, i.e. *exposition, complication, climax, anti-climax* and *denouement* or *catastrophe*, more or less, coincide with the five customary acts. By the end of the 19th century, the traditional five-act drama was abandoned and later dramatists like Henrik Ibsen, Bernard Shaw, John Galsworthy and Anton Chekhov reduced the number of acts to four or three. A one-act play is a step forward toward further reduction. Finally some modern playwrights have dispensed with acts altogether and have remained satisfied with scenes only. The Nigerian playwright Wole Soyinka, in his *A Dance of Forests* (1663), has totally done away with even scenes. Only stage settings denote the change in locale in the play. However, his play is divided into two parts that may serve as acts or scenes.

Aestheticism/Estheticism A 19th century literary movement of a group of artists who believed in the theory called "Art for art's sake" in opposition to the belief that art must be morally or practically valuable. The two key figures of the English aesthetic movement were Walter Pater (1839-1894) and Oscar Wilde (1854-1900). It is believed that the movement was a strong reaction against prevailing utilitarian social philosophies what were commonly perceived as the ugliness and 'philistinism' of the industrial age. Its roots lie in the German theory outlined by Emmanuel Kant (1724-1804) that aesthetic contemplation is indifferent both to morality and utility of the beautiful. The vanguards of the movement include such authors as Charles-Pierre Baudelaire (1821-1867), Gustave Flaubert (1821-1880), Théophile Gautier (1811-1872), Stéphane Mallarmé (1842-1898), Edgar Allan Poe (1809-1849), Algernon Swinburne (1837-1909), and Maz Beerbohm (1872-1956), etc. The American-born painter James McNeill Whistler (1834-1903) raised the movement's ideal of the cultivation of refined sensibility to its highest point. Cyril, a character in Oscar Wilde's play, *The Decay of Lying* (1889), frankly propagates the author's view that art "never expresses anything but itself." The philosophy, i.e. a literary or artistic work is an end in itself, was later adopted by proponents of the New Criticism school in the 1920s. This notion, also known as *autotelism*, insists that an artwork is "complete in itself" and can exist without any external reference to it. Since the theory stresses on aesthetic quality of a piece of art rather than its didactic potential, the followers of Pre-Raphaelitism, whose poems show an unconditional appreciation for colour, shape and beauty, in a way, too are adherents of this philosophy.

However, some schools, including the Marxist, vehemently opposed the basics of the movement. Bernard Shaw too openly declared that for art's sake alone he would not take the toil of writing even a single line. Some other critics of aestheticism included William Morris and John Ruskin. In Russia, Leo Tolstoy questioned the value of art divorced from morality. Some American *moral-aesthetic critics*—Edmund Wilson, Kenneth Burke, Malcolm Cowley, Morton D Zabel, Newton Arvin and FO Matthiessen, etc tried a balance between aesthetic concerns and social or moral issues. They were interested both in analyzing and in evaluating literary works, i.e. how a literary work was constructed and also to place it in a larger social or moral framework.

Ref: AC Bradley, "Poetry for Poetry's Sake", *Oxford Lectures on Poetry* (1909). William Gaunt, *The Aesthetic Adventure* (1945). Frank Kermode, *Romantic Image* (1957). Lionel Lambourne, *The Aesthetic Movement* (1996).

Aesthetics/Esthetics A branch of philosophy that studies the principles of beauty and taste, especially in different art forms. The English word *aesthetics* is derived from Greek term *aesthetikos* or *aisthanomai*, meaning sensory perception or to perceive (hence *anesthetic* is a medicine that decreases sense perceptions). Alexander Baumgarten in his *Reflections on Poetry* (1735) first used the term. Aesthetics was one of the two branches of the study of knowledge, i.e. for the study of sensory experience coupled with feeling, which Baumgarten argued was a different kind of knowledge from idea studied by logic. In its scope aesthetics is broader than philosophy of art. It does not deal with nature and value of the art alone but also with those reactions to natural objects that find expression in the language of the beautiful and the ugly. Now, aesthetics as a subject has come to refer to a set of investigations concerning beauty, their values as well as modes of cognition related to a piece of art. However, in terms of the concept and its interpretation there are ample difference of opinions and hence such variations as Western aesthetics, Marxist aesthetics, Black aesthetics and Eastern aesthetics, etc. have proliferated in the world of criticism. [Cf. aestheticism]

Ref: MM Bakhtin, *Questions of Literature and Aesthetics* (1975). Ayn Rand, *The Romantic Manifesto: A Philosophy of Literature* (1971). Satya Dev Chaudhuri, *Glimpses of Indian Poetics* (2002).

Affective/Sympathetic Fallacy A method of judgment of literary works. For many, especially those who have advocated for New Criticism, judging the merit or demerit of a literary work on the basis of its psychological effect on the reader, known as affective fallacy, is a defective way of criticism. William K Wimsatt and Monroe C Beardsley first used the term. The error or fallacy results from shifting the importance of the work from its inner qualities as a created object to its effect upon the reader: "The Affective Fallacy is a confusion between the poem and its results..., a special case of epistemological skepticism" which "begins by trying to derive the standard of criticism from the psychological effects of the poem and ends in impressionism and relativism" with the result that "the poem itself, as an object of specifically critical judgment, tends to disappear." To be precise, in this form of criticism the focus of attention is moved from what the *art* is to its effect upon the reader—how it *moves* a reader emotionally or, as a literary work, what it *does* upon the reader. The school of New Criticism, accordingly, does not approve of Aristotle's theory that tragedy evokes "pity and fear" to restore an emotional balance. However, Reader-response Criticism that recognizes the reader's authority in making a sense of texts has attested the theory of affective fallacy; for it is a reader's privilege to appreciate a text as it appears to him. For him, therefore, it is not a fallacy.

Ref: Robert Con Davis and Ronald Schleifer, *Contemporary Literary Criticism: Literary and Cultural Studies* (1989). WK Wimsatt &

Monroe Beardsley, "The affective fallacy", *The Verbal Icon: Studies in the Meaning of Poetry* (1954). William Keast, "Review of the Verbal Icon." *Modern Language Notes* 8 (1956).

Alamkara An Indian aesthetic term referring to the embellishing and decorative factors that add to the charm and/or quality of poetry. In Indian classical literature and criticism *alamkara* has always been given much importance as part of an artist's craftsmanship. In its modern meaning it comes very close to many of the aspects dealt with in English *Figures* of Speech. In this sense *Rupaka* (metaphor), *Anuprasa* (alliteration), *Upama* (simile) and *Slesa* (paronomasia), etc are all alamkaras, which decorate both the body and soul of poetry. However, the term has wider sense in which, according to Dandin, "the definition of alamkara is that every kind of characteristic which provides any sort of brilliance to a piece of poetry." Thus the concept includes both poetry and its exposition. On the basis of this notion Indian poetics is often called *Alamkara-sastra*. Bhamaha (6th-7th CE), the author of *Kavyalankara*, is regarded as the first eminent Indian scholar of the Alamkara School.

It may be noted that both Hindu and Buddhist philosophies were, by nature, integrated and comprehensive in all aspects they dealt with. In them both body and mind appeared to be under the same laws. They were not exclusive of each other, but invariably interdependent. The tradition of Patanjala, too, spoke of such mental operations as *bhava* and *rasa* purely in terms of bodily experience. Bharata (3rd BCE-1st CE) extensively borrowed from both the *Yoga-Sutra* and *Charaka-Samhita*, none of which looked at body and mind as distinctly separate entities. *Alamkara* theory, too, thus was as integrated philosophy of art. The modern reader, very largely influenced by Descartes, has learnt to look at body and mind, or say, form and content, as two distinct entities. [Cf. *Rasa*]

Ref: Dr. V Raghavan, *Studies on Some Concepts of the Alamkara Sastra* (2009). Kapil Kapoor, *Literary Theory: Indian Conceptual Framework* (1994). RK Sen, *Aesthetic Enjoyment* (1966). Satya Dev Choudhury, *Glimpses of Indian Poetics* (2002).

Alexandrine/Iambic Hexameter An iambic line of six feet, originally a popular French metrical form of the heroic verse structure set by Tort's *Roman d'Alexandre* (c.1200 CE) and was revived by Pierre de Ronsard (1524-1585). The term *Alexandrine* is possibly derived from the fact that certain 12th century French poems on Alexander the Great were written in this particular metrical scheme. This leading meter in French poetry consists basically of a line of twelve syllables with major stresses on the sixth (which precedes the medial caesura) and on the last syllable and a *secondary accent* in each half line. Since six syllables make a normal breath group and the secondary stresses can be on any other syllable in the line, the Alexandrine is an elastic form, adjustable to a wide range of subjects. Its structural standard is based on stress according to sense and thereby making it suitable for simple or complex emotion, narrative description and pompous, patriotic or heroic sentiment.

In English versification, an Alexandrine or iambic hexameter contains six *primary accents*, rather than the two major and two *secondary accents* of the French tradition. Though it was introduced into England in the 16th century and was adapted to German and Dutch poetry in the 17th century, its success outside France was limited. This meter has sometimes been used throughout a whole poem, as in Michael Drayton's *Poly-Olbion* (1612-22); but it is more generally employed to complete certain stanzas with shorter iambic verses. The standard Spenserian stanza is often finally rounded up with an Alexandrine. Pope's *Essay on Criticism* offers this exemplary comment on the Alexandrine: "A needless Alexandrine ends the song/ That, like a wounded snake, drags its slow length along." Some other examples of this metrical category are—"Was Knighthood's dauntless deed, and Beauty's matchless eye" (Scott), "The dew was falling fast the stars began to blink" (Wordsworth) and "She knelt, so pure a thing, so free from mortal taint" (Keats).

Ref: Raymond Macdonald Alden, *English Verse: Specimen Illustrating its Principle and History* (1903).

Allegory A Figure of Speech and a literary style of reference that suggests parallel actions, meanings or abstract ideas irrespective of the literary form employed—poetry, fiction or drama. Usually allegory uses recognizable types, symbols and narrative patterns to indicate that the meaning of a text is to be found not in the text alone but also in a body of cultural and conventional ideas and beliefs or in an extra-literary context. John Bunyan's *Pilgrim's Progress* (1678) and Tennyson's *Idylls of the King* (1842-85) may exemplify this technique. Two types of allegories—*political/historical* and *abstract*—were quite common during the middle ages. It continued to be used as a narrative device even today. William Golding's *Lord of the Flies* (1954) succeeds brilliantly in its intention of creating an allegory on the state of civilization, but on the surface level the novel is an adventure story with a narrative line as straightforward as those found in children's comics. Essentially metaphoric in style, allegory is distinguished from metaphor and parable as an extended story that may sustain interest for the story on the surface level alone. The additional meaning and actions that an allegory offers are an extra attraction. [Cf. beast fable, fable]

Ref: Angus Fletcher, *Allegory: The Theory of the Symbolic Mode* (1964). Morton W Bloomfield, Ed. *Allegory, Myth and Symbol* (1981). Stephen Greenblatt, *Allegory and Representation* (1981).

Alliteration A Figure of Speech, the use of which produces a rhyme-pattern inside a verse line by repeating similar sounds in a sequence of words. When the initial consonant sound is alliterated, it is called *initial rhyme* or *head rhyme*. Its use was the most outstanding feature of the Anglo-Saxon and old German poetry. Even modern poets often consciously or unconsciously make use of it and the use is mostly limited to creating powerful musical effects. An example from Pope—"Puffs, powders, patches, bibles, billet-doux"—may give an idea of the effect alliteration may produce. In the second half of the 14th-century England the general increase or surge in *alliterative verse* is often described as *alliterative revival*. Many think that a surge of regionalism or nationalism encouraged northern poets to return to the older alliterative type of poetry during the middle and late-1300s. During this time, *Piers Plowman, Sir Gawain and the Green Knight* and other important medieval poems were written which exemplify profusion of alliterations. However, when lines crowded with alliterations, like "Peter Piper picked a peck of pickled peppers," that are difficult for smooth pronunciation, are often called *tongue twisters*. [Cf. consonance, versification]

Ref: Richard Lanham, *A Handlist of Rhetorical Terms* (1991).

Allusion <*Ludere,* to play or jest> A Figure of Speech based on similarity, a brief and indirect reference to a person, place, thing or thought of historical, cultural and literary significance. Its brief or implicit reference to something outside the text is a matter of rhetorical device, a kind of play with the reader's knowledge; and there lies the relevance to its etymology. For example: "Now we clap/ Our hands, and cry, 'Eureka', it is clear" (Byron)—takes the reader to the exclamation of Archimedes when he found out how to test the purity of king Hiero's gold crown. Keats's "Ode to the Grecian Urn" is rich in allusions:

Sylvan historian, who canst thus express
A flowery tale more sweetly than our rhyme:
What leaf-fringed legend haunts about thy shape
Of deities or mortals, or of both,
In Tempe or the dales of Arcady?

The use of allusions—*Sylvan, Tempe* and *dales of Arcady*—no doubt, enriches or broadens the impact of the statement. However, the device presupposes the reader's knowledge of the intended reference. While discussing Ngugy wa Thiongo's novel, the critics, Bill Ashcroft and others, show how the use of allusion can help to create a distance between the text and the reader who is not familiar with what is depicted or the vocabulary used: "Allusion can perform the same function of registering cultural distance in the post-colonial text.... An example of this is Ngugy wa Thiongo's novel *A Grain of Wheat*...."

Ref: Preminger & Brogan, *The New Princeton Encyclopaedia of Poetry and Poetics* (1993). Allan H Pasco, *Allusion: A Literary Graft* (1994).

Ambiguity <Latin *Ambiguus,* double meaning> A style often known as *affective ambiguity.* It is a state of having more than one possible meaning; usually resulting from something being stated in such a way as denies a fixed judgment. In poetry specially, it functions to enhance the richness and refinement of language and to "imbue it with a complexity that expands the literal meaning of the original statement." Blake's lines—"Piping songs of pleasant glee/ On a cloud I saw a child"—for example; contain a clear ambiguity as there is no answer as to who is really piping, the child or the speaker. However, the richness and complexity of literature often tend to rely on ambiguity as it opens up new dimensions. Line nine of Spenser's *Amoretti* sonnet 67: "There she beholding me with mylder looke" too is slightly charged with ambiguity. It is not clear who makes the conquest possible by becoming milder, the hunter or the hunted, until the uncertainty is resolved in the eleventh line. Gerard Manley Hopkins' poem, *The Bugler's First Communion*, exemplifies almost all the types of ambiguity in varying degrees. "The Sick Rose", a short poem by William Blake, is full of ambiguities: The reader does not know for sure what "crimson bed of joy" means there; neither can he be sure about the clarification of "dark secret love". The ambiguous nature of such phrases allows readers to explore for deeper meanings of the poem. Often known as *plurisignation* or multiple meanings, ambiguity has become a major issue in interpreting poetry. William Empson defended ambiguity as a merit rather than fault. His work happens to be one of the most powerful critical works of the early 20th century. Empson's affirmation is that uncertainty or the overlapping of meanings in the use of a word enriches a poetic text. The critical school known as New Criticism is somehow indebted to this method of textual analysis. Empson further validated his critical method in his later works. The basis of Empson's analyses is based on the view that poetry derives its emotional undertone primarily from the "ambiguities and complexities of its cognitive and tonal meanings." [Cf. ambivalence]

Ref: William Empson, *Seven Types of Ambiguity* (1930), *Some Versions of Pastoral* (1935) & *The Structure of Complex Words* (1951).

Ambivalence <Latin *ambi,* duality + *valentia*, vigour> An attitude reflecting the coexistence of opposing feelings or uncertainty. In psychology the word has special significance and is used for all sorts of conflicts that involve disagreeing factors in the human mind—a crisis moment, very much like Hamlet's "To be or not to be" situation. The word was introduced into psychology by the Swiss psychiatrist, Paul Eugen Bleuler (1857-1939). Sigmund Freud reserved the word for conflicts involving love and hate. Carl Jung used the word to apply to images as well as to instincts and his concept of ambivalence dovetails cleanly with his ideas of complexes and of compensation.

In recent literary criticism the term has gained some weight; it indicates more than one possible attitude being displayed by the writer towards a character, theme and idea, etc. Specially in terms of postcolonial studies the term is more meaningful. Conrad has often been severely criticized for his racist discourse; but his ambivalence in *The Heart of Darkness* gives him some defence. His attitudes and feelings about the wilderness, the African people and even the white society is quite complex; and the complexity arises mostly from the literary use of imagery of various types and a layered narrative. The ambivalence perhaps postpones a definite answer or decision. In Rhys' case, her novel *Wide Sargasso Sea* reveals the mutual trauma of the colonised and the colonizer. Walcott's poetry elucidates dualities of the formerly colonised subjects towards the European cultural legacy he has inherited in part—ambivalence which drives his mind and fuels the building up of a new, plural cultural identity in the aftermath of colonialism. Historicizing the concept for aesthetic experience, thus, highlights the essential pattern of ambivalence in modern subjectivity. [Cf. ambiguity]

Ref: Christine Gallant, *Shelley's Ambivalence* (1989). Homi Bhabha, *The Location of Culture* (1994). Lisa Mendelman, "Ambivalence and Irony: Gendered Forms in Interwar America", *Arizona Quarterly: A Journal of American Literature, Culture and Theory,* Vol. 71, No. 4 (2015).

American Renaissance A very fruitful American literary period beginning from the 1830s and lasting to the end of the Civil War (1865). This period gave birth to an acute sense of Americanness in literary activities. What is commonly known as American Renaissance is the emergence of a national literature, which examined American experience from various points of view. Americans attempted at freeing themselves from the British cultural legacy and in place of British models American models began to evolve and perfect themselves. In this context the Transcendentalists provided a good example; they reinterpreted the British Romanticism in the context of American scenario.

The main figures that lent active hands in configuring American Renaissance were such New Englander doyens as Mark Twain, Herman Melville, Walt Whitman and the like. A new spirit inspired them all and their achievements reached a great magnitude. Partly this was because they were in some way influenced by the democratic concepts that in 1829 triumphed in Andrew Jackson's (1767-1845) swearing in as President and also because in this American Romantic period of emphasis upon native scenes and characters in literature they put much of America into their creative works. Particularly full of vibrant touches were the works of two groups of American humorists who appeared between 1830 and 1867. One group created several down-east Yankee characters that used common-sense arguments to comment upon the socio-political scenario. The most representative of this group were Seba Smith, James Russell Lowell and Benjamin Shillaber. In the old Southwest, such writers as Davy Crockett, Augustus Baldwin Longstreet, Johnson Hooper, Thomas Bangs Thorpe, Joseph Baldwin, and George Washington Harris drew lively pictures of the cheerful frontier and showed interest in the common man that was a part of Jacksonian democracy.

Ref: FO Mattheissen, *American Renaissance: Art and Expression in the Age of Emerson and Whitman* (1968). David S Reynolds, *Beneath the American Renaissance: The Subversive Imagination in the Age of Emerson and Melville* (1988).

Anachronism <Greek *ana,* back + *chronos,* time> An unintentional or deliberate disregard of chronology or sense of time while narrating or projecting something literary. Ordinarily, it is most frequently found in works of imagination that rest on historical narratives. The reference to a clock striking time in Shakespeare's *Julius Caesar* is a classic example of anachronism. Artists often tend to depict old characters in terms of their own time, culture and nationality; and thus the Virgin has been pictured both as an Italian peasant and as a Flemish housewife; Alexander the Great appeared on the French stage down to the time of Voltaire in the full costume of Louis XIV. In painting a classic example of anachronism is the long table in *The Last Supper* (1498) by Leonardo da Vinci. This kind of table was unknown at the time and place of Jesus Christ. Anachronism is also introduced deliberately for a burlesque or satiric effect, such as Mark Twain's writing of a Connecticut Yankee visiting King Arthur's court. [Cf. anachrony and archaism]

Ref: Anthony Grafton, *Forgers and Critics: Creativity and Duplicity in Western Scholarship* (1990).

Anachrony An alteration of time sequence, contrasted with a traditional linear storyline. Narratologist Mieke Bal has termed this as "chronological deviations." This anachronous narrative technique has plot construction that recounts events without a chronological sequence. This discrepancy between the order of events in a story and the order in which they are presented in the plot may be termed as anarchy in terms of time. Anachrony has three distinct types: [1] *analepsis,* the insertion of scene that has taken place in the past, known as flash-back in the cinematic language; [2] *prolepsis*, insertion of scene that preview future events, also known as flash-forward and [3] *ellipsis*, a gap indicating that something has been omitted. [Cf. anachronism and archaism]

Anacrusis An extra *unaccented syllable* inserted at the beginning of a line in which the metrical pattern would normally not accommodate it. For example: "*Wĕ* | | lóok bĕ | | fóre ănd | | áf-tĕr." This extra unaccented syllable—'we'—is usually not counted as part of the metrical scheme. Normally the pattern follows a trochaic versification. The reverse is *acephalous,* a metrical verse line that lacks the first expected syllable. Examples of anacrusis are often found in the old English poetry and it is not unusual in later iambic pentameter versifications as well. In the same fashion, in a musical phrase, one (or more notes) preceding the first downbeat is called anacrusis. [Cf. catalexis]

Anadiplosis/Doubling Back A Figure of Speech evident by doubling or folding up of words. The rhetorical repetition of one or several words, specifically, repetition of a word that ends one clause and begins the next is anadiplosis: "Men in great place are thrice servants: servants of the sovereign or state; servants of fame; and servants of business"—Francis Bacon. A modern example from Frank Zappa, the American musician film-maker goes: "Information is not knowledge, knowledge is not wisdom, wisdom is not truth, truth is not beauty, beauty is not love, love is not music and music is the best."

Anagnorisis/Recognition <Greek *discovery*> A reference to some startling revelation that suddenly leads the protagonist to a changed situation, may be a moral crisis. His/her journey from ignorance to knowledge leads him/her to a new context in which entire scheme of things requires readjustment of a kind never conceived of previously. It is discussed by Aristotle in *Poetics* as an essential part of the plot of a tragedy, although it occurs in comedy, epic and, at a later date, the novel as well. As part of his discussion of peripeteia, Aristotle defines anagnorisis as "a change from ignorance to knowledge, producing love or hate between the persons destined by the poet for good or bad fortune." Anagnorisis usually involves disclosure of the true identity of a person previously unknown, e.g. a father recognizes a stranger as his son or vice versa. One of the finest examples occurs in Sophocles' *Oedipus Rex* when a messenger reveals to Oedipus his true birth and Oedipus recognizes his wife Jocasta as his mother, the man he slew at the crossroads as his father, Laius, and himself as the tainted sinner who found himself responsible for bringing disaster on Thebes. This kind of recognition is artistically more satisfying because it is accompanied by a peripeteia, the shift in fortune from good to bad that moves on to the tragic catastrophe. An anagnorisis is not always accompanied by a peripeteia, as in *The Odyssey,* when Alcinous, ruler of Phaeacia, has his minstrel entertain a shipwrecked stranger with songs of the Trojan War, and the stranger begins to weep and reveals himself as none other than Odysseus. Aristotle has discussed of several kinds of anagnorises employed by dramatists. The simplest kind, used "from poverty of wit," is recognition by scars, birthmarks or tokens. More attractive are those that arise logically or unobtrusively from incidents of the plot. Similarly, the plot of many novels involves critical recognitions and discoveries. For example, Pip's discovery, in Charles Dickens' *Great Expectations* that Magwitch rather than Miss Havisham has been his secret benefactor, remakes the psychological and social positions of the character. However, in classical tragedy, anagnorisis is not just a kind of surprise element; it accelerates the play toward the catastrophe and facilitates the desired tragic objective.

Ref: Aristotle's *Poetics*. HDF Kitto, *Greek Tragedy* (1954). Northrop Frye, *Fables of Identity: Studies in Poetic Mythology* (1963). http//:www.britannica.com

Anagram A word or phrase formed by transposition of letters of another word or phrase. It is the result of rearranging the letters of a word or phrase to produce a new word or phrase, as *heart* is an anagram of *earth.* Anagram is often a game of words popular with learners of certain age groups. Thus *neat* and *leg* are anagrammatic productions from *elegant*. Anagrams have often been considered merely an exercise of one's ingenuity, but sometimes writers use anagrams to conceal proper names or messages. Samuel Butler's *Erehwon* (> *nowhere* rearranged) is in fact an example of anagram. Anagrams are in themselves a recreational activity, but they also make up part of many other games, puzzles and game shows, etc. William Drummond of Hawthornden, in "On the Character of a Perfect Anagram", tried to lay down some basic rules for permissible substitutions. William Camden provided a definition of 'Anagrammatisme' as "dissolution of a name truly written into his letters, as his elements, and a new connection of it by artificial transposition, without addition, subtraction or change of any letter, into different words, making some perfect sense applyable to the person named." [Cf. acronym]

Ref: Henry Benjamin Wheatley, *Of Anagrams: A Monograph Treating of Their History from the Earliest Ages to the Present Time* (1862).

Anapaest A tri-syllabic metrical foot/ measure in which one *accented syllable* is preceded by two unaccented ones:

"Lĭke ă chíld | | frŏm thĕ wómb, | |
lĭke ă ghóst | | frŏm thĕ tómb," or,

'Twăs thĕ níght | | bĕ-fŏre Chríst | |
măs, whĕn áll | | thrŏugh thĕ hóuse

Nŏt ă créa | | tŭre wăs stír | | ĭng,
nŏt év | | ĕn ă móuse".

Lord Byron has extensively employed this pattern in his poem "The Destruction of Sennacherib". Usually anapaests tend to be used in a rising rhythmic scheme. Anapaestic words are less common in English. They are, however, more commonly found in other languages, such as French. In the English language anapaestic trimeter and anapaestic tetrameter are more common whereas anapaestic hexameter is very rare. Rhythmically seen, anapaestic meter has a particular sing-song resonance often closely reminding one of the sounds of a trotting horse.

Anaphora A Figure of Speech, meaning 'carrying back' in Greek. It is the repetition of a word or phrase at the beginning of successive phrases, clauses or lines: "We shall not flag or fail. We shall go on to the end. We shall fight in France, we shall fight on the seas and oceans, we shall fight with growing confidence and growing strength in the air.... We shall never surrender"—Churchill. In contrast, an *epiphora* is repeating words at the end of the sentence. The combination of anaphora and epiphora results in *symploce*. Anaphora as a rhetorical device has some poetic and emotive value as it adds rhythm to a number making reading a smooth journey and an easier to remember affair. Perhaps the most striking and outstanding example of this rhetoric is Martin Luther King's (Jr.) well-known delivery: "I have a dream" that occurs some eight times throughout the speech. [Cf. antistrophe]

Anastrophe <Greek *anastrophê*, a turning back or about> A Figure of Speech, in which transposition of normal word order occurs, most often found in Latin in the case of prepositions and the words they control. Anastrophe is a form of hyperbaton: "The helmsman steered, the ship moved on; / yet never a breeze up-blew..."—Coleridge. Another example from *The Rime of the Ancient Mariner* will clarify how the usual English syntactical order of subject-verb-object is changed to one of object-subject-verb order. It is deliberately altered to draw some extra poetic force from the line: "He holds him with his skinny hand,/ 'There was a ship', quoth he./ 'Hold off! unhand me, grey-beard loon!'/ Eftsoons his hand dropt he".

Ref: Herbert Weir Smyth, *Greek Grammar* (1920).

Angry Young Men A group of British writers of the 1950s, often known as the "new university wits", whose works voiced anger and disenchantment with social traditions. The term, originally coined by Leslie Allen Paul, refers to the prevailing all-pervasive yet unfocussed resentment and frustration that was characteristic of the post-war youth in England. The angry young men were a new breed of intellectuals, mostly from the working class or the lower middle-class origin. Although some had been educated at universities—a few from even Oxford—they shared a candid derision for the British class system, its pedigreed families and the university elitists. They showed an equally uninhibited disdain for the drabness of the post-war welfare state, and their writings articulated anger and frustration as the post-war reforms failed to meet exalted aspirations for a genuine change. Common to their works is an antihero who resists the rotten social order and strives for personal integrity. The term has been used to describe writers like Kingsley Amis, John Osborne, Colin Wilson, Harold Pinter and John Wain. Other writers included in the group are the novelists John Braine, Alan Sillitoe, the playwrights Bernard Kops and Arnold Wesker. Kenneth Tynan's observation on John Osborne's play, *Look Back in Anger* (1956), reflects much of the malady of the time and the unfocussed reaction of the youth to it: "*Look Back in Anger* presents post-war youth as it really is... the drift towards anarchy, the instinctive leftishness...the casual promiscuity, the sense of lacking a crusade worth fighting for...." However, the term was ordinarily applied to a big, 'disjointedly united' group, i.e. the writers of this group did not generate a united movement. On the contrary there were several disagreements among them which often resulted in direct or indirect attack and counterattack. [Cf. problem plays, kitchen-sink drama, sociological novel]

Ref: Colin Wilson, *The Angry Years* (2007). Humphrey Carpenter, *The Angry Young Men: A Literary Comedy of the 1950s* (2002). William Van O'Connor, *The New University Wits and the End of Modernism* (1963).

Antagonist/Villain A character in a play or story, often the second most outstanding person. He/she is known as antagonist or villain and his function in a play is almost specific against the protagonist. His career turns out to be as one who constantly tries to frustrate the protagonist or hero/heroine. The idea of the antagonist as an evil force is rooted in all traditional legends and myths. Even in the Bible, Satan has been entrusted with the responsibility of an antagonist. The simple moral scheme that pitted virtues against vices in the interludes was never entirely submerged in more sophisticated drama, and Vice, the tricky villain of the *morality play,* survives in different shapes and proportions in later works.

Shakespeare's Aaron, in *Titus Andronicus,* is an early example of a complex antagonist who relishes every opportunity to create mayhem and misery. He devises plots to kill Bassianus and then frames Titus' sons Quintus and Martius for the murder. Before his death he gives a speech lamenting his failure to wreak even more disaster during his lifetime. In *Hamlet*, Claudius is a hypocrite, but he is successful in his role. A very shrewd villain as he is, his deception equals that of an accomplished politician. He is not dramatically shown as being in any way unworthy of his position; he upholds his part with dignity. He is a smiling villain and is not exposed until the catastrophe. The jealous Hamlet heaps abuse upon him, but Shakespeare makes Claudius the self-controlled murderer. Thus, theatrically, the situation is much more exciting.

The introduction of an antagonist or villain is embedded in the very concept of dramatic art itself. Since a dramatic plot is basically conceived upon the conflict between two opposing forces, the requirement of an antagonist is a natural choice. Both antagonist and protagonist are the archetypal characters always present in a narrative, play or a movie. Either in a concrete or an abstract form, every play or story needs at least one antagonist against the protagonist. Hamlet has Claudius before him, Antonio has Shylock; so has Maurya, the sea—all are situated to frustrate the protagonists. However, in those works in which the protagonist himself is an incarnation of evil force, the antagonist represents the good. In *Macbeth,* Macduff has this remarkable position. Similarly, in Marlowe, Doctor Faustus happens to be the evil protagonist of the play and possibly the Christian doctrine is in the theoretical position of an antagonist there.

Ref: Aristotle, *Poetics*. HDF Kitto, *Greek Tragedy* (1954). Sam Smiley, *Playwriting: The Structure of Action* (1971). Bernard Spivack, *Shakespeare and the Allegory of Evil: The History of a Metaphor in Relation to his Major Villains* (1958).

Anticlimax A Figure of Speech that records a deliberate descent from an elevated to a lower emotional height. The figure may refer to an event, speech, topic or even a tone resulting in disappointment or reversal of expectation. The incongruity exposed thereby produces comic, even ludicrous effect: Byron's *Don Juan* frequently exploits this device. Here is an example: "Though every wave roll'd menacing to fill,/ And present peril all before surpass'd,/ They grieved for those who perished with the cutter/ And also for the biscuits-casks and butter." The instances of anticlimax may either be intentional or it may just happen on the part of the narrator or author. The effect of an unintentional application of anticlimax at a time when the writer actually attempts at the sublime is known as bathos.

In a traditional plot construction, anticlimax refers to the progress of a plot between climax and dénouement. Usually the end of the third act or the beginning of the fourth act in a five-act play is reserved for anti-climactic developments. Gustav Freytag, in his treatment of dramatic art, had termed anti-climax as 'falling action'. His famous diagram illustrating the dramatic action is as follows:

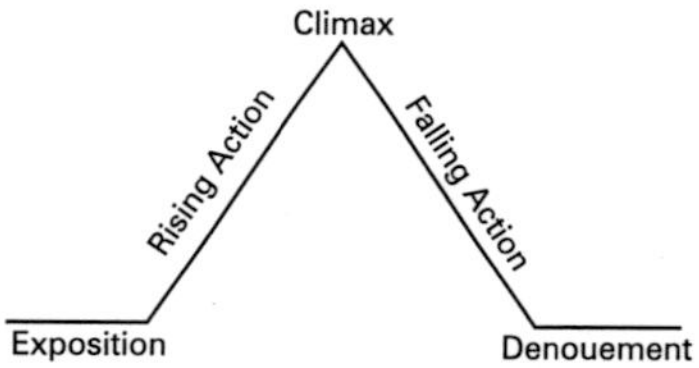

Ref: Gustav Freytag, *Die Technik des Dramas* (1863).

Antihero/Antiheroine The central character in a dramatic or narrative work; but seriously lacking in such qualities as ability, nobility and magnanimity the traditional heroes are endowed with. What is special about an antihero is that he cannot defend a cause heroically and he easily succumbs to the pressure of circumstances. Although there are predecessors of an antihero in such work as Miguel de Cervantes' *Don Quixote* (1605) and Gustave Flaubert's *Madame Bovary* (1857), the proliferation of this unheroic hero is to be found in the human situations of modern and postmodern eras. James Joyce's *Ulysses* (1922) provides outstanding examples of the unheroic ordinariness and inadequacy. Modern drama too has experimentations with antiheroes in the works of Albert

Camus, Samuel Beckett, Eugène Ionesco and the like, who are often associated with the Theatre of the Absurd. Though no formal absurdist movement existed as such, dramatists of this group and others including Jean Genet, Arthur Adamov, Harold Pinter, Arthur Miller shared a pessimistic vision of humanity struggling vainly to find a purpose and to control its fate. The Angry Young Men too produced the disgruntled heroes and heroines who, more or less, give vent to their anger but never think themselves qualified enough to uphold the challenge of the occasions heroically. Humankind is left feeling hopeless, bewildered and anxious. These Prufrocks, to borrow from Eliot, do not, in any sense match their classical and Shakespearean predecessors. They become their shadows—shape without intrinsic quality. Frye believes that the antihero emerged as a foil to the traditional hero archetype, a process that he called the fictional "centre of gravity." The transition marked a literary change in heroic ethos from the feudal aristocrat to the urban democrat, as was the shift from epic to ironic narratives.

However, the modern antiheroes realistically portray biographies of modern 'hollow men', and pathetically fail to live up to any of the expectations and myths of his family and social milieu as narrator and protagonist. The twentieth century fiction abounds with antiheroes and is perhaps more outstanding than in the drama. With the failure of the Russian Revolution (1905), Mikhail Petrovich Artsybashev developed pessimism and cynicism that overtook the Russian literary scene. In his novels *Sanin* (1907) the antihero Sanin adopts a lifestyle of selfish and cynical hedonism. In the same way, Theodore Dreiser's novel, *An American Tragedy* (1925), Amis Kingsley's *Lucky Jim* (1954) and *That Uncertain Feeling* (1955) have identical antiheroes. However, an antihero should not be confused with an antagonist. [Cf. Antagonist]

Ref: David Simmons, *The Anti-Hero in the American Novel* (2008). Martin Esslin, *Absurd Drama* (1965). Northrop Frye, *Anatomy of Criticism* (1957). https://en.wikipedia.org/wiki/Antihero

Antimetabole <Greek *turning about,* also called *epanados*> A rhetorical scheme involving repetition in reverse order: "One should eat to live, not live to eat." Or, "Beauty is truth, truth beauty." The witches in *Macbeth* give voice to their devilish mirth in an antimetabolic chant when they declare: "Fair is foul and foul is fare" etc. In *Love's Labour's Lost* (I.ii.) Moth uses the rhetoric device when he asks, "I pretty, and my saying apt? or I apt, and my saying pretty?" Antimetabole often overlaps with chiasmus. One must remember that while antimetabole is an inversion of repeated words in successive clauses, chiasmus is an inversion of parallel grammatical structures. Havelock Ellis's chiasmus, "Charm is a woman's strength; strength is a man's charm," clears the confusion between the two terms. Here the two clauses give opposite meaning; it cannot be an antimetabole.

Ref: Edward PJ Corbett, *Classical Rhetoric for the Modern Student* (1971)

Antinovel/Nouveau Roman The term nouveau roman was used by Jean-Paul Sartre (1905-1980) and later antinovel was used by Charles Sorel to mean almost the same thing. They describe some contemporary experimental fictional works that deviate from popular conventions and norms of the novel. The antinovel usually fragments, distorts and confuses the experience of its characters, forcing the reader to assemble and make sense out of confusion and a disordered narrative. This type deliberately deviates from the established standards and the moral frame of reference. The author generally rejects the use of traditional elements of novel structure, especially in regard to development of plot and character. In literature such deviations began to come up during the post-war scenario and the works coincided with the frustrations and general deterioration of general life and standard. Some French examples of such nouveau Romans include the works of S Beckett, A Robbe-Grillet, N Sarraute and M Butor. The best-known antinovels are Alain Robbe-Grillet's *Le voyeur* (1955), John Hawkes' *The Blood Oranges* (1971) and Uwe Johnson's *Mutmassungen über Jakob* (1959), *Speculations about Jacob* (1963), etc. The characters in this type are all vaguely identified; they are uncertain about their mission of life and they deliberately frustrate conventional literary expectations.

Antistrophe A Figure of Speech with repetition of a word or phrase at the end of successive clauses: "In 1931, ten years ago, Japan invaded Manchukuo— without warning. In 1935, Italy invaded Ethiopia—without warning. In 1938, Hitler occupied Austria—without warning. In 1939, Hitler invaded Czechoslovakia—without warning. Later in 1939, Hitler invaded Poland—without warning. And now Japan has attacked Malaya and Thailand—and the United States—without warning" (Franklin D Roosevelt).

In *Pindaric ode*, it means something slightly different: antistrophe is the second stanza of the Greek choral musical dance, which followed the *strophe* (or stanza), and at this moment the chorus turned from left to right. [Cf. anaphora, ode]

Antithesis <Greek word *antithenai*, to oppose> A Figure of Speech that projects opposition, or contrast of ideas or words in a balanced or parallel construction: "Extremism in defense of liberty is no vice, moderation in the pursuit of justice is no virtue"—Barry Goldwater's statement is an example. John Dryden's "Too black for heaven, and yet too white for hell" is another classic example of antithesis. Incidentally, Alexander Pope's poems abound in antithetical versifications. Charles Dickens in his own style opens *A Tale of Two Cities* with a series of antithetical statements: "It was the best of times, it was the worst of times, it was the age of wisdom, it was the age of foolishness", etc. In philosophy, however, it is the second stage in the Hegelian dialectic contradicting the *thesis* before resolution by the *synthesis*. [Cf. oxymoron]

Apocalypse/Apocalyptic <Greek *apokalypsis,* uncovering> An ancient substitute for the modern English word *revelation*. In religious context apocalypse is a vision of heavenly secret that has some earthly connotation. Apocalypse refers to the Revelation, the last book of the *New Testament*. Therefore, any vision of catastrophic end of this world is by nature apocalyptic. By extension any form of prediction, revelation, uncovering and prophesying about the future of the world is included in the term. Thus, William Blake's "The Book of Thel," "Jerusalem," William Butler Yeats' "The Second Coming," John Keats' "Hyperion," PB Shelley's *Prometheus Unbound*, HG Well's *The War of the World*, etc come within this category of Apocalypse. [Cf. epiphany]

Ref: Joshua W Brooks, *Dictionary of Writers on the Prophecies* (1835). Tina Pippin, *Apocalyptic Bodies: The Biblical End of the World in Text and Image* (1999).

Apollonian & Dionysian A set of concepts that refer to Nietzsche's theory of dichotomy in philosophical and literary works. Apollo and Dionysus, in Greek mythology, are sons of Zeus; but they represent two contradictory concepts —order and chaos respectively. In the classical era it was believed that these impulses guided authors of the tragic drama. Apollonian is named after Apollo, the Greek god of light and beauty and the symbol of intellectual order; whereas the unrepressed passion is named after Dionysus, the Greek god of wine and the symbol of uninhibited forces of nature. While the Apollonian impulse is positive as it refers to a rational, harmonious world, the Dionysian is a negative impulse inspiring irrational forces of human nature. The Greeks did not consider the two forces as distinctly separated; rather they were entangled by nature. Friedrich Nietzsche (1844-1900) used them in *The Birth of Tragedy* to designate contrasting elements in Greek tragedies.

Aposiopesis A Figure of Speech meaning "becoming silent" in the midst of a speech. It can be defined as a verbal device, forced or unforced, in which the speaker breaks off abruptly and leaves the speech unfinished. The unfinished part is, however, comprehensible to the listener. The situation may arise as a deliberate need of the speaker not to tell the whole sentence or it may occur under pressure of exasperation, excitement, passion or fear, etc. Such example as—"My lords... my ladies... and everybody else"—after the words "my lords" and "my ladies," there are brief breaks that serve to give respect to the lords and ladies in the audience and, therefore, is not an aposiopesis. But in such sentence as—"No, I don't know anything; if you press further for even once, I'll..."—is an aposiopesis. There is something unuttered, may be a threat, and that part can be predicted by the listener from the context and the specific feeling of the speaker.

Apostrophe <Latin from Greek *apostrephein*, turning away> A Figure of Speech used to mark a moment when a speaker turns away from the main line of dialogue, usually in order to address a real, imaginary, a dead person or even an idea or object: "O pardon me, thou bleeding peace of earth/ That I am meek and gentle with these butchers" —Shakespeare. Here in this case, Antony, in *Julius Caesar*, occasions the apostrophe in front of dead Caesar. Jane Taylor's well-known nursery rhyme: "Twinkle, twinkle, little star,/ How I wonder what you are" is often considered as a beautiful apostrophe as the poem is a child's address to a twinkling star, almost an imaginary entity. One must not confuse the apostrophe which is a Figure of Speech with the apostrophe which is a punctuation mark, i.e. (')—as in *don't*.

Arcadia A place name that comes from the mythological figure Arcas and it refers to a mountainous region in central Peloponnes, Greece, which was believed to be the blissful home of Pan, the Greek god of the shepherds. In literature Arcadia is always associated with simplicity and is usually seen as a retreat from the complexities of sophisticated life in the court or the city. After the fall of the Roman Empire, Arcadia became part of the Byzantine Empire and it was famous as a beautiful and quiet area with simple herdsmen as its inhabitants leading a simple yet happy lives. Arcadia was first recreated in literature by the Greek poet Theocritus (BCE 300-260) in his *Eidyllia* and later by the Roman poet Virgil (BCE 70-19) in his *Eclogues*. Virgil, however, turned it into an ideal pastoral environment. Renaissance poets such as Edmund Spenser and Sir Philip Sidney exploited the Arcadian settings and themes liberally. It was, of course, Sir Philip Sidney (1554-1586) who almost immortalized the name in the English speaking world with his work *The Countess of Pembroke's Arcadia*, a combination of pastoral romance and poetry. It is still a celebrated work to the learned readers of English literature. Even today the word suggests the supposed Golden Era of blissful simplicity in the midst of nature. [Cf. dystopia, el dorado and utopia]

Ref: Joan Rees, *Sir Philip Sydney and Arcadia* (1991).

Archaism A deliberate mismatching of time, event and/or space. It should not be confused with anachronism. In anachronism something is placed out of a chronological order or context; whereas archaism refers to using an obsolete word or expression. It is often a result of an author's love of classical or old literature. Sometimes authors deliberately use archaic words or expressions to give the subject matter a proper historical context and create an appropriate setting for the plot. Thus dress, mannerism, even a thought too can be archaic. In Coleridge's *Rime of the Ancient Mariner*, for instance, the deliberate use of archaic words like *stoppeth, spake*, etc help to evoke a medieval image of the world which best suits the ballad. Shakespeare, John Milton, Thomas Hardy and Charles Lamb have made proper use of the archaic words and style. However, the English versions of the Bible still remain the best manifestation of archaic practices. [Cf. Anachromism]

Archetypal/Myth Criticism A related forms of criticism based on myth and Carl Jung's (1875-1960) theory of the archetype (< Greek *arche*, origin, and *typos*, type, pattern, etc>) which is a symbol, image, theme, setting, character-type that has so constant and recurring appearance in folktale, folklore, literature, rituals and cultural constructs as to have acquired a status as an element of essential and collective human experience. It studies each literary work as part of the whole literature. Some psychologists argue that there are two levels of the unconscious: [1] the personal, which comprises repressed memories that are part of an individual's psyche, and [2] the archetypal, which comprises the racial memory of a collective unconscious, a storehouse of images and patterns, vestigial traces. All human beings inherit this and this finds symbolic expression in all human art.

Archetypal criticism begins with the speculations in the British anthropologist JG Fraser's book, *The Golden Bough* (1890-1915), and also from the studies of the Swiss psychologist Jung (1875-1961). Myth criticism explores the nature, function and significance of the primordial archetypal patterns. Mythological critics look for underlying recurrent patterns in literature that reveal universal meanings and basic human experiences for readers regardless of when and where they live. They may normally specialize in areas such as classical literature, philology, anthropology, psychology, and cultural history. Whereas Jung focuses on the genesis of these archetypes, myth critics, such as Northrop Frye, focus on their analysis. For Frye, an archetype is "a symbol, usually an image, which recurs often enough in literature to be recognizable as an element of one's literary experience." Frye devises an elaborate taxonomy of modes, symbols, myths and genres, establishing a complex and broad association between the basic genres, such as comedy, romance, irony and tragedy and the myths and archetypal patterns associated with the seasonal cycle of spring, summer, fall and winter. Archetypal critics approach a text from a broader perspective, identifying archetypal images manifested in a wide variety of works. In a sense, archetypal criticism anticipates structuralism in that the latter believes that language constructs reality rather than reflects it. Similarly, it comes partially close to reader-response criticism, which too emphasizes that the author does not control the whole meaning of his/her text; the reader too is a source of meaning which is conditioned by his/her cultural experience, conscious or unconscious, social roles and ideological position, etc.

Ref: James G. Frazer, *The Golden Bough: A Study of Magic and Religion* (1890-1915). Maud Bodkin, *Archetypal Patterns in Poetry* (1934). Northrop Frye, *Anatomy of Criticism: Four Essays* (1957). Wilson Knight, *The Starlit Dome: Studies in the Poetry of Vision* (1959) & *The Wheel of Fire* (1963).

Aristotolian Criticism A primary and major system of literary evaluation in Europe. In response to Plato's (BCE 428/427-348/347) theory, Aristotle (BCE 384-322), in his *Poetics*, formulates his approach to tragedy in particular and poetry in general. Aristotelian criticism highlights on both the form and logical structure of a work apart from its historical or social context. The poet, he believes, creates types and situations that, while imitating nature, are, nonetheless, akin to the universal; that is, the poet describes what is possible as though it were both likely and necessary. Aristotle also permits the analogy of poetry to oratory as well as the consideration of the moral, political, and educational effects of both. Tragedy, which is the only kind of poetry analyzed in detail, and is defined in terms of its form, not in terms of its purpose, as a kind of imitation rather than as a mode of persuasion or excitation. Thus it imitates a serious action of great magnitude in a dramatic form and accomplishes the catharsis of the emotions of pity and fear. John Crowe Ransom and Cleanth

Brooks and others, accept only the formal aspects of the Aristotelian criticism for textual analysis. Aristotle's argument, in the specialized sense, is based on the plot or sequence of ideas that forms its conceptual structure.

Ref: Monroe C Beardsley, *Aesthetics from Classical Greece to the Present: a Short History* (1972). SH Butcher, *Aristotle's Theory of Poetry and Fine Art* (1951). WB Stanford, *Greek Tragedy and the Emotions: an Introductory Study* (1983).

Aside A dramatic convention, usually a short comment or statement, often a speech of moderate length, by a character, directed either to a particular character or the audience, which by convention is supposed to be inaudible to other characters on the stage. A related stage device is soliloquy, in which a character expresses his thoughts or feelings aloud while either alone upon the stage or with the other actors keeping silent. Soliloquy and aside were for long accepted dramatic conventions, especially in the theatre of the 16th, 17th and 18th centuries. The basic difference between these two devices is whereas aside has an intended audience, soliloquy has apparently none. It is a convenient aid for the dramatist to convey directly to the audience information about a character's motives, intentions and the state of his inner mind. This way an aside is a short speech of a character, whereas a soliloquy is a speech of the character by the dramatist for the audience. Shakespeare has extensively used this convention with confidence and greater success than many other dramatists. For example, in *Julius Caesar* (III.i) Cassius and Brutus talk together in the form of aside. Purpose of the aside is obvious—Cassius does not want Antony hear this part of his secret suggestions to Brutus. However, no matter if it is an aside or a soliloquy, the audience has the full share of it all. The devices like aside and soliloquy fell into a slight disfavour after much exaggeration and overuse in the plays of the Elizabethan (1550-1660) and Restoration (1660-1685) periods; but it remained useful for revealing the inner life of characters. Finally with the emergence of a more naturalistic drama in the 19th century, aside and soliloquy as dramatic devices almost ceased to exist when growing demands that plays convey the illusion of real life forced the playwrights to exploit alternative means for conveying necessary information to the spectator.

Assonance & Dissonance A couple of sound effects used in poetry. Assonance is repetition of identical vowel sounds, usually in *stressed syllables*, followed by differing consonant sounds in proximate words or phrases: *frame/fate*. The examples of double assonance: *argues/cargoes* and also triple assonance: *mincingly/trippingly* are often available in English verses, but very frequent in Spanish versification. Assonance produces an *imperfect rhyme*. For further example, *frame* and *fate* produce assonance, whereas *fate* and *late* give *perfect rhyme*. Dissonance, on the other hand, is harsh, inharmonious *rhythm*, or a juxtaposition of unmatched sounds to create a special poetic effect or to create an interesting variation from what is rhythmically expected. Robert Browning has often skilfully used dissonance while Tennyson was in favour of assonance.

Consonance too comes very close to these forms. [Cf. rhyme]

Asyndeton & Syndeton <Greek word *asyndeton* means 'unconnected' and *syndeton* means the opposite> An associated set of Figures of Speech. Asyndeton is marked by lack of conjunctions between coordinate phrases, clauses or words: "We shall pay any price, bear any burden, meet any hardships, support any friend, oppose any foe to assure the survival and the success of liberty"—JF Kennedy. The lack of conjunctions may occur between words and phrases as well as between sentences and clauses. Mostly used in speech, asyndeton may speed up the rhythm of verse also. Whereas Syndeton includes addition of multiple conjunctions such as "He drinks and dances and sings and sleeps", asyndeton does away with conjunctions: "He drinks, dances, sings, sleeps."

Auchitya An Indian aesthetic term, meaning *propriety,* used in literary and art criticism. The term can be traced in Bharata's dramatic theory *A Treatise on Theatre,* originally known as *Nāṭyaśāstra*, a classical Indian Poetics written in the Sanskrit language. Bharata did not deal with the concept at length. The term is developed only recently from the study of classical Indian literature. However, the sage, believed that the rules of 'Auchitya' (propriety) must be maintained so that Rasa (emotions) in art could be evoked in due proportion. In a sense the greatest Guna (merit) of poetry is *Auchitya* and it comprehends all the other *gunas*. On the other hand, *dosha* (demerit) is its absence, *Anauchitya*. Thus the theory of Auchitya is actually a sturdy prescription of some do's and dont's while composing poetry. There are some twenty-seven forms of Auchitya; but the concept is often reduced to five main categories: *Bhasha Auchitya*, (propriety of diction), *Saundarya Auchitya* (propriety of aesthetics), *Vyakaran Auchitya* (propriety of grammar), *Samskriti Auchitya* (propriety of culture) and *Pratibha Auchitya* (propriety of creative genius). Each of the five categories includes the various constituents of language and artistic embellishment in them. Each of them again can be discussed in terms of *Antaranga* (internal) and *Bahiranga* (external) processes.

The concept of Auchitya, however, is not a very simple issue. Several other finer ideas are associated with the concept and they make it a complex whole. The employment of the *anubhavas* (feelings) in relation to the subject matter is a major creative drive and is a part of the artistic process. The concepts of *Nitya* and *Anitya* —meaning permanent and transitory *dosha* (demerits) and *guna* (merits) respectively—too are responsible for bad and good art. All these constituents—say, rasa, riti, guna, alamkara when move in the right direction together as a whole, it produces good poetry. Another ancient theoretician, Kuntaka, admits that Auchitya as guna or quality brings out the excellence of poetry. Kuntaka holds that propriety pervades in the world of sense and the entire poetical composition. If the composition or a part of it suffers from impropriety, Auchitya fails to lead to the desired aesthetic end. Some of the salient features of the concept seem to be very intimately similar to the Western classical theory of art and poetry.

Ref: Natalia Lidova, *Natyashastra* (2014). RK Sen, *Aesthetic Enjoyment: Its Background in Philosophy and Medicine* (1966). Wallace Dace, "The Concept of Rasa in Sanskrit Dramatic Theory", *Educational Theatre Journal* 15/3 (1963).

Augustan A term applied to late the 17th and the early 18th century English literature, implying its similarity to the great age of Latin literature under Emperor Augustus (BCE 27-14 CE). The epoch of Virgil, Horace and Ovid showed a concern for decorum, urbanity and correctness. Major British authors of this period (1700-1745) are Pope, Swift and Dryden. Because of too much adherence to the classical formalities of the Augustan Era, the Age of Pope in English literature (1700-1745) is often termed as the Neo-classical Era. English literature, therefore, has no classical era as such; it inherits the common classical tradition of the Greeks and the Romans. The decline of quality in moral and cultural standard following this period is termed as decadence. [Cf. Neo-classicism]

Ref: Donald Greene, *The Age of Exuberance: Backgrounds to Eighteenth Century Literature 1660-1785* (1970). Oliver Goldsmith, "Account of the Augustan Age in England" (1759). Paul Fussell, *Rhetorical World of Augustan Humanism* (1965).

Autobiographical Novel A self-written biography of an author, often in the form of a novel, or a novel based on the author's own life, at least partly, if not wholly. This is also known as *autofiction*. Many novelists include in their works people and events from their own lives. Accordingly, the author has more freedom to offer fictitious incidents too. A personal story of the emergence, with its implicit motifs of struggle, conflict, suffering and success, has an inevitable appeal for the novelist. It is often seen that many first novels are autobiographical and they attempt to generalize the author's own experiences into a kind of universal symbol of the growing and learning processes. Charles Dickens (1812-1870) embodies a whole bildungsroman in his works like *David Copperfield* (1850) and *Great Expectations* (1861). Mark Twain's (1835-1910) *Tom Sawyer* and *Huckleberry Finn*, Maxim Gorky's (1868-1936) *My Childhood,* James Joyce's (1882-1941) *Portrait of the Artist as a Young Man* and Lucy Grealy's *Autobiography of a Face* (1995) are all brilliant examples of how personal experiences are transmuted into fictional forms. However, the writers normally tend to make his life story the ingredients of fiction and thereby the elements undergo certain changes irrespective of the writer's conscious efforts in favour of creating fiction or otherwise. The literary technique itself is distinguished from an autobiography or memoir by the requirements of being fiction. Some other examples of this genre are George Orwell's *Down and Out in Paris and London*, DH Lawrence's *Sons and Lovers* and Mircea Eliade's *La Nuit Bengali,* etc. [Cf. diary]

Ref: Carolyn Barros, *Autobiography: Narrative of Transformation* (1998). Philippe Lejeune, *On Autobiography* (1989). Roy Pascal, *Design and Truth in Autobiography* (1960).

Automatic Writing A theory and practice of writing that is carried out without a preconceived strategy in an effort to capture every random thought. Authors who engage in automatic writing typically do not revise their work, preferring instead to preserve the revealed truth and beauty of spontaneous expression. Automatic writing is also known as or *psychography*. It is described, in psychology, as a psychic ability allowing a person to create extempore written texts without consciously writing them. The technique is often practiced while the person writing is in a state of trance. Gertrude Stein approached her work through studies of the rambling writing of asylum inmates. During the 1920s with the followers of Dadaism, automatic writing became a credo and later Surrealism (notably, the French poet Robert Desnos) gave formulas for achieving it. Since causality and motivation found no room in the theory, the writers relied much on accident or chance for the growth of their works. Comparable in this connection is Wordsworth's Romantic theory of poetry as being 'spontaneous overflow of powerful feelings recollected in tranquillity'. If it is a fact that Coleridge's "Kubla Khan" was written in a state of dream or an inspired mood, the poem may have legitimate claim as a model of automatic writing. Other Romantics like Shelley and Keats also believed that it was better to destroy a poem if it needed corrections or if it did not come out naturally like the growth of a leaf. The Classical method of meticulously verifying a literary product goes against this theory.

Ref: Robert Todd Carroll, "Automatic writing", *The Skeptic's Dictionary* (2003).

Avant-Garde A French term meaning *vanguard*. It is used in literary criticism to describe a new writing that rejects traditional approaches to literature in favour of innovations in style or content. The term, thus, can be loosely applied to any innovative experiment that marks a recognizable shift from the fashionable tradition either in criticism or creative writing. For example, modernist works are often called avant-garde, a label that has also been applied to more radically experimental postmodernist works written in the demoralizing wake of World War II. Other 20th century examples of the literary *avant-garde* include the Black Mountain School of poets, the Bloomsbury Group, and the Beat Movement etc.

B

Ballad <French *chanson ballade*> An old story meant for singing, either composed for occasions out of a repertory of traditional motifs or phrases or anecdotes conserved by memory and handed down by the wandering minstrels. The ballad is a short narrative folksong of the primitive tradition whose distinctive style was crystallized in Europe in the late Middle Ages and that persists to till date in areas where literacy, urban contacts and mass media have not yet affected the habit of folk singing. France, Denmark, Germany, Russia, Greece and Spain, as well as England and Scotland, possess impressive ballad collections. In no two language areas, however, are the formal characteristics of the ballad identical. For example, British and American ballads are invariably rhymed and strophic (divided into stanzas); the Russian ballads known as *byliny* and almost all Balkan ballads are unrhymed and unstrophic. Again, though the ballads of Spain, romances and the Danish *viser* are alike in using assonance instead of rhyme, the Spanish ballads are generally unstrophic while the Danish are strophic, structured into either quatrains or couplets.

During the 16th century, *broadside ballad*, a popular song printed on one side of a single sheet dealing with some current event usually hawked on the streets, was meant for the populace. Since 18th century onwards, educated poets outside the folk-song tradition, notably Goethe and Coleridge have written imitations of the popular ballad form and style to produce what is known as literary ballads. A literary ballad is a narrative poem written by an urban poet in deliberate imitation of the form and spirit of the popular ballad. The Romantic poets composed some of these outstanding literary ballads. Though relatively more expanded than popular ballads, Coleridge's *Rime of the Ancient Mariner*, Scott's "Proud Maisie" and Keats' "La Belle Dame sans Merci" belong to the urbanized sophisticated ballad tradition. The story in a ballad is told simply, impersonally and often with vivid dialogues. The frequently used stanza form, called the ballad stanza is composed in quatrains with alternating four-stress and three-stress iambic lines, with a varying number of unstressed syllables in a line. Here is an example from *The Rime of the Ancient Mariner*:

I looked upon the rotting sea,
And drew my eyes away;
I looked upon the rotting deck,
And there the dead men lay.

Technically speaking, musical quality in a ballad is a must, since a ballad is not theoretically a ballad unless it can be sung. Though tunes and texts are dynamically interdependent, it is not unusual to find the same version of a ballad being sung to a variety of tunes of suitable rhythm and meter or to find the same tune being used for several different ballads.

Ref: David Atkinson, *The English Traditional Ballad: Theory, Method and Practice* (2002). Eric Nebeker, *The Broadside Ballad and English Literary History, 1540-1700* (PhD Diss. 2009). Paul Franklin Baum, *Principles of English Versification* (1929).

Bard A poet. The word has its origin in Welsh *Bardd* and Irish *Bard.* In this sense he is a Celtic poet of olden days, a singer with a harp in his hand reciting a ballad or a heroic verse. In ancient times these bards were the oral historians, political critics, eulogizers and entertainers much like the *minstrels*, who were professional entertainers of the late medieval Europe, either itinerant or settled at a noble court. They were entrusted with responsibilities for celebrating such national events as heroic actions and victories. In modern usage the word has become synonymous with poet. Shakespeare in particular is often referred to as the Bard of Avon in spite of the fact he wrote during the Renaissance England, long after the halcyon days of the Celtic bards. The modern time has seen a sort of revival of bardic performances since 1822, when Wales arranged for contests on the ancient tradition. In Welsh these contests are called *Eisteddfodau* (singular *Eisteddfod*) and *bard* refers to any participant who has competed in an Eisteddfod.

Baroque <Portuguese *baracco*, rough pearl> A lavishly ornate style used more precisely in music, architecture and art than in literary criticism. In literature it refers to an artificial poetic style and glitzy diction that threaten to outshine the balanced Renaissance elements. This particular style is often known as *Gongorism* and *Marinism* (after Spanish poet Gongora and Italian poet Marini). Baroque works typically express tension, anxiety and violent, even grotesque emotion relying much upon the elaborate, ornate, even grotesque presentation and intricate, fantastic conceits. The Baroque Age designates a period in Western European literature beginning in the late 16th century and ending about one hundred years later. Baroque is almost a catch-word frequently applied to elaborate verses and extravagant conceits of poets like Crashaw in England. The poems of Donne, especially some of his divine poems in which apocalyptic vision is imagined are labelled as baroque. In European continental context the term simply refers to the crisis of sensibility during the late Renaissance period. Examples of Baroque works include Richard Crashaw's poem "The Weepers," John Lyly's *Euphues: The Anatomy of Wit,* Luis de Gongora's *Soledades,* and Shakespeare's *As You Like It.*

Ref: Robert Harbison, *Reflection on Baroque* (2000). Michael J Horswell, *Baroque and Neo-baroque Literary Tradition* (2013).

Bathos A Figure of Speech derived from the Greek origin *bathys,* deep (as in *bathyscape, bathymetric*). In literature it refers to a failed attempt at sublimity or sudden descent from the exalted to the banal or ridiculous, either in style or content. The term was first used in this sense by Pope in his treatise *Peri Bathous,* or, *The Art of Sinking in Poetry* (1728). Pope undertakes to lead his readers "as it were by the hand...the gentle down-hill way to Bathos; the bottom, the end, the central point, the *non plus ultra*, the true Modern poetry!" Bathos may result from an inappropriately dignified treatment of the commonplace, the use of elevated language and imagery to describe trivial subject matter, or from such an exaggeration of pathos as to become blatantly sentimental or ridiculous. In ordinary speech the basic difference between bathos and anticlimax is that whereas bathos is clearly a lapse or often an inadvertent fault, anticlimax is a deliberate attempt to make a definite poetic effect. Whereas bathos can happen any time in a narrative; anticlimax happens only after climax has been achieved thoroughly.

Even great poets occasionally lapse into bathos. Lord Tennyson's long narrative poem "Enoch Arden" is an example. Though the poem is serious throughout all sixty-five stanzas, and told through a serious tone, the very final three-line stanza reduces the solemn sentimentality completely by referencing to the cost of Enoch's funeral:

So past the strong heroic soul away.
And when they buried him the little port
Had seldom seen a costlier funeral.

Sir Richard Blackmore (1654-1729), English physician-writer, has provoked retorts from Alexander Pope and his friends and earned his reputation as "father of the Bathos, indeed the Homer of it."

Beast Epic/Beast Fable A genre beginning with Aesop's fables (BCE 6th century) and very common in the Middle age literary map. It comprises a sequence of tales in which the principal characters are animals with human properties and characteristics. Read as an allegory, a beast fable can convey proper meaning and a moral. Many of Aesop's tales, Chaucer's "The Nun's Priest's Tale" which is said to have been adapted from Pierre de Saint-Cloud's *Roman de Renart* (1173), etc. easily fit into the category of beast fable or beast epic. Aesop, Jean de La Fontaine and Joel Chandler Harris are quite known beast fabulists. George Orwell's allegorical novel *Animal Farm* is often read as a strong step towards writing a modern beast fable in which political discourses are personified as animals like pig and sheep etc. [Cf. parable]

Ref: HJ Blackham, *The Fable as Literature* (1985). Jan Ziolkowski, *Talking Animals: Medieval Latin Beast Poetry, 750-1150* (1993).

Beat Movement A school and a period of American cultural scenario. It featured a group of poets and novelists of the 1950s and 1960s, such as Jack Kerouac, Allen Ginsberg, Gregory Corso, William S Burroughs, and Lawrence Ferlinghetti, who rejected dominant culture, conventional social and literary principles. They publicly advocated anti-intellectual, anti-political and antiestablishment views. The term *beat* has two-fold connotation: [1] a feeling of oppression, *beaten down*, and [2] a desire for the *beatific*. Using such techniques as the stream of consciousness, writing and jazz-influenced free-verse and focusing on unusual or abnormal states of mind—generated by religious ecstasy or drugs—the Beat writers aimed to create works that were unconventional in both form and content. They heavily drew materials from outside sources. PB Shelley and William Blake are often cited as especially influential on the development of the Beat aesthetic. The Beat Generation (a member is a *beatnik*) had a general tendency to defy the prevalent conventions of the time by riding motorcycles, smoking marijuana and importing tenets from foreign sources. Allen Ginsberg (1926-1997) is the most famous poet of the generation, and Jack Kerouac's *On the Road* (1957) is the best-known novel ever written by a beatnik. Some other beatniks are: William S Burroughs (1914-1997), Ken Kesey (1935-2001), and Carl Solomon (1928-1993), etc. The Beat Generation has never been a large group in terms of numbers, but in influence and cultural status they are more visible than many other groups opposing aesthetic status quo.

Ref: Sanders, Ed. *Tales of Beatnik Glory* (1990). Matt Theado, Ed. *The Beats: A Literary Reference* (2002).

Belles-Lettres A French style of *billets doux* is the origin of belles-letters, meaning *fine letters* or *beautiful writings*. It is often used as a synonym for literature, typically referring to imaginative, creative and artistic rather than scientific or expository writing—especially fiction, poetry, drama, or essays—valued for their aesthetic qualities and originality of style and tone. Current usage sometimes restricts the meaning to light or humorous writing and appreciative essays about literature, the kind of which flourished in the late 19th and early 20th century England. Many essays of Max Beerbohm (1872-1956) and some of Andrew Lang's writings exemplify this type. The author of belles-lettres is known as *belletrist*. The main focus of the *Belletristic rhetoric theory* is on analyzing the technical style, beauty, sublimity and aesthetic property of a work that affect the emotion and reasoning of the reader.

Biblical Criticism A literary study and criticism surrounding the biblical literature, *exegesis*. Biblical criticism lays the groundwork for meaningful interpretation of the Bible. At least five major types of biblical criticism are mentioned: [1] *textual criticism,* concerned with establishing the original or most authoritative text; [2] *philological criticism*, the study of the biblical languages; [3] *literary criticism*, focuses on the various literary genres to uncover evidence concerning date of composition, authorship of the Bible; [4] *tradition criticism*, the development of the oral traditions that preceded written texts; and [5] *form criticism*, that classifies the written material according to the pre-literary forms, such as parable or hymn. Other schools include *redaction criticism*, which studies how their final authors and editors assembled the documents; and *historical criticism*, which seeks to interpret biblical writings in the context of their historical settings.

In the 20th century, Rudolf Bultmann and Martin Dibelius initiated approaches to the study of historical circumstances surrounding biblical texts. The rapid development of philology in the 19th century, later together with archaeological discoveries, has revolutionized biblical criticism.

Ref: Robert McQueen Grant, David Tracy, *A Short History of the Interpretation of the Bible* (1984). Walter Brueggemann, *The Prophetic Imagination* (1978). Wayne Grudem, *Systematic Theology: An Introduction to Biblical Doctrine* (1994).

Bildungsroman <German for *formation novel*> A novel that attempts at tracing the development of its hero from his early childhood or adolescence through a troubled quest, often a spiritual crisis, into adulthood or maturity and the recognition of his role in the world. The term, Bildungsroman, is often used synonymously with such terms as *formation novel, apprenticeship novel, pedagogical novel* and *character development novel,* etc. Generally the protagonist of these novels is a young man who matures and learns the ways of the world. The term was popularized by Wilhelm Dilthey in the 1900s.

Goethe's *Wilhelm Meisters Lehrjahre* (1795-96) set the pattern for later Bildungsroman. Although the fictional form arose in Germany, it soon became a popular form in Europe and many other places. Many outstanding novels of the late 19th and early 20th centuries followed the bildungsroman format. Dickens' *David Copperfield* (1849-50) and Somerset Maugham's *Of Human Bondage* (1915), for example, are often classified as *formation novels*. An example from modern American fiction may include the Native American writer Scott Momaday's work, *A House Made of Dawn* (1969), which portrays the native hero, Abel's identity crisis and settlement in the changing world of America. Starting with Mr. Biswas on his deathbed, in *The House for Mr. Biswas* (1961), VS Naipaul goes back to his early life, a bildungsroman in reverse, almost setting a new trend of this kind. In many cases, this type of novels tends to come close to what is known as *autobiographical novel*. A 21st century example of the form is Khaled Hosseini's *The Kite Runner* (2003).

However, it is noteworthy here that when the novel describes the formation of a 'young artist', as in Joyce's *A Portrait of the Artist as a Young Man* (1916), it is called a *Künstlerroman*. Bildungsroman often overlaps with Künstlerroman in the sense both the types portray the development of the protagonist. However, whereas Bildungsroman depicts the hero or the heroine from childhood to adulthood, Künstlerroman depicts an artist of any description as the central character of a literary piece, in which he/she recognizes his artistic destiny and achieves mastery of his/her craft through a detailed process. The question of attaining maturity remains a common factor in both the types. Thomas Mann's *Doktor Faustus* (1947) may serve as a classic example of this. In its essential characteristics, *Erziehungsroman, novel of education*, too is very similar to these categories of novels. However, terms like *Künstlerroman, Erziehungsroman* and *Entwicklungsroman* or even *novel of upbringing* are only variations of an almost similar motif and the points of basic difference between these terms and Bildungsroman are so slight that they are sometimes used interchangeably.

Ref: David Madden, "Bildungsroman", *A Primer of the Novel: For Readers and Writers* (1980).

Binary Opposition A linguistic concept of Roman Jakobson, borrowed by the promoter of poststructuralism, Jacque Derrida (1930-2004), that the Western linguistic and cultural structures lead to and express ideas in terms of contrary pairs or polarities. Saussurean structuralist theory too has its share to contribute to the concept. According to Ferdinand de Saussure, the binary opposition is the means by which the units of language have value or meaning. In theoretical argument binary oppositions "provide a way of bringing dynamics and process into theory." It helps to explain the numerous pairs of related antonyms and exclusive opposites, such as, good/bad, hot/cold, high/low, right/wrong, dark/light, subject/object and so on. In asking about size, one asks, "How big is it?" about weight, "How heavy is it?" It is also possible to ask, "How small, or how light is it?"—and get an answer; but it is usually not done. The second set of questions mostly relies on the other (and *negative*) side of a thing—more of an evaluating and balancing than contradictory nature. However, when the two opposite concepts are coupled together the result is a process of interaction between the individual and society at large. One cannot understand 'good' unless one does know what 'bad' is. The deconstruction of philosophy critiques many of these hierarchical oppositions and aims to erase the boundary between binary oppositions and thus those tacit assumptions on which Western discourse rests. This idea has lent support to the feminist criticism as many such pairs of linguistic constructs, as he/she, male/female, reason/emotion, masculine/feminine, etc have all tacit agreement with the sexist social conventions. [Cf. structuralism]

Ref: Jonathan Culler, *Structuralist Poetics: Structuralism, Linguistics, and the Study of Literature* (1975). Jack Goody, *The Domestication of the Savage Mind* (1977). Peter Barry, *Beginning Theory: An Introduction to Literary and Cultural Theory* (2009).

Biographical Criticism An approach to literature mostly based on the author's personal life. Biographical criticism suggests that knowledge and information about the author's life and his/her experience can be of great aids to the understanding of his/her work. Literary works, they believe, often reflect the author's cognition of the world, and therefore, the author's knowledge can throw light on the subjects he deals with. The basic premise of the approach is, therefore, that the events and experiences of an author's life have a bearing on his literary work and hence the study of author's life is relevant. For example, John Milton's sonnet, "On His Blindness," can best be appreciated when it is read against the author's own blindness. The form of criticism is a venerable form of approach and it dates back to Samuel Johnson's publication of *Lives of the English Poets* (1779-1781). Soon the form of criticism gained popularity and was esteemed through the 19th century until challenged first by the formalist school of New Criticism and later by Structuralist and Post-structuralist critics. For IA Richards, for example, the fundamental object of criticism was only the text, and nothing outside it. For structuralist like Roland Barthes biography too was a construct like a text and, therefore, not acceptable for criticism. For Jacques Derrida a text can be made meaningful only through the consistent suppression of alternate possible meanings in them and the relevance of the biographical information to the text was only one among myriad possible meanings. Michael Foucault too proposed that the idea of the author was itself part of a field of authoritarian and disciplinary discourses around a text aimed at controlling the production of meaning in it. The followers of this school, however, believe that learning about the life of the author can often enrich a reader's assessment of the author's work.

A slightly sophisticated form is the *Historical-Biographical Criticism*, the basic tenets of which were clearly formulated by the 19th century French critic HA Taine. Put simply his theory of *race, milieu* and *moment* sees a literary work chiefly as a reflection of its author's life and times of the characters in the work. Thus the topical quality of Milton's another sonnet, "On the Late Massacre in Piedmont," enriches the sonnet with a concrete topicality; thereby making the poem more meaningful than the poem without context and background can do. [Cf. Formalist criticism]

Ref: Jackson J Benson, "Steinbeck: A Defense of Biographical Criticism," *College Literature* 16.29 (1989). John Worthen, *The Art of Literary Biography* (1995). Terry Eagleton, *Literary Theory* (1985).

Biography <Bio, life + Graph, writing> A detailed narrative that tells a person's life story, usually from birth to death. In a good biography attempts are made to offer a coherent picture of the person concerned. A biographer typically aims to be objective and closely detailed. Biographies are distinctly different from autobiographies and memoirs. Somebody other than the person who is described in the narrative writes a biography, whereas an *autobiography* is a self-written account of the writer. The autobiographer relies mostly on his/her memory while writing the story. Another crucial point of difference is that biography is expected to be an objective study of a person's life, while autobiography has chances of romanticizing personal incidents and experiences. Some celebrated autobiographies are written by some best minds of the world: Benjamin Franklin's *The Autobiography of Benjamin Franklin;* Charlie Chaplin's *My Autobiography;* Nelson Mandela's *Long Walk to Freedom;* Mahatma Gandhi's *The Story of My Experiments with Truth;* Maya Angelou's *I Know Why the Caged Bird Sings;* Ernest Hemingway's *A Moveable Feast* and Helen Keller's *The Story of My Life,* etc are just a few examples. To come back to biography, with an exception of Plutarch's *Parallel Lives*, which focuses on statesmanship in ancient times, the Greek and the Roman biographers, more or less, stressed on the moral character of a person and during the middle Ages the attention was mainly confined to writing *hagiography*, i.e. the narration of saints' life. It is only during the Renaissance and after, a new focus on individual man prepared the real grounds for this genre. During the 17th century, this form of art became popular in England. Samuel Johnson's fifty-two biographical studies and James Boswell's *Life of Samuel Johnson* (1791) are still thought to be the greatest biographies of all time. Only a few other examples of notable biographies are: Irving Stone's *The Agony and Ecstasy* (1961), a biography of Michelangelo; Walter Jackson Bate's *John Keats* (1979) and Doris Kearns Goodwin's biography of Franklin and Eleanor Roosevelt, *No Ordinary Time* (1994), etc. [Cf. autobiographical novel, memoir]

Ref: Frederic Regard, *Mapping the Self: Space, Identity, Discourse in British Auto/Biography* (2003). Hermione Lee, *Biography: A Very Short Introduction* (2009). DA Stauffer, *The Art of Biography in Eighteenth Century England* (1941). PB Daugliane, Ed. *Essays in Eighteenth-Century Biography* (1968). W Shumaker, *English Autobiography* (1954).

Black Aesthetic/Black Arts Movement A period and phase of artistic and literary development among the African-Americans in the 1960s and 1970s. In its narrowest sense black criticism covers the study of African-American literature and corresponding cultures and theories. In its wider sense it includes the study of postcolonial literatures and cultures. The underlying assumption is that race is a fundamental and deciding category of literary and cultural analysis in the same way feminist critics take gender as one. However as a movement this was the first major Afro-American artistic movement since the Harlem Renaissance. It closely coincided with the civil rights and Black power movements. The black aesthetic writers attempted to produce works of art that would be meaningful to the Black American masses. Key figures in Black aesthetics included one of its founder poet and playwright, Amiri Baraka, formerly known as LeRoi Jones; poet and also essayist, Haki R Madhubuti, formerly Don L Lee, poet and playwright Sonia Sanchez and dramatist Ed Bullins. Works representative of the Black Aesthetic Movement include Amiri Baraka's play *Dutchman,* a 1964 Obie award-winner, *Black Fire: An Anthology of Afro-American Writing* (1968), edited by Baraka and playwright Larry Neal, and Sonia Sanchez's collection of poems, *We a BaddDDD People* (1970).

However, the movement failed to achieve a definite goal. In the mid-1970s many began to accuse the movement of chauvinism, introspection and Marxist rhetoric. They tried to see it as a Marxist "literary theory in which the concept of race is substituted for the Marxist idea of class." [Cf. post-aesthetic movement]

Ref: Addison Gayle, Ed. *The Black Aesthetic* (1971). Amiri Baraka, "The Myth of a 'Negro Literature,'" *Home: Social Essays* (1966). Henry Louis Gates, Jr, *The Signifying Monkey: A Theory of Afro-American Literary Criticism* (1988). Richard Wright, "Blueprint for Negro Writing," *New Challenge* 2 (1937). WEB Du Bois, *The Souls of Black Folk: Essays and Sketches* (1903).

Black Comedy/Dark Comedy A variety of dramatic and also non-dramatic work, depicting sinister and ominous subject matter with a kind of bitter amusement. Since the main purpose of this kind of literature is to produce shock and fright among the reader and audience, all unpleasant issues like death, disease, war and disaster, rape, sex, homo-phobia, sodomy, drug abuse, etc. are treated meticulously in the works under the head. Philosophically the practitioners seem to have been influenced by pessimistic view of life and everything seems to have gone beyond human understanding and control. This type aims at making serious and taboo subjects light provoking vulgar issues first and then amusing the audience. The characters act without any positive motive and no moral standard is set before them. Some works like Jean Jenêt's *The Maids* (1954) and *The Blacks* (1958), Harold Pinter's *The Homecoming* (1965) and Joe Orton's *Entertaining Mr. Sloane* (1964) etc. can be bracketed in this variety. Comedians like Lenny Bruce have been labelled for using 'sick comedy' by mainstream critics and have been considered flag bearers of the black comedy. [Cf. black humour]

Ref: Vanessa M Merhi, *Distortion as Identity from the Grotesque to L'humour Noir* (2006). Patrick O'Neill, *"The Comedy of Entropy: The Contexts of Black Humor"*, Dark Humore, Ed. *Harold Bloom & Blake Hobby* (2010).

Black Humour A form of humour that relies much on cruelty and moral disorder and often places grotesque elements side by side amusing ones in an attempt to shock the reader, forcing him to laugh at the horrifying reality of a chaotic world. In literature an artistic combination of the morbid and the grotesque with humour and farce gives a disturbing result and convey the absurdity and cruelty of life. The Gothic mixture of horror and cruel passions, often known as *roman noir*, comes very close to this category. Many think that horrors one sees cannot be escaped by familiarity, or ameliorated by despair; but they can be overcome by laughter. The ugly, as Aristotle thinks, can be aesthetically acceptable once artistically treated and thus capable artists can make use of black humour too for artistic purposes. Many of the works, however, as Ionesco terms, remain *tragic farce*, in which the events are simultaneously comic, brutally horrifying and absurd without a presentable mission—either artistic or otherwise. Joseph Heller's novel *Catch-22* is considered an outstanding example of brilliant use of black humour. Other well-known authors who are black humourists include, among others, Kurt Vonnegut, Edward Albee, Eugene Ionesco, Harold Pinter and even Gunter Grass to certain extent. Antecedents to black humour include the comedies of Aristophanes and Voltaire's *Candide* (1759). [Cf. black comedy]

Ref: André Breton, *Anthologie de l'humour noir* or *Anthology of Black Humour* (1940). Harold Bloom, "On Dark Humour in Literature," *Dark Humour* (2010).

Black Mountain School/Poets A group of poets that formed a vital component of the avant-garde American poetry in the 1950s. Their poems were innovative yet disciplined, many of which were published in the *Black Mountain Review* (1954-57), a leading forum for experimental verse, which was edited by Robert Creeley. The impetus of the movement gathered around such poets as Robert Creeley, Robert Duncan and Charles Olson while they were teaching at Black Mountain College in North Carolina. They discarded the poetic tradition espoused by TS Eliot and followed the freer style of William Carlos Williams. Charles Olson's essay "Projective Verse" (1950) became their credo. Olson emphasized the creative process, in which the poet's energy is transferred through the poem to the reader. In the papers, he called for poetry of 'open field' composition and discarded customary closed poetic forms. Intrinsic in this new form of poetry was the reliance upon decidedly American conversational language.

Ref: Anne Day Dewey, *Beyond Maximus: the Construction of Public Voice in Black Mountain Poetry* (2007).

Blank Verse A verse style close to what the Italian poet Giovanni Rucellai first understood by the term *versi sciolti*. Some experiments in the 16th-century Italy were the tragedy, *Sofonisba* (1514-15) by Gian Giorgio Trissino and the didactic poem, *Le api* (1539), by Giovanni Rucellai. It soon became the standard meter of Italian Renaissance drama, used in such major works as the comedies of Ludovico Ariosto, *L'Aminta* of Torquato Tasso, and *Il pastor fido* of Battista Guarini. Blank verse was adapted from the unrhymed Greek and Latin heroic verses along with other classical meters. It is an unrhymed *iambic pentameter*, the preeminent dramatic and narrative verse form in English and also the standard form for dramatic poetry in Italian and German traditions. Its richness and versatility depend on the skill of the poet in varying the stresses and the position of the caesura in each line, in catching the shifting tonal qualities and emotional overtones of the language, and yet in echoing the natural rhythm of speech.

Henry Howard, Earl of Surrey, brought the meter to England perhaps for the first time while translating Book II and IV of Virgil's *Aeneid* (1557). Especially the Elizabethan period witnessed the linguistic and lyrical upsurge of the verse form with a new liberating tone of freedom from the intricate metrical verse of the *miracle plays*. John Skelton's versification in *Magnificence* (1516) marks the beginning of the blank verse in English drama. Thomas Sackville and Thomas Norton used it for the first English tragic drama, *Gorboduc* (1561) and Christopher Marlowe developed its musical qualities and emotional power in *Tamburlaine, Doctor Faustus* and *Edward II*. Shakespeare transformed the line and the instrument of blank verse into the *vehicle* for the greatest English dramatic poetry. First, he combined it with prose and a ten-syllable rhymed couplet; later he refashioned it depending on stress rather than syllabic length. Shakespeare's poetic expression in his later plays is rather flexible, approximating the rhythms of speech, yet capable of conveying the subtlest human emotions. Below is just an example of unrhymed blank verse from *Hamlet*:

To be or not to be—that is the question;
Whether 'tis nobler in the mind to suffer
Or to take arms against a sea of troubles...

King Richard II is almost all written in blank verse. Often rhymed examples are too glaringly present:

Thou canst help time to furrow me with age,
But stop no wrinkle in his pilgrimage;
Thy word is current with him for my death,

But dead, thy kingdom cannot buy my breath.

After a short period of degradation, John Milton, in *Paradise Lost* (1667), restored blank verse to its former splendour. Milton's verse is intellectually complex, yet flexible, using inversions, Latinized words, all kinds of stress, line length, variation of pause and paragraphing to gain descriptive and dramatic effect. In the 18th century, James Thomson used blank verse in his descriptive poem *The Seasons* (1726-30) and Edward Young in *Night Thoughts* (1742-45) with power and passion. Later, Wordsworth wrote his autobiography of the poetic spirit, *The Prelude* (1850), in blank verse; Shelley used it in his play, *The Cenci* (1819), as did John Keats in *Hyperion* (1820). The extreme flexibility of blank verse is almost universal, ranging from the high-keyed Shakespearean tragedies to the low-keyed verbal tone of Robert Frost in *A Masque of Reason* (1945).

Ref: Paul Fussell, *Poetic Meter and Poetic Form* (1979). Robert Burns Shaw, *Blank Verse: A Guide to its History and Use* (2007).

Bloomsbury Group A scholarly group of a few upper middle class English writers, artists and intellectuals who held informal artistic and philosophical discussions in Bloomsbury, a district of London, from around 1907 to the early 1930s. The Bloomsbury Group had no strong uniform philosophical platform; it was a commonly shared aversion to moral prudery and a desire for greater social tolerance that brought them together with Vanessa Stephen and her sister Virginia Stephen (later Virginia Woolf). A shared understanding of the central passage of GE Moore's "Principia Ethica" further strengthened the bond. At various times the circle included such celebrities as Virginia and Leonard Woolf, EM Forster, Clive Bell, Lytton Strachey, Duncan Grant and even John Maynard Keynes. They heavily drew from GE Moore's philosophy that one's chief objects in life were love, the creation and enjoyment of aesthetic experience and the pursuit of knowledge. Incidentally, EM Forster too was somehow affected by the group philosophy and his 'Only Connect' theory (*Howards End,* 1910) was mostly based on the liberal beliefs of the group.

Ref: Bell Quentin, *Bloomsbury* (1986). David Gadd, *The Loving Friends: A Portrait of Bloomsbury* (1974).

Bon Mot French term for *good word* (*bon* = good + *mot* = word). A bon mot is a witty repartee, a clever observation or something well said. Charles Lamb, Oscar Wilde, Winston Churchill, Bernard Shaw and the like are often remembered for their bon mots. The contribution of Francis Bacon (1561-1626) to this area is no doubt matchless. His essays are store house of proverbial sayings. Here is an example from his essay 'Of Adversity': "Certainly virtue is like precious odours, most fragrant when they are incensed or crushed; for Prosperity doth best discover vice, but Adversity doth best discover virtue." Another example—"Americans always try to do the right thing after they've tried everything else" is by a master of this art, Mr. Winston Churchill (1874-1965). Many bon mots tend to become *proverbs* in due course of time. When an epigrammatic statement can be attributed to an authorship it is called *aphorism*; and when the authorship is lost but the bon mot gains wide popularity, it becomes a *proverb*. A statement, if tends to offer a piece of behavioural advice, is called a *maxim*.

Burlesque <Italian *burlesco burla*, meaning 'a joke'> A deliberate comic imitation, or even distortion of a popular or celebrated literary style, or of human action with a view to ridiculing by incongruity of style and subject. The term appeared in England during pre-Restoration era to refer to a robust spirit of humour rather than a true literary method. Now it is used for literary works of any description in which men, manners and institutions are made to appear ridiculous by way of incongruous imitation, i.e. "disproportion between the style and the sentiment" (Johnson). While *high burlesque* involves a high style for a low subject (e.g. *Don Quixote*, *The Rape of the Lock), low burlesque* does a low style for a high subject, as is found in many political satires or iconoclastic writings (e.g. Monty Python's *Life of Brian*, 1979). Shakespeare's *A Midsummer Night's Dream* and John Gay's *The Beggar's Opera* (1728) burlesque the traditions of *interlude* and Italian opera respectively. Burlesque overlaps in meaning with caricature, parody and travesty.

Ref: Jane Briggeman, *Burlesque: A Living History* (2009).

C

Cacophony/Euphony A couple of sound effects. Whereas cacophony is harsh and discordant consonant-based sound used in verse to achieve some harsh impact, euphony is achieved through the use of vowel and vowel dominated sounds in words of generally serene imagery. The combinations of words that require a staccato, explosive delivery produce cacophony. Inadvertent cacophony is a mark of defective style. Used skilfully for a specific effect, however, it vitalizes the content of the imagery used. A line from Coleridge's *Rime of the Ancient Mariner* illustrates cacophony: "With throats unslaked, with black lips baked, / Agape they heard me call." Another example from a politician's prose utterance—"We want no parlay with you and your grisly gang who work your wicked will" (Churchill)—shows how cacophonous words can add to the weight of a resolution. On the other hand, euphony is pleasing and harmonious sound effect usually achieved through the use of vowels in words of generally tranquil descriptions. Vowel sounds, which are more easily pronounced than consonants, are euphonious. The longer vowels are the most melodious. Liquid and nasal consonants and the semivowel sounds and *l, m, n, r, y, w,* are also considered euphonious. An example from "The Lotos-Eaters" by Tennyson—"The full-juiced apple, waxing, over-mellow, / Drops in a silent autumn night."—illustrates how euphony can add to a soothing effect. Keats' "Ode to Autumn" thrives on euphony liberally whereas many poems of Done and Browning have deliberate cacophonous verse lines.

Cadence A natural flow and rhythm of language caused by the alternation of *accented* and *unaccented syllables*, i.e. rise and fall of pronounced syllables. Modern poetry, notably free verse, deliberately manipulates cadence to create complex rhythmic effects. James Macpherson's "Ossian Poems" are richly cadenced, as are the poems of the symbolists, Walt Whitman, and Amy Lowell. Here is an example from Emily Dickinson's poem:

Light laughs the breeze
In her Castle above them–
Babbles the Bee in a stolid Ear,
Pipe the Sweet Birds in ignorant cadence–
Ah, what sagacity perished here!

[Cf. foot, meter]

Caesura <Latin *cutting off*> A strong pause in prosody, typographically indicated, within a poetic line that breaks the regularity of a metrical scheme. It is represented in scansion by the sign | |. Caesura is often used to emphasize the formal meter of a line, but more often it introduces the cadence of natural speech patterns and habits of phrasing into the metrical order. Caesuras may coincide with conventional punctuation marks, as in the following Shakespearean line, in which a strong pause is demanded after each comma for rhetorical expression: "This blessed plot, | | this earth, | | this realm, | | this England…" It is not always necessarily set off by punctuation mark as in this line from John Keats: "Thou foster-child of silence | | and slow time."

In Germanic and Old English alliterative poetry, caesura was a formal device dividing each line centrally into two half lines, as in this example from "The Battle of Maldon" (c. 991):

Hige sceal þe heardra, | | hearte þe cenre,
Mod sceal þe mare, | | þe ure mægen lytlaþ.
(Mind must be firmer, | | heart the more fierce,
Courage the greater, | | as our strength diminishes).

In Romance and Neoclassical verse, the caesura occurs most frequently in the middle of the line (*medial caesura*), but in modern verse its place is flexible; it may occur near the beginning of one line (*initial caesura*) and near the end of the next (*terminal caesura*). A *masculine caesura* follows a stressed syllable while a *feminine caesura* follows an unstressed syllable. There may be several caesuras within a single line or none at all. Thus, it has the effect of interposing the informal and irregular patterns of speech as a subtle counterpoint to the poem's regular rhythm. A caesura prevents metrical monotony and underlines the sense of lines. In classical prosody, caesura refers to a word ending within a metrical foot, in contrast to *dieresis*, in that the word ending and the foot ending coincide. It is strictly a metrical element, not an element of expression.

Calypso <Greek *kalypto*, to cover, hide or deceive> A song or ballad sung by the West Indians on any festival or public occasions, such as carnivals, fêtes, elections and even cricket or football matches. Incidentally, the name of the nymph who captivated Ulysses on the island of Ogygia is also Calypso. The similarity is no more than just a matter of coincidence. However, the name has its definite origin in Greek classical mythology. Calypso was a nymph and the daughter of Atlas. She tempted and detained Odysseus for almost seven years in her island Ogygia. She also bore Odysseus two sons and finally released him only when Athena and Zeus interfered. Calypso is remembered mostly for her role in Homer's *Odyssey*.

Canon A biblical term for an authentic model. Originally it refers to [1] the laws of a church and [2] the collection of writings of books of a religion that are considered to be God's words and that set forth the standards of faith. On the analogy of this biblical concept, canon (Scripture, as opposed to the *Apocrypha*), the term *literary canon* refers to those works of literature regarded as possessing authentic merit and authority. Outside theology it refers to works that are superior, central, or most worthy of study in a culture. Thus the canon of Shakespeare plays includes 37 plays generally considered to be certainly his; but some works that lack quality and authenticity (e.g. anonymous *Arden of Faversham*), are *apocryphal*, or noncanonical. The Marxist, feminist and postcolonial criticisms are now questioning the validity of the concept associated with canon. First, the canonical body is thoroughly dominated by the DWEM (dead, white, European & male) and the accusation is that women and minorities and non-Western writers have been deliberately disregarded. Secondly, the concept of canon has always been qualified by political, cultural and race ideologies and hegemonic predisposition. The recent developments, such as emergence of postcolonialist discourses and non-European literatures from the periphery penetrating into the centre, have challenged the European canonical concept.

Ref: Harold Bloom, *The Western Canon: The Books and School of the Ages* (1995). Jan Gorak, *The Making of the Modern Canon: Genesis and Crisis of a Literary Idea* (2013). Trevor Ross, *The Making of the English Literary Canon from the Middle Ages to the Late Eighteenth Century* (1998).

Caroline Age/Poets An adjective form to refer to the age of Charles I (1625-1649) or the poets of his period. The term is derived from the Latin version of Charles, i.e. *Carolus*. Historically speaking, the period is a part of Stuart period (1603-1714) that followed the Jacobean era and was followed by the Civil War (1642-51). Caroline poets included a group of versifiers whose works may in the bulk or roughly assigned to the reign of Charles I, though as a matter of fact many of them continued to produce poetry even later. The most important of them, Robert Herrick (1591-1674), wrote both religious and secular poems with equal ease. Other poets of this group include such writers as Thomas Carew (1598-1639), Andrew Marvell (1621-78), Richard Lovelace (1618-58), George Herbert (1593-1633), Richard Crashaw (1613-49), John Suckling (1609-42) and others. They are a miscellaneous group; but all are delightful in their naturalness and spontaneity, their exquisite fancy and their lyrical charm and grace. Another most common singular feature among them is their striking absence from contemporary political activities in a period that was marked with political strife between the Cavaliers, King's supporters, and the Roundheads, supporters of the parliament. The poets who were associated with the court are better known as the Cavalier poets. Important names of this group include authors working between the later Metaphysical and early Miltonic eras: Marvell, Carew, Lovelace, and the like. John Donne's name does not figure in this group as his poetic career had come to an end before Charles I came to power. In literature as a whole and especially in drama the Caroline period has often been regarded as a diminished continuation of the trends of the previous era dominated by Shakespeare and Jonson. The civil war and puritan attacks too weakened dramatic art to a great extend.

Ref: Basil Willey, *The Seventeenth Century Background* (1934). David Cressy, *Charles I and the People of England* (2015). ED Jones, Ed. *English Critical Essays: 16th-18th Centuries* (1922). Sir Herbert Grierson, *Cross Currents in English Literature of the Seventeenth Century* (1964).

Carpe Diem <*Carpe diem, quam minimum credula postero* = seize the day, do not trust tomorrow> An attitude to life, which has its origin in *Odes* (i.xi) of Horace (BCE 65-08). It means 'make the best of the present time.' The motif refers to and stresses on a particular philosophy of life and is commonly found in many European lyric poems. The speaker of a carpe diem poem prefers to argue and substantiate, often to a hesitant virgin, that life is very short and therefore pleasures of life should be accomplished without inhibitions while there is time. The classic example of a carpe diem motif is to be found in the poem, "To His Coy Mistress" (1681), written by Andrew Marvell, in which the impatient poet urges his mistress to abandon her false modesty and submit to his embrace before time and death rob them of the opportunity to love:

Had we but world enough, and time,
This coyness, lady, were no crime…
But at my back I always hear
Time's wingéd chariot hurrying near;
And yonder all before us lie
Deserts of vast eternity …
The grave's a fine and private place,
But none, I think, do there embrace…

By nature the poem is metaphysical; and some other metaphysical poets who have versified the carpe diem motif include Robert Herrick. His "Counsel to Girls" (1648) declares the carpe diem theme in the very opening line: "Gather ye rose-buds while ye may." Interestingly, the reference to the rose occurs passim in the poets of this group. It becomes an emblem of the brevity of physical beauty and finality of decay and death. However, Herrick's poem has its original in Spenser: "Gather therefore the Rose, whilst yet is prime" (*Faerie Queene*, II.xii. 74-75). Samuel Johnson's poem—"A Short Song of Congratulation"—to a callow heir is at once lively and wry in its ironic treatment of the carpe diem theme. Many think that Gabriel García Márquez's *Love in the Time of Cholera* (1985) is a modern variation of the Carpe Diem theme.

In some Christian poems and sermons, the carpe diem motif warns us to prepare our soul for death, rather than our bodies for bed. An *Ubi sunt* theme that questions—"where are those who were before us?"—comes very close to carpe diem motif. The ubi sunt poetic motif meditates nostalgia, the transitory nature of youth, mortality and beauty. Originally proliferated in Medieval Latin poems, because of some common human issues, it attracted poets of all ages and languages. [Cf. metaphysical poetry]

Ref: Joseph J Moldenhauer, "The Voices of Seduction in 'To His Coy Mistress': A Rhetorical Analysis", *Texas Studies in Literature and Language* 10.2 (1968). Robert H Ray, "Marvell's 'To His Coy Mistress' and Sandys' Translation of Ovid's Metamorphoses" *The Review of English Studies,* New Series, 44.175 (1993).

Catachresis <Greek for *semantic misuse*> A Figure of Speech, an incorrect or strained use of a word, often inviting an illogical metaphor extending the use of it beyond its capacity. It is often a misapplication of a word: ordinary usage like "tooth of a comb" or "I listen vainly, but with *thirsty ear*"—MacArthur. Thus the use of an unnatural and especially paradoxical Figure of Speech, such as *thirsty ear or blind mouths*, is normally covered within the definition of catachresis. Poets use catachresis to achieve a stylistic effect or exert great compression in both comic as well as serious writing. [Cf. Malapropism, personification]

Catalexis/Catalectic A prosodic name. A catalectic line omits the final *unstressed syllable* or syllables of a verse line. Shelley's "To a Skylark" has several instances of catalectic verses. In the following trochaic tri-meter composition, the second and the fourth line lack one (unaccented) syllable each at the end which could complete the prosodic pattern in respect of the metrical scheme applied in the first and the third line:

Líke ă | | glów-wŏrm | | gól-dĕn
Ín ă | | déll ŏf | | déw,
Scátt-ĕring | | ún-bĕ | | hól-dĕn
Ít's ă | | ré- ăl | | húe.

The first and third lines of the above quote are *acatalectic* since in terms of syllables they are complete. So the second and fourth lines are examples of catalexis; and the pattern, accordingly is catalectic. When the number of syllables missing is more than one, it is called *brachycatalectic*; and when the verse has additional syllables, it's called *hypercatalectic*. [Cf. anacrusis]

Catastrophe <Greek *kata* = down + *strophe* = turning> A position in traditional plot construction—the final act of a play, where the ultimate resolution is achieved. Catastrophe is often called dénouement [day-nu-mah]; it marks the closure of a tragic play, usually involving the death of the hero or the protagonist. Many critics prefer to employ the term catastrophe to tragedy only, and dénouement is applied to both tragedy and comedy. Conventionally, a tragic plot construction is divided into five divisions, technically known as acts. The acts have corresponding technical categorization, e.g. [1] *exposition,* [2] *complication* or *rising action,* [3] *climax*, [4] *anti-climax* or *falling action* and [5] *catastrophe* or, *denouement*. The plot construction in a typical Elizabethan drama, following the Senecan tragedy, was similar to this formula of construction. The fate of the protagonist is finally determined at the end of the tragedy. Therefore, catastrophe of a play gives the final shape to the tragic vision involved in it. For example, in *Macbeth* the catastrophe occurs in the penultimate scene of the 5th act in which Macbeth dies during a sword scuffle with Macduff. Since death and destruction are the common events in tragedies, the word *catastrophe* suits the outcomes of tragic plays better than *dénouement* does. [Cf. act, anticlimax]

Catharsis/Katharsis <Greek *katharsis,* purgation> A widely discussed term in connection with Aristotelian concept of tragedy. In the therapeutic sense it means purgation, and purification in the ethical. In literary criticism Aristotle (384-322 BCE), in his *Poetics*, metaphorically used this term to illustrate the effects of tragic play on the spectator. Aristotle states that tragedy rouses "pity and fear" in the minds of the spectators and thereby activates the catharsis of these unhealthy emotions. It is similar to the principle of *similia similibus curantur* (like cures like). Aristotle's contention has evoked a great many critical deliberations over the centuries. The German dramatist and literary critic Gotthold Lessing (1729-1781) has upheld the view that catharsis transforms excess of "pity and fear" into an equilibrium leading to healthy disposition of mind. FL Lucas rejects the medical metaphor and says "theatre is not a hospital." However, he and Herbert Read regard it as a safety valve. In his lecture on the *Poetics*, Humphrey House stresses on its moral implication and for him catharsis means a process that brings about 'a quantitative evacuation' or a 'qualitative change' of the body and mind. In his preface to *Samson Agonistes* (1671), Milton views that the function of tragedy is "to temper and reduce" pity and fear "to just measure with a kind of delight stirred up by reading or seeing the passions well imitated." Other critics see tragedy as a moral lesson in which "pity and fear" energized by the tragic hero's fate serve to caution the witness not to attract destiny in a similar fashion. The interpretation generally accepted is that through experiencing the vicarious display of "pity and fear" in a controlled artistic manner, the spectator's own moral angst is directed outward and through sympathetic identification with the tragic protagonist, his insight and outlook are enlarged. Tragedy then has a healthy and humanizing effect on the spectator or reader.

In a way the effect of catharsis as revolutionary; non-acceptance and non-compliance with the status quo is a common factor in great tragedies. It asserts the dignity and greatness of man. Shakespeare's heroes perish unreconciled and unrepentant; Henrik Ibsen (1828-1906) creates a feeling of protest and revolt; the storm and stress of the passion rage furiously with unsettling effect on the human mind and the aesthetic applicability of catharsis remains valid for all categories of tragedies of all times. Freud continued to believe in the cathartic method although he found hypnosis difficult. In recent times further focus has been given on the psychological aspect of the theory and the release of repressed emotions by acting out, as in behaviour or the imagination, is believed to be effective through the cathartic process. The general conclusion is that catharsis is at least effective for producing attitudinal and behaviour change. [Cf. tragedy]

Ref: A Blatner, "The Dynamics of Catharsis", *Journal of Group Psychotherapy, Psychodrama & Sociometry* (1985). FL Lucas, *Tragedy: Serious Drama in Relation to Aristotle's Poetics* (1927). Elder Olson, *Tragedy and the Theory of Drama* (1961). Robert Boies Sharpe, *Irony in the Drama: An Essay on Impersonation, Shock, and Catharsis* (1975). Jean-Michel Vives, *Catharsis: Psychoanalysis and the Theatre* (2011).

Cavalier Poets A school of poets of the 17th century associated with the court of Charles I, connoisseur of the fine arts. He supported poets who created the art he craved. In literature the age is known as Caroline Age (1625-1649). The Cavaliers were Royalists and were pitted against the Round heads who were Puritan supporters of Cromwell. The word cavalier does not have the old 14th century meaning of a well armed knight here; but has the sense that the group of poets meant to portray themselves as animated gallants. The term was thus little insulting to those who supported Charles. A special feature of this school of poets was that they concentrated upon royal issues and expressed happiness in poetically celebrating festive rather than usual serious poetic issues like philosophy, arts and life in general. Cavalier poetry is straightforward, yet refined. Many of the poems concerned with sensual, romantic love and also the idea of carpe diem. To the Cavalier poet, enjoying life was far more important than following moral codes. They did not hesitate to combat the Roundheads who supported the Parliament to oppose the king. The poets often drew inspiration mostly from the Roman masters of the classical era, such as Horace, Cicero and Ovid, etc and practised allegorical style tinged with classical allusions. Later as the Civil War in 1642 raised the conflict between the two groups to a serious height and the balance tilted towards the monarchist, the Cavalier group of poets came to the limelight. The main poets belonging to this group were Thomas Carew, Sir John Suckling, Robert Herrick, Richard Lovelace, Edmund Waller, etc.

The most influential poets of this era were, of course, Ben Jonson and Jon Donne. While Ben Jonson stressed on the classical tradition of poetry; John Donne initiated a new style, now known as Metaphysical. Jonson was clearly with the Cavalier group and he had a band of followers behind him. The Followers, specially the dramatists, are known as *Tribe of Ben.* If not all, many of the Cavalier poets belonged to this tribe. Others poets associated with the Cavalier tradition were Lord Herbert, Aurelian Townshend, William Cartwright, Thomas Randolph and Sir Richard Fanshawe, etc.

Ref: DL Peterson, *The English Lyric from Wyatt to Donne* (1967). John Stubbs, *Reprobates: The Cavaliers of the English Civil War* (2012). WR Keast, Ed. *Seventeenth Century English Poetry* (1962). ER Miner, *The Cavalier Mode from Jonson to Cotton* (1969).

Celtic Renaissance/Twilight <Irish Revival/Literary Renaissance> A period of Irish literary and cultural history in the last part of the 19th century to counter long drawn British cultural hegemony. It sought to reconstruct an independent and nationalistic Irish literary tradition. Followers of the movement aimed at creating a romantic vision of Celtic myth and legend. The most significant works of the Celtic Renaissance typically present a dreamy, unreal world usually in reaction against the unpleasant reality of contemporary social life. *Celticism* thus emerged as a philosophy that stressed on the renewed interest in native culture and 'Irishness', and the concept was viewed against the Englishness present in the cultural scenario. William Butler Yeats' *The Wanderings of Oisin* is one among the most significant works of the Celtic Renaissance movement. Other leaders of the movement include Lady Gregory, JM Synge, Sean O'Casey and even James Joyce. The Irish Literary Theatre, 'The Abbey Theatre' and Irish National Literary Society were all founded during this period. However, the British have perceived Celtic revival in the modern era as part and parcel of an anti-British sentiment. [Cf. American renaissance and renaissance]

Ref: Phillip L Marcus, *Yeats and the Beginning of Irish Renaissance* (1970). Una Ellis-Fermor, *The Irish Dramatic Movement* (1954). EA Boyd, *Ireland's Literary Renaissance* (1916), Matthew Arnold, *On the Study of Celtic Literature* (1866).

Character A person in a narrative or dramatic work. Characters simply refer to the people or persons who actually happen to be responsible for or identifiable with the happenings. The character in a dramatic or narrative work may be fictional or real. EM Forster, in his *Aspects of the Novel* (1927), divides characters into two types—*flat* and *round*. A flat character is usually built around "a single idea or quality" and is presented in outline without much individualizing detail. A round character, on the other hand, is complex in temperament and motivation and is represented with subtle particularity. These types are often referred to as *static* and *dynamic* characters. However, the characters play the part given them by the plot. Jane Austen's *Pride and Prejudice* has both the types: Charles Bingley exemplifies the *flat* type. He is static, and he stands as a representative of a particular class or group of people. Fitzwilliam Darcy, on the other hand, is dynamic, and he does exemplify the *round* type. The former does not develop, the latter 'grows and matures' with experience. The chief character, on which our interest centres, is called the protagonist or hero, and if he is pitted against an important opponent, that character is called the antagonist or villain. May be noted here, sometimes animals or even natural objects can be made to play the role of characters. For example, in Herman Melville's *Moby Dick* the real hero is a whale.

It was once accepted that without character there could be no fiction. Since World War II, the creators of the French nouveau roman, i.e. new novel, or antinovel, have deliberately reduced the human element, claiming the right of objects and nonhuman elements. Thus, in books termed *Chosiste* (literally "thing-ist"), they make the furniture of a room more important than its human occupants. Aristotle considered the plot to be the soul of a tragedy with character in second place. There are more shifts and changes in the recent times. The introduction of the LGBT characters in central positions, for example, has opened up new dimensions in terms of characterization as well as literary interpretation of a text. [Cf. dramatis personae]

Chiasmus <Greek *chi*, often *chiasm*, meaning *crossing*> A Figure of Speech, two corresponding pairs of phrases arranged not in parallels (a-b-a-b) but in inverted order (a-b-b-a), when repeated or subsequently referred to in a sentence: "And singing still dost soar, and soaring ever singest" (Shelley) or, "They fall successive, and successive rise" (Pope). A very commonplace example is: "One should eat for living and should not live for eating." The term is taken from the Greek letter *chi,* which typographically looks like the structure of an X, suggesting the interchangeability of positions. The style of the rhetoric device was popular in old Greek, Hebrew and Latin texts. In common oratory the practice may prove very effective because the balancing structure of the statement gives only two clear options to choose from.

Ref: John Welch, *Chiasmus in Antiquity: Structures, Analyses, Exegesis* (1981).

Chicago Critics/School A group of literary critics whose works as theorists and historians of criticism were a major influence in the development of literary criticism of modern America. The group, which was associated since the 1940s with the University of Chicago, is frequently called Aristotelian or *Neo-Aristotelian*, because of its debt to Aristotle, in particular to his method of analyzing the parts of a text in terms of their relative significance in producing the author's chosen effect. This practical approach enabled the Chicago critics to underline the author's success in terms of his responses and solutions to specific artistic problems involved in the construction of a given text. The most decisive expression of the group's critical approach is set forth in *Critics and Criticism: Ancient and Modern* (1952), its manifesto, edited by Ronald Crane. A full exposition of the theoretical basis of the group's method is to be found in Crane's *Languages of Criticism and the Structure of Poetry* (1953). Wayne C Booth made a brilliant application of the principles to fiction in *The Rhetoric of Fiction* (1961). The school agrees with the Formalistic criticism insofar as it stresses on the individual basis of a work, but disagrees with them insofar as its interest in historical matters is particularly nonformalist. [Cf. Aristotelian criticism]

Ref: Raman Selden, *A Reader's Guide to Contemporary Literary Theory* (1993). René Wellek, *American Criticism, 1900-1950* (1986).

Children's Literature <also Juvenile Literature> A body of written texts, often with accompanying illustrations, in order to entertain or instruct young readers. The genre encompasses a wide range of works, including picture books and easy-to-read stories, nursery rhymes, fairy tales, lullabies, fables and folk songs, etc. Relatively a later phenomenon, the beginnings of English children's literature is dated from the first decade of the 18th century with a 12-page, undated book, *A Little Book for Little Children,* by TW. Later developments owe much to *Émile* (1762), which in accordance with Rousseau's philosophy does not insist on accelerating children's adulthood too soon. Since then between nursery rhymes like Taylor sisters' "Twinkle, twinkle, little star" and the latest JK Rowling's *Harry Potter*, the corpus of children's literature is amazingly vast. Notable works that have contributed to the vastness are John Newbery's *Little Pretty Pocket-Book*, Lewis Carroll's *Alice in Wonderland,* William Blake's *Songs of Innocence* (may not be meant for children), etc. A realistic shift may be noted in the family novel, *Holiday House*, by Catherine Sinclair, in which there are children who are noisy, even naughty. Poetry too has its contribution. At the opening of the 19th century it was not Blake's; but *Original Poems for Infant Minds* (1804) by "Several Young Persons," including Ann and Jane Taylor dominated the scene. The Taylor sisters, though adequately moral, struck a new note of sweetness and humour. Their works (*Rhymes for the Nursery*) have been memorized and actually liked by many generations. JB Barrie's Peter Pan stories, some of which were published in *The Little White Bird* (1902), still remain on high demand. Only recently the youthful Peter Pan has been given a fresh life in the form of an officially sanctioned sequel by award-winning British author Geraldine McCaughrean, who retains the original Barrie style. Wendy is now a wife and mother; the *Lost Boys* are the old Boys and that the mythical Neverland is now an autumnal, polluted landscape, where the eternally youthful Peter Pan still lives.

However, children often read *adult* novels, e.g. *Gulliver's Travels* and many 'adult' authors too have something for the children, e.g. John Ruskin's *King of the Golden River* (1851). The acid test for selection of a children's novel is that it must be interesting to and, at some level, accessible by children. Other works that have always been children's favourite are *Cinderella*, Oscar Wilde's *Happy Prince*, Mark Twain's *Tom Sawyer*, LM Montgomery's *Anne of Green Gables*, Catherine Marshall's *Christy*, CS Lewis' *Perelandra*, GK Chesterton's *The Man Who Was Thursday*, Walter de la Mare's *Songs of Childhood* and *Peacock Pie*, Eleanor Farjeon's *When We Were Very Young,* Bodie Thoene's *In My Father's House*, Enid Blyton's *The Famous Five* series, etc. In India, children's stories in English are not quite unknown. Ruskin Bond is one of the leading authors of this genre in English and all regional languages have their own literature for children. During the British era, Mary Martha Sherwood (1775-1851), who stayed in India for quite some time, wrote quite a good many books for children, specially Anglo-Indian children.

Ref: DL Kirkpatrick, Ed. *Twentieth Century Children's Writers* (1978). Jack Zipes, Ed. *The Oxford Encyclopedia of Children's Literature* (2006). Kimberley Reynolds, *Children's Literature: A Very Short Introduction* (2011). Peter Hunt, *Criticism, Theory, and Children's Literature* (1991).

Chivalry <French *cheval*, horse> A quality very much associated with medievalism. It is an idealized code of military and social conduct prescribed for the medieval knights. The word *chivalry* is derived from Old French *cheval* (horse), and thus *chivalry* literally means *horsemanship*, which was, of course, associated with certain other qualities than sportsmanship. Normally, only rich feudal lords could afford the expensive armour, weaponry and warhorses necessary for tournaments and combats. The ideals involved sparing non-combatants, such as women, children, and the helpless; the protection of the church; honesty in words and in deeds; loyalty to one's liege; dignified behaviour, bravery and combat between noble opponents who had a quarrel, mainly over love affairs, etc. Other associated chivalric virtues included gentlemanly duels supervised by witnesses and heralds, behaving according to the manners of polite society, courtly love and brotherhood in arms, etc. The right to knighthood in the late medieval period was either inherited, or awarded by the king or a lord for laudable services. However, over a long period of time in Europe the meaning of the word got gradually refined to mean social and moral virtues with or without heroism. English literature abounds in chivalric references and allusions: Spenser, Keats, Tennyson and even TS Eliot have exploited the chivalric tradition quite successfully. [Cf. knight, romance]

Ref: Christopher Gravett, *Knight: Noble Warrior of England 1200-1600* (2008).

Chorus A group of artists in a dramatic performance. In ancient drama and music, the performing artists who performed vocally in a group as opposed to those who performed singly. The chorus in classical Greek drama was a group of actors who described and commented upon the main action of a play with song, dance and recitation. In Greek tragedy some 50 men danced and sang dithyrambs. Choral performances continued to dominate the early plays until the time of Aeschylus (5th c. BCE), who added a second actor and reduced the chorus from 50 to 12. Sophocles, who added a third actor, increased the chorus to 15, but reduced it to a commentarial role only in most of his plays. The chorus in Greek comedy numbered 24 and interspersed songs displaced its function eventually. The distinction between the passivity of the chorus and the activity of the actors is central to the artistry of the Greek tragedies. While the tragic protagonists act out their defiance of the limits subscribed by the gods for man, the chorus expresses the fears, hopes, and judgment of the polity, the average citizens. Their judgment is the verdict of history.

As the importance of the actors increased, the choral odes became fewer in number and tended to have less importance in the plot, until at last they became mere decorative interludes separating the acts. During the Renaissance the role of the chorus was revised. In the drama of Elizabethan England, for instance, the name chorus designated a single person, often the speaker of the prologue and epilogue, as in Christopher Marlowe's *Doctor Faustus*. The use of the group chorus has been revived in a number of modern plays, such as Eugene O'Neill's *Mourning Becomes Electra* (1931) and TS Eliot's *Murder in the Cathedral* (1935).

Ref: Arthur Elam Haigh, *The Attic Theatre: a Description of the Stage and Theatre of the Athenians, and of the Dramatic Performances at Athens* (1898). HDF Kitto, *The Greek Tragedy: A Literary Study* (1939). J Gould, "Tragedy and Collective Experience", *Tragedy and the Tragic*, Ed. M Silk (1996).

Christian Novel A novel that either directly or indirectly deals with Christian faith and theme. Though not a distinct genre, a good many novels can be listed under the head—Christian Novel. It often contains a plot revolving around the Christian life, evangelism, or conversion stories, the Christian concept of sin, suffering and salvation, or anything related to some cardinal aspects of Christianity. Sometimes the plots are directly religious and sometimes they are allegorical or symbolic. For examples, John Banyan's (1628-1688) *Pilgrim's Progress* (the second part is called *Christiana*), Charles Sheldon's *In His Steps,* Lloyd C Douglas' *The Robe,* Dickens' *Christmas Carol*, Somerset Maugham's *Cakes and Ales*, Graham Greene's *The Heart of the Matter* and *The Power and the Glory*, Nathaniel Hawthorne's *The Scarlet Letter*, William Faulkner's *The Unvanquished* and *The Sound and the Fury*, Henryk Sienkiewicz's *Quo Vadis,* Fyodor Dostoyevsky's *Crime and Punishment* and Par Lagerkvist's *Barabbas,* etc. are only a few of this type of novel. English fiction generally is much influenced by the basic Christian concepts. Many secular novelists, Dickens for instance, have often, written updated versions of the Good Samaritan motif and many Victorian novels are much concerned with the old conflict between the good and the evil. It is a fact that European literature as a whole has been greatly inspired by the biblical narrative; and perhaps no other single source is found as motivating as the Bible for the writers. Some of the very recently published novels justify the statement: Jeanette Winterson's *Boating for Beginners* (1985), Michele Robert's *The Book of Mrs. Noah* (1987), Christopher Brookmyre's *Not the End of World* (1998), Will Self's *The Book of Dave* (2006) and Meg Rosoff's *There is No Dog* (2011), etc have clear biblical analogues to deal with in the texts.

Ref: Piero Boitani, *The Bible and Its Rewritings* (1999).

Christian Play A dramatic work dealing deliberately with Christian or related religio-spiritual matters evolved out of rich symbolic liturgy of the church. By the time of the Norman Conquest (1066) a form of Christian drama, which had already established itself in France, found its way to England. Its purpose was directly didactic; that is, it was initially the work of ecclesiastical authors, who used it as a means for instructing the unlettered masses in the truths of their religion. The early Christian found in the drama a suitable form for propaganda of Christianity. Initially the original purpose was to represent the Biblical stories with the help of simple dialogues and gestures, but gradually, with the introduction of characters into the plot, dramatic quality began to emerge; and during the late 13th century the plays began to follow the classical rules partially.

What began as a religious performance by the clergy extended itself to include performers from outside the clergy folk. In the Middle Ages the performance gradually became buoyant during the festival; the clergy came to be excluded from participating in such merry celebrations. The exclusion of the clergy entailed the relaxation of church control over such performances, leading to the secular growth of what was essentially Christian drama. At this stage plays based on stories from the Bible and the Gospel were called *Mystery Plays* (e.g. *Second Shepherds' Play*). Most of such plays were probably performed in the local languages. The stories enacted were based on subjects such as the Creation, Adam and Eve, the murder of Abel and the last Judgment. Often the plays were performed together in cycles which could last for days at a stretch.

Gradually *Miracle plays* or *Saint's plays* became distinguished from mystery plays as they specifically re-enacted miraculous interventions by the saints, particularly St. Nicholas or St. Mary, into the lives of ordinary people, rather than biblical events. Some examples were *The Harrowing of Hell* and *Mary Magdalene*, etc. WH Hudson observes: "This distinction is accepted on the Continent; but has never been established in England, where the current name for the religious drama in general has been miracle play." And whether they were evolved from alternating songs sung in the church or were spontaneous expression of the dramatic instinct is a point where scholars vary. However, these religious plays had their most fruitful time up to the 16th century and there is good reason to think that Shakespeare must have witnessed one or two of the performances.

A new form, i.e. the *Morality Play*, marks a later stage in the evolution of the drama. In an indirect way, the *Morality Play*, which was allegorical, also served the same didactic purpose. Its characters, instead of being taken from sacred narrative or the legend of the saints were personified abstractions like Five Senses, Seven Deadly Sins, Vice and Virtue, etc. *The Castle of Perseverance* and *Everyman* are the examples of this genre. The rise of this form of drama was very natural at a time when allegorical poetry was immensely popular. One very common element in all these three types of early forms of dramatic art was the depiction of eternal conflict between Good and Evil for possessing mastery over the human soul. This was basically a Christian idea and found more elaborate treatment in the Renaissance tragedies in England. The basic idea has continued in Edmund Spenser's poem (*The Faerie Queene*), as well as in plays of Christopher Marlowe (*Doctor Faustus*), John Bunyan's novel (*The Pilgrim's Progress*) and other later dramatic/non-dramatic works up to TS Eliot (*The Murder in the Cathedral*).

What is known as the *Interlude* was also a late product of the dramatic development of the morality play. There is some confusion as to the exact scope and proper use of this term as interludes are often no more than only modified forms of the morality; but in its more specific sense it seems to mean any short dramatic piece, satiric rather than directly religious or ethical and in tone and purpose far less serious than the morality proper. It was usually performed between two courses of feasts or two longer dramatic items. John Heywood's *Four P's* (c. 1520), a dialogue in which a Palmer, a Pardoner, a Pothecary and a Pedlar exchange racy stories and finally enter into a competition as to which of them can tell the biggest lie, is the most amusing specimen of its class. Other examples are *Interlude of the Four Elements* and *Thersytes*. These Christian plays, in due course, played an important role in the development of the English regular drama that flourished soon after. First from the sacred building of the church, then to the courtyard, and finally to the open stage, the story of the English drama has a long history.

Ref: Karl Young, *The Drama of the Medieval Church,* 2 Vols (1933). OB Hardison, Jr., *Christian Rite and Christian Drama in the Middle Ages* (1965). Rosemary Woolf, *The English Mystery Plays* (1972). R Potter, *The English Morality Play* (1975).

Chronicle <Greek *chronos*, time> A record of events presented in chronological order without analysis. It is more or less a kind of marginal historical notations attached to calendars. In early history the pagan Romans, the Greeks and the Hebrews had developed their chronicles. The medieval practice developed from the *Chronicon* of Eusebius of Caesarea and the practice continued till the Renaissance. Scholars often categorize the genre of chronicle into two subgroups: [1] *live chronicles* and [2] *dead chronicles*. A *dead* chronicle is one that ends with the end of an individual writer; whereas a *live* chronicle is one that is continued by other writers even after the death of one writer and the process may continue for quite a few generations. Because of the immediacy of the information, historians tend to value live chronicles, such as annals, over dead ones. Although the scope and level of details provided vary greatly among the chronicles surviving from ancient times, a few, such as the *Anglo-Saxon Chronicle,* feature brilliant narrations of important events. Other examples include Geoffrey of Monmouth's *Historia Regum Britanniae* (*History of the Kings of Britain*), Andrew of Wyntoun's *Orygynale Cronykil* and Raphael Holinshed's *Chronicles of England, Scotland, and Ireland*. These were composed in prose or verse and in addition to providing valuable information about the period; they provided important source materials to playwrights like William Shakespeare and Christopher Marlowe.

During the Elizabethan era, many plays, appropriately called chronicle plays, were based on materials from the available chronicles. Early examples of the chronicle play include *The Famous Victories of Henry the Fifth, The Life and Death of Jacke Straw* and *The Troublesome Raigne of John King of England*, etc. The genre came to maturity with the work of Christopher Marlowe and William Shakespeare. Marlowe's *Edward II* is based in part on Raphael Holinshed's *Chronicles of England, Scotland, and Ireland* (1578). For the primary sources of many of his historical plays including his first *tetralogy* (*Henry VI,* three parts, *Richard* III) and second tetralogy (*Richard II*, *Henry IV* two parts and *Henry V*) Shakespeare too depended mostly on the chronicles of Edward Hall and Raphael Holinshed. In *An Apology for Actors* (1612), the dramatist Thomas Heywood wrote that chronicle plays "are writ with this ayme, and carryed with this methode, to teach their subjects obedience to their king, to shew the people the untimely ends of such as have moved tumults, commotions, and insurrections, to present them with the flourishing estate of such as live in obedience, exhorting them to allegiance, deporting them from all trayterous and fellonious stratagems." The genre is characterized by its assumption of a national consciousness in its audience. It has flourished in times of intensely nationalistic feeling, notably in the late 16th and early 17th century England. The term is often synonymously used with *chronicle history* and history play. [Cf. historical novel, history play]

Ref: Lister M Matheson, *The Prose Brut: The Development of a Middle English Chronicle* (1998). Graeme Dunphy, Ed. *The Encyclopedia of the Medieval Chronicle* (2010).

Chronotope <Greek *chronos*, time, and *topos*, place> A new "reality of timespace" in literary works, as defined and illustrated by Mikhail Bakhtin (1895-1975) in "Forms of Time and Chronotope in the Novel" (*The Dialogic Imagination*). Bakhtin describes this term as "the intrinsic connectedness of temporal and spatial relationships that are artistically expressed in literature." In Bakhtin's theory, this term acquires a special meaning, namely, the indivisible unity of time and space. In fairy tales, time and space are beyond our experience while in fantasy the time and space relationship in that world creates a contrast to reality. In other words in literature spatial and temporal indicators are fused together in an inseparable entity. Time becomes almost "artistically visible" and space "responsive to the movement of time." The concept is rather complicated and it has been interpreted copiously leading only to further confusion.

Ref: MM Bakhtin, *The Dialogic Imagination: Four Essays* (1981). Simon Dentith, "Chronotope", *The Literary Encyclopedia* (2001).

Circular Structure A type of artistic structure of a literary piece in which a sense of completeness or closure does not arise with the conclusion. Rather the concluding part takes the reader back to the subject matter with which the piece begins. The circular structure is not limited to any particular literary genre; it may be fiction, drama or a piece of poetry, or in fact, any of the popular genres. Leigh Hunt's poem, "Jenny Kissed Me" is an example of a circularly structured poem, since it ends with the same words that open the speaker's ecstasy. The structure of Langston Smith's poem "Evolution" is circular in two ways: [1] technically, the concluding phrase, "When you were a tadpole, and I was a fish", is also the opening phrase; and [2] thematically, by implication the cycle of reincarnated love is suggested. In many ways, the smaller tales within a larger narrative, or frame, functions as a tool to highlight the circular structure, because each small tale begins by taking the reader away from the main theme, and again at the end returning him to the broader theme. The Native American writer, Scott Momaday's *A House Made of Dawn* (1969) is often seen as a circular novel. The protagonist Abel returns to his community after a long circular journey. He is finally able to recover his faith in his tribe and tradition. Momaday himself comments on this aspect of his work: "I see the novel as a circle. It ends where it begins and it's informed with a kind of thread that runs through it and holds everything together."

Classic/Classical <Latin *classicus*> A term that refers to an art, a style or person of the *superior* grade. For example, the 'Mona Lisa' by Leonardo da Vinci is the archetypal masterpiece of classic painting. In its strictest definition in literary criticism, it refers to works of ancient Greek or Roman literature, such as Homer's epics, *The Iliad*, *The Odyssey*, Greek tragedies, including Aeschylus' *Agamemnon*, Sophocles' *Oedipus Rex*, and Euripides' *Electra* and Virgil's Roman epic, *The Aeneid*, etc. The list of classical works from non-European cultures includes *The Arabian Nights*, Confucius' *Tao Te Ching*, Indian epics *The Ramayana* and *The Mahabharata*, etc. However, the term has gone beyond its restricted meaning nowadays. Any work, literary or otherwise, which has gained widespread and lasting appreciation and both critics and readers over a period of long time have agreed that the work has transcended its time and space by virtue of its artistic merit, is regarded as a classic work. In this sense works of William Shakespeare, Charles Dickens, Fyodor Dostoyevsky, Guy de Maupassant, Mark Twain, JW von Goethe, Anton Chekov, Rabindranath Tagore and many other artists are regarded as classic.

Classicists still believe that the ancient artists achieved a standard of excellence that has never been surpassed by later artists. Therefore, the term classic refers to intrinsic excellence of a piece of art that aims at achieving that old standard. Whether a work is classical or not is best determined by time and the way readers receive them later. Thus the most censured work of a particular period may achieve the status of a classic or a classical work later. Vladimir Nabokov's *Lolita* (1955) and DH Lawrence's *Lady Chatterley's Lover* (1960) exemplify this group. Though such expression as 'modern classics' is not rare, there is a general tendency to refer back to the past time to credit something as a classic or classical. [Cf. Classicism]

Ref: Steven Shankman, *In Search of the Classic: Reconsidering the Greco-Roman Tradition, Homer to Valéry and Beyond* (1994). TS Eliot, *What Is a Classic?* (1946).

Classicism A term coined by the Latin author Aulus Gellius (2 CE): "scriptor classicus" in his *Noctes Atticae* and contrasted it with another term, "scriptor proletarius," to differentiate the aristocratic writers from the proletariat. Gradually *classicus* attained new connotations and referred to works worthy of prescribing for the academics. Hence the great Greek and Roman authors constituted the classics and the spirit of classicism. The most common factors that tied those works of antiquity together and associated with the term classicism typically exhibit [1] restraint on the part of the author, [2] unity of design and purpose, [3] clarity and simplicity of expression, [4] logical coherence in organization, and above all, [5] unquestioning respect for tradition. Now, when used to refer to aesthetic attitude, classicism invokes those characteristics normally associated with the art of antiquity—harmony, clarity, restraint, universality and idealism. Because of the high regard accorded to ancient art and artistry, classicism is used to refer to similar qualities and standards, at least comparable, in art and literature. By extension, classic and classicism are also sometimes used to refer to a spirit and stage of development that some historians and aestheticians have identified as a regular feature of what they have seen as the circular development of all styles.

Nevertheless, whenever artists have referred to antiquity, they have carried the problems and ideals of their own time with them, interpreting in different ways what antiquity had to offer. Classicism has historically been seen as one of any number of polar opposites. These polarities may designate aesthetic or critical oppositions (*classic* versus romantic, *classic* versus avant-garde), or they may indicate historical oppositions, such as, Renaissance versus Gothic, *High Renaissance* versus Mannerism, etc; the first term of each pair being able to embody the aesthetic characteristics of Classicism.

Thus classicism has always been a target for artistic goal, an ideal. Although for a certain period, deviations may lead artists away from it, it is a temporary phase; artists may come back with new enthusiasm to embrace the old. The classical spirit had oppositions, but was not extinguished during the Middle Ages.

The resolute efforts of the 15th and 16th century Italians revived the classicism of antiquity; the Italian Renaissance was the outcome. The 15th century architect Leon Battista Alberti equated classicism and beauty and defined beauty in architecture as "the harmony and concord of all the parts achieved by following well-founded rules...and resulting in a unity such that nothing could be added or taken away or altered except for the worse." The examples of antiquity and of the Renaissance in Rome provided the standard of classicism for the next two centuries in Europe. Examples of literary classicism include Cicero's prose, the dramas of Pierre Corneille and Jean Racine, JW von Goethe and others. In England the Neo-classical poetry of John Dryden and Alexander Pope attempted at recreating the flavour of old poems of the Augustan era. In the early 20th-century Europe and the US there was a renewed interest in Greek and Roman literature, and classical models were somewhat revived, as in the work of Ezra Pound and TS Eliot. [Cf. classical, romanticism]

Ref: Craig Kallendorf, *A Companion to the Classical Tradition* (2007). G Highet, *The Classical Tradition* (1949). Paul Oskar Kristeller, *Renaissance Thought: The Classic, Scholastic, and Humanist Strains* (1961). Roberto Weiss, *The Renaissance Discovery of Classical Antiquity* (1988).

Cliché A hackneyed or trite phrase and expression repeatedly used or misused. A word is never coined as cliché; once it is overused and it loses its original force, it is clichéd in the process and treated as a less reputable word among educated people. Robert Burn's famous line, for instance, "My luve's like a red, red rose," has become a cliché for overuse and probably misuse of the phrase. Incidentally, phrases like "sincerely yours" are perhaps the worst hit words if overuse is the question; but they are standard expressions and are parts of formal requirement and never treated as clichés. *Cliché rhymes* are rhymes that are considered trite or predictable. Cliché rhymes in poetry include endings like *love/dove, moon/soon, trees/breeze*, etc. Incidentally Alexander Pope has an interestingly satirical comment on cliché rhymes:

> Wherever you find "the cooling western breeze,"
> In the next line it "whispers through the trees;"
> If crystal streams "with pleasing murmurs creep,"
> The reader's threatened (not in vain) "with sleep."

Sometimes, to avoid such cheaper stuff, poets may go at hyperbolic lengths, such as the tri-syllabic rhymes, as is found in Lord Byron's *Don Juan*. [Cf. dead metaphor]

Ref: Margery Sabin, "The Life of English Idiom, the Law of French Cliché," *The Dialect of the Tribe* (1987).

Climax A Figure of Speech. In the Greek language, *climax* means ladder. In rhetoric, climactic effect is achieved by the arrangement of words, phrases, clauses or sentences in an ascending order of importance. By the figure the sense rises by degrees to what is more and more important and impressive. Gibbon's (1737-1794) statement—"A heart to resolve, a head to contrive and a hand to execute"—shows an ever-rising movement from a determination to action, whereas Tennyson's—"To strive, to seek, to find, and not to yield"—shows how determination is gradually further consolidated.

In a dramatic or a non-dramatic work, the point of development of the plot at which usually the highest level of interest and emotional response is achieved is also identified with the term climax. In the structure of a play the climax, or crisis, is the decisive moment, or turning point, at which the rising action of the play is reversed to falling action. It may or may not coincide with the highest point of interest in the drama. In *Hamlet*, for example, the location where climax happens to take place is as soon as Hamlet can ascertain the guilt of Claudius (III.ii). In the influential pyramidal outline of five-act dramatic structure, advanced by the German playwright Gustav Freytag (1816-1895) in *Die Technik des Dramas* (1863), the climax, in the sense of crisis, occurs close to the conclusion of the third act. By the end of the 19th century, when the traditional five-act drama was abandoned in favour of the three-act, both the climax and the emotional crisis were placed close to the end of the play. [Cf. act, anticlimax, catastrophe and denouement]

Comedy <Greek *kōmōidía*> One of the two major types of dramatic art, the other being tragedy. Aristotle did not comment on comedy at length. However, according to him, comedy deals with "some defect or ugliness that is not painful or destructive." The most important comic dramatist of ancient Greece was Aristophanes and his works with their pungent political satire and abundance of sexual and scatological innuendo, effectively define the genre today. Henri Bergson (1859-1941) thinks that comedy expresses a lack of adaptability to society; any individual is comic who defies social convention. The purpose of laughter is to wake him from his dream. The essential difference between comedy and tragedy, says Bergson, invoking a distinction that goes back to that maintained between ethos and pathos, is that tragedy concerns with individuals and comedy with classes. And the reason that comedy deals with the general is bound up with the corrective aim of laughter: the correction must reach as great a number of persons as possible. To this end, comedy focuses on peculiarities that are not indissolubly bound up with the uniqueness of a single person. However, during its long journey, the word comedy has developed various shades of meanings. In the Middle Ages it meant a tale with a happy ending. Thus some of Chaucer's tales and Dante's (1265-1321) poems are called comedies. Subsequently the term was applied to *mystery plays* with a happy ending. The modern usage combined this sense with one in which Renaissance scholars applied it to the ancient comedies.

The complexity that comedies show cannot be properly dealt with by any definition that sees it as aiming simply at exciting laughter. Laughter is undoubtedly associated with comedy, but it has more than just laughter in it. The different kinds of the comedy derive actually from differences in the attitudes and intentions of dramatists: When the intention is to ridicule, satirical comedy emerges; satire of social convention creates the comedy of manners; satire of conventional thinking produces the *comedy of ideas*. Progress from troubles to the triumph of love in a happy outcome produces romantic comedy. Shakespeare's own brand of romantic comedy is suffused with a mellow humour rather than wit. Mediaeval theory of humour helps Jonson to create his own brand of comedy of humours. The comedy of intrigue derives from a dominant intention of providing amusement and excitement with an intricate plot of reversals with contrived situations. In case the author wants to exploit serious issues sentimentally, sentimental comedy results. Tragicomedy combines elements of the tragic and the comic.

The drama during the 18th and 19th centuries continued with the development of the English theatre. Important playwrights are Sheridan and Goldsmith. Heading into the 20th century it is George Bernard Shaw with his dramatic basket of robust humour and social messages. By the middle of the 20th century English comic theatre was rather turgid, but in 1950s, it was shaken out of its complacency by John Osborn (*Look Back in Anger*) and other angry young men. Simultaneously so-called black comedy and absurd drama reflected existentialist concerns. Musical comedy, in which true comedy is often subservient to broad farce and spectacular effects, has been popular in Great Britain and the US since the late 19th century. Of course, these are not mutually exclusive; elements of one or more may appear in other items. Today, English theatre is rich with playwrights like Tom Stoppard and companies like the Royal Shakespeare Company and the National Theatre. However, whenever comedy comes as a general issue, for good reasons, dear old Shakespeare's name is still remembered with admiration.

Ref: AH Thorndike, *English Comedy* (1929). Elder Olson, *The Theory of Comedy* (1968). GW Knight, *The Crown of Life* (1947). Louis Kronenberger, *The Thread of Laughter* (1952). Northrop Frye, *Anatomy of Criticism* (1957). Robert Bernard Martin, *The Triumph of Wit: A Study of Victorian Comic Theory* (1974).

Comedy of Humours A sub-genre of comedy based on the eccentricities of characters whose temperaments are distorted in proportion to an imbalance among the bodily humours. The comedy of humours was based on the humour theory of the Middle Ages and the Renaissance. One of the most extensive treatments of the subject was Robert Burton's *Anatomy of Melancholy*. Moliere ridicules this dilemma in his play, *L'Amour Médecin*. Virchow's theory of cellular pathology superseded the Hippocratic model in the 19th century. Humour theory believed that the proportion of humours—blood, phlegm, yellow bile and black bile—determined a man's personality. An imbalance in proportion affected him in a very specific way. By nature comedy of humours is satiric as human nature is subjected to severe analysis on the stage. The early part of the 17th century in England saw the rise of a comedy based on observations of contemporary manners and mores. Masterminded by Ben Jonson, these comedies were overtly didactic. Comedy, as Jonson learned from Cicero's works, was an imitation of life, a glass of custom; it held the mirror up to nature and reflected things so that society might recognize its shortcomings and set about its improvement. The point is well raised by Harry Levin when he observes: "The induction to *Every Man out of His Humour* sets forth the full argument for comedy as a social purgative. It is perhaps as relevant to Johnson's work as psychoanalysis is to the dramas of Eugene O'neill." Jonson's great plays, such as *Every Man in His Humour* (1598), *Volpone* (1606), *Epicoene* (1609), *The Alchemist* (1610) and *Bartholomew Fair* (1614) offer a richly detailed contemporary account of the follies and vices that are always part of human behaviour. The victims are almost embarrassingly eager to be victimized. Each has his ruling passion, his humour and it serves to set him more or less mechanically in the path that he will unmistakably pursue. Presumably, Shakespeare's Falstaff, has a dominance of blood, while Hamlet seems to have an excess of black bile. Jonson's plays are usually referred to as have been affected by the humour theory, whereas Shakespeare's are not.

It may be noted that this popular theory behind the comedy of humours comes from ancient and mediaeval Greek medical theories. According to the theory the four humours and the elements they serve are as follows: blood–air; phlegm–water; yellow bile–fire; black bile–earth. All these humours again represent four corresponding human natures and psychological frame of mind: Blood – sanguine disposition; Phlegm – phlegmatic disposition; Yellow Bile – choleric disposition, and Black Bile – melancholic disposition. When the humours are harmonious, balanced and working well together, that is a condition called *eucrasia,* or "good mixture." When these humours are unbalanced, aggravated, or out of sorts, that is a condition called *dyscrasia* or "bad mixture." [Cf. humour]

Ref: AA Berger, *An Anatomy of Humor* (1993). Richard Cave, Ed. *Ben Jonson and Theatre: Performance, Practice and Theory* (1999). TC Veatch, *"A Theory of Humor"*, *Humor* (1998).

Comedy of Manners A witty form of comedy that depicts and satirizes manners and affectations of society. A comedy of manners is concerned with social manners and whether or not characters meet certain social standards. Often the social standard is morally trivial but exacting. The plot of such comedies, usually concerned with illicit love affairs or similarly scandalous matters, is subordinate to the play's atmosphere, witty dialogue, and pungent commentary on human foibles. The comedy of manners has historically thrived in periods and societies that combined material prosperity and moral latitude. Such was the case in ancient Greece when Menander (c. 342-292 BCE) inaugurated New Comedy, the forerunner of comedy of manners. One of the greatest exponents of the comedy of manners was Molière, who satirized the hypocrisy and pretension of the 17th century French society in such plays as *L'École des femmes* and *Le Misanthrope*.

In England the variety had its halcyon days during the Restoration period (1660-1700). Though influenced by Ben Jonson's comedy, the *Restoration Comedy* of manners was lighter and more vivacious in tone. The masterpieces of the genre were plays of William Wycherley (*The Country-Wife*) and William Congreve (*The Way of the World*). In the late 18th century Oliver Goldsmith (*She Stoops to Conquer*) and Richard Sheridan (*The Rivals, The School for Scandal*) revived the form. The tradition was carried on by Oscar Wilde in *Lady Windermere's Fan* (1892) and *The Importance of Being Earnest* (1895). Incidentally, many novels too have tried to offer similar social dramas in fictional form; they too are often called comedy of manners. Jane Austen's novels exemplify this genre with great success. In the 20th century the dramatic examples of comedy of manners re-emerged in the amusing drawing-room plays of the British dramatists Noel Coward and Somerset Maugham and the Americans, Philip Barry and SN Behrman.

Ref: Bonamy Dobrée, *Restoration Comedy* (1924). J Palmer, *Comedy of Manners* (1913). William Hazlitt, *English Comic Writers* (1819).

Comic Relief A brief emotional relief from dramatic tension as continued stress and tragic atmosphere for quite a length of time often prove too much for the audience. Comic relief is, thus, a short light speech or scene appreciably meant for relieving the excruciating tension created by a tragic play. The practice was almost universal in Elizabethan plays. Often the comic elements were simply intrusive for the purpose of alleviating tension or adding variety. In quality classics, however, they are made very much integral to the plot and in effect they further enhance the tragic significance of the play by way of contrast and counterpoint. Best examples of comic relief from Shakespeare are perhaps the gravediggers' scene in *Hamlet* (V.i) and the drunken porter's speech in *Macbeth* (II.iii). The speeches of the Fool in *King Lear* too serve almost a similar function. The technique was so popular during Shakespeare's time that almost all tragic plays had something to do with one or more provisions for comic relief.

It is quite obvious that provision for comic relief in a comedy would be ridiculous. It needs serious and tensed atmosphere around for exact effect. Shakespeare has managed to make a slot for this in his a little less comic comedy, *Measure for Measure* (1623). Elbow is a ridiculous character, much given to malapropisms, as in II.i, when he brings before Angelo and Escalus "two notorious benefactors," the fools, Pompey and Froth. His abuse of the English language provides a bit of comic relief in what is otherwise a grim comedy, if not black comedy.

Ref: John Morreall, *Comic Relief: A Comprehensive Philosophy of Humour* (1974).

Commonwealth Literature A body of English literature written by writers of the former British colonies. Commonwealth Literature is thus used to cover the literary works from territories that were once part of the British Empire; but excludes books from the UK unless these are produced by resident writers who originate from a former colony. The original grouping started in 1931 and comprised Australia, Canada, South Africa and New Zealand, the countries, while self-governing, pledged allegiance to the British Crown. Today Commonwealth is a loose alliance of fifty-three countries. In the 1950s some courses in American, Commonwealth, Irish and African literatures were offered in a few 'provincial UK universities' and that was the first official attempt to accept Commonwealth literature academically. The nearest definition of Commonwealth literature, as Salman Rushdie once argued, is that "body of writing created...in the English language, by persons who are not themselves white Britons, or Irish, or citizens of the United States of America." However, Pakistan was not a member of the Commonwealth; but Pakistan's English writings were a part of the body. On the other hand, England was a member of the group, but its literary output remained outside this definition.

However, situation changed and the problem of nomenclature provoked critics for alternative terms. In a famous and scathing essay, the India-born writer Salman Rushdie asserted that "Commonwealth Literature Does Not Exist". His claim had some meaning. It is obvious that colonization in one form or the other was responsible for the use of English in the colonized regions which already had their indigenous forms of literature. Thus the English language literature produced a new head to the body of native literature of erstwhile colonies—India, Kenya, Nigeria, Australia, New Zealand, Canada and many more countries. Here comes a new name for all these writings—*New Literatures* in English. Now, somehow assimilated into the existing body of English literature, the new literatures are perceived as enriching and invigorating. In fact many of the best literary works of England in the last few decades have been produced by writers from or with roots in the colonies. Many of these works are again part of what is known as *postcolonial literature*. Almost all genres of literature are available in this group; but the domination of fiction is evidently visible.

Some important names of the group and their works include Salman Rushdie, India (*Midnight's Children*); Ngugi wa Thiongo, Kenya (*A Grain of Wheat*); Chinua Achebe, Nigeria (*Things Fall Apart*); Nadine Gordimer, South Africa (*Burger's Daughter*); Michael Ondaatje, Sri Lanka (*The English Patient*), Jean Rhys, Caribbean (*Wide Sargasso Sea*) and Patrick White, Australia (*The Solid Mandala*), etc. These works, no matter whether they are recognized as Commonwealth Literature, or New Literature or even Postcolonial Literature, are expected to be critically approached with new canons and critical tools.

Ref: Bruce King, Ed. "Introduction", *The Commonwealth Novel Since 1960* (1991). CD Narasimhaiah, *Essays in Commonwealth Literature* (1999). Salman Rushdie, "Commonwealth Literature Does Not Exist", *Imaginary Homelands* (1991). William Walsh, "Preface", *A Manifold Voice: Studies in Commonwealth Literature* (1970).

Conceit <Old word for *concept*> An elaborate, intellectually ingenious and emotionally unpredictable poetic comparison, such as analogy or metaphor in which, say a beloved is compared to a ship, planet, etc. Helen Gardner defines conceit as "a comparison whose ingenuity is more striking than its justness, or, at least, is more immediately striking." Two major types of conceits abound: [1] The *Metaphysical conceits* frequently uses erotic and often commonplace references in an uncommon manner.

John Donne, in his poem "The Flea" uses a flea to reckon the sexual union, and in fact makes a smart dig at the concept of a woman's chastity. John Donne and other Metaphysical poets established connections between many aspects of the new scientific discoveries, commerce, and human experience. [2] The *Petrarchan conceit* (after the name of Petrarch) employs analogy, hyperbole or oxymoron to depict lovers in an uneven relationship. The exaggeration of beauty and cruelty of the ladylove and the anguish of the lover-worshipper are common features of the tradition. Certain fashionable comparisons, such as that of the lover to a storm-torn ship, are so recurrent that they have become common clichés. Here is a stanza from Donne's "A Valediction of Weeping":

On a round ball
A workman that hath copies by, can lay
An Europe, Afric, and an Asia,
And quickly make that, which was nothing, all;
So doth each tear
Which thee doth wear,
A globe, yea world, by that impression grow,
Till thy tears mix'd with mine do overflow
This world; by waters sent from thee, my heaven dissolved so.

Here a drop of tear is compared to the globe. The quantity of tears grows into an amazing proportion and it takes the form of almost a biblical deluge. The incongruity is patent and the readers find it difficult to see the similarity between the two things brought into comparison. Spenser, in his *Amoretti* sonnets, has extensively used the Petrarchan conceits. Shakespeare's comment, "My mistress' eyes are nothing like the sun," mocks popular Renaissance conceits. [Cf. discordia concours]

Ref: ER Miner, *The Metaphysical Mode from Donne to Cowley* (1969). FR Leavis, "The Line of Wit," *Revaluation* (1964). George Lakoff & M Turner, *More than Cool Reason: A Field Guide to Poetic Metaphor* (1989). KK Ruthven, *Conceit* (1969).

Concrete Poetry/Verse A kind of poetry in which visual elements play a large part in its presentation and also in forming the poetic effect. In addition to the usual poetic devices, punctuation marks, letters, or words are so arranged on a page as to form a visual appeal: a cross, for example, a bumblebee, or a pyramid. Word play, various fonts and juxtapositions are set upon posters, wallpaper, rubber stamps and strange media. In the 1950s Swiss artist Eugene Gomringer and the Brazilian Décio Pignatari were among the early leaders of the experimentation. Haroldo de Campos and Augusto de Campos are among the latest known authors of concrete poetry. Some anthologies of concrete verses include E Williams' *An Anthology of Concrete Poetry* (1968), Marshall McLuhan's *Verbi-Voco-Visual Explorations* (1968) and Mary Ellen Solt's *Concrete Poetry* (1969), etc. The experiment has stopped to flourish further.

Confessional Literature A piece of literary work, may be poetry, a novel or whatever, in which the author reveals very personal, intimate, sometimes shocking information about himself or herself. Not a literary genre properly speaking;

by nature confessional literature is autobiographical. Rousseau's *Confessions* (1781-88), De Quincey's *Confession of an English Opium Eater* (1821), etc are the most outstanding and major works of this kind. Many of Anne Sexton, Sylvia Plath, Robert Lowell and John Berryman's poems set the confessional tone in poetry and they are often termed as *confessional poetry*. The idea of St. Augustine's *Confessions*, reinforced by the autobiographical *The Seven Storey Mountain* (1948) of Thomas Merton, a monk, gave rise to confessional form of fiction. From Fyodor Dostoyevsky to André Gide, Jean-Paul Sartre, Albert Camus, Saul Bellow and many heavyweights have in fact written confessional novels.

Conflict A dramatic tension within a character, or between characters. "No conflict no drama"—conflict, for example, between the police and the criminal, the stupid father and the pretty young daughter, America and Iraq, etc are the staple food for drama. This notion, of course, has validity only so far as the action is built on the tension inherent in a piece of dramatic work. In a play it is a kind of resistance that on the one hand restricts the movement of the hero, and on the other, supplies the hero with necessary impetus for struggle for a particular objective. In popular comedies and tragedies the conflict is easier to recognize as it takes place between the hero and the villain, in other words, between good and evil. In *The Merchant of Venice* the clash between Antonio, a Christian nobleman and Shylock, a Jewish usurer, happens to be the major area of conflict. In *Hamlet*, Prince Hamlet is the protagonist and King Claudius, the murderer of Hamlet's father, is the antagonist. The play depicts how the two powerfully opposing forces clash and lead the story neatly toward the catastrophe. This scheme of a tussle between two opposing forces is a popular motif in all types of dramatic works, be it a grand tragedy or a light comedy or even a television serial.

It is, however, not an obligatory requirement that conflict must arise from a crude tussle between the hero and the villain, or between good and evil in their objectified shapes. For example, a hero/heroine in a Greek tragedy has to struggle against heavy odds imposed on him or her by an inscrutable force, called Fate. In such cases conflict arises out of man's indomitable will power against divine forces. A man's mind often becomes the battlefield of conflicting forces, and in such cases, the two aspects of human mind have often been objectified as Good Angel and Bad Angel, or Tempters, as in *Doctor Faustus* and *Murder in the Cathedral*. In JM Synge's play, *Riders to the Sea*, it is a conflict between Maurya, an old woman, and nature, the sea. Sophocles' (c. 496-404 BCE) *Antigone*, on the other hand, concerns the conflicting obligations of civic versus personal loyalties and religious mores. While interpreting *Antigone*, Hegel tries to locate the conflict in Antigone as being not between so-called good and evil, but between two goods. She finds herself in a moral conflict—tossed between her positions as King Creon's subject and her obligation to her dead brother, Polyneices. It is a *Hegelian conflict* to achieve a more comprehensive good. Obeying all her instincts of love, loyalty and humanity,

Antigone defies Creon and dutifully buries her brother's corpse. It is, therefore, explicit that the dramatic conflict may be internal within the mind itself, or external in the objective world or passing from the one to the other. Whatever is the nature of the conflict in a play, it definitely accentuates the aesthetic and emotional value of a dramatic work.

In our times technology too becomes a force in literature and, therefore, character is confronted with the machines and/or artificial intelligence created by man himself. Isaac Asimov's science fiction, *I, Robot,* offers a classic example of a modern conflict—fear of robots and artificial intelligence.

Connotation & Denotation A set of linguistic terms used in terms of deriving meaning of a word. Connotation goes beyond its dictionary meaning and it depends on association(s) which may be evoked or which may be derived from a specific context as opposed to the literal sense or its strict dictionary definition. Connotation refers to the attitudes, emotions and values attached to the word in a particular culture and context and also an extra meaning tactfully imposed on it. The denotation, on the other hand, is the dictionary definition. The word *wall* denotes an upright structure, which encloses something or serves as a boundary. When used connotatively the word *wall* can mean an attitude or actions, which prevent becoming emotionally close to a person. In Robert Frosts' "Mending Wall," *wall* is both a boundary (denotation) and a barrier that prevents the speaker and his neighbour from getting to know each other, a force prohibiting involvement (connotation).

Consciousness Criticism/Geneva School An approach to literature mainly associated with critics like Georges Poulet, Wolfgang Iser and Cary Nelson. During the 1950s growing out of Russian formalism and phenomenology the "Geneva School" used the phenomenological method to analyze works of literature as representations of deep structures of an author's mind and consciousness. The form of criticism tends to extend the study of a particular text beyond it. The critic gives focus on the whole range of texts of an author, or his/her groups so that the critics' consciousness can identify with the author's consciousness in its totality. During the 1950s and 1960s, associated with the consciousness school is the approach known as Geneva School, which is often a kind of expressive criticism, known as phenomenological criticism. The critics of this school attempted to almost "get into the author's head" in search of an intuitive understanding of the author's mind. They believed that each poet had a unique mind, somehow different from the minds of all other poets. Critics' responsibility, therefore, was to experience that unique mindscape of an author. To achieve that goal they sought to verify the author's all creative enterprises, including the structural unity in his works, letters and diaries, etc. Many of the close-knit group were attached to the University of Geneva. Some critics of this group were persons like Albert Béguin, Marcel Raymond and Jean-Pierre Richard. [Cf. genetic criticism]

Ref: Terry Eagleton, *Literary Theory: An Introduction* (1983).

Consonance A harmony of sound, opposed to dissonance. It is a repetition of a sequence of two or more consonants, but with a change in the intervening vowel. The repetition of consonantal sounds at the end of lines or words after different accented vowels at a regular interval to make a pattern is known as consonance: *pressed / past, shadow / mellow*, and even, *litter / letter*, etc. Auden's poem gives a fuller example:

"Out of this house"—said rider to reader,
"Yours never will"—said farer to fearer,
"They're looking for you"—said hearer to horror,
"As he left them there, as he left them there."

Consonance is frequently used in ballads, folk and popular songs. [Cf. assonance]

Convention A characteristic of a literary genre, realistic or unrealistic, any literary norm that is understood and accepted by the author and reader/audience. The acceptance comes from tradition, because it has come through practice for a long time and is recognized as a familiar technique. For example, the division of a play into acts and scenes is a dramatic convention, as are soliloquies and asides. Flashbacks and foreshadowing are other examples of literary conventions, so are stanzas and paragraphs. Those who break away from established norms are avant-gardes, and readers and audience may not immediately accept them. [Cf. canon]

Couplet A couple of poetic lines. As a literary term it refers to two rhyming verse lines that are self-contained linguistically and thematically. A couplet may be formal or closed or it may be run-on, with the meaning of the first line continuing to the second (enjambment). A *closed couplet* must be a rhymed one and that must form a complete thought or syntactic unit itself. Such couplets taken out of longer poems too may be treated as meaningful by virtue of their being independent in terms of construction and meaning. They are parts of a poem and they can safely be used out of the context as well. Example abounds in Pope's poems; one of them is taken from his *Essays on Criticism*:

True wit is nature to advantage dressed,
What oft was thought, but ne'er so well expressed.

Thus the simple difference between a *closed couplet* and an *open couplet* is both syntactical and semantic. While the closed couplet gives each line an independent status, the open couplet normally extends its meaning to the second line. However, since they lend themselves to condensed and succinct statements, they are often composed as independent poems or function as parts of other verse forms, such as the Shakespearean sonnet, which is concluded with a couplet. In French narrative and dramatic poetry, the rhyming alexandrine is the dominant couplet form, and German and Dutch verses of the 17th and 18th centuries reflect the influence of the alexandrine couplet. The term *couplet* is also commonly substituted for stanza in French versification. A *square couplet*, for example, is a stanza of eight lines, with each line composed of eight syllables. However, the greatest English couplet is the heroic couplet, two rhyming lines of iambic pentameter with a caesura, usually medial, in each line. Introduced by Chaucer in the 14th century, the heroic couplet was perfected by John Dryden and Alexander Pope in the late 17th and early 18th centuries. An example from Pope's *An Epistle to Dr Arbuthnot* is:

Ăs yét | | ă chíld, | | nŏr yét | | ă foól | | tŏ fáme,
Ĭ lísp'd | | ĭn núm | | bĕrs, fór | | thĕ núm | | bĕrs cáme.

Couplets were also frequently introduced into the blank verse of Elizabethan and Jacobean drama for heightened dramatic emphasis at the conclusion of a long speech or in running dialogue. An example from Shakespeare's *Richard II*:

Think what you will, we seize into our hands
His plate, his goods, his money, and his lands.

Ref: J Walker, *Walker's Rhyming Dictionary of the English Language* (1936). Philip Hobsbaum, *Metre, Rhyme and Verse Form* (1996).

Courtier Poets A group of poets during the 2nd half of the 16th and 1st half of the 17th centuries. These poets were associated with the court and the crown. Until modern times there were strong incentives to patronize poets and other writers wherever the seat of power was renowned as a centre of culture. Courtly protocol and ritual often required the use of highly ornamented poetry. The royal lifestyle demanded the production of texts to provide entertainment, as well as instruction. Most of the well-known poetry of this period was written by courtiers and by highly educated gentlemen, and was not always published. Poetry was composed for a small circle of friends or nobility. There is some controversy about how important their self-perception as poets was to them and to the social implications of this perception. It is perhaps true that some poets of the Elizabethan era—from Thomas Wyatt, Walter Raleigh to John Davies—were first courtiers and then poets. During the period of Henry VIII, important courtier poets were Sir Thomas Wyatt (1503-1542) and Henry Howard, Earl of Surrey (1517-1547). During Elizabeth's time Sir Edmund Spenser (1552-1599) and Sir Philip Sidney (1554-1586) and finally partly during Elizabeth I and James I the major courtier poets were Sir Walter Raleigh (1552-1618), Fulke Greville (1554-1628) and Lord Brooke (1554-1628), etc. Most of the writings were sonnets on Italian models, literature on courtly life and behaviour, classical type of poetry or religious writings. It must be remembered that self-deprecation was part of the poetic convention of the time and never taken very seriously by the audience.

Ref: DM Loades, *The Tudor Court* (1986). Janay Miller, *Courtly Literature* (1999, online). Steven W May, *The Elizabethan Courtier Poets: The Poems and Their Contexts* (1991).

Courtly Love A mediaeval concept of love transformed during the English Renaissance. In his *Symposium* and *Phaedrus*, Plato has deliberated on ideal love. Later Plotinus has further developed the idea that continued until the medieval practice of courtly love displaced it. Héroët Antoine, Renaissance court poet, whose works are representative of the amalgam of Platonism and Christian humanism produced the modern concept of courtly love.

In the 16th century Sir Wyatt and the Earl of Surrey translated Petrarch's works into English and it proved vastly influential. The sonnets initiated a new fashion of love poetry. In the centre of chivalric love a beautiful mistress, almost a deity, presided and the lover unconditionally served his mistress for the sake of love itself. This is found in troubadour poetry of Aquitaine and Provence in France toward the end of the 11th century. The concept rapidly spread to almost every part of Europe via Italy. The basic tenets of courtly love are: [1] the celebration of infidelity; [2] near deification of the mistress; [3] the lover unrequited in his love; and [4] paradoxically, the celebration of faithful service to the beloved. Some reasons behind courtly love are often mentioned: [1] a few women in a castle dominated by large number of male making the lady a common object of male admiration; [2] Catholic imagination of Virgin Mary; and [3] pre-Christian tribal conception of a women as powerful being, etc led to the lady's love being a quasi-divine object, especially in poetry. It is from this peculiar conjunction of social and historical factors that the poetry of courtly love carries the paradoxical discourses of adultery and fidelity; intense physical passion celebrated in an idealized mode. The literary convention of courtly love can be found in lyrics, romances and allegories of most of the representative poets of the Middle Ages. Among the English, Geoffrey Chaucer, John Gower, Sir Thomas Malory's names are to be found easily. Later Shakespeare and Spencer too celebrated this discourse of love in their sonnets.

Ref: Andreas Capellanus, *The Art of Courtly Love* (1964). CS Lewis, *The Allegory of Love: A Study in Medieval Tradition* (1936). D Kelly, *Medieval Imagination: Rhetoric and the Poetry of Courtly Love* (1977).

Criticism A systematic study and evaluation of literary works, usually based on a specific method or set of principles. The practice of criticism is a living process and it has given rise to numerous theories, methods, schools and traditions, sometimes producing conflicting, even contradictory interpretations of literature in general, as well as of individual works. Even such basic issues as what constitutes a poem or a novel have been the subjects for numerous debates over centuries. Some major and seminal texts of literary theory and criticism include Plato's *Republic,* Aristotle's *Poetics,* Sir Philip Sidney's *An Apology for Poetry*, John Dryden's *An Essay of Dramatic Poesy,* Alexander Pope's *An Essay on Criticism*, William Wordsworth's "Preface" to the second edition of his *Lyrical Ballads,* ST Coleridge's *Biographia Literaria*, PB Shelley's *A Defence of Poetry*, Matthew Arnold's *The Study of Poetry*, and TS Eliot's "Tradition and Individual Talent," etc. Some major schools of critical approach to literature are: aesthetic, antithetical, archetypal, biographical, Chicago school, classicist, contextual, cultural, deconstruction, dialectical, dialogical, disability studies, eco-criticism, existentialist, expressive, expressionist, feminist, formalist, gender, genetic, Geneva school, gynocriticism, historicist, humanist, imagist, impressionistic, judicial, Jungian, Marxist, mimetic, modernist, naturalist, neoclassicist, new criticism, new historicism, objective, personal, phenomenological, postcolonial, postmodernist, poststructuralist, practical, pragmatic, psychoanalytic, queer theory, reader-response, realist, rhetorical, romantic, semiotic, socialist, structuralist, textual, theoretical, transcendental, etc.

Seen from practical point of view, all these schools can be reduced to two major approaches only: [1] textual and [2] extra-textual approaches. The first approach gives importance to the text only without much regard to time, space or social, philosophical backgrounds, whereas in extra-textual approach the text is studied in terms of author's biography, time, historical contexts, ideology, etc.

Ref: A Ford, *The Origin of Criticism: Literary Culture and Poetic Theory in Classical Greece* (2002). MH Abrams, *The Mirror and the Lamp* (1953). Lionel Trilling, *Literary Criticism: An Introductory Reader* (1970). Rene Wellek, *A History of Modern Criticism* (1955), Terry Eagleton, *Literary Theory: An Introduction* (1983). WK Wimsatt, Jr. & Cleanth Brooks, *Literary Criticism: A Short History* (1957).

Cultural Criticism/Culture Studies An approach to literature that focuses on interdisciplinary fields concerned with the role of social institutions in the shaping of culture. In other words, this method analyses literature and other art forms in their political, economic and socio-institutional contexts. As Patrick Brantlinger points out, it is not a tightly coherent, unified movement with a fixed agenda; but rather a loosely coherent group of tendencies, issues and questions. Often the method analyses the interrelationships between varieties of cultural discourses. Originally identified with the Centre for Contemporary Cultural Studies, University of Birmingham (1964) and with such scholars as Richard Hoggart, Stuart Hall, and Raymond Williams, today cultural studies is recognized as a discipline or area of concentration in many academic institutions and has had broad influence in sociology, anthropology historiography, literary criticism, philosophy and art criticism. Among its central concerns is the place of race (or ethnicity), class, and gender in the production of cultural knowledge. The broad areas under which the critical approach can be categorized are: [1] Cultural studies transcend the confines of a single discipline such as literary criticism. Thus it cuts across diverse social and political interests and addresses many of the struggles within socio-intellectual scene. [2] It is on principle a political engagement as it seeks to restructure relationships between the dominant and the subordinated cultures. [3] It rejects the traditional notions of high and low or elite and popular culture. All forms of cultural production are studied in relation to other cultural practices. [4] It analyzes not only cultural production, but also the means of production. Thus culture studies come close to such para-literary questions as have been raised by the Marxists. A distinction between the two terms—*culture studies* and *cultural criticism*—often limits the second one to the field of art and literature, while the first one is applied as a broader term to include many other human interests and issues. [Cf. sociological novels]

Ref: Jeff Lewis, *Cultural Studies: The Basics* (2008). Raymond Williams, *Keywords: A Vocabulary of Culture and Society* (1985). Toby Miller, Ed. *A Companion to Cultural Studies* (2006).

Cyberfiction/Cyberpunk Fiction A relatively recent term that has developed hand in hand with the spread of information technology, specially the internet. Often interchangeably used with cyberpunk and hypertext fiction, cyberfiction simply means any fictional text, new or old, either published or not published before, that is uploaded on the website for public consumption. The spread of modern computer culture has somehow broadened public access to literature, although the old book form still continues to enjoy superiority. Cyberpunk, on the other hand, mainly refers to a variety of science fiction that gained popularity during the last three decades. The first popular cyberpunk, a novel, *Neuromancer*, composed by William Gibson, was cyber-published in 1984. The term is a hybrid formation having the first part from *cybernetics* and the second from *punk*, an antiestablishment group of activists in Europe during the 1970s. The specialty of the cyberpunk fiction is that the authors, like many science fiction writers, visualize a future society peopled by cyber fanatics immersed in a cyborg world, a world characterized by linked network, in which man and robot cease to have many distinctions. Characters are normally technologically proficient and life is mainly experienced through the virtual reality of cyberspace. Some of the cyberpunk fiction writers are William Gibson (*Neuromancer* 1984, *Mona Lisa Overdrive* 1988), Bruce Sterling (*Islands in the Net* 1988, *The Difference Engine* 1990), and Neal Stephenson (*Snow Crash* 1992, *The Diamond Age* 1995, *Cryptonomicon* 1999).

Ref: Edward James, *Science Fiction in the 20th Century* (1994). Larry McCaffery, *Storming the Reality Studio: A Casebook of Cyberpunk and Postmodern Science Fiction* (1992). Nigel Wheale, *The Postmodern Arts: An Introductory Reader* (1995). Stephen Graham, *The Cybercities Reader* (2004).

D

Dactyl/Dactylic A tri-syllabic metrical foot of one strong stress followed by two unstressed ones. Here is a couplet from Lord Tennyson's "The Charge of The Light Brigade" to exemplify the scheme:

> Bóld-ly̆ thĕy | | róde ănd wĕll
> Ín-tŏ thĕ | | jáws ŏf dĕath.

Dactylic hexameter is mostly used in classical epics; in English poems Dactyl has often been used as rhythmic variants. Dactyl means *finger* and the measure is so called because it consists, like a finger, of one long division followed by two shorter ones—the middle finger being the index for the stressed syllables and two smaller fingers on both sides representing unstressed syllables. [Cf. Scansion]

Dadaism An antiestablishment avant-garde movement in creative art and literature. Founded by Tristan Tzara in Zurich, Switzerland, 1916, Dadaism is characterized by an attempt to curb ordinary logical relationship between thought and idiom. After the First World War, the movement gained momentum rapidly in Europe and Paris became the headquarters of the Dadaist theorists and followers. The followers of the movement expressed their outrage at the destruction brought about during the First World War by revolting against various forms of social conventions. Mainly limited to painting and visual art, they offered artistic works marked by calculated madness and colourful nonsense, and insisted on total freedom of expression, mostly through primitive display of emotion and illogical phrases. Shock and awe seem to have been their modus operandi. None of the Dada art that survives can be called aesthetically pleasing and that was perfectly what they wanted—not to be pleasing was after all their motto. "For us, art is not an end in itself...but an opportunity for the true perception and criticism of the times we live in"—was how Hugo Ball expressed the creed behind the doctrine. And as George Grosz commented Dadaism meant nothing. "We want to change the world with nothing." The movement, however, ended soon after the war and the flag of Dadaism was embraced by surrealism. Proponents of Dadaism include Andre Breton, Louis Aragon, Philippe Soupault and Paul Éluard. Many critics try to associate the term with *father* (Dadaism <*dada*>, daddy, childish word for *father*) and think that Dadaism propagates and injects masculinity into literature. [Cf. surrealism]

Ref: Dietmar Elger, *Dadaism* (2004). Hugo Ball, *Flight Out of Time: A Dada Diary* (1927).

Dalit Aesthetics A new area of aesthetics and literary theory only recently penetrating into the Indian literary contexts. The word *Dalit* means *crushed, downtrodden* and thereby refers to a vast populace—marked as the untouchable, the scheduled caste, the Harijans, etc.—which for generations has been subjected to oppression and exploitation of the so-called upper caste people. The word gained currency as a marker of identity in 1972 when "Dalit Panthers of Bombay," a small group of Dalit activists, emerged as a force. The existence of Dalit literature is to be found in India's traditional folk cultures and oral literatures in regional languages such as Hindi, Marathi, Punjabi, Telegu and Gujarati, etc. The written texts are a recent phenomenon. However, with the emergence of a vast quantity of such texts that mainly focus on the marginality of the Dalit existence and the sub-human living condition they are subjected to, a kind of artistic yardsticks becomes a necessity since the traditional aesthetical tools appear inadequate to explain a Dalit experience. Despite initial difficulties, since 1990s onwards, an urgency to formulate a different aesthetics and literary theory has been felt both by Dalit writers and sympathizers. Critics like Sharankumar Limbale and Omprakash Valmiki have tried to formulate what may be called a Dalit literary theory. It is true that in various ways Dalit literature has been ostracized by Indian canonical criticism. Now that Dalit literature is a reality both quantitatively and qualitatively, Dalit aesthetics too is evolving as a viable factor. The aesthetics is imbued with Dalit consciousness of the surrounding reality. Limbale insists on the need to instrumentalize Dalit aesthetics and employ it as a cultural and social weapon against the so-called mainstream critical theories. As against 'pleasure' as the ultimate goal of literary works as is conceived of in the mainstream criticism, Dalit aesthetics stresses on the exposure of 'pain and anguish', its transportation beyond local boundaries and the portrayal of the Dalit aspirations as its ultimate aims. Dalit aesthetics demands thorough knowledge of the context in which a Dalit text is produced. The theory articulates the "ideological position of the Dalit writer, draws up the aims and goals of Dalit literature and defines its basic credo."

The rejection of the Gandhian Harijan concept is the starting point in formulating the school's critical tools. The radical ideas of Jyotirao Phule and Dr. BR Ambedkar's worldview have lent philosophical stability to the Dalit movement and they have set the cultural aspiration of the Dalit in motion. It is often apprehended that a standard Dalit aesthetics is difficult to formulate as the vast Dalit populace of India is divided and subdivided into many regional, cultural, linguistic and ethnic groups with diverse aspirations. However, the concept of Black aesthetics in the American context may help in understanding the background and development of Dalit aesthetics in India. Whereas in America the expatriation and colour of skin are strong unifying factors among the Black people, the Dalit populace in India has the same marginality of existence and oppression of the upper caste people before them. The traditional concept of race in America has its equivalent in the form of caste in India. Thus Dalit aesthetics seems to be a potential factor not just as a cultural phenomenon, but as a socio-political issue too. [Cf. Black aesthetics]

Ref: BR Ambedkar, "The Great Conversion: Speech on the Eve of the Great Conversion Held on 15 October 1956," *Thus Spoke Ambedkar: Selected Speeches,* Vol II (1969). Omprakash Valmiki, *Dalit Sahitya ka Soundaryashashtra* (2001). Sharankumar Limbale, *Towards an Aesthetic of Dalit Literature* (2004).

Dalit Literature <Dalit = underdog, oppressed class> A subaltern or a working class literature in India. The word 'Dalit', however, makes the literature somewhat dissimilar from one of the working class type. In India the Dalits are those who have been traditionally considered to be of so-called lower caste origins and hence have been deprived of basic human dignity and opportunities by the reactionary elements of the upper caste. The organized system of torture upon the Dalit was made a part of the mainstream culture. The literatures of this group of people emerged only during the 1960s and now have found some platforms even in the university syllabi. This literature is to be found in almost all Indian languages though it is in the Marathi language that had the first official voice of this genre. Silenced for centuries by caste prejudice and social oppression, the Dalits have only in the last fifty years found a powerful tone in Marathi literature. The revolutionary social movement launched by their leader Dr Ambedkar was paralleled by a wave of Dalit writing. For ages, Dalits have had their tales told by upper-caste writers. For examples, Premchand wrote of Dukhi, Mulk Raj Anand of Bakha, Arundhati Roy of Velutha and Mahasweta Devi of Doulati, etc. These are not Dalit literature in a strict sense. Dalit literature is the literature of the Dalit, by the Dalit and for the Dalit—i.e. literature written by Dukhies, Bakhas, Veluthas and Doulaties.

However, literature of the Dalit is not a new phenomenon. Because of social injustice such literary works too were suppressed and looked down upon. One of the first Dalit writers was Madara Chennaiah, an 11th century cobbler-saint who is often regarded the father of *Vachana Poetry*, or oral poetry. Another poet was Dohara Kakkaiah. The origins of the Dalit writing can also be traced back to Buddhist literature. However, in 1958, the term "Dalit literature" was used at the first conference of 'Maharashtra Dalit Literature Society' in Mumbai. Baburao Bagul (1930-2008) wrote in Marathi. His first collection of stories, *Jevha Mi Jat Chorali (When I Concealed My Caste*), published in 1963, depicted a cruel society and thus brought in new momentum to Dalit literature in Marathi. Another model collection of the new genre *The Poisoned Bread* (Ed. Arjuna Dangale 1992) became almost the literary manifesto of the Dalit class representing their plight and consciousness as well as their creative capability.

Ref: Amarnath Prasad & MB Gaijan, *Dalit Literature: A Critical Exploration* (2007). Sharankumar Limbale, *Towards an Aesthetic of Dalit Literature* (2004). Murali Manohar, *Critical Essays on Dalit Literature* (2015).

Susie Tharu & K Satyanarayana, *The Exercise of Freedom: An Introduction to Dalit Writing* (2013).

Dead Metaphor An overused Figure of Speech. Too frequent use of a figure may turn it into a popular cliché and thus, in due course of time, may turn it into a very commonplace tool. Gradually it may lose its figurative implication. As the meaning becomes too obvious, its metaphoric charm is lost. In such circumstances it becomes a dead metaphor. Such examples as "head of the family," "a fall in the trade," etc are frequently found in common usage. The basic difference between a dead metaphor and a cliché is that a dead metaphor has to be a metaphor, whereas any expression, metaphor or otherwise, can become a cliché. However, overuse is a common factor both the terms share between them.

Decadence A phase of moral and artistic decline towards the end of the 19th century following a period of greatness. The negative overtone of the term has its origin in the decline of quality in Hellenistic Greek and post-Augustan Latin literature since the present period and the past had a common feature to share with—decline in moral and literary standards. However, the literary movement referred to by the term had its beginnings in French Aestheticism. Decadent literature displays a fascination for the perverse and gloomy state of affairs and the new thrill. Major artists are found preoccupied with mysticism and a belief in the meaninglessness of human existence. A self-consciously refined style, polished ornamentation over substance received the major thrust and thus theoretically it closely associated itself with the doctrine known as *Art for Art's Sake*. The concept of fin de siècle of 1880s and 1890s too has a thematic link with decadence since it too connotes an emphasis on the decline of something, a concern with the overblown, the over-brightness and the luxuriance of decay. Major French decadence artists are Charles Baudelaire and Arthur Rimbaud. English decadents include Oscar Wilde, Ernest Dowson and Frank Harris.

Ref: Jacques Barzun, *From Dawn to Decadence: 500 Years of Western Cultural Life, 1500 to the Present* (2000). Mario Praz, *The Romantic Agony* (1930).

Deconstruction A method of philosophical and literary analysis, derived mainly from works of the French scholar Jacques Derrida (1930-2004) that questions the fundamental conceptual distinctions or oppositions in Western philosophy through a close examination of the language and logic of philosophical and literary texts.

In the 1960s Derrida initiated his major critique of Western metaphysics. To "deconstruct is to take an idea, institution and value, and understand its mechanisms by removing the cement that makes it up." The process involves the inquiring of many hierarchical binary oppositions i.e. *cause/effect, presence/absence* and *speech/writing,* etc in order to expose the bias of those tacit assumptions on which Western metaphysics rests. Deconstruction exhibits a process that reveals how a text undermines itself since every text includes unconscious *traces* of other positions exactly opposite to that which it sets out to uphold. The deconstruction displaces the opposition by showing that neither term is primary; the opposition is a product or a construct of the text rather than something given independently of it. The *speech/writing* opposition, according to which speech is present to the speaker or author and writing absent, is a manifestation of what Derrida calls the *logocentrism* of Western culture—i.e., the general notion that there is a world of *truth* existing prior to and independent of its representation by linguistic signs. To *deconstruct* an opposition, thus, is to explore the tensions and contradictions between the hierarchical ordering assumed in the text and other aspects of the text's meaning, especially its figurative or functional aspects. In discussions about intellectual trends of the late 20th century, deconstruction was sometimes used pejoratively to suggest nihilism and frivolous skepticism. In popular usage the term has come to mean a critical dismantling of tradition and traditional modes of thought.

Many American scholars took deconstruction as a logical step beyond New Criticism, and it inspired such scholars as Paul de Man and J Hillis Miller. Others, who are often referred to in connection with Derrida's discourse, are Geoffrey Hartman, Catherine Belsey, Harold Bloom, Eugenio Donato, Shoshana Felman, Michel Foucault, Barbara Johnson, Jonathan Culler and Gayatri Spivak.

Ref: David Lodge, Ed. *Modern Criticism and Theory* (1989). Jonathan Culler, *On Deconstruction* (1987). Terry Eagleton, *Literary Theory: An Introduction* (1983).

Dénouement The concluding part in which clearing up or untying of the complications takes place in a dramatic work. All mysteries, confusions and doubtful destinies are clarified. This phase, to be very precise, ranges from the anti-climax to the end of the last scene of the play. Like an orchestral symphony, in the dénouement, incidents and motifs treated in the earlier parts of a work are finally synthesized. Many critics use the two terms—catastrophe and dénouement as synonyms, though some prefer to restrict the use of catastrophe to tragic plays only, whereas dénouement is treated as a more universal term —applicable to tragedy, comedy and even fiction. As Aristotle has viewed, the dénouement is a logically deducted aesthetic product of a good dramatic plot. In tragedy particularly, elements of emotional interest that is what dénouement aims at is a combination of some aesthetic experiments on the part of the dramatist. Very often peripeteia and anagnorisis together makes the dénouement more powerfully effective.

Although Schopenhauer's views have very limited application to tragic dénouements in general, Hegel sounds remarkably like Racine when he claims that, in the tragic dénouement the necessity of all that has been experienced by particular individuals is seen to be in complete accord with reason and is harmonized on a true ethical basis. But where Neoclassicism was preoccupied with the unities of time and place, Hegel's concerns, like those of other Romantics, are inward. For him, the dénouement of tragedy is not the misfortune and suffering of the protagonist but rather the satisfaction of spirit arising from reconciliation. However, the modern dramatists, along with many other traditional structural elements of dramaturgy, have done without the dénouement part. Artists like Samuel Beckett in *Waiting for Godot* (1955) and Harold Pinter in *The Caretaker* (1960) prefer to opt for rather open-ended ambiguous closings of plays which raise questions than answer them. [Cf. catastrophe]

Detective Fiction/Story A narrative featuring a crime, solving the mystery shrouding it and locating the identification of a criminal. The conventions of the detective story comprise the detective's scrupulous use of logic while investigating the mystery; incompetent or ineffectual police; a suspect who appears guilty at first but is later proved innocent; and the detective's friend or confidant, often the narrator, whose delay in interpreting clues emphasizes by contrast the detective's brilliance. In England Dickens's protégé, Wilkie Collins is sometimes referred to as the "grandfather of English detective fiction." His mystery novels, *The Woman in White* and *The Moonstone* had a great fan following including TS Eliot. Edgar Allan Poe's "Murders in the Rue Morgue" is normally regarded as the first American example of this type. With this work, Poe established many of the conventions of the genre of detective fiction, which are still in operation. Other practitioners and literary examples of this vast and extremely popular genre include Sir Arthur Conan Doyle's *The Hound of the Baskervilles* featuring Sherlock Holmes is arguably the most famous of all detective stories. Agatha Christie's *Murder on the Orient Express* and Dorothy Sayers' *Strong Poison*, etc. are great examples in this category. The detective fiction, however, is a subgenre of crime fiction and mystery fiction in which an investigator or a detective investigates a crime, often murder. The type was flourished mainly during the mid-19th century. Although its basic pattern remains the same stories of this category are known by different names—espionage, gothic, psychological suspense, murder, police procedural, conspicuously and, even to a certain degree, the horror story.

Ref: LeRoy Panek, *An Introduction to the Detective Story* (1987). Susan Oleksiw, *A Reader's Guide to the Classic British Mystery* (1988).

Deus Ex Machina & Coup De Theâtre A couple of popular devices used in dramatic literature. In some ancient Greek dramas, essentially inexplicable crises were often solved by the involvement of a god, often brought on stage by an elaborate piece of equipment. This 'god from the machine' was literally a deus ex machina. No modern work introduces deities hanging by wires from the ceiling and coming to the aid of the afflicted hero, but the term deus ex machina is still used when a playwright uses some unlikely measure to sort out a dramatic impasse. When the cavalry comes charging over the hill or when the impoverished hero is relieved by an unexpected inheritance, it's often called a deus ex machina. In George Eliot's *Adam Bede*, when it was all set to execute Hetty Sorrel, the sudden arrival of Arthur with a new order serves as a modern form of deus ex machina. Coup de theâtre, on the other hand, is an unexpected and theatrically startling event, such as the sudden leap into activity of the supposedly invalid and sick wife of General St. Pé in Jean Anouilh's play *La Valse des Toréadors*. Since surprise is the common factor in both the devices, it is often difficult to distinguish between the two. However, basic ideas involved are: [1] in deux ex machina, the solution usually comes from outside; whereas in coup de theâtre it comes from within, and [2] in the development of the plot the former is more decisive than the latter. [Cf. peripety]

Dialogic/Monologic Criticism An approach to literature. The terms *dialogic* and its opposite 'monologic' have been given currency by the Russian scholar Mikhail Bakhtin (1895-1975). According to Bakhtin language is always social in that by nature it presupposes dialogue with others. He sees the novel as the most dialogical form in its capacity to subvert the *monological* (single) discourse or voice of the author. In dialogic works the dominant social or cultural ideology may vie with the discourses of popular culture. Therefore dialogic criticism tends to recognize other voices that are normally suppressed by the ruling voice, or the *monologic discourse*, either by the author or the narrator. He believes that no work can absolutely be monologic since the narrator, though he may represent the official voice, invariably discloses a range of viewpoints. He contrasts the monologic novels of writers such as Leo Tolstoy (1828-1910) with the dialogic works of Fyodor Dostoyevsky (1821-1881). Instead of subordinating the voices of all characters to an overriding authorial voice, a writer such as Dostoyevsky creates a polyphonic discourse in which the author's voice is only one among many and the characters are allowed free speech. Bakhtin developed his theory in the 1920s, but the theory could not affect much the mainstream Western critical thought until the 1980s. [Cf. polyphonic, subtext]

Ref: I Marková, *Dialogicality and Social Representations: The Dynamics of Mind.* (2003). Mikhail Bakhtin, *Problems of Dostoevsky's Poetics* (1929), trans. Caryl Emerson (1984).

Diary <Latin, *diarium dies*, day> A form of informal and purely personal writing, a regularly kept record of a person's private activities and reflections. As such, a diary is supposedly not intended for public consumption. Though not treated as a regular literary genre, the diary may have immense literary and socio-political merits. Often diary, memoir and autobiography jostle together for a common space. The earliest existing diary in Europe is the anonymous French *Journal d'un bourgeois de Paris de 1405 à 1449* written by a priest, which was a valuable reference to Charles VI and VII. The earliest English diary is dated 1442. In striking contrast to the West, the Middle East practice of diary writing goes back at least to the 9th century as a source for systematic historiography and Hadith criticism. Analyst Al-Haitham Ibn Adi (c. 747-821) was a pioneer figure in this respect. Interestingly, in Europe the practice of writing dairies flourished only after the Renaissance. The individualism of the Renaissance, in contrast to the communalism of the Middle Ages, shifted man's attention from God to himself and secular aspects of life. Some early instances of published dairies of merit include *Memorials of the English Affairs* by the lawyer and parliamentarian Bulstrode Whitelocke (1605-75), the diary of the French Marquis de Dangeau (1638-1720), etc.

The English diarist John Evelyn is surpassed only by the greatest diarist, Samuel Pepys, whose diary (1660-1669) is an astonishingly candid self-analysis and depiction of life in London. Jonathan Swift's *The Journal to Stella* (1766-68) has extraordinary emotional interest, ambition, affection tinged with wit. The novelist Fanny Burney's (Madame d'Arblay) diary (1842-46) and James Boswell's *Journal of a Tour to the Hebrides* (1785) are some of the best examples ever written in English. In the 19th century some diaries of unusual literary interest include the *Journal* of Sir Walter Scott (1890) and that of Henry Crabb Robinson (1869) having much biographical material on his literary acquaintances, including Johann Wolfgang von Goethe (1749-1832), Friedrich von Schiller (1759-1805), Wordsworth, and Coleridge.

The posthumous publication of the diaries of the Russian artist Marie Bashkirtseff (1860-84) produced a great sensation in 1887, as did the publication of the diary of the Goncourt brothers, beginning in 1888. In the 20th century, the Journal of *Katherine Mansfield* (1927), the two-volume *Journal of André Gide* (1939, 1954), and the five-volume *Diary of Virginia Woolf* (1977-84) are among the most notable examples. The *Journals of Dorothy Wordsworth* (1855) showing her influence on her brother Wordsworth and *The Diary of Anne Frank* (1947) are examples of well-known diaries discovered and published posthumously. Many writers have used the form as a deliberate literary device, as in Nikolai Gogol's (1809-1852) story "Diary of a Madman."

Ref: Bruce Mary, "The Literary Diary as a Genre", *The Maynooth Review* Vol. 5, No. 1 (1979). J New, *Drawing from Life* (2005). George Makdisi, "The Diary in Islamic Historiography: Some Notes", *History and Theory,* Vol. 25, No. 2 (1986). Ronald Blythe, *The Pleasures of Diaries: Four Centuries of Private Writing* (1989). William Matthews, *British Diaries: An Annotated Bibliography of British Diaries Written between 1442-1942* (1950).

Diaspora/Diasporic <Greek *dispersion*> A dispersion or mass migration of people from homeland. Though the term is originally associated with the forced displacement of the Jewish outside Israel from the 6th century BCE by the Babylonians, it is no more restricted to religious dispersion alone; now it encompasses a wide variety of people—expatriates, immigrants, the expelled, political refugees and alien residents. William Safran has thrown further light on the issue and argued that it is a dispersal of people from a specific, original and ethnic *centre* to one or more peripheral or foreign regions, retaining vestiges of a collective memory or vision, myth of the original homeland. The diasporic life is further complicated by an identity crisis in the host country. For the diasporic, going back home is almost impractical, though frequently making home a constant referral point continues. Diaspora is a part of colonial and postcolonial history—the huge volume of diasporic population includes movements of the African slaves, the Indian plantation labours, Chinese unskilled manual workers and even modern technical professionals, teachers, doctors, etc. to the US, West Indies, Fiji and Mauritius and many European countries. However, the colonial expansion and the movement of the colonizers to the colonized country and their settlement have normally been kept outside the scope of diaspora. The basic diasporic conditions of displacement and its aftermath, however, do not theoretically rule out the colonial ruling class from becoming diasporic.

Life in diaspora, the experience of the participants, their hopes, despairs, their attitudes to homeland and host country, and their love-hate relationship there, have given birth to a great body of literature, known as *diasporic literature*. Some principal names of authors in this category are Bharati Mukherjee, Salman Rushdie, Meena Alexander, Michael Ondaatje, Jhumpa Lahiri, Neil Bissoondath, Vijay Lakshmi, MG Vassanji and many others.

Ref: Robin Cohen, *Global Diasporas: An Introduction* (2008). William Safran, "Diasporas in Modern Societies: Myths of Homeland and Return," *Diaspora* (1991). I. H-Shihan, "Anglo-Indian Fiction: A Study of the Ruling Class in Diaspora," *English Studies in Albania* (ESSA), 2011, Volume 2, No. 1.

Diction A choice of words in a literary work depending on the author's targeted meaning and discourse. There are four general types of diction: *formal*, used in scholarly or lofty writing; *informal*, used in relaxed but educated conversation; *colloquial*, used in everyday speech; and *slang* containing newly coined words and other terms not accepted in formal usage. An author normally prefers formal diction that consists of a dignified, impersonal and elevated status; it follows the rules of syntax exactly and is often characterized by complex words and lofty tone. The subject matter however may demand words from informal, colloquial or even slang vocabulary. *Poetic diction* refers to the way poets sometimes employ an elevated diction that deviates significantly from the common speech and writing of their time, choosing words for their supposedly inherent poetic qualities. Since the 18th century, however, poets have been incorporating all kinds of diction in their works and so there is no longer an automatic distinction between the language of a poet and the language of everyday speech. In English it was Chaucer who first used colloquial languages suitable to his tales. *Metaphysical poetry* too preferred rugged ordinary poetic diction and finally Wordsworth, according to his theory—"Poet is a man speaking to men"—advocated for common everyday language in his poetry. Victorian culture once again preferred standard diction for literature; but only to be replaced by ordinary language with the trends of modernity. Since then very formal and high sounding diction is considered to be a mark of snobbery and artificiality.

Didactic A work of art that is instructive or that provides recommendation or lesson. The term is often used to define literary works that aim to teach some moral, religious, political or practical lesson. Although didactic elements, more or less, are often inseparably present in all forms of literature, the term didactic usually refers to literature in which the message is more important than literature itself. Examples of didactic literature include John Bunyan's *Pilgrim's Progress,* Alexander Pope's *Essay on Criticism,* Jean-Jacques Rousseau's *Emile* and Elizabeth Inchbald's *Simple Story.* Some writers, however, prefer to be overtly didactic. Bernard Shaw, for example, made his mission clear in his unequivocal statement that for art's sake *alone* he would not take the toil of writing a single line. Long ago Aristotle focuses his attention on the problem. He believes immature mind views things didactically. It is not that every writer announces his intention and that the purpose must be judged from the work. He suggests that if it appears that the idea is old, the form is new, then it is didactic; if the form before the idea, the work is precious; and if the idea and form take shape together, the work is pure art. [Cf. aestheticism, exemplum, fable and parable]

Dirge <ME Classical Latin *dirige*, to direct—"Direct my way in your sight, O Lord my God" (Psalm 5:8) > A sad song appropriate for a funeral performance. It refers to the first words of an *antiphon* in Christian music in the form of a chant, specially sung for the burial service. Simply speaking it is a solemn lyric or song commemorating a death, expressing grief. The ancient Roman and Greek counterparts were *nenia* and *epicedium*. They were originally sung at funerals by family members and later by hired wailing women. Finally dirge came to mean a simple mournful lyrical composition with some musical qualities. A dirge is often made part of a dramatic piece as in Shakespeare's *Tempest*: "Full fathom five thy father lies;/ Of his bones are coral made" etc. "Why were you born when the snow was falling"—a poem by Christina Georgina Rossetti is another example of the subgenre. A dirge is always much shorter than an elegy and whereas an elegy signifies a personal meditation, a dirge commemorates a death of a person or a thing. Among the famous dirge writers one easily remembers: Shakespeare (Come away come away, death,/ And in sad cypress let me be laid), Tennyson (Now is done thy long day's work;/ Fold thy palms across thy breast) and Shelley (Rough Wind, that moanest loud/ Grief too sad for song), etc. It is, however, often said that many oral traditions are richer in dirge poetry and that nowhere in the corpus of oral poetry have there been more works of delicate originality than the African dirge forms.

Discordia Concours A Latin phrase meaning "discord in harmony." The term was coined by the English writer Samuel Johnson (1709-1784), in *The Lives of Poets,* to describe "a combination of dissimilar images or discovery of occult resemblances in things apparently unlike." Johnson created the expression by reversing a phrase by the Latin poet Horace. The metaphysical poetry of John Donne, Richard Crashaw, Abraham Cowley, George Herbert and Edward Taylor, among others, contains many examples of discordia concours. For example in his poem "A Valediction" Donne compares his union with his ladylove to a draftsman's compass and thus becomes the butt of some critics' harsh attack as the comparison is most improbable, something incompatible, as it were "yoked by violence", not by the naturalness of poetic harmony.

Discourse <Latin *discursus*, running to and from> A key concept in semantics, a linguistic unit composed of several sentences. In other words, discourse is composed of conversations, arguments or speeches. Conventional phraseology often characterizes discourse as a learned deliberation. Discourse refers to the words in a text or narrative, as opposed to its story line, that projects an ideological position within a given narrative and underlines a certain point of view or defends a given value system. While analyzing the concept, contemporary literary critics maintain that society is generally made up of a number of different discourses, one or more of which may be dominant or serve the dominant ideology at a given time. Discourse has recently become a key concept in analyzing colonial and post-colonial texts. The major and influential discussions on this issue are to be found in Edward Said's *Orientalism* (1978). Modern criticisms argue that no field of enquiry is ever completely neutral, but is shaped by institutions which support it. In a colonial context this is particularly relevant because knowledge about the colonized peoples was entwined with a sense of authority over them and this, in turn, justified the need for their control. Thus to analyze colonial discourse is to study how colonized peoples were constructed, represented and even silenced within colonial literature. Joseph Conrad's *Heart of Darkness* (1902), for example, is not an isolated piece of writing. Once put in the context of 'Africanist' and then 'primitivist' discourse, the reader comes to know that the text is not a straightforward reflection of Africa, but actually part of the process by which Africa is constructed and invented in the European imagination. Therefore, discourse is a system by which knowledge of a particular field is organised and the subject is constructed. Such knowledge is produced from a distance and supports the prejudices and assumptions of the dominant group. [Cf. dialogic criticism, orientalism]

Ref: A McHoul & W Grace, *A Foucault Primer: Discourse, Power, and the Subject* (1993). J Sunderland, *Gendered Discourses* (2004).

Dithyramb An improvised song in honour of the wine god Dionysus sung by banqueters in Greece, 7th century BCE. It was contrasted with the more sober *paean*, sung in honour of Apollo. The dithyrambs began to achieve literary distinction when the poet Arion gave them names and formally presented them with a dithyrambic song accompanied by circular dances performed around the altar of Dionysus by choruses composed of 50 men and boys at the Great Dionysia competitions at Corinth. By the end of the 6th century BCE, the dithyramb was a fully recognized literary genre. Its most famous composer was Lasus of Hermione, who is said to have been one of Pindar's teachers. From about 450 BCE onward, dithyrambic poets employed ever-more-startling devices of language and music; until for ancient literary critics the dithyrambic acquired the connotations of *turgid* and *bombastic*. True dithyrambs are rare in modern poetry, although John Dryden's "Alexander's Feast" (1697) may be said to bear a coincidental resemblance to the form. [Cf. chorus]

Documentary Fiction A form of fiction often confused with *docu-fiction* that features a great amount of documentary materials such as newspaper items, trial transcripts and legal reports, etc. This form may portray fictionalized slices or may contain a fictional story in which the author incorporates real-life information or events. Examples of documentary fiction include the works of Theodore Dreiser (1871-1945), Emile Zola (1840-1902), John Dos Passos (1896-1970), and James T Farrell (1904-1979). An example of a nonfiction literary documentary is James Agee and Walker Evans's *Let Us Now Praise Famous Men* (1941). A documentary film, or better known as *docu-film*, too can be made of the similar stuff.

Doggerel A verse type or a lesser kind of a poem, ordinarily a poem without any specific rhythm, maybe with some forced rhyme pattern; a low, or trivial form of verse, loosely constructed. The poems are written either for evoking fun or some burlesque effect; otherwise it has no efficacy. Most probably the name is a derivative of 'dog'. One of the earliest examples of the word is found in the 14th century in the works of Chaucer, who applied the term *rym doggerel* to his "Tale of Sir Thopas". The mechanics play in *A Midsummer Night's Dream* has a crude and bawdy sort of verse; they call it doggerel; and Shakespeare uses doggerel in *The Comedy of Errors* to help establish the intellectual and socioeconomic status of the Dromio twins. Geoffrey Chaucer's 'Tale of Sir Thopas,' goes like this:

> Sir Thopas was a doughty swain,
> White was his face as paindemain,
> His lippes red as rose.
> His rode is like scarlet in grain,
> And I you tell in good certain
> He had a seemly nose.

Drama A work primarily designed to be presented by actors on the stage, in which characters enact their roles through actions and dialogues. The drama denotes a broad literary genre that includes a variety of forms, from pageant and spectacle to tragedy and comedy, as well as countless types and subtypes. More commonly, in modern usage, however, a drama is a work that treats serious subjects and themes but does not aim at the grandeur of tragedy. This use of the term originated with the 18th century French writer Denis Diderot, who used the word *drame* to designate his plays about middle-class lives. Thus drama typically features characters of a less exalted stature than those of tragedy. Examples of classical dramas include Menander's comedy *Dyscolus* and Sophocles' tragedy *Oedipus Rex.* Contemporary dramas include Eugene O'Neill's *The Iceman Cometh,* Lillian Hellman's *Little Foxes,* and August Wilson's *Ma Rainey's Black Bottom.*

Sometimes it is possible that a piece of drama is not meant for the stage at all. Although written in the form of a regular drama, it is intended to be read. This type is called *closet drama*. Some poets like Milton (*Samson Agonistes*), PB Shelley (*Prometheus Unbound*) and Lord Byron (*Manfred*) have tried this form. Another variety of drama is *poetic drama*, in which in place of prose dialogue, poetry is used. Most of the dialogues in English poetic dramas are framed in blank verse.

A poetic drama may either be tragedy or comedy. TS Eliot's *Murder in the Cathedral* is an example of this genre. [Cf. comedy of manners, epic farce, melodrama, revenge tragedy, theâtre]

Ref: A Nicoll, *A History of Early Nineteenth Century Drama IV, 1800-1830* (1952). GP Deshpande, *Modern Indian Drama: An Anthology* (2000). JW Cunliffe, *Modern English Playwrights: A Short History of English Drama from 1825* (1969). Peter Devison, *Contemporary Drama and the Popular Dramatic Tradition in England* (1982). Philip Whaley Harsh, *A Handbook of Classical Drama* (1944).

Dramatic Irony A form of irony, a language device based on indirectness, either spoken or written, in which the real meaning is concealed or contradicted by the literal or contextual meaning. There are several kinds of irony though they fall into two major categories—*verbal* and *situational*. Verbal irony arises from a sophisticated or resigned awareness of contrast between what is and what ought to be and expresses a controlled pathos without sentimentality. It is a form of indirection that avoids overt praise or censure as in the casual irony of the statement—"The brotherly love of our enlarging Christianity is proved by the multiplication of murder" (Ruskin). In a theatrical situation too there is an incongruity between what is expected and what occurs. Dramatic irony, therefore, is not by itself a category; it is an irony embedded in a dramatic situation rather than in a verbal deal.

Dramatic irony, as noted above, depends on the structure of a work rather than its use of words. In plays or in narrative works the ironic effect is often created by the audience's awareness of a fate in store for the characters that they themselves are not properly aware of. For example, when Agamemnon accepts the flattering invitation to walk upon the purple carpet (that is to become his shroud), although Agamemnon does not know it, the audience is fully aware of what tricky situation Agamemnon is in. The surprise ending of an O Henry short story, "The Gift of the Magi," is also an example of dramatic irony, as is the more subtly achieved effect of Anton Chekhov's story "Lady with the Dog," in which an accomplished Don Juan engages in a routine flirtation only to find himself seduced into a passionate lifelong commitment to a woman who is no different from all the others. In Shakespeare, the use of dramatic irony is often very subtle: Desdemona is too innocent and she advocates for Cassio's case when Othello is very disturbed. It is ironical that she tries to please her angry husband with something that itself is the reason for his anger. Without her knowledge she adds fuel to the fire. Or, when Duncan betrays full faith on Macbeth—"He was a gentleman on whom I built/ An absolute trust"—he was in fact betraying his ignorance about human nature and also about the prophecy of witches that Macbeth was going to be the king after murdering him whereas the audience knows about the prophecy! The irony in *Oedipus the King* too consists in the relation between the audience's knowledge of the protagonist's situation and his own ignorance of it. But Shakespeare's readiness to remark on the "mind's fainter and involuntary utterances" is so great, says Schlegel, that nobody ever painted so truthfully as he has done the facility of self-deception, the half self-conscious hypocrisy towards ourselves, with which even noble minds attempt to disguise the almost inevitable influence of selfish motives in human nature. [Cf. irony]

Ref: Wayne Booth, *A Rhetoric of Irony* (1974). John Lippitt, *Humour and Irony in Kierkegaard's Thought* (2000).

Dramatic Monologue <Greek *mono*, one & *logos*, speech> A dramatic technique when a lone character reveals his or her inner mind and feelings, through a speech, otherwise hidden throughout the course of the story line. This speech, where only one character speaks and the person spoken to is neither present nor audible, somehow records the reactions of the listener too. It is like a telephonic conversation in which one can listen to one person only and can gather what comes from the other end. When such listener or audience is imaginary, he is often called *internal audience*. Dramatic monologue, however, is often introduced during a climactic moment in a work and often reveals hidden truths about characters, their history and their relationships. Also it can further develop a character's personality and also be used to create irony. The most famous examples of this special type of monologue can be found in Robert Browning's poems, such as "My Last Duchess," "The Bishop Orders his Tomb," and "Andrea Del Sarto". Browning's use of dramatic monologue had a special appeal to his readers because of his craftsmanship over the form and subject matter. However, in one of the most influential and controversial definitions, Robert Langbaum saw the dramatic monologue technique as a continuation of an essentially Romantic "poetry of experience" in which the reader experiences a tension between sympathy and judgment. One problem with this approach seems to arise from the fact that modern readers of Browning's poems found them vastly different from Langbaum's Wordsworthian model. Among other big poets whose works included dramatic monologues the names of Robert Frost and TS Elliot come readily. [Cf. monologue, soliloquy]

Ref: Robert H Garratt, "Browning's Dramatic Monologue: The Strategy of the Double Mask," *Victorian Poetry* 11, 1973. George P Landow, *Dramatic Monologue: An Introduction*, www.victorianweb.org (Seen 21-December-2017). SS Curry, *Browning and the Dramatic Monologue* (1908).

Dramatic Poem/Poetry A lyrical composition that employs elements of the drama such as dialogue, action or characterization, but excluding works that are intended for stage presentation. Victorian poet Robert Browning's many poems are regarded as dramatic poems. A monologue is a form of dramatic poetry. Almost a similar kind of dramatic writing is meant for *readers' theatre*, in which actors read out or recite without decor before an audience (not to be confused with *closet drama*, often a dramatic poem that assumes dialogue form; e.g., Milton's *Samson Agonistes*, not meant for the stage). The essential discipline of the circuit of communication with an audience is what distinguishes drama as a genre and when this essential quality is dressed in the poetic form, it becomes poetic drama. To be precise, dramatic poem is basically a poem with dramatic quality within a play or in a book of poem; whereas poetic drama is a piece of dramatic work further qualified by poetry. [Cf. dramatic monologue]

Dramatis Personae A customary list of characters in a literary work, particularly a drama. The characters' names printed on the first page of the text of a play or announced in the programme are the dramatis personae. The list is descriptive; it mentions short description of the characters and their relationship with other characters in the work. So far as written and published books are concerned, names of major characters appear on the page just preceding the text of either the play's opening scene or the prelude.

Dystopia/Utopia A couple of fictitious places. Dystopia, instead of being a paradise, is a horrible place where everything has gone awry in an attempt to create a perfect hellish society. The characters lead dehumanized, fearful lives. Jack London's *The Iron Heel,* Yevgeny Zamyatin's *My,* Aldous Huxley's *Brave New World,* George Orwell's *Nineteen Eighty-four,* HG Wells's *The Time Machine* and Margaret Atwood's *Handmaid's Tale,* etc portray versions of dystopia. These anti-utopian novels are called *Dystopian* novel. Dystopian literature warns us of a dangerous future ahead. Utopia, on the other hand, is an ideal place that does not exist in reality. Utopia has its origin in Greek words *outopia* (no place) and *eutopia* (good place). Utopian literature is an escape from reality and it depicts author's vision of an ideal place. Early literary utopias were included in Plato's *Republic* and Sir Thomas More's *Utopia,* and Francis Bacon's *The New Atlantis*, while more modern utopias can be found in Samuel Butler's *Erewhon,* Theodor Herzka's *A Visit to Freeland,* HG Wells' *A Modern Utopia,* Charlotte Perkins Gilman's *Herland*, and Edward Bellamy's *Looking Backward: 2000-1887.* [Cf. arcadia, el dorado]

E

Ecocriticism A study of the relationship between literature and the physical environment. Ecocriticism tries to focus on certain geocentric interrogations, such as, how nature is represented in a poem; how the physical setting contributes to the plot of a story; how the values expressed in a dramatic work is consistent with environmental wisdom and how the metaphor of the land influences the way we treat nature, etc. Therefore, the theoretical discourse rests mostly on the interrelation between nature and culture or, in other words, between the human and the nonhuman. Beginning with the Association for the Study of Literature and Environment (ASLE), the theory gained momentum in the 1990s in the US and some other western countries. One of the theoreticians of the school, Rueckert thinks that man's tragic flaw is his anthropocentric vision that dictates him to violate, conquer, domesticate nature and exploit it of its resources for his consumption. A global ecological crisis has endangered human existence; not because how ecosystems function but because how man's ethical systems malfunction. Getting through the crisis requires two things: [1] Understanding the impact of human interference with nature; and [2] Commitment to apply that understanding to restore the system. Literary scholars, along with the scholars of other branches of learning can help mobilize the understanding and thus may help repair the creative bond between nature and man. Therefore, as Christopher Cokinos believes, "like feminism at its best, ecocriticism is fundamentally an ethical criticism and pedagogy, one that investigates and helps make possible the connections among self, society, nature, and text." Thomas Dean believes that "eco-criticism is a response to the need for humanistic understanding of our relationships with the natural world in an age of environmental destruction." In terms of the academy, the movement is a reaction to "scholarly specializations that have gone out of control" and eco-criticism seeks to reattach scholars and scholarship to the real concerns of the world. However, the newness of the term is more apparent than real; it is a sophisticated rephrasing of the rudimentary theories already worked out by philosophers and poets like Rousseau, Wordsworth, Thoreau and the like. As a literary theory ecocriticism has limitations. The theory may not be relevant for wide ranging literary texts. The texts that may fit easily within its structure are the epic poems, the Bible, elegy, pastoral and Romantic poetry and also the texts that have treated nature with a philosophy or used nature extensively as backgrounds as in Thomas Hardy and JM Synge, etc.

Ref: Cheryll Glotfelty & Harold Fromm, Eds. *The Ecocriticism Reader: Landmarks in Literary Ecology* (1996). Dana Phillips, "Ecocriticism, Literary Theory, and the Truth of Ecology", *New Literary History,* Vol. 30, No. 3 (1999). Laurence Coupe, Ed. *The Green Studies Reader: From Romanticism to Ecocriticism* (2000). William Rueckert, "Literature and Ecology: An Experiment in Ecocriticism." *Iowa Review* 9.1 (1978).

Ecofeminism A compound word derived from *ecology* and *feminism*. The eco-feminist activists emerged as an academic and social force between 1980s and 1990s. The philosophy of ecofeminism is in fact an extension of the environmental movements of the 1970s and merger of the same with the feminist movement of the 1980s. Some important publications that are responsible for proliferation of the philosophy are: Mary Daly's *Gyn/Ecology* (1978), Susan Griffin's *Women and Nature* (1978) and Carolyn Merchant's *The Death of Nature* (1980). It is worthwhile to refer to Mary Mellor's definitive observation on the issue and see how nature and women issues are synchronized in this philosophy: "Ecofeminism is a movement that sees a connection between the exploitation and degradation of the natural world and the subordination and oppression of women. It emerged in the mid-1970s alongside second-wave feminism and the green movement. Ecofeminism brings together elements of the feminist and green movements, while at the same time offering a challenge to both. It takes from the green movement, a concern about the impact of human activities on the non-human world and from feminism the view of humanity as gendered in ways that subordinate, exploit and oppress women." Mellor's argument is sizeable. She associates women with biology and nature and argues that the relationship between women and the environment can refine our understanding of the relationship between humanity and the natural world. She, therefore, stresses that there is within the feminist and green movements the basis of a new radical prospect which draws on the principles of both the philosophies. The advocates of the school are insistently verbal against paternalistic and capitalistic society as both, according to them, have led to a harmful divide between nature and culture. Early ecofeminists propagated that the divide could only be repaired by the feminine intuition for nurture and holistic awareness of nature's action. Therefore, the crucial issue of ecofeminism finds in gender discrimination and environmental evils a common connection—i.e. paternalistic social organization. Some literary works of Margaret Atwood, Jean Auel, Octavia Butler, Ursula K Le Guin, Toni Morrison and Alice Walker, etc. are examples of ecofeminist consciousness. In the Indian social context, the 1973 Chipko movement led by rural womenfolk to protect forests is one of the burning examples of ecofeminist perception.

Ref: Karen J Warren, *Ecofeminist Philosophy: A Western Perspective on What It Is and Why It Matters* (2000). Mary Mellor, *Feminism & Ecology* (1997). Rosemary Radford Ruether, *Integrating Ecofeminism Globalization and World Religions* (2005). Susan Griffin, *Woman and Nature: The Roaring inside Her* (1978).

El Dorado <*Gilded place*> An amazing place often referred to as 'The Great and Golden City of Manoa' by the Spaniards. However, the legend of El Dorado predates the arrival of Spaniards in South America. The legendary place, supposed to abound in gold, was believed to have existed on the banks of the Amazon or the Orinoco. The first expedition in search of El Dorado was led by Francisco de Orellana in 1541. Orellana named the Western hemisphere's largest river, the Amazon, and followed it across South America to the Atlantic Ocean; but he could not trace the fabled city of El Dorado. It is said that Sir Walter Raleigh (1552-1618) undertook an expedition to the Orinoco in search of gold. His expedition failed and at the demand of the Spanish ambassador, Raleigh was arrested and executed. However, his exaggerated account of his experience in a book that added to the legend of El Dorado. Since the place is still undiscovered, it still means an imaginary place, a dreamland, where all the best things conceivable could be found. El Dorado smoothly made its way into literature. In *Candide,* a novel by the French writer Voltaire, the main character accidentally discovers the rich city. Edgar Allan Poe's poem *Eldorado* refers to the legend, as does *Paradise Lost* by poet John Milton. The latest addition in the long series is Baroness Orczy's *Eldorado* (1913), a story of escape. [Cf. arcadia, utopia]

Ref: Robert Silverberg, *The Golden Dream: Seekers of El Dorado* (1985).

Electra & Oedipus Complex A set of psychological make-ups frequently referred to in literary discussions. *Electra Complex* is used to describe the psychological conflict of a daughter's unconscious rivalry with mother for her father, with whom she develops an obsessive attachment. The name comes from the Greek Electra myth, the source of all Electra plays by Aeschylus, Euripides and Sophocles in which Electra avenged the death of her father, Agamemnon, by plotting the death of her mother, Clytemnestra. Since Sigmund Freud (1856-1939) the term Electra Complex has replaced what he referred to as *female Oedipus Complex*. On the other hand, *Oedipus Complex* refers to a son's amorous obsession with his mother. The phrase is derived from the story of the ancient Theban hero Oedipus, who unknowingly killed his father and married his mother. Literary treatments of the Oedipus complex include Andre Gide's *Oedipe* and Jean Cocteau's *La machine infernale,* as well as the most famous, Sophocles' *Oedipus Rex.* In English, Lawrence's novel *Sons and Lovers* is often treated as a story based on the Oedipus complex.

Ref: Andrew M Colman, *A Dictionary of Psychology* (2008). B Tobin, *Reverse Oedipal Complex Analysis* (1988). Seymour Keitlen, *Oedipus Complex: A Philosophical Study* (2003).

Elegy A sombre poem, originally a Greek funeral tribute, *elegos*, lament, written in couplets of hexameter followed by a pentameter. The word *elegy* was later applied by Ovid to describe love poems such as his *Amores*. In English, the modern and restricted meaning of lament for a departed soul or a tragic event has been current only since the 16th century. Donne's elegies followed Ovid's and were sometimes witty and ribald. Generally the term elegy signified a sad meditation on love inflected with a sense of mortality. *Adonaïs: An Elegy on the Death of John Keats* is a pastoral elegy, written by Shelley in 1821, is widely regarded as one of Shelley's best and most well-known works. Shelley, while writing this elegy, followed another great elegy of English tradition—Milton's *Lycidas* (1638) which was dedicated to Edward King, his friend. However, "Elegy Written in a Country Churchyard" by Thomas Gray and "When Lilacs Last in the Dooryard Bloom'd" by Walt Whitman are the two most admired examples of elegy from both sides of the Atlantic. [Cf. dirge, pastoral elegy]

Ref: Jahan Ramazani, *Poetry of Mourning: The Modern Elegy from Hardy to Heaney* (1994). Karen Weisman, Ed. *The Oxford Handbook of the Elegy* (2012). Peter M Sacks, *The English Elegy: Studies in the Genre from Spenser to Yeats* (1987).

Elision/Deletion A deliberate omission of a part of a word's sound, vowel, consonant or even a phrase to make a line conform to a metrical scheme: *o'er* = over, *ne'er* = never, etc. In linguistics elision and deletion are frequently used interchangeably. In English, an elision is normally marked by the sign called apostrophe, as in *don't*. The colloquial English and sometimes written form as well have numerous examples of such deliberate or natural omissions. For examples: 'going to' > 'gonna' is an elision whereas 'do not' > 'don't' is a contraction. In phonology the opposite of elision is *epenthesis*, whereby sounds are inserted into a word to ease pronunciation. This occurs passim in the French language. The specialists often make a slight difference between the two terms. For them an elision is normally used in linguistics to show the changes in a contemporary living language; whereas deletion is used to mark the change of sound over a long period. Deletion also means an item that has been or will be deleted or an act of deleting. This phenomenon is relevant to almost all known languages.

Empathy <German *einfühlung*> Empathy is an emotional ability to put oneself in another's place and *feel into* his/her experience, ideas, affliction and ecstasy, etc. The term is coined in the early 20th century, investing in it the nuance of the German *einfühlung* and was modelled on *sympathy*. The term is applied with reference to a strongly felt aesthetic experience. The way one may feel before the Greek statue Discobolus to flex muscles to hurl the discus is an automotoractive response and this is an emphatic response in terms of aesthetic experience. A good actor too genuinely feels into the role he performs. With other works of art too, a viewer may, by introjections, identify himself with what he observes or contemplates. In *Venus and Adonis,* Shakespeare's description of the snail, whose tender horns being hit, shrinks backward in pain and some of the physical sensations evoked in the description of the movement of the falcon in Manley Hopkins's *The Windhover* may exemplify the use of empathy in literature. Carl Rogers, American psychologist, applied empathy as a part of his counselling technique. Empathy is an unconscious psychic process by which a person incorporates into his/her own psychic device the characteristics of another person or object or can feels from the position of the person or object in view. [Cf. synaesthesia]

Ref: Mark H Davis, *Empathy: A Social Psychological Approach* (1996).

End-Stopped Line A well-knit pattern of sentence structure in a line of a poem. It is contrary to enjambment. It refers to a poetic verse or line in which the end of the line coincides with the end of the grammatical structure, usually the sentence. In other words the end of the line is marked with a clear punctuation mark and also the end of the metrical unit involved in the line. Here is an example from Robert Southey's poem, 'The Scholar': "My never-failing friends are they,/ With whom I converse day by day." The idea comes to a completion here and it does not run on to the next line as it happens in case of an enjambment. Many of Pope's couplets too have rigid end-stop lines. In fact end-stopped line pattern was the most popular fashion of the art of poetry and run-on patterns are a later discovery. Shakespeare's early works are all composed as end stopped lines and later he experimented with enjambments. Free verse does not offer much scope for tight end-stopped line patterns.

Enjambment A French poetic term for *striding over*, an expression that spans over more than one line. It is a line that ends before grammatical and semantic unity has been achieved and therefore the sense carries on to the next line without a pause. Such lines are ordinarily called *run-on lines,* and are clearly distinguished from end-stopped line. The opening of Coleridge's "Kubla Khan" boldly exemplifies the use of enjambment: "In Xanadu did Kubla Khan/ A stately pleasure-dome decree;/ Where Alph, the sacred river, ran/ Through caverns measureless to man/ Down to a sunless sea."

Enlightenment A 17th and 18th century trend in philosophy and literature mostly rooted in faith in the human reasoning faculty. It began in France but had a wide impact throughout Europe and America. Thinkers of the Enlightenment valued reason and believed that both an individual and society could achieve a state of perfection. Corresponding to this essentially humanist vision was a resistance to religious authority. Edmund Burke termed this as the age of "sophisters, economists, and calculators." Some historians have ascribed in it not only Jacobean authoritarianism, but also a kind of totalitarianism. It may be that the movement that helped to free man from the past and its "self-incurred tutelage" (Kant) failed to prevent the development of new systems and techniques of tyranny. This intellectual odyssey should, however, be seen to be related to the growth of the state, the advancement of science and the subsequent development of an industrial society. For their ill effects, the Enlightenment cannot be held to be mainly responsible. Rather it should be viewed as an integral part of a broader historical process. Important figures of the Enlightenment were Rousseau, Diderot and Voltaire in France; Lessing and Moses Mendelssohn in Germany; Edward Gibbon, Locke, Newton, Johnson and David Hume in England; and Thomas Paine and Thomas Jefferson in the US. To round off the issue, it can be said that Enlightenment was a collective effort of the post Renaissance west to understand the natural world and humankind's place in it solely on the basis of reason without turning to religious belief. The movement claimed the allegiance of a majority of thinkers during the 17th and 18th centuries. At its heart it became a conflict between religion and the inquiring mind that wanted to know and understand through reason based on evidence and proof. Science and religious dogma had a head on collision for the first time in human history. Many believe that Enlightenment was a natural continuation of the Renaissance. In English literature it was Pope's time. Here is a typical poetic voice of the Age of Reason; his poetic account of the Newtonian universe:

All are but parts of one stupendous whole,
Whose body nature is, and God the soul
All nature is but art, unknown to thee;
All chance, direction, which thou cannot see.
All discord, harmony not understood;
All partial evil, universal good
And, spite of pride, in erring reason's spite,
One truth is clear: Whatever is, is right.

In his *Essay on Man* (1733) Pope thus expressed his robust optimism and good faith in reason that marked the era.

Ref: Dorinda Outram, *The Enlightenment* (1995). Hackett Lewis, *The European Dream of Progress and Enlightenment* (1992). Louis Dupre, *The Enlightenment & the Intellectual Foundations of Modern Culture* (2004). Stephen Bronner, *The Great Divide: The Enlightenment and its Critics* (1995). William Burns, *Science in the Enlightenment: An Encyclopædia* (2003).

Epic <Latin 'epicus' and Greek 'epikos'> A long narrative poem in a grand style celebrating valiant feat and treating themes of historical, national or legendary impact. It can be distinguished from the briefer heroic lay, the less ambitious folktale and ballad, and the more consistently extravagant and fantastic medieval romance, though in the narrative poetry of Ariosto, Boiardo and Spenser the categories tend to merge. One may also distinguish *primary* or *traditional epic*, shaped from the legends and traditions of a heroic age, from *secondary* or *literary epic,* self-consciously produced by sophisticated poets adapting aspects of traditional epic for specific literary and ideological purposes. Homer's *Iliad* and *Odyssey* are primary epics; Virgil's *Aeneid* and Milton's *Paradise Lost* are secondary. The Homeric poems (900-750 BCE) are usually regarded as the first important epics and the main source of epic conventions and distinctiveness in the secondary epics of Europe. In India two great epics *The Ramayana* and *The Mahabharata* still remain the masterpieces of the genre in Asia. These heroic adventure tales have surprising durability over time.

The main aspects of the epic convention are the centrality of a hero, sometimes semi-divine, of military, national or religious importance; an extensive, perhaps even cosmic, geographical setting; heroic battle; extended and often exotic journeying and the involvement of supernatural beings in the action. Epics usually begin with a statement of the theme, invoking the assistance of a muse and then plunge into the middle of the story, filling in the earlier stages later on with retrospective narrative. Since epics tend to be traditional, this permits immediate dramatic involvement without bewildering the audience. Catalogues and processions of heroes, often associated with specific localities, are common, and when such heroes speak, it is often in set speeches delivered in formal circumstances. Epic narrative is often enriched by extended *epic similes,* in place of one, a series of similes put together, that go beyond an initial point of correspondence to elaborate a whole scene or episode drawn from different areas of experience.

Primary epics registering heroic experience in the vernacular languages of Europe continued to appear long after Virgil popularized *secondary epics*. The mid-12th century Spanish *Poema de mio Cid* celebrates the hero of the wars against the Moors in the 11th century; the 12th-century French *La Chanson de Roland* commemorates an 8th-century battle in the Pyrenees between Charlemagne's army and the Saracens; the 13th-century German epic *Nibelungenlied* recounts a story that derived ultimately from the war between the Burgundians and the Huns in the 5th century; and the Anglo-Saxon *Beowulf* refers to historical characters and events of the 6th century as it describes Beowulf's struggles against the monsters that threaten the heroic fellowship of the mead-hall.

The epic tradition is extinct now, but the scope and majesty of the genre have occasionally been exploited either in the mock epic form or in such narrative works as Frank Norris' unfinished trilogy of novels *The Epic of the Wheat* (1901-03), Sergey Eisenstein's film *Ivan the Terrible* (1944-1958), JRR Tolkien's fantasy trilogy *The Lord of the Rings* (1954-56), and Shashi Tharoor's narrative work, *The Great Indian Novel* (1989).

Ref: CM Bowra, *From Virgil to Milton* (1945). Colin Burrow, *Epic Romance: Homer to Milton* (1993). David Quint, *Epic and Empire: Politics and Generic Form from Virgil to Milton* (1993). EMW Tillyard, *The English Epic and its Background* (1954). Jan de Vries, *Heroic Song and Heroic Legend* (1963). Thomas M Greene, *The Descent from Heaven: A Study in Epic Continuity* (1975).

Epic Theatre <German episches> A form of dramatic presentation introduced by the 20th-century German playwright Bertolt Brecht (1898-1956). Brecht fashioned a type of drama that the audience could watch with complete detachment. The type was essentially political and deliberately responded to the contemporary political environment in Europe. Brecht exploited what he termed *alienation effects* to create an emotional distance between the spectator and the action on stage. For this the two main measures he attempted were: short, self-contained scenes that keep the play from building to a cathartic climax; and songs that comment on the action and techniques of acting that prevent the actor from developing an emotional identity with his role, etc. Epic theatre includes a manner of acting that exploits what Brecht calls *gestus*. One of Brecht's most-important aesthetic innovations prioritised *function* over the barren opposition between *form* and *content*. Besides the plays of Bertolt Brecht (*The Threepenny Opera, Mother Courage*, etc.), other plays that utilize epic theatre conventions include those of Georg Buchner, Frank Wedekind, Erwin Piscator and Leopold Jessner. However, the term "epic theatre" comes from Erwin Piscator who coined it during his first year as director of Berlin's Volksbühne. Erwin encouraged playwrights to address contemporary social issues as a measure to derive public response.

Ref: Anthony Squiers, *An Introduction to the Social and Political Philosophy of Bertolt Brecht: Revolution and Aesthetics* (2014). Peter Brooker, "Key Words in Brecht's Theory and Practice of Theatre", *Cambridge Companion to Brecht* (1994).

Epigram <Greek *epigramma,* meaning *inscription*> An inscription and often it is referred to mean a short poem. An epigrammatic use refers to a polished, terse and witty remark that packs generalized knowledge into short compass. It is more personal and specific than a *proverb* and less profound than an apothegm. Ordinarily the term has been associated with any pointed pithy saying in prose or verse. The epigram is a bon mot and it thrives on the compactness of its expression. Coleridge has a beautiful couplet on its definition which is well worth quoting: "What is an epigram? a dwarfish whole,/ Its body brevity, and wit its soul." It's a pithy saying that easily catches the imagination of the reader or listener. Benjamin Franklin puts this aspect of an epigram so beautifully: "Little strokes/ Fell great oaks." As a Figure of Speech, epigram is closely allied to antithesis and paradox: An epigram as a figure refers to a concise, witty, statement often having an apparent contradiction which by causing a temporary shock finally delivers an interesting meaning from the same construction: "In the midst of life we are in death", or "Behind every great fortune there is a crime." [Cf. antithesis, paradox]

Epigraph <Greek *epi*, upon + *graph*, writing> It is a short quotation from great writings cited at the start of a book, chapter or a poem to prefigure its theme and associate its content with learning. It can also be an inscription on a monument or building explaining some aspect related to it. An epigraph tends to set the tone or establish the theme of the text or whatever it presides over. For example, TS Eliot, in many of his poems such as "The Love Song of J. Alfred Prufrock," "Gerontion" and "The Hollow Men", etc. has made use of epigraph from classical writings and Shakespeare's plays. In "Gerontion" for example, the epigraph is—"Thou hast nor youth nor age/ But as it were an after dinner sleep/ Dreaming of both" (*Measure for Measure*). Normally, an epigraph makes a subtle preface to the text that follows. It strikes the key note of the main work.

Epilogue & Prologue A set of two literary technical conventions in the classical tradition of dramatic art. Whereas the prologue introduces a narrative, epilogue sums it up. Epilogue is the concluding section of a long poem, fable, play or any literary work to wrap up the poem or the work. Thus the terms are antonyms to each other. Often prologue gives the background information for the help of the reader or spectator and epilogue requests an appreciation of the audience. In medieval divisions of a *peroration*, i.e. concluding speech or epilogue is the fifth and the last division. Chaucer and many others poets and dramatists have used both prologue and epilogue in their works. Shakespeare and Marlowe were not much particular about the use the convention in their major plays. Marlowe faithfully followed the device only in *Dr. Faustus*, if not in other plays. Although a prologue presupposes an epilogue, or vice versa, there are exceptions also. For example, Ben Jonson's play *Volpone or the Foxe* has a distinct prologue in the beginning; but no epilogue. However, the last six lines of the play, a speech by Volpone himself seeking applause from the audience, may serve the purpose of an epilogue. Shakespeare's play, *The Tempest,* on the other hand, does without a prologue; but the play has a distinctly marked epilogue spoken by Prospero—"Now the charms are all o'erthrown", etc. Modern plays normally stay away from the convention. [Cf. frame]

Epiphany <Greek *epiphaneia*, manifestation> Epiphany means manifestation and refers to the incarnation of a divine soul. Now it is a Christian festival celebrated on January 6th as one of the three oldest festival days of the Christian calendar (other two being Easter and Christmas). It commemorates the first manifestation of Jesus Christ to the Gentiles, represented by the Magi and the manifestation of his divinity, as it occurred at his Baptism in the Jordan River and at his first miracle at Cana in Galilee. The evening preceding Epiphany is called Twelfth Night. The figurative inference often drawn in literature is that epiphany suggests a renewed communication with society on a higher and more informed level of understanding after an estrangement. The theme has been used by James Joyce to mean a sudden realization of what reality is or what revelatory experience is. It is also applied to a work that deals with such an experience. James Joyce's story "Araby" and Virginia Woolf's novel *Mrs. Dalloway* have adequately exploited the theme of epiphany in its secular sense. Closely related theological words are: *hierophany,* a manifestation of the sacred; and *theophany*, an appearance of a god. [Cf. apocalypse]

Episode A short story introduced into a narrative or poem to give variety, an interesting incident, a passage affording relief from the principal subject yet adding to it, an incident or period detachable from a novel play, etc. As an incident, however, an episode makes a part of a long story and is significantly related to it. Episodes may be either self-contained narratives or events that depend on a larger context for their purpose, meaning and importance. This may seem to be a digression in an otherwise well-knit long story, such as the founding of Wilmington in Charles Reade's *The Disinherited*

Heir. The individual events comprising the picaresque novels and medieval romances too are episodic in nature. Thus a work containing a series of episodes that are rather loosely connected within the larger narrative structure is called *episodic structure*, the opposite of which is *thematic structure*. Most of the travel narratives (e.g. Lawrence Durrell's *Sicilian Carousel*), pornographic texts (e.g. Anne Rice's *The Sleeping Beauty* trilogy) are based on episodic structure.

Epistolary Novel <*Epistle,* letter> A novel written in the form of a series of letters or one that is based on letters. The form manifests how the dramatic possibilities of the novel are derived from the use of letters within the narrative framework. The novels of Samuel Richardson (1689-1761) arose out of his pedagogic vocation and his trade of a printer—the compilation of manuals of letter-writing technique for young ladies, or as models for country readers, a volume that has become known as *Familiar Letters on Important Occasions*. Occasionally he hit upon continuing the same subject from one letter to another and, after a letter from "a father to a daughter in service on hearing of her master's attempting her virtue," he supplied the daughter's answer. This was the germ of his novel *Pamela.* His age regarded letter writing as an art form and expected the literary concern almost appropriate to the essay or fiction. For Richardson, the creation of epistolary novel form required only a step forward from the actual world into that of the imagination. Richardson's *Pamela* (1740) and *Clarissa* (1748) won phenomenal success and were imitated all over Europe and the epistolary novel with its liberated outburst of the heart was an aspect of early romanticism. Smollett's *The Expedition of Humphrey House* (1771) can be comfortably placed in the category. In the 19th century, when the letter-writing art had not yet fallen into disuse, it was possible for Wilkie Collins to tell the mystery story of *The Moonstone* (1868) in the form of an exchange of letters; but it would be hard to conceive of a detective novel using such a device in the 20th century when the well-wrought letter is considered artificial. Attempts to revive the form have not been successful and Christopher Isherwood's *Meeting by the River* (1967), which has a profoundly serious theme of religious conversion, seems to have failed because of the excessive informality and chattiness of the letters in which the story is told. The 20th century's substitute for the long letter is the transcribed tape recording—more, as Beckett's play *Krapp's Last Tape*—indicates a device for expressing alienation than a tool of dialectic. But it has common with Richardson's epistolary design the power of seeming to grant direct communication with a fictional character, with no apparent interference on the part of the true author. The popular epistolary method has the advantage of allowing the characters to tell the story in their own words, but it is hard to resist the uneasy feeling that a kind of divine editor is sorting and ordering the letters into his own pattern.

American writer Alice Walker's *The Color Purple* (1982) is a classic model of modern epistolary novel. In it there are ninety-four letters in all—from Celie to God, from Nettie to Celie and from Celie to Nettie. Ruth Prawer Jhabvala's *Heat and Dust* (1975) does not contain letters but it has epistolary elements in the sense that Olivia's letters make the source material of the main story. Two old French examples of the epistolary tradition are Jean Jacques Rousseau's *Julie: ou, la nouvelle Héloïse* (1761) and Pierre Choderlos Laclos's *Les Liaisons dangereuses* (1782).

Ref: David Lodge, *The Art of Fiction* (1992). Gaston Bachelard, *Epistolary Fiction in Europe, 1500-1850* (1999). Janet Gurkin Altman, *Epistolarity: Approaches to a Form* (1982).

Epitaph An inscription in verse or prose upon a tomb, and by extension, anything written as if to be inscribed on a tomb. Probably the earliest surviving are those of the ancient Egyptians, written on the sarcophagi and coffins. Ancient Greek epitaphs are of considerable literary interest, tender in feeling, rich and varied in expression and epigrammatic in form. They are usually elegiac in tone. Roman epitaphs, in contrast, contained a record of facts and figures only. In England, a familiar 18th-century epitaph was the one of twelve lines ending of Thomas Gray's "An Elegy Written in a Country Churchyard." Perhaps the most-noted modern epitaph was that written by William Butler Yeats for himself in "Under Ben Bulben"—"Cast a cold eye/ On life, on death./ Horseman, pass by!" The art of writing epitaph was largely lost in the 20th century.

Epithalamion/Prothalamion A set of wedding songs in the form of the ode. The epithalamion dates back to classical Greek literature and was probably first used by the Greek poetess Sappho (630-570 BCE). The term is derived from the Greek words *epi,* outside + *thalamus,* chamber, and referred to the song sung by the throng of wedding celebrants as they escorted the couple to the bridal chamber. Spenser composed his epithalamion to celebrate his marriage to Elizabeth Boyle in June 1594. Epithalamion also celebrated the consummation of the married couple. In this context the poems often tended to become suggestive with sexual innuendo. Prothalamion is invented by Spenser, in order to differentiate his poem by that name from his own bridal songs written earlier (*pro,* prior). The word is, therefore, a Spenserian *neologism*. However, the meaning remains almost the same. His Prothalamion was written on the occasion of the wedding of Elizabeth and Catherine Somerset, daughters of Edward Somerset, the Earl of Worcester. While Spenser's own epithalamion carries elements of eroticism, his prothalamion is qualitatively almost different poem and is devoid of any erotic suggestiveness. It is rather a disguised complaint poem. Both the types use a personal setting, a river side and a couplet as refrain, etc. While writing his poems, Spenser maintains traditional conventions of the poetic form. Like Catullus and other writers of epithalamia, he begins his own poem with an invocation of the muses. He asks for their assistance in his artistic endeavour; but he also entreats them to round-up all the nymphs they can find and to urge his sleeping love to wake. It is part of tradition that such poems frequently refer to the passage of time by the mention of positions of the sun or by any other means.

Ref: A Kent Hieatt, *Short Time's Endless Moment: The Symbolism of the Numbers in Edmund Spenser's 'Epithalamion'* (1960). Enid Welsford, *Spenser: 'Fowre Hymnes', Epithalamion: A Study of Spenser's Doctrine of Love* (1967).

Essay A prose composition with a focused subject for discussion. The term was coined by Michel de Montaigne who wrote his 1580 collection of brief, informal reflections on himself and on various topics relating to human nature. As a literary genre it is very flexible in its form and content. Many critics think that anything in any form, if it is not technically suitable for any other recognized genre, can be an essay. *Personal essays*, such as Charles Lamb's, mostly rely on the charm of the essayist's personality; whereas *objective essays*, such as Francis Bacon's, on the discursive and argumentative qualities. An essay can also be a long, systematic discourse. An example of a longer essay is John Locke's *An Essay Concerning Human Understanding*. Some major essayists in English are Joseph Addison, Sir Richard Steel, Aldous Huxley, TS Eliot, EM Forster, GK Chesterton, EV Lucas, AG Gardiner, Robert Lynd, JB Priestly and so on. The 18th century England had the greatest proliferation of this literary form. Three major journals that were associated with the growth and development of this genre in English were *The Tatler, The Spectator* and *The Rambler*.

Ref: AC Ward, *20th Century English Literature 1901-60* (1974). Huge Walker, *The English Essay and Essayists* (1915). John D'Agata, Ed. *The Lost Origins of the Essay* (2009). Theodor W Adorno, "The Essay as Form", *The Adorno Reader* (2000).

Ethnicity A set of common cultural factors and characteristics that connect a group or groups of people together emotionally. Although *race* comes close to it, ethnicity is rooted in the idea of societal groups, marked especially by shared nationality, tribal affiliation, religious faith, common language, cultural and traditional origins and backgrounds, whereas *race* is rooted in the idea of biological classification. Often it is used to justify real or imagined historic ties as well. In a diasporic condition, ethnic identity strengthens bond among own people and the same identity often threatens an immigrant's interests. In English, ethnicity goes far beyond the modern ties of a person to a particular nation and focuses more upon the connection to a perceived or shared past and culture. In other languages, the corresponding terms for ethnicity and nationhood can be closer to each other. The 19th century saw the development of the political ideology of ethnic nationalism, when the vague concept of race was tied to nationalism, first by German theorists including Johann Gottfried von Herder. Even today, in a diasporic context, the terms *ethnic* and *ethnicity* are frequently referred to. Race, Ethnicity and Post-colonial condition point to three different possible emphases in literary and cultural analysis, but they share a commitment to challenge coercion based on cultural identity, seeking to enrich understanding of the diverse knowledge and rich traditions of all ethnic groups and peoples. Racism and ethnocentrism have been plaguing almost all societies and regions of the world, as differences in appearance, colour, language and customs have been used to assign groups of *us* and *them* with the unique characteristics of *them* perceived as a threat to security and interest of *us.* The ethnic analysis thus explores the complex relationship between a text and its social context locating the many ways in which the belief system of a time and place are reflected and altered by literary and other forms of representation.

Ref: Fredrik Barth, Ed. *Ethnic Groups and Boundaries* (1969). Gary Craig, et al. Eds., *Understanding 'Race' and Ethnicity: Theory, History, Policy, Practice* (2012). Joseph F Healey & Eileen O'Brien, *Race, Ethnicity, Gender, and Class: The Sociology of Group Conflict and Change* (2014).

Euphemism A Figure of Speech. Substitution of a mild or less negative word or phrase for a harsh or blunt one is known by this figure. For example, one can use *pass away* instead of *die*, or *washing* can soften *abortion*. The basic psychology of euphemistic language is the desire to put something bad or embarrassing in a better or at least neutral light. Thus many terms referring to death, sex, crime, bribe and excremental functions are examples of euphemisms. Since euphemism is often chosen to give something of a disagreeable nature a portable pack, the satirists, for the use of irony and exaggeration, exploit it. [Cf. innuendo]

Euphuism A highly ornate style of writing popularized by John Lyly's *Euphues.* The style is characterized by balanced sentence construction, rhetorical *tropes*, and multiplied similes and allusions. Usually frequent use of similes, alliteration, antithesis and parallel and balanced construction makes it look catchy and enthusiastic. Euphuism should not be confused with euphemism.

Exemplum <Latin, plural *exempla*> A tale with a moral, message or an anecdote that supports a moral point or sustains an argument, often used in sermons. This variety of literary sermonizing flourished during the Middle Ages. When exempla appeared in collections was known as *example-books*. The works of Geoffrey Chaucer are full of *exempla.* The Biblical parable of the Good Samaritan is probably the most well-known moral exemplum in Christian literature. In it, a man asks Jesus what it means to live morally; Jesus simply says, "Love thy neighbour as thyself" and finally exemplifies his moral by telling the parable of the Good Samaritan to explain the definition of neighbour. Common people respond to stories better than dry facts or philosophy, hence the efficacy of exemplum. [Cf. didactic, fable]

Existentialism/-list A 20th century philosophy redefining the nature and opinion of human existence. There are two major strains of existentialist thought—atheistic and religious. Followers of atheistic existentialism believe that the individual is alone in a godless universe and that the basic human condition is one of suffering and loneliness. Nevertheless, because there are no fixed values, individuals can exercise free will to create their own values. The atheistic strain culminates in and is popularly associated with the works of Jean-Paul Sartre (1905-1980). The Christian existentialists believe that only God may free people from suffering. The common factors between the two opposing views are: [1] existence cannot be fully understood empirically; [2] anguish is universal; [3] individuals must bear responsibility for their actions; and [4] there is no common standard of behaviour or perception for religious and ethical matters. Existentialist thoughts figure prominently in the works of such authors as *Jean-Paul Sartre* (1905-1980), Fyodor Dostoyevsky (1821-1881), Eugene Ionesco (1909-1994), Franz Kafka (1883-1924), Simone de Beauvoir (1908-1986), Samuel Beckett (1906-1989) and Albert Camus (1913-1960).

Ref: David Cooper, *Existentialism: A Reconstruction* (1999). Viktor Frankl, *Man's Search for Meaning* (1946). Jean-Paul Sartre, *Being and Nothingness* (1943). Robert C Solomon, Ed. *Existentialism* (2005).

Exit/Exuent A couple of a very common technical terms frequently used in dramatic literature. They basically refer to stage direction for characters when they are supposed to leave the stage. These Latin stage directions are found in the margins of Shakespearean and other English popular plays also. Exit refers to a single person's exit, "he/she goes out." Exuent is the plural form—meant for more than one dramatis personae or actor leaving the stage. Often the phrase is accompanied with explanatory remarks, such as *exuent omnes* (everybody goes out), or *exit solus* (he/she alone goes out).

Expressionism A German movement that found its most congenial media in painting and the drama in the first half of the 20th century. The basics of this avant-garde group are to be found in the works of Vincent van Gogh, Edvard Munch and James Ensor, each of whom in the period 1885-1900 evolved a highly personal painting style although behind the movement there was the potent influence of the Italian critic Benedetto Croce. According to him art is expression and criticism is the study of that expression. The theory stresses that an artist's aim is to express or convey the essence of a particular theme to the exclusion of such secondary considerations as fidelity to real life. In this philosophy human character is less important than the idea of humanity, and probability of action in the old realist sense is the least of the writer's concerns. The emotional atmosphere is high-pitched, even ecstatic, and the tone is more appropriate to propaganda than to art. The term applies to almost any mode of unconventional, highly subjective writing that distorts reality in some way. Advocates of expressionism include dramatists Bertolt Brecht, George Kaiser, Ernst Toller, Luigi Pirandello, Federico Garcia Lorca, Eugene O'Neill, and Elmer Rice; poets George Heym, Ernst Stadler, August Stramm, Gottfried Benn, and Georg Trakl; and novelists Franz Kafka James Joyce and others.

Ref: Bram Dijkstra, *American Expressionism: Art and Social Change, 1920–1950* (2003). Charles L Kuhn, *German Expressionism and Abstract Art: The Harvard Collections* (1957). D Anfam, *Abstract Expressionism* (1990). Lakatos Gabriela Luciana, *Expressionism Today* (2011).

External/Internal Evidence A twin set of evidences used in literary criticism.

An evidence that is not derived from the text, for authorship, intended meaning, circumstances of production, or date of a particular literary work is external evidence. It covers biographical information, as well as evidence from analytical and other bibliographical studies and from publishing history, or any source other than the text itself. On the other hand, internal evidence is an evidence of the authorship, intended meaning, circumstances of production or date of a particular literary work derived from the text itself. No evidence gathered from other sources comes within this category. The stylistic features, reference to events contemporary with the writing or from any possible analysis of the text may form internal evidence. These forms are related to textual and non-textual forms of criticism.

F

Fable A fictitious moral tale or legend of ancient origins. It can be either in prose or verse, but a specific point or lesson expressed at the end of the tale via an epigram is the familiar feature in a fable. The fable often features personified animals as their principal characters and for this it is often called beast fables. Some scholars have used the term *apologue* as a synonym for beast fable. There it differs from parable. A parable does not introduce anthropomorphized animal or inanimate objects. In a fable animals and natural agents speak and behave like human being. Aesop's *Fables* are, no doubt, the best-known examples, and Rudyard Kipling's *Just So Stories* (1902) too embodies the spirit of the old literary tradition. [Cf. exemplum]

Fairy Tale A tale about elves, dragons, hobgoblins nymphs and other fantastic magical beings set vaguely in the distant past of a pseudo-medieval world. The prince is changed into a bird and flies to his love and sings. Popular conventions include magic, charms, disguises, talking animals and a hero/heroine who overcomes obstacles to live happily ever after. It is often difficult to distinguish between tales of literary and oral origins, because folktales have received literary treatment from early times, and, conversely, literary tales have found their way back into the oral tradition. The most famous compilers include Hans Christian Anderson (Denmark), the Grimm brothers (Germany) and Charles Perrault (France). Examples from the European tradition include the tales of Prince Charming, Red Riding Hood, Puss in Boots and Cinderella. An example from Middle-Eastern tradition would be Ali Baba tales. In spite of the stories' surface simplicity, many critics note that the fairy tales often embody psychological depth, especially in terms of childhood anxiety and wish fulfilment. The art form was cultivated in the period of German Romanticism by Goethe, Ludwig Tieck, Clemens Brentano, and ETA Hoffmann and in Victorian England by John Ruskin (*The King of the Golden River,* 1851) and Charles Kingsley (*The Water-Babies,* 1863); but few of these tales have found permanent popularity. Shakespeare's *A Midsummer Night's Dream* has thrived much on the tradition. The master of the art, whose works rank with the traditional stories in universal popularity, is the Danish writer Hans Christian Andersen. Though his stories have their roots in folk legend, they are personal in style and contain elements of autobiography and contemporary social satire. JK Rowling's Harry Potter series has its story lines often based on magic, fantasy and water-dragon that give the stories a clear-cut fairy tale look. [Cf. fable, fantasy]

Ref: JRR Tolkien, "On Fairy-Stories", *The Tolkien Reader* (1966). Vladimir Propp, *Morphology of the Folktale* (1928, English Trans 1958).

Fancy/Imagination While discussing the definition and role of primary and secondary imaginations, Coleridge, in his *Biographia Literaria*, Chapter XIII, differentiates Fancy from imagination: "Fancy...has no other counters to play with, but fixities and definites. The Fancy is indeed no other than a mode of Memory emancipated from the order of time and space; while it is blended with, and modified by that empirical phenomenon of the will, which we express by the word CHOICE. But equally with the ordinary memory the Fancy must receive all its materials ready made from the law of association." Coleridge, while trying to distinguish between mechanical and organic processes of artistic creation, uses these terms. Fancy, according to him, is the inferior mental faculty. It first follows a mechanical law of the association of ideas and then merely reproduces the "fixed and dead" items given to consciousness through observation and recollection. Imagination, the superior faculty, on the other hand, is creative and organic. It 'dissolves, diffuses, and dissipates, in order to recreate.' A mechanical form is an inflexible idea imposed by fancy, whereas imagination is an organic form and is esemplastic by nature. It improves the creative faculty revealing itself in the balance or reconciliation of opposite or discordant qualities. Applied to works of literature as an operative doctrine, Coleridge's discrimination between Fancy and Imagination accordingly led him to the discrimination between two kinds of poems—one that draws upon sense impressions and memory and the other involves the higher faculty of the Imagination.

Ref: Raymond L Brett, *Fancy and Imagination: A Study of Coleridge* (1969).

Fantasy A form of fiction or any other literary form set in the earth, moon or a non-existing fairy land found in the tradition of mythology and folklore. Fantasy literature is typically peopled with men as well as magical figures like elves, dwarves, trolls, beasts, known and unknown creatures, talking dragons as well as hobbits and it features supernatural beings and strange activities, anything between the funny and the horrible. It is often quite difficult to make a clear boundary among such genres as fantasy, fairy tale and folklore. However, the modern fantasy fiction is usually said to have begun with the Scottish author, George MacDonald (author of *The Princess and the Goblin* and *Phantastes*). MacDonald was a major influence on both Tolkien and CS Lewis. Another major fantasy writer William Morris, a popular English poet and novelist, is famous for his fantasy title, *The Well at the World's End.* Notable examples of fantasy literature are JRR Tolkien's *The Hobbit, The Lord of the Rings*, Stephen Donaldson's trilogies

The Chronicles of Thomas Covenant the Unbeliever, Mervyn Peake's *Gormenghast* trilogy, and Diana Wynne Jone's *Fire and Hemlock*, etc. Modern examples must include works of Harry Potter series by JK Rowling. A very recent example of paranormal fantasy novel is *No Hero* (2011) written by Jonathan Wood. Among the modern genres, the cyberfiction often comes very close to this category. Fantasy as a genre is a broad category under which come such subgenres as dream vision, fable, fairy tale, romance and science fiction, etc. Since the second half of the 20th century fantasy fiction has become one of the most commercially viable literary genres.

Ref: CN Manlove, *Modern Fantasy: Five Studies* (1975). Deborah Chester, *The Fantasy Fiction Formula* (2016). Everett Bleiler, *Checklist of Fantastic Literature* (1948). Lin Carter, *Imaginary Worlds: The Art of Fantasy* (1973).

Farce A comic work, generally low comedy intended to evoke laughter mainly through gesture, buffoonery, action, etc. Broad humour, outlandish incidents, and often crude vulgarity are the basic ingredients here. Whereas a regular comedy depends much on language, development of plot and characterization, farce can do without them. Expectedly its appeal is limited to a small group. Brandon Thomas' *Charley Aunt* (1892) is still recognized as the masterpiece of the genre. However, the origin of farce is often traced back to the 15th and 16th century *Interludes.* They were often invested with farcical elements and were usually very short plays performed in the intervals of banquets and royal entertainments and are often regarded as transitional between *morality plays* and comedy. Some examples of such farcical type are Shakespeare's *Comedy of Errors*, Oliver Goldsmith's *She Stoop to Conquer*, John Heywood's *The Four P's* (Palmer, Pardoner, Pothecary and Pedlar, who join a lying contest), *Johan Johan the Husband*, etc. Much of the 'comedy' in film and television could more accurately be described as farce. [Cf. humour]

Ref: Robert Metcalf Smith, *Types of Farce-Comedy* (1928). Leo Hughes, *A Century of English Farce* (1956). Louis Kronenberger, *The Thread of Laughter* (1952).

Feminist Criticism An approach to literary criticism and scholarship that seeks to explore or expose the predominantly male-dominated critical perspective with a feminist consciousness and assert its own system of values. If postcolonial criticism invites a reappraisal of colonial texts and develops a vocabulary for discussing postcolonial literature, then feminist criticism extends that process to include an analysis of how women are represented in literary texts. The purpose behind this is to challenge assumptions and stereotypes about women both in literature and society. Male writing can be seen as often reflecting the values of the patriarchal society to which it belongs. During the 1970s the feminist school emerged with well-defined self-regulating discourse, although the French, the British and the American counterparts of the movement varied widely in terms of the interests and assumptions associated with the doctrine. Elaine Showalter divides the form of criticism into two varieties: *women as reader* and *woman as writer*. The common assumption was that all the social institutions including language, literature and other cultural practices were *sexist* in the sense they promoted stereotyping of social roles on the basis of gender in a demeaning way and they served the patriarchal positions against women. Feminist criticism, therefore, places literature in a social context and uses a broad range of disciplines including history, sociology, psychology and linguistics, etc to provide a perspective sensitive to feminist issues. Feminist theories also attempt to understand representation from a woman's point of view and to explain women's writing strategies as specific to their social conditions. While doing so, some feminist critics worried that using approaches such as psychoanalytic, formalist, Marxist, etc would prevent feminist theory from being accepted as *equal*, but many denied the need for a unifying feminist theory. A wide range of feminist critics, beginning with Lisa Tuttle, Kate Millett, Ellen Moers, Sandra Gilbert, Susan Gubar, Virginia Woolf, Elaine Showalter, and so on, have direction to new gender-based approaches to past and present writers.

The feminist literary criticism has a particular relevance in a post-colonial context. Though both colonialism and patriarchy have been closely entwined historically, an end to formal empire has not guaranteed an end to the oppression of women in the former colonies. On a literary level, post-colonial feminists point to the ways in which women continue to be stereotyped and marginalized, ironically even by postcolonial authors, who might themselves claim to be challenging a culture of domination. [Cf. lesbian criticism]

Ref: Alice Walker, *In Search of Our Mothers' Gardens: Womanist Prose* (1984). Helen, Cixous, "The Character of Character", *New Literary History* (1974). Elaine Showalter, *The New Feminist Criticism: Essays on Women, Literature and Theory* (1985). Josephine Donovan, Ed. *Feminist Literary Criticism* (1975). Maggie Humm, *Feminist Criticism: Women as Contemporary Critics* (1986). Simone de Beauvoir, *The Second Sex* (1949).

Femme Fatale A popular French term which literally means *fatal woman*. A femme fatale is a sensuous and alluring woman who often leads men into danger or trouble. A classic example of the femme fatale is the nameless character in Billy Wilder's *The Seven Year Itch,* portrayed by Marilyn Monroe in the film adaptation. The mysterious woman in Keats' "La Belle Dame Sans Merci" has associations of a femme fatal. However, Keats depicts a supernatural fairy woman, whereas the concept of femme fatal is not necessarily associated with a fairy or supernatural being. A femme fatale is an archetype in literature and art. The classic femme fatale resorts to murder to free herself from an agonizing relationship with her predator who would try to possess and control her, as if she were a piece of property or a pet. In some cases she herself takes up the role of the predator to destroy her male victim. The most well-known archetypal figure of a femme fatale is Eve, who with her beauty and sexuality, tempts Adam to eat the forbidden fruit and thus accelerates destruction. Some other examples in western literatures are: [1] Homer's Circe; [2] Spenser's Acrasia;

[3] Coleridge's Geraldine; [4] Sheridan Le Fanu's Carmilla; [5] Mary Elizabeth Braddon's Lady Audley; [6] Oscar Wilde's Salome, and the like. In Hindu mythology the seductive Mohini played the role of a femme fatale as she could enchant gods, demons and sages with equal ease. However, an American critic of modern culture, Prof. Camille Paglia, thinks that "the mystique of the femme fatale cannot be perfectly translated into male terms."

Ref: Mario Praz, "La Belle Dame Sans Merci", *The Romantic Agony*, Chapter IV (1930). Toni Bentley, *Sisters of Salome* (2002).

Fiction Any story that is more a product of imagination rather than a documentation of fact. The characters and events in fiction may be based on real life but their ultimate form and configuration is a creation of the author. It may be defined as the art or craft through written words of contriving and representing human life that instructs and/or diverts. The various forms that fiction may take are best seen less as a number of separate categories than as a continuum or, more accurately, a cline with some such brief form as the *anecdote* at one end of the scale and the longest conceivable novel at the other. The earliest ancestry of fiction is to be found in such ancient Roman works as Petronius' *Satyricon* (1st century) and Lucius Apuleius' *Golden Ass* (2nd century) that contain many of the popular elements that distinguish the novel from its nobler born relative, the epic. Geoffrey Chaucer's *The Canterbury Tales,* Laurence Sterne's *Tristram Shandy* and even Margaret Mitchell's *Gone with the Wind* are basically fiction. Fiction has almost always been treated as synonymous and interchangeable with the novel. Walter Allen thinks, "At the heart of confusion is the fact that the story is common to both. So long as men have told stories there has been fiction, whether in verse or prose and only to this extent is it true to say that any work of fiction written before about 1670 in England is in some sense an ancestor to the novel. But the novel itself is something new."

Fiction is rather a hold-all term; it may include among, other things, genres and subgenres like short stories, fables, legends, myths, fairy tales, epic and narrative poetry, romance and even plays. In the present time it has widened its scope thanks to the development of technology and, therefore, it encompasses comic books, many animated cartoons, films, videos and some television programmes, etc. *Literary fiction* is defined as fictional works that are deemed to be of literary value, as distinguished from most commercial or 'genre' fiction. The distinction, however, may be somewhat controversial. Literary fiction, in its attempts to be reliable to the reader or because of the gradual deterioration of the imaginative faculty, involves social commentary, political criticism or reflection on the human condition. In general it focuses on introspective, in-depth studies of "interesting, complex and developed" characters and comes very close to what we nowadays call realistic fiction. Accordingly, the traditional boundary between fiction and nonfiction is narrowing every day. [Cf. novel]

Ref: Geir Farner, *Literary Fiction: The Ways We Read Narrative Literature* (2014). FR Leavis, *The Great Tradition* (1967). H Thomas

Milhorn, *Writing Genre Fiction: A Guide to the Craft* (2006). Northrop Frye, *Anatomy of Criticism* (1957). Robert Scholes & Robert Kellogg, *The Nature of Narrative* (1966). WC Booth, *The Rhetoric of Fiction* (1961).

Figure/Figurative Language A way of using language, in which the speaker or writer temporarily takes the words away from their etymological sources, disrupts the popular order, structure or meaning and invest some extra significance to it for artistic or practical purpose. This interruption or hijacking of language turns literal language into a figurative language. Since ancient times figurative language has been divided into two types: [1] *Figures of Speech* or *Rhetorical Figures* and [2] *Tropes* or *Figures of Thought.* A Figure of Speech is an ornamental language; it is a deviation from plain and ordinary way of speaking for greater effect. For example, "I will drink life to the lees" simply mean "I will enjoy life fully". It is a metaphor, a figure of speech. Trope, on the other hand, has come to be used for describing commonly some recurring literary and rhetorical devices motifs or clichés in creative works. Some figures of speech are treated as tropes; but tropes do not include all the figures. The figures of speech that come within the definition of tropes are metaphor, metonymy, irony, personification, simile, hyperbole, litotes, and synecdoche, etc. Originally a musical term, trope, during the Middle Ages, was used to exemplify the verbal amplifications of liturgical texts and now it is a flexible word that may derive its figurative meaning from the textual matrix. Figurative use allows poetry to be concrete and specific as well as universal and general. An urn can be both an ordinary object and a metaphor/trope for the eternal durability of art. Poetic language thus reconciles the ordinarily opposed elements of the concrete and the universal. Such reconciliation is possible in connotative poetic tropes. The study of tropes is called *tropology*.

Ref: J Hillis Miller, *Tropes, Parables, and Performatives* (1990). Sam Glucksberg, *Understanding Figurative Language: From Metaphor to Idioms* (2001).

Fin De Siècle A French term meaning *end of century*. The term specially refers to the last decade of the 19th century, a transition period when writers and artists in Europe and also America abandoned old established conventions associated with the Victorian era and looked for new artistic techniques and objectives. The adoption of the French term, rather than its English equivalent 'end of the century' may help to trace particular critical content—it continues to be associated with those writers and artists whose work displayed a debt to French decadent, symbolist or naturalist writers and artists. Two English writers frequently associated with the fin de siècle mindset are Oscar Wilde and George Bernard Shaw. It is said that the German philosopher Arthur Schopenhauer's philosophy influenced much the culture of *fin de siècle*. Dodd and Atkinson observe that much of *fin-de-siècle* writing tended to assume that the passing of the nineteenth century would represent a fundamental historical discontinuity, a clear break with the past. Interestingly the departure from standards was not limited to the physical world alone, but it hinted at the change of human body and mind as well. The most representative works of this period includes: Robert Louis Stevenson's *Strange Case of Dr Jekyll and Mr Hyde*, Oscar Wilde's *The Picture of Dorian Gray*, Arthur Machen's *The Great God Pan*, HG Wells' *The Time Machine* and Bram Stoker's *Dracula*, etc. All these works have a common platform—the themes of change, pessimism, mutation, corruption and decay in relation to the human body and mind. [Cf. aestheticism, decadence]

Ref: Gail Marshall, Ed. *The Cambridge Companion to the Fin de Siècle* (2007). Shearer West, *Fin de Siècle: Art and Society in an Age of Uncertainty* (1994).

Flashback & Flash-Forward A set of devices used in narrative technique or in the cinema that allows the writer/director to present events that happened before or after the time of the current narration or the current events. Flashback technique that takes the story back in time includes memories, dreams, stories of the past told by characters, or even authorial sovereignty. Flashback is useful for exposition of the past time, to fill in the reader about a character or place, or about the background to a conflict. It is a form of *analepsis*, one of the three major types of anachrony. The technique has its origin in the ancient epic tradition of beginning a work *in medias res*, i.e. in the middle of things, and then moving back to the beginning. The opposite convention, the evocation of something to take place much later, is flash-forward. Good novelists and storytellers make use of the techniques as narrative tools. For example, in Arundhati Roy's *God of Small Things* the way in which the story unfolds does not follow a conventional route from beginning to middle to end. Instead, Roy employs alternating narrative threads, flashbacks and flash-forward's to unfold her story out of sequence in a non-linear fashion.

Fliting/Flyting A popular pastime in which two people try to outdo each other in the richness of their rhetorical scorn. Originally it was a form of poetical invective, specially an exchange of abusive verse by two poets as *The Flyting of Dunbar and Kennedie* (1908). It was also a diatribe often found in epic poems, e.g. that between Beowulf and Unferth.

Foil A character whose qualities or actions serve to emphasize those of the protagonist or some other character by providing a strong contrast with them. In the dramatic art of characterization the use of foils is very frequent, the main purpose being highlighting the protagonist from as many angles as possible. Shakespeare has made extensive use of the technique with greater success than many of his fellow dramatists. In *Much Ado about Nothing* (1600) the hero is docile and the heroine ingenuine. Conventional in character, she and her beloved Claudio are foils to the play's sparring couple, Beatrice and Benedick. However Shakespeare's use of the foils in *Hamlet* (1604) is often multidimensional in effect. The son of Polonius and brother of Ophelia, Laertes serves as a foil to Prince Hamlet. Caught up in events beyond his control, Laertes attempts to avenge his father's death and finally destroys himself. More interesting is the fact that there are other foils to Hamlet also. Hamlet's height has been further highlighted from so many points of view in the play very artistically. Besides

Claudius, set off against Hamlet is Polonius. He is wrong in his judgments, one after another and this leads to the audience's rejection of his political and human acumen. In all circumstances he seems slightly ridiculous—foil for Claudius as he is for Hamlet. His astuteness suffers by comparison with that of the King. His philosophical view of life is hollow compared with Hamlet's. Hamlet has as many general maxims as Polonius's; but Hamlet's seem to be the product of a far more refined sensibility and of an ability to respond truthfully to experience. The novelists too have later exploited the tradition of making use of foils.

Folio & Quarto A set of two terms associated with the manuscripts of a drama of the Shakespearean era. When a large size printer's sheet of paper is folded and stitched so as to make two leaves of four pages, and then bound together, is called a folio. On a single sheet, the page visible on the right-hand side of an open book or the top of such a page is called the *recto* (Latin right), and the reverse or bottom side of such a page (the page visible on the left-hand side of an open book) is called the *verso*. If the folio is folded in half once more, it becomes a quarto. Thus, a quarto is a sheet of material folded twice to create four leaves of eight pages, which results in a medium-sized book. Folios are typically large books, twice the size of a quarto and four times the size of an *octavo* printing. The collected editions of Shakespeare's plays, published after his death as distinct from the earlier unauthorized quarto editions, are often referred to as folios. Texts of many such plays as have both the editions often vary textually to some extent.

Folklore/Folk Tale A product of folk culture. Generally Folklores contain songs, stories, beliefs, ritualistic tenets and even myths preserved in a culture or group of people. Typically, these are passed on orally from one generation to the next in various forms, such as legends, charms, ballads, songs and proverbs, or preserved in customs, rituals and ceremonies, specially those of preliterate early societies and social classes. For a long time folklores have been received as products of "low culture." WJ Thomas first used this term in 1846. Sir James Frazer's *The Golden Bough* (1890) is a wonderful record of folklores of the British islands. Folk tale, on the other hand, is usually a short narrative originating in oral tradition of a primitive ethnic group. Folk tales fall into a variety of categories, including legends, ghost stories, fairy tales, Fables and anecdotes often based on historical figures and events. Examples of folk tales include Giambattista Basile's *The Pentamerone,* which contains the tales of "Puss in Boots," "Rapunzel," "Cinderella," "Beauty and the Beast" and Joel Chandler Harris's *Uncle Remus* stories, which represent transplanted African folk tales and American tales about such characters as Mike Fink, Johnny Appleseed, Paul Bunyan, and Pecos Bill. However, one must not confuse between folk tale and folklore. Folklore is a greater category in which folk tale is only a part. Whereas folklore refers to the traditional beliefs, practices, folk tales, legends, myths and even superstitions of a community that have passed down from one generation to the other through words of mouth; folk tales refer only to the stories that have been passed down from ancestors of an particular group of people to the younger generations through words of mouth. An interesting feature of folk tale and folklore is that similar oral materials can be located in Europe, America, Africa and Asia. In the recent past these items have been treated and analyzed seriously by scholars of cultural studies. [Cf. fairytale, folk tale]

Ref: Barre Toelken, *The Dynamics of Folklore* (1979). John M Wickersham, Ed. *Myths and Legends of the World* (2000). Richard Dorson, *Folklore and Fakelore: Essays toward a Discipline of Folk Studies* (1976). Robert A Georges & Michael Owen Jones, *Folkloristics: An Introduction* (1995). Vladimir Propp, *Morphology of Folk Tale* (1928).

Foot A basic rhythmic unit of a metrical verse line. It is a unit of a line measured in terms of *stressed* and *unstressed syllables* for analysis of a metrical structure. The variation of feet within a line (or passage) affects its rhythm; the repetition within the poem determines the meter. There are three general groups of feet: [1] *falling*, when the accented syllables precede the *unaccented* (Trochee); [2] *rising*, first unaccented then accented (Iamb); and [3] *rocking*, accented syllable in the middle (Amphibrach). The frequently used foot names and patterns used in English versification are listed below: ᴗ (breve) means unaccented and ˊ (acute) means accented:

Iamb (iambic) disyllabic foot: (rĕ-fér)

Trochee (trochaic) disyllabic foot: (sú-ffĕr)

Anapest (anapestic) trisyllabic foot: (rĕ-fĕ-rée)

Dactyl (dactylic) trisyllabic foot: (réf-ĕr-ĕnce)

Amphibrach (amphibrachic) trisyllabic foot: (rĕ-fér-ĕr)

Other metrical feet like Spondee (disyllabic, both accented syllables) and *Pyrrhic* (disyllabic, both unaccented syllables) are exceptions to the general rule of English versification. *Amphimacer* (trisyllabic foot with accented, unaccented and accented syllables) too is exceptional. According to the basic principle of English prosody there must be *only one* accented syllable in a foot. However, some unusual use of these two types, if any, may mean a variation or exceptional use under unavoidable circumstances. Besides these three unusual feet there are *Tetrasyllabic* (with four syllables) feet like *Choriambus* (accented, unaccented, unaccented and accented) and *Paean* (accented, unaccented, unaccented and unaccented), which are again very rare and not much favoured by the English poetic style. [Cf. accent, metre, scansion]

Foreshadowing A device used in literature to prepare the reader for future events or to lay down an explanation of later developments. In Charles Dickens's *Great Expectations,* the graveyard encounter at the beginning of the novel between Pip and the escaped convict Magwitch foreshadows the baleful atmosphere and events that comprise much of the narrative. Almost all narrative varieties of literature use this technique; but suspense stories, gothic tales and detective fiction need it more than other forms do. Shakespeare in *Hamlet, Macbeth* and other plays has used foreshadowing with mastery. This technique has been exploited in postcolonial texts also. In Chinua Achebe's *Things Fall Apart* there are several instances of foreshadowing: The early account of Ikemefuna as 'ill-fated boy' foreshadows his ultimate murder by Okonkwo; the arrival of the locusts foretells the influx of the colonizers and Obierika's prediction that Okonkwo kill himself presages Okonkwo's suicide. However, *side-shadowing* is a kind of diversion from the main track of story mostly used in epic poetry or story of a grand scale and it refers to an aspect that may not be immediately relevant to the issue at hand. The exact opposite of foreshadowing is *back-shadowing*, a literary technique that shows how a past event affects the future. These techniques are both literary and cinematic. [Cf. flash-forward]

Formalistic Criticism A literary theory developed largely in reaction to the "practice of interpreting literary texts by relating them to 'extrinsic' issues, such as the historical circumstances and politics of the era in which the work was written, its philosophical or theological milieu or the experiences and frame of mind of its author" (Murfin). In the early 20th century the Moscow and Prague Linguistic Circles are mainly responsible for this approach. The Russian Formalists believe that content is the *motivation* of form and the literary work is a grouping of devices which function within an independent textual scheme. Literariness of a text does not come from outside the text, but emerges from within when the literary devices are fore-grounded— i.e. brought into distinction to such an extent as to produce an effect of estrangement or *defamiliarization*. Literature, by baring the device, deautomatizes one's perceptions, its language composing a deliberate set of departures from the models of ordinary language. In its hybridization, mixture of devices, conventions, forms, and techniques, literature, in the words of Roman Jakobson, is an "organized violence committed on ordinary speech." In a general sense, formalism is applied to any critical approach that regards the text as a self-independent space of discourse, subject to interpretation without reference to biographical or historical context. The formalists concentrate their analyses on the interplay and relationships between the text's essential verbal elements. Critics associated with the movement include IA Richards, William Empson, John Crowe Ransom and RP Blackmur. [Cf. new criticism, biographical criticism, cultural criticism]

Ref: Frank Lentricchia, *After the New Criticism* (1980). Wayne Booth, *The Rhetoric of Fiction* (1961). WK Wimsatt & Monroe Beardslet, *The Verbal Icon: Studies in the Meaning of Poetry* (1954).

Frame <*Frame* story, often *cornice*> A story within a story that provides a setting and exposition for the main narrative, a kind of justification or an apology. Often, a narrator describes where he found the manuscript of the novel or where he found the story he is about to narrate. The frame helps control the reader's perception of the work and the device has been used in the past to help give credibility to the main section of the novel. Examples: Geoffrey Chaucer's *Canterbury Tales*, Mary Shelley's *Frankenstein* and

Nathaniel Hawthorne's *The Scarlet Letter.* [Cf. prologue, subplot]

Free Indirect Style A technique of narrating the thoughts of character that blends both the first and the third person narrative. The purpose is to be intimate yet detached at the same time. EM Forster, in *A Passage to India* (1924), has used this technique to mime as well as comment on Ronny's limited language and imagination. It is, of course, difficult to get inside multiple characters' heads while also maintaining the proverbial reportorial narrative of the third person omniscient. Master story tellers Johann Wolfgang von Goethe, Jane Austen and Gustave Flaubert have shown the way much ahead. *Madame Bovary* (1857) is generally recognized as the model for the intracranial technique. The technique is now called the "Free Indirect Style." The narrative technique allows embedding a character's speech into a third-person narrative. The narrative, thus, moves back and forth between "the narrator telling us what the character is thinking and showing us the character's conscious thoughts, without denoting which thought belongs to whom." The result is a story that reads almost like it shares two "brains." <https://litreactor.com/columns/the-benefits-of-free-indirect-discourse>.

Free Verse/Vers Libre A verse structure which lacks regular metrical and rhyme patterns and relies on parallelism, cadences and stresses of everyday speech instead. The form allows a poet to exploit a variety of rhythmical effects within a single poem. French artist Victor Hugo (1802-1885) first experimented with this structure. In English the application dates back to King James translation of the Psalms and Song of Solomon. Macpherson's "Ossian Poems" were in fact richly rhythmic prose and Aloysius Bernard first attempted the prose poem as a specific form in his *Gaspard of the Night* (1836). The new form, however, had to wait for formal recognition until American poet Walt Whitman's *Leaves of Grass* first appeared in 1855. It eliminated much of the artificiality and some of the aesthetic distance of poetic expression and substituted a flexible formal organization suited to the modern idiom and more casual tonality of the language. Free-verse technique has been widely used in the 20th century by such writers as Ezra Pound, TS Eliot, Carl Sandburg and William Carlos Williams. WH Auden has an interesting comment on free verse: "The poet who writes 'free' verse is like Robinson Crusoe on his desert island: he must do all his cooking, laundry and darning for himself. In a few exceptional cases, this manly independence produces something original and impressive, but more often the result is squalor—dirty sheets on the unmade bed and empty bottles on the unswept floor." TS Eliot too observes that "No *vers* is *libre* for the man who wants to do a good job." [Cf. blank verse]

Ref: G Burns Cooper, *Mysterious Music: Rhythm and Free Verse* (1998). HT Kirby-Smith, *The Origins of Free Verse* (1996). Philip Hobsbaum, *Metre, Rhythm and Verse Form* (1996). Robert Wallace, *Writing Poems* (1982).

Futurism/-ist <Italian *futurism*> An early 20th century artistic movement started in Italy that emphasized the spirit of modernity. The significant results of the movement were found in the visual arts and poetry. In 1909, the Italian poet Filippo Tommaso Marinetti first announced the new manifesto in the Paris based newspaper *Le Figaro* that unambiguously glorified the new technology of the automobile and the beauty of its speed, power, movement, dynamism, energy, change and restlessness of modern life in general. He exalted violence and conflict and called for the sweeping repudiation of traditional socio-cultural and political values and the destruction of such cultural institutions as museums and libraries. The manifesto's rhetoric was passionately bombastic; its tone was aggressive and inflammatory and was purposely intended to inspire public anger and amazement, to arouse controversy and to attract widespread attention. Futurist writers include Filippo Tommaso Marinetti, Wyndham Lewis, Guillaume Apollinaire, Velimir Khlebnikov, and Vladimir Mayakovsky. In Russia the movement had the strongest influence, specially in the works of Boris Pasternak, and of Vladimir Mayakovsky, who, for a time, adhered to the official school of communist art.

Ref: Emilio Gentile, *The Struggle for Modernity: Nationalism, Futurism, and Fascism* (2003). Gunter Berghaus, *Futurism and the Technological Imagination* (2009). John Rodker, *The Future of Futurism* (1927).

G

Gay/Lesbian/Queer Criticism A few relatively new and well-defined terms related to *gender criticism.* The approaches are intersected with the feminist criticism which is concerned with issues of sexuality and of gender identity. For a time, the movements seemed to share a common ground with the feminist school; as women, lesbians and gays were objects of oppression by a dominant male heterosexual agenda. But in some other respects there were grounds for differences. All these approaches have a common problematic trend in that the antagonistic and preconceived feelings of a critic may lead to a less than unbiased response to the work. However, these critical approaches are also powerful tools to illustrate the effect that mainstream literature has on those who have been, or feel they have been, disenfranchised. The gay/lesbian approach to literature focuses on how homosexuals and lesbians are represented in literature, how they read literature and whether sexuality, as well as gender, is culturally constructed or innate. In the late 1960s and into the early 1980s these schools flourished. The gay and lesbian scholars began to peel away the layers of prejudice that had made almost impossible, before the Stonewall riot, to study the history of gay and lesbian writing or to analyze how the life and experience of the gay and lesbian were distorted in the mainstream cultural history. The emergence of the school coincides with the publication of Eve Kosofsky Sedgwick's *Between Men: English Literature and Male Homosocial Desire* (1985). Other scholars include Gayle Robin, Michael Foucault, Judith Butler and Lee Edelman. These schools along with gender studies have discussed three broad areas of work in literary and cultural theory: [1] The examination of history of repression of practitioners of sexualities other than those deemed normal by the mainstream heterosexual group; [2] the exploration of the counter cultures of gay and lesbian writing that existed in parallel with the heterosexual culture; and [3] the analysis of the instability and indeterminacy of all gender identities, such as *normal* heterosexuality and *abnormal* multiple sexuality, etc.

While theorizing gender issues, specialists nowadays prefer to stress on 'sexualities' rather than 'sexuality'. In the process a new coinage *queering* has come into existence. Queering is the process of defying the postulation that heterosexuality as the only norm. Queer now refers not only to gay and lesbian issues but other practices as well—it includes everything that has been marginalized in society including bisexuality, sadomasochism, the transgendered and even the transsexual. [Cf. feminist criticism]

Ref: Beatriz Preciado, *Manifesto Contra-sexual* (2002). Judith Butler, *Bodies that Matter: On the Discursive Limits of 'Sex'* (1993). Teresa de Lauretis, "Queer Theory: Lesbian and Gay Sexualities", *Differences: A Journal of Feminist Cultural Studies* (Summer, 1991).

Genetic Criticism A serious approach to literature evolved in France. Although its raw material is a writer's manuscript, genetic criticism owes more to structuralist and poststructuralist notions of textuality than to philology and textual criticism. Its main objective is the reconstruction and analysis of the writing process. For this, writer's notes, sketches, drafts, manuscripts, typescripts, proofs and even correspondences are brought to the analysis as additional aids. Genetic engineering of human body and that of a literary text have been brought together and the search for an ideal text has become something like the search for an ideal body. David Greetham ("The Philosophical Discourse of [Textuality?]") and Joseph Grigley ("Editing Bodies") are the leading scholars in this school. The approach is often viewed as the European alternative to the conflicting Anglo-American perspectives of intentionalism and sociological editing. Genetic criticism does not focus on one particular state of the text, but rather in the process by which the text came into being. [Cf. Geneva school]

Ref: Dirk van Hulle, *Textual Awareness: A Genetic Study of Late Manuscripts by Joyce, Proust and Mann* (2004). Jed Deppman, Daniel Ferrer, et al. Eds., *Genetic Criticism Texts and Avant-textes* (2004).

Genre A literary kind or class or category with which a work can be associated. In critical theory, genre may refer to both the content of a given work (tragedy, comedy, or pastoral, etc.), and to its form (poetry, fiction, or drama, etc.). This term also refers to types of popular literature (science fiction, detective story, etc.). During the Renaissance and after, till the 19th century, it was a common custom to judge a work of art in terms of the genre it belonged to. Later many critical traditions have been evolved to judge a work irrespective of its generic characteristic. Ludwig Wittgenstein defines genre in terms of family resemblance. Modern literary genres are rather loose and arbitrary and often either offshoots or subcategories defined according to different criteria: formal structure (sonnet, epic), style (allegory, baroque), length (novella, limerick), intention (satire, mock-heroic), effect (comedy, tragedy), subject (science fiction, romance), hybridity (tragicomedy, black comedy), ideology (didactic, postcolonialist), cross-cultural (Indian-English, diasporic), etc.

Ghost Word A word, which does not really exist in the vocabulary of a language. The great 19th century editor of medieval texts, WW Skeat, coined the term. Ghost words or *phantom words* are often the results of errors made by copyists, printers and editors: *Will he? Nill he?*—thus becomes *willy-nilly*. Mostly the errors that give birth to such spurious words are inadvertent, although ignorance on the part of the person responsible for such words may have some role in the breaking and making of words: *bacon and eggs* > *bekendecks*.

Gothic A term pertaining to a Germanic tribe, the Goths, who invaded the Roman Empire. Retrospectively it also refers to architectures in the style that was popular in Western Europe from the 12th to the 16th century. The name, originally a term of abuse, appears to have been taken in the first instance from the French and employed to denote any style of building that was not classical. The application of the term to literature, specially fiction, is a further shift from the previous meaning, i.e. fiction written in the style popular in the 18th and 19th centuries, which describes romantic adventures in mysterious or frightening surroundings. To be precise, the Gothic novel is a class of novel dealing with the frightening and the supernatural, and chiefly associated with Horace Walpole's *The Castle of Otranto* (1764) and the works of Ann Radcliff (*Mysteries of Udolpho*, 1794), MG Lewis (*The Monk*, 1796) and CR Maturin (*Melmoth the Wanderer*, 1920). Walpole, like some later writers, called his novel a "Gothic story" only to highlight the traces of mediaeval elements in the work. The popularity of such works, due in part to their supernatural elements, led to the identification of Gothic with the supernatural. Many works with only a very slight mediaeval element or none at all, thus, came to be called Gothic.

However, the Gothic novel specializes in the treatment of the ruins, haunted castles, frightening landscapes, claustrophobic atmosphere, treatment of the magic, the grotesque and the like. Some of its elements of atmosphere or characterization can be traced back to other and earlier genres, such as Jacobean tragedy and 18th century graveyard school of poetry. There are Gothic elements in Smollett's *Ferdinand Count Fathom* (1753). The Gothic novels and its readers are satirized in Jane Austen's *Northanger Abbey* (1818). The 19th century exponents of the Gothic novel, in one form or another, include Mary Shelley, Charlotte Brontë, Edgar Allan Poe and Sheridan Le Fanu. And much of the horror fiction of our own time may also refer back to this tradition. [Cf. holocaust literature, supernaturalism]

Ref: Chris Baldick, "Introduction", *The Oxford Book of Gothic Tales* (1993). David Punter, *The Gothic* (2004). Maggie Kilgour, *The Rise of the Gothic Novel* (1995). Carol Margaret Davison, *Gothic Literature 1764–1824* (2009).

Graveyard School A group of 18th-century English poets, who, unlike their contemporary neoclassicist, wrote long, picturesque meditations on death. They emphasized subjectivity, mystery, melancholy and gloom, etc. Many of the poems were in fact set in graveyards. Their works were designed to cause the reader to ponder immortality. The most famous work of this school is Thomas Gray's *Elegy Written in a Country Churchyard.* Some poems of the Graveyard School or Churchyard School are: Thomas Parnell's *A Night-Piece on Death* (1721), Edward Young's *Night Thoughts* (1742) and Robert Blair's *The Grave* (1743), etc. Generally speaking, this school was not much successful in terms of quantity and quality. Grey's elegy and Elizabeth Rowe's *Friendship in*

Death: In Twenty Letters from the Dead to the Living (1728) were exceptional in this respect. By 1840 Rowe's epistolary work went through some 89 print/editions. Some other poets of this group are William Cowper, William Collins, Oliver Goldsmith and Thomas Warton, etc.

Ref: Eric Parisot, *Graveyard Poetry: Religion, Aesthetics, and the Mid-Eighteenth-Century Poetic Condition* (2013). James Huff, *The Graveyard School of Poets* (1912).

Grotesque An adjective referring to something ugly and repulsive. In literary criticism the term (grotesque/grottoesque), since the 18th century, in French, German and English, has come to be used as a general adjective for the strange, fantastic, incongruous, unpleasant, or disgusting, etc. It refers to the subject matter of a work or a literary style characterized by overstatement, distortion, freakishness and disorder. The grotesque often includes an element of comic absurdity. Victor Hugo's *Hunchback of Notre Dame* is one of the most celebrated grotesques in literature. Dr. Frankenstein's monster can also be considered a grotesque. Some other examples of literary grotesque include Francois Rabelais's *Pantagruel* and *Gargantua* and Thomas Nashe's *The Unfortunate Traveller,* Sterne's *Tristram Shandy*, etc. Edgar Allan Poe, Evelyn Waugh, Eudora Welty, Flannery O'Connor, Eugene Ionesco, Gunter Grass, Thomas Mann, Mervyn Peake, Joseph Heller and others exploit this device with artistic neatness. The term *Theatre of the Grotesque* refers to an anti-naturalistic school of Italian dramatists, writing in the 1910s and 1920s, who are often seen as precursors of the Theatre of the Absurd school. [Cf. black humour]

Ref: Wolfgang Kayser, *The Grotesque in Art and Literature* (1957). Geoffrey Galt Harpham, *On the Grotesque: Strategies of Contradiction in Art and Literature* (1982).

H

Hamartia/Tragic Flaw <Greek *hamartanein,* to err> A technical term that refers to an inherent defect or weakness in a tragic hero, who is in many other respects a superior being favoured by fortune. This particular defect or weakness in the character of a hero is something very elemental and it is this defect that finally counts for his downfall.

Aristotle introduced this concept of hamartia in his *Poetics* while describing the tragic hero as a noble man of high rank whose misfortune is not brought about by villainy, but by some error of judgment, 'weakness of the flesh', any omission or commission on his part. This imperfection came to be interpreted as hamartia or a moral flaw, such as Othello's jealousy or Hamlet's irresolution. Most great tragedies, however, defy such a simple interpretation. However, the hero's suffering and its far-reaching reverberations are far out of proportion to his flaw. An element of cosmic collusion among the hero's flaw, chance, necessity and other external forces are essential to bring about the tragic catastrophe.

In Greek tragedy the nature of the hero's flaw is even more indefinable. Often the tragic deeds are committed unwittingly. The circumstances under which Oedipus kills his father and marries his own mother are a matter of custom rather than anything else. And even when such deeds are committed knowingly, they are not committed by choice. Orestes is under obligation to Apollo to avenge his father's murder by killing his mother. Also, an apparent weakness is often only an excess of virtue, such as an extreme probity or zeal for perfection. It has been suggested in such cases, since the tragic hero is never passive but struggles to resolve his tragic difficulty with an obsessive dedication, that he is guilty of hubris—i.e. presumption of being godlike and attempting to overstep his human limitations.

Recent scholarship has suggested that the interpretation of hamartia as a fatal flaw is itself flawed, and that the word more properly means any disproportion in the character's makeup that leads to downfall. Thus an excess of a valuable or virtuous quality can in some circumstances be seen as hamartia. However, the Greek concept has no Christian basis, as human being is by nature a sinner and, therefore, imperfect. The question of excess virtue in man has, therefore, no Christian basis. It must be, however, noted that the Greek idea of tragedy preceded Christianity by some four centuries.

Ref: AC Bradley, *Shakespearean Tragedy* (1904). JM Bremer, "Hamartia." *Tragic Error in the Poetics of Aristotle and in Greek Tragedy* (1969). Samuel H Butcher, *Aristotle's Theory of Poetry and Fine Art* (1902).

Harlem Renaissance/Negro Renaissance <Also NEW NEGRO MOVEMENT> A cultural outpouring of the Black gaining momentum of a literary movement in America. The Harlem Renaissance of the 1920s is normally considered the first major movement of the Black writers and artists in the US. According to Abraham Chapman, from "the writers of the 20's to 30's to Wright, Ellison, Baldwin and the younger negro writers who are now coming up, we can appreciate the literary validity and continuing historical significance of the Renaissance." The Harlem Renaissance is usually dated from 1925 to 1935 the year of the Harlem riots. During this period, new and established Black writers published more literary works than ever before. The first influential Black literary journals, such as *Crisis* and *Opportunity,* heralded their appearance and the Black authors and artists received their first widespread recognition and serious critical attention both from inside and outside the US. Although New York City was its centre, it drew writers from other cities as well. Many see this as a strong reaction against racial violence and atrocities against the Black which found its worst shape in the 1920s. Alaine Le Roy Locke's *The New Negro*, which has five important essays, "Foreword," "The New Negro," "Negro Youth Speaks," "The Negro Spirituals," and "The Legacy of the Ancestral Arts" established the mood and spirit of the movement. Among the major writers associated with this period are Claude McKay, Jean Toomer, Countee Cullen, Langston Hughes, WEB Du Bois, Arna Bontemps, Nella Larsen, and Zora Neale Hurston. Works representative of the Harlem Renaissance include Arna Bontemps's poems "The Return" and "Golgotha Is a Mountain," Claude McKay's novel *Home to Harlem,* Nella Larsen's novel *Passing,* Langston Hughes's poem "The Negro Speaks of Rivers," etc. [Cf. black aesthetic movement, negritude].

Ref: A Baker, Jr., *Afro-American Poetics: Revisions of Harlem and the Black Aesthetic* (1988). Abraham Chapman, "The Harlem Renaissance in Literary History," *CLA Journal XI* (1967). Arthur P Davis, *The Dark Tower: African American Writers* (1974). Houston David Levering Lewis, Ed. *The Portable Harlem Renaissance Reader* (1995).

Hegemony <Greek *hegemonía,* leadership, domination, etc> A concept, mostly political and cultural, referring to ruling group's apparatus of domination upon the ruled without direct oppression. In ancient Greece, hegemony was political domination of a City State over other City States. The dominant City State was recognized as *hegemon.* In the 5th century BCE the City State of Sparta was an example of hegemon as it exerted hegemony over other states. In modern cultural theory the term refers to the idea of the ruling class's management of value systems and customs of the dominated society. In cultural imperialism the leading state controls the domestic affairs and regulates social standards of the subordinate state. The mechanism or the process through which the process is manipulated constitutes the hegemonic area of influence. The modern concept of hegemony, however, is developed by the Italian Marxist political thinker, Antony Gramsci (1891-1937). Peter Childs and RJP Williams have clarified the concept as: "Gramsci's term for the force by which people are convinced of the naturalness or rightness of their position and that of their rulers.... The political leadership of a hegemonic group is through the consent and acceptance of the ruled.... Culture is the site on which the struggle for hegemonic power is conducted." Hegemony, therefore, can be viewed as a model for understanding how dominant cultural concepts of the colonizer become imbued by the colonized and how colonial power becomes gradually accepted. Importantly, hegemony helps to explain the collusion of colonized groups and their acceptance of colonial discourse. Coercing, but voluntary, institutions like educational institutions and areas of job opportunities play a major role in instituting hegemonic power and thereby 'brain washing' the colonized. Many postcolonial writers have had major concern with both the psychological and cultural effects of colonialism and how its dominant values were internalized by colonial subjects. Chinua Achebe, RK Narayan and Franz Fanon, etc are just a few examples.

Ref: Edward Said, *Orientalism* (1976). Jonathan Joseph, *Hegemony: A Realist Analysis* (2002). Peter Childs & RJ Patrick Williams, *An Introduction to Postcolonial Theory* (1997). Richard Howson, Ed. *Hegemony: Studies in Consensus and Coercion* (2008).

Hellenism & Hebraism A set of two related terms used by Matthew Arnold (1822-1888). Hellenism refers to an idiomatic style, free from all excesses. Hellenism, after the Greek model, is devoid of solecism, barbarism and foreign expressions. It also refers to an approach to life that focuses on the growth and development of the intellect and values. It prefers that reason should be applied to examine human experience in pursuit of "sweetness and light." Hebraism opposes Hellenism. It is an attitude to life based on obedience without proper sense of development of human resources. Arnold in his *Culture and Anarchy* (1869), Chapter IV, has deliberated on these two rival forces in history of human culture: "The governing idea of Hellenism is spontaneity of consciousness; that of Hebraism is strictness of conscience." Hence Hebraism promotes narrow-mindedness and develops propensity toward material prosperity at the cost of intellectual creativity, giving rise to *philistinism,* as Arnold likes to call it. Arnold's attack was aimed mainly at the cultural barrenness of the British middle class people of his generation.

Hemistich & Stichomythia <*Hemi,* half and *stich,* verse> A couple of methods of versification. Hemistich is half of a verse, often half of an Alexandrine line, either unfinished or deliberately finished that way with a caesura for greater dramatic or poetic effect. The Latin poet Virgil used this pattern of lines in *Aeneid* to express great duress in his characters, specially when they were emotionally so caught up that they could not utter full sentences. Many Old English *alliterative verses* are in fact divided into two equal sized hemistiches—a-verse and b-verse with a clear caesura in the middle: "The dew was falling fast the stars began to blink" (The dew was falling fast | | the stars began to blink). In dramatic terms, a very short dialogue, or half a line is known as *hemisticomythia*. When the poetic line conveys an uninterrupted thought without a caesura, it is known as *monostich*. Stichomythia, on the other hand, has quick successions of usually short single-line *repartees*. Often characterized by antithesis, a quick exchange of dialogues is frequent in orthodox plays. For example, the opening of Hamlet's meeting with his mother (III.iv) exemplifies stichomythia:

Queen: Hamlet, thou hast thou father much offended.
Hamlet: Mother, you have my father much offended.
Queen: Come, come, you answer with an idle tongue.
Hamlet: Go, go, you question with a wicked tongue.

[Cf. Caesura]

Ref: TVF Brogan, et al., "Hemistich", *The New Princeton Encyclopaedia of Poetry and Poetics* (1993).

Hendiadys A Figure of Speech, originally a Greek device, in which use of two substantives are connected by a conjunction, instead of subordinating one to the other, to express a single complex idea: "His look drew audience and attention" (Milton); or "we drink from cups and gold," which might have been expressed by a noun qualified by an adjective—"we drink from *golden cups*." The figure is often called "the *figure of twins*." In Genesis 23:4 there is a nice example of this device uttered by Abraham to the Anatolian people when he wants to bury his wife Sarah: "I am a *stranger and a sojourner* with you: give me a possession of a burying place with you, that I may bury my dead out of my sight."

Heptameter/Fourteener A metrical verse line of seven iambic feet used widely in England during the 16th century before *pentameter* replaced it. The heptameter has the advantage of being readily divided in groups of four feet, then three, as often found in ballads. An example of simple heptameter from Tennyson: Ănd sweét | | ĕr fár | | ĭs deáth | | thăn lífe | | tŏ mé | | thăt lóng | | tŏ gó. It is sometimes called fourteener for it has fourteen syllables.

Hero/Protagonist A chief character of dramatic or narrative work. He/she is usually the centre of the reader or spectator's attention and sympathy. In cases where there are both the hero and the heroine, the plot usually gives major focus on one of them; he or she is the protagonist. In Shakespeare's *Hamlet*, Hamlet is unquestionably the hero and the protagonist, and the position of the heroine, Ophelia, is secondary. In Bernard Shaw's *Mrs. Warren's Profession*, it is the heroine who happens to be the protagonist. The deciding question should be—who is in the centre of action? It is the protagonist from where all action emerges and to whom all action diverges. In the first case, Ophelia is the heroine, but Hamlet is the hero and the protagonist, whereas in the second case, Mrs. Warren is the heroine and the protagonist. Seen from her importance in the plot she is the protagonist, as good as a hero; but here the preference for the word *heroine* is a question of gender only.

Aristotle, in his *Poetics*, has described the qualities that can make someone the hero or the protagonist of a tragedy. His moral virtue, social status, etc are the prerequisites there. As Aristotle believes, a hero is the person next to none in the play, be it a tragedy or a comedy. In his time hero's social hierarchy mattered. In modern times it is the personal quality of a person, irrespective of his background; and his role in the plot that are the deciding factors. Sometimes, however, the deciding factors are controversial. For example, in Shakespeare's play, *Julius Caesar,* both Caesar and Brutus seem to vie for the position. In experimental works writers sometimes try to play game with the reader or spectator. A modern example is the character of Marion in Alfred Hitchcock's film, *Psycho*: Marion is in the position of the hero; but suddenly he disappears to the utter shock of the spectator. Then there is a great work like Leo Tolstoy's *War and Peace* in which some fifteen major characters have been treated with equal share in the narrative. The reader has to decide who is who. [Cf. antihero, antagonist]

Heroic Couplet/Verse A pair of rhymed verse lines of *iambic pentameter*. Though Geoffrey Chaucer is the first English poet to exercise it, it has its heyday only during the 18th century. Many of heroic couplets are *closed couplets*, each line rhyming with the other and together forming a logical whole. Alexander Pope is one of the best practitioners of this form of verse: "And when I die, be sure you let me know/ Great Homer died three thousand years ago." Other poets, Chapman and Dryden too have excelled in this verse style. Like heroic couplet, there is *heroic quatrain* in which a group of four lines are taken together instead of two lines. In a quatrain of this kind the rhyme scheme normally looks like: a-b-a-b, c-d-c-d, etc. [Cf. couplet]

Ref: Philip Hobsbaum, *Metre, Rhythm and Verse Form* (1996).

Hiatus & Lacuna A stylistic and phonological feature. The words are almost similar in meaning—they refer to 'gap' or 'break.' Hiatus is a gap, or a missing section in a manuscript. A simple pause or break in speech or writing, for emphasis or for the purpose of highlighting what comes next or even for proper pronunciation is again a hiatus (not lacuna). By extension a pause between two successive vowels is also hiatus. For example when we say, "the examination,"—the first word ends with a vowel and the second begins with another; thus two successive vowel sounds are brought together. One needs a slight break, a hiatus, for perfect utterance. However, in some similar cases of hiatus often a consonant is used to make the pronunciation smooth: The *n* in *an* (*an* example) is covering the hiatus; otherwise the 'n' in 'an' has no meaning. In the French language the use of liaison or an insertion of a consonant sound between two vowels—one ends a word and the other begins the next one—is numerous. Thus 'ce objet' becomes 'cet objet', this object. Lacuna, on the other hand, is simply a gap, break or missing element in a text, often referring to an ancient manuscript. Thus a lacuna in the inscription makes interpretation difficult. Weathering, decay, etc causing damage to old manuscripts or inscriptions are often responsible for lacunae. An example of such lacuna is the eight-leaves-long 'Great Lacuna' in the *Codex Regius*, a major source of Norse mythology. The plural form of lacuna is *lacunae* or *lacunas*.

Higher/Lower Criticism A form of Biblical Criticism. In biblical studies a higher criticism is that which touches upon the intellectual, aesthetic, pedagogic and spiritual properties of a text; whereas a lower criticism limits discussions only to the text and the mechanism involved in it. In the 18th century Biblical criticism, the term higher criticism was commonly used in mainstream scholarship in contrast with 'lower criticism.' This form of criticism is also known as *Historical Criticism*. In the present time, historical criticism is the more commonly used term for higher criticism, while textual criticism is more common than the loose expression 'lower criticism.' The main issue of the criticism is to employ history or historical events and circumstances as a means to the understanding of a literary work. Such criticism moves beyond both the facts of an author's personal life and the text itself in order to scan the social and intellectual environment in which the author has composed the work. The study of a work based on its impact on the world of a period in which it was written together with the impact of history on the work is a norm of historical criticism. The main concern of historical criticism is to ascertain the text's unique meaning in its original historical context and its literal sense. The next important concern is to create a reconstruction of the historical situation of the author and the readers of the text. Examples of postmodern historical criticism can be found in the work of Michel Foucault, Hayden White, Stephen Greenblatt, and Jonathan Goldberg. [Cf. culture studies, Marxist criticism, new historicism, postcolonial criticism]

Ref: Ernest Cadman Colwell, "Biblical Criticism: Lower and Higher", *Journal of Biblical Literature,* Vol. 67, No. 1 (1948). HEW Turner, *Historicity and the Gospels* (1963). Ronald Nash, *Christian Faith and Historical Understanding* (1984). Ted F Peters, "The Use of Analogy in Historical Method", *Catholic Biblical Quarterly* 35 (1973).

Historical Novel A novel in which fictional characters take part in actual historical events and interact with real people from the past or one that makes use of historical personages and events in a fictitious narrative. The work may deal with actual historical personages, as does Robert Graves's *I, Claudius* (1934) or it may contain a mixture of fictional and historical characters or situations, as does Charles Dickens' *A Tale of Two Cities* (1859). Focus may be on a single historic event too, as does Franz Werfel's *Forty Days of Musa Dagh* (1934), which dramatizes the defence of an Armenian stronghold. More often it attempts to portray a broader view of a past society in which great events are reflected by their impact on the private lives of fictional individuals. In serious examples of this type, historical facts and events are not just decorative in nature; in fact, they are very central to the development of the story and thereby historical vision of the novelist or dramatist. In English literature it was Sir Walter Scott who first achieved greatness in this field. His works like *Waverly* (1814), *The Heart of Midlothian* (1818) and *Ivanhoe* (1819), etc give him unique position among the English writers of historical novels. Thomas Carlyle has thus commented on his novels: "These historical novels have taught all men this truth…that the bi-gone ages of the world were actually filled by living men, not by protocols, state papers, controversies, and abstractions of men."

Another English writer, Winston Graham's historical novels chronicle several generations of the Poldark family in the 18th and 19th centuries in Cornwall. These include *Ross Poldark* (1945), *Jeremy Poldark* (1950), *The Grove of Eagles* (1963), *The Black Moon* (1973), *The Miller's Dance* (1982) and *The Twisted Sword* (1990), etc. In the 1970s the Poldark saga was adapted into a popular television series in England. Other works, such as, Victor Hugo's *The Hunchback of Notre Dame*, William Makepeace Thackeray's *Barry Lyndon*, Herman Wouk's *The Winds of War* and more recent James McBride's *Miracle at St. Anna* (2002) substantiate the popularity of this genre of the novel. Some more examples of this genre are Arthur Koestler's *The Gladiators* (1939), Zoé Oldenbourg's *Destiny of Fire* (1960) and Mary Renault's *The King Must Die* (1958), etc. Though some historical novels, such as Leo Tolstoy's *War and Peace* (1865-69), are of the highest artistic quality, many fail to achieve that standard. George Lukács, in *The Historical Novels* (1937), tries to explain this category in terms of Marxist discourse and Scott is seen as "a radical innovator because he succeeds in showing how the historical meaning of human destiny is constituted as concrete narrativity." [Cf. history play]

Ref: George Lukács, *The Historical Novel* (1937). Harry E Shaw, *The Forms of Historical Fiction: Sir Walter Scott and His Successors* (1983). Jerome de Groot, *The Historical Novel* (2009). Sarah L Johnson, *Historical Fiction: A Guide to the Genre* (2005).

Historicism A philosophical discourse that holds that knowledge and cognition are historically conditioned both spatially and temporally. Often used negatively, the term first appeared in the 18th century Germany, coined by Karl Schlegel. The concept challenges a progressive view of history that views history as linear. The major concepts of the Enlightenment were built upon the hypothesis that there is only one kind of rationality applicable to all people and cultures. Giambattista Vico (1668-1744) and JG Herder (1744-1803), the founder members of the Historicism school, reject this notion and develop the archetypal models of historicism. Vico and Herder criticize the concept that truth transcends history and argue that truth is conditioned by human history and thus reject central ideas of the Enlightenment, such as a historical view of humanity, concept of universal rationality and belief in the progress of human history with the development of reason. They give importance to individual historical period and culture, a unique value system that particular culture contains. History is conceived as the aggregate of diverse, unique histories.

Herder believes "a poet is the creator of the nation around him; he gives them a world to see and has their souls in his hand to lead them to that world." To him poetry had its greatest purity and power in nations before they became civilized, as shown in the Old Testament, the Edda and Homer and he tries to find such virtues in ancient German folk songs, Norse poetry and mythology. Since literature is part of man's cultural heritage, it has to have its historical contexts. History shapes literature: every novel, play or poem is influenced by the socio-political context in which it is written. Roland Barthes, in *The Death of the Author*, acknowledges that an author is always a product of his time and he "can only imitate a gesture that is always anterior, never original." Historicism argues that the meaning of a text can only be revealed by contextualizing it around other discourses from the same period. If *The Canterbury Tales* is read from a purely formalist viewpoint, the rich resource of art and intimate knowledge of a particular age behind the text will be disregarded. While the formalists judge literary work on its aesthetic value, historicism results in literary and non-literary texts being given equal weight, unbiased and aware of all aspects surrounding a work. Historicism contextualizes a text like Orwell's *Animal Farm,* for example. The allegory of *Animal Farm* is rendered pointless without considering Russia of a particular era. The Austrian-English philosopher Karl Popper denounced historicism and the Post-structuralists used the term New Historicism, which has some associations with both anthropology and Hegelianism.

Ref: Isaiah Berlin, *Vico and Herder: Two Studies in the History of Ideas* (1976). Mises Ludwig von, *Theory and History* (1957). Wesley Morris, *Toward a New Historicism* (1972).

History Play A play or a dramatic work representing events based on history or historical figure. Frequently referred to as history play, it was earlier known as *chronicle play*. The Elizabethan chronicle plays are so called because many of them were constructed upon the available chronicles. Shakespeare has the best to offer in this category: *Hamlet, Macbeth, King Lear* and *Julius Caesar*, etc. Many of the plays of this category are, in fact, dramatic treatment of the materials found in chronicles of Raphael Holinshed. Later works of this group, which are better known as history plays, include even Schiller's *Maria Stuart* (1800), John Osborne's *Luther* (1961), Arthur Miller's *The Crucible* (1953) and also David Hare's *Licking Hitler* (1978), which is later reprinted with two other works under the title *The History Plays* (1984). [Cf. chronicle, historical novel]

Ref: EMW Tillyard, *Shakespeare's History Plays* (1946). Irving Ribner, *The English History Play in the Age of Shakespeare* (1965). Lily B Campbell, *Shakespeare's Histories* (1947).

Hollywood Novel A type of novel that depicts the Hollywood world of motion picture, its activities and relationships emerging in the filmdom. Many novelists have often associated themselves with Hollywood film industries as scriptwriters and in many cases scriptwriters too have emerged as novelists. For example, Bud

Schulberg was initially a scriptwriter and later with *What Makes Sammy Run*? (1941) he emerges as a powerful novelist. The novel, about an unprincipled motion picture studio mogul, was a great success. On the other hand, the novelist Scott Fitzgerald's novel about Hollywood, *The Last Tycoon* (1941), is another classic of this genre. The career of its hero, Monroe Stahr, is based on that of the producer Irving Thalberg. This is Fitzgerald's final attempt to create his dream of the promises of American life and of the kind of man who could realize them. *The Beloved Infidel* by Fitzgerald too deals with the author's love affair with Sheilah Graham and it makes an excellent film. It must be noted that the film and the novel are two different media. A film script is different from a novel and even a novel has to be rewritten before it is made into a film. The art of fiction depends more on artistic handling of the materials than on sets or atmosphere, local colour or the exaggeration of the life it describes. The term Hollywood Novels refers only to some novels and it has nothing to do with film scripts.

Ref: Anthony Slide, *The Hollywood Novel* (1994).

Holocaust Literature A rather indistinctly formulated genre, works mostly influenced by or written about the holocaust of World War II. War and its aftermath are the common factors that bring a lot many works under this umbrella. This type may include true stories of survival in the combat zone, concentration camps, escape and life after the war or fictional works and poetry. All epics, in a broader sense, come under this head. Representative modern works of holocaust literature include Saul Bellow's *Mr. Sammler's Planet,* Anne Frank's *The Diary of a Young Girl,* Erich Maria Remarque's *All Quiet on the Western Front,* Jerzy Kosinski's *The Painted Bird,* Arthur Miller's *Incident at Vichy,* Czeslaw Milosz's *Collected Poems,* William Styron's *Sophie's Choice,* Ford Madox Ford's *Parade's End* and Art Spiegelman's *Maus*, etc. The poems of Wilfred Owen that mostly thrive on "the pity of war" too may be counted in this category. However it remain a problem area in the study of war fiction as to what is true and what is not. The word 'fiction' as a synonym for 'lies' poses it antithetically to truth and reflects negatively on the expressive possibilities of a particular literary form when applied to the world of actual events.

Ref: Bernard Bergonzi, *Heroes' Twilight: A Study of the Literature of the Great War* (1965). Saul S Friedman, Ed. *Holocaust Literature: A Collection of Critical, Historical and Literary Writings* (1993). Sara R Horowitz, *Voicing the Void: Muteness and Memory in Holocaust Fiction* (1997). Sue Vice, *Holocaust Fiction* (2006).

Homily/Sermon <Greek *Homilia,* to have communion, talk & Latin *Sermo,* discourse> A discourse or a short, exhortatory talk, a religious discussion to be read/talked before a group of listeners in order to instruct them spiritually or morally. Normally the speech is delivered by the priest after the scripture readings that help the congregation relate to the message of the Bible. The terms are often interchangeably used; though they have shades of differences. A homily is a reflection on the scripture or its part; whereas sermon uses scriptural passages to explain a religious idea. Sermon is more of a formal lecture and homily is a simple talk or discussion. During the Middle Ages, the homiletic lectures were the popular means for preaching at the congregations. However, homilies are simple and easily understood by common people and they are considered better means than sermons for interweaving Sacred Scripture. These days the church normally uses the word homily more than sermon. The basic concept of homily/ sermon is not limited to Christianity alone. The Indian sacred book, the Bhagavad Gita is a storehouse of sermons and homilies that have been interpreted and reinterpreted for generations. Krishna's counsels to Arjuna have the basics of homilies and all his guidance is relevant for all people. Even today they are used as exemplary lessons. A frequently used example: "Set thy heart upon thy work, but never on its reward" (Krishna-Dwaipayana Vyasa). Islam too has similar models. Here's a quote from Al-Bukhari (Hadith: 1623, 1626, 6361): "O People, lend me an attentive ear.... Beware of Satan, for the safety of your religion.... All mankind is from Adam and Eve, an Arab has no superiority over a non-Arab nor a non-Arab has any superiority over an Arab; also a white has no superiority over black nor a black has any superiority over white except by piety (taqwa) and good action...." This is the most celebrated and last homily or *Khutba* of Prophet Muhammad, which he delivered on a Friday in mount Arafat's Uranah Valley.

Literary examples of homilies and sermons in secular writings are not very frequent, but available. Chaucer himself takes two Latin tracts on penitence, translates and turns them into a sermon by placing the text in the mouth of the Parson in "The Parson's Tale" (*The Canterbury Tales*). Writings based on Christian thoughts, like old morality plays, *Doctor Faustus, The Pilgrims Progress* and *Murder in the Cathedral,* even pure fiction like *Huckleberry Finn* have instances of homiletic lessons in various forms. Jonathan Edwards in *Sinners in the Hands of an Angry God* emphasizes the idea that God has given a chance to humanity to rectify their sins, as will of God has kept them away from depths of hell. [Cf. didactic]

Ref: Bishop John Jewel, *Second Book of Homilies* (1571). Craner, *First Book of Homilies* (1547). Keith A Francis and William Gibbon, *The Oxford Book of British Sermon 1689-1901* (2012). Hans J Hillebrand, Ed. *The Oxford Encyclopedia of Reformation* (1996).

Hubris/Hybris <Greek *hybris*> An *insolence* or *arrogance* inviting disaster. In fact, the concept is closely associated with an extreme form of tragic flaw, or hamartia. In classical Greek ethical and religious thought it is supposed that hubris or overweening, is by itself a moral flaw since it suggests an impious disregard of the limits governing human action in an orderly universe. It is the sin to which the great and the gifted are most susceptible and in Greek tragedy it is often the hero's tragic flaw. The protagonist's transgression leads him eventually to his or her downfall, which may be understood as divine retribution or *nemesis*. Perhaps the simplest example occurs in *The Persians* of Aeschylus, in which the arrogance of Xerxes in building a bridge of ships across the Hellespont flaunts nature by turning sea into land.

He is punished by the crushing defeat of the Persians at Salamis. In most other Greek tragedies the hero's hubris is very subtle, and sometimes he appears wholly blameless.

However, the act of defying a moral code of conduct may often be regarded as a merit in terms of human consideration. Very often the struggle of the tragic hero is posited against the status quo of all kinds including moral laws, and as such, the indomitable spirit of a human being challenging an otherwise irrelevant order is more of a merit than demerit. In essence the spirit of hubris is revolutionary. Only from an orthodox moral point of view, thus, hubris is a flaw, whereas seen from humanistic philosophy; it is often a quality that man, since the Renaissance and then the Enlightenment, aspires to attain. That is why many Shakespearean heroes may be destroyed, but not only do they emerge at the end nobler figures than what they were at the beginning; but also they foreshadow the establishment of a new order. In its simple meaning hubris means excessive pride combined with arrogance and lack of the sense of humility. Hubris in literature is perhaps best illustrated in Milton's *Paradise Lost*, where Satan attempts to force other angels to worship him and asserts: "Better to reign in hell than serve in heaven." [Cf. hamartia, tragedy]

Ref: Douglas L Cairns, "Hybris, Dishonour, and Thinking Big", *Journal of Hellenic Studies,* 116 (1996). Nick Fisher, *Hybris: A Study in the Values of Honour and Shame in Ancient Greece* (1992).

Humanism A new form of human aspiration and human standing the Renaissance aspired for. Interests in human culture, education and reason, sparked by a revival of interest in classical Greek and Roman literature, culture and language gave birth to this philosophy. Human nature and the dignity of man were exalted and emphasis was placed on the present life as a worthy event in itself (as opposed to the medieval emphasis on the present life merely as preparation for a future life). Humanism from the beginning developed on two main lines: [1] Some, like Erasmus, embraced the rational wisdom of antiquity, and [2] Many, like Montaigne, found in the classical wisdom sanction for scepticism and naturalism. But humanism, either religious or secular, became a comprehensive doctrine of social and intellectual order. In our time, humanism is attuned with secularism. Some 20th century critics such as Ezra Pound, Hulme and TS Eliot specially considered humanism to be sentimental "slop" or "an old bitch gone in the teeth" and wanted to go back to a manly, authoritarian society such as existed in the Middle Ages.

However, literature, presumably, was one of the areas in which humanistic doctrine found its expression. It led to the rise and development of Neoclassicism; and writers and readers developed a common consciousness of rich literary and cultural heritage behind them. Humanist thought is represented in the works of Marsilio Ficino, Ludovico Castelvetro, Edmund Spenser, John Milton, Dean John Colet, Desiderius Erasmus, John Dryden, Alexander Pope, Matthew Arnold, Irving Babbitt and many other writers.

Ref: Tony Davies, *Humanism: The New Critical Idiom* (1997). Paul Oskar Kristeller,

The Renaissance Philosophy of Man (1950). Robert Proctor, *Defining the Humanities* (1998).

Humour/Humor A physiological stimulus. In our times, humour has almost nothing to do with its early medieval western psychological theory upon which Ben Jonson based his plays. Now, humour can be simply defined as a type of stimulation that tends to elicit the laughter reflex. One might call it a *luxury reflex*. Its only function seems to be to provide relief from tension. Humour lies in oddity and in the perception of incongruity. This incongruity may be between the ideal and the real, between illusion and reality, between the language modes, between the genteel and the vernacular, etc. The characteristic features may expose cultural and social pretensions to make them appear ridiculous and artificial. This is exactly where literary artists have exploited it artistically. Humour is the only form of communication in which a stimulus on high levels of complexity produces a stereotyped, predictable response on the physiological reflex level. Since the step from the sublime to the ridiculous is reversible, the study of humour provides clues for the study of creativity in general. In its most ordinary use it simply refers to something purely comic. The purpose of humour in this sense is just to evoke sympathetic laughter or just laughter that ends in itself. May be, sometimes humour is what makes a man laugh and another grind his teeth in anger. It is a kind of amusement at the cost of another's distress or frailty. Humour has to have an astringent flavour like characters in great plays that hurt in order to amuse or amuse in order to hurt. Humour and wit often come very close to each other. Whereas wit is always verbal, humour may be ascribed to a comic appearance or a mode of behaviour too. Charlie Chaplin, the actor, and Falstaff, the character, are perhaps still the greatest figures in this respect. Humour can be intended for serious and curative purpose, wit cannot. The greatest comic characters have all good sense of humour, be it Mrs. Malaprop, Micawber or Polonius. [Comedy of Humours]

Ref: AA Berger, *An Anatomy of Humour* (1993). A Klein, *The Healing Power of Humour* (1989). A MacC Armstrong, "The Idea of the Comic", *British Journal of Aesthetics* 25/3 (1985). Noël Carroll, *Humour: A Very Short Introduction* (2014). Richard Alexander, *Aspects of Verbal Humour in English*, Vol. 13 (1997).

Hybridity A creation of new form from previously distinct elements; it is a mixed, eclectic and mongrel form. It refers, indirectly to disintegration of notions of fixed or pure forms of culture. Hybridity gives birth to new transcultural forms within the contact zones produced by colonial expansion. Whereas pre-colonial world is characterized by distinct categories like East/West, civilized/savage and European/non-European, etc, the post-colonial world by a breakdown of such distinct categories yielding space to mixed formations on both cultural and literary levels. Rather than seeing texts as part of a dominant or resistant culture, critics who emphasize hybridity, prefer to see the eclectic nature of postcolonial writings in terms of both style and content. It may take many forms, such as linguistic, cultural, political and racial, etc. *Pidgin* and *creol* are its linguistic examples. The following passage from *The God of Small Things* can be an interesting example of how once ideologically ill-assorted ideas can naturally coexist in postmodern texts: "So there it was. History and Literature enlisted by Commerce. Kurtz and Marx joining hands to greet rich guests as they stepped out off the boat." While analyzing the colonizer/colonized relationship, Homi Bhabha stresses on their interdependence and the mutual construction of their subjectivities and contends that all cultural statements and systems are constructed in a space, the "third space of enunciation." The position often creates ambivalence, the ambiguous way in which the colonizer and the colonized look at one another. The colonizer regard the colonized as inferior, exotic, backdated; while the colonized regard the colonizer as corrupt, cruel yet enviable. In the context of hybridity this often generates a mixed sense of curse and blessing. However, the in-between space may carry the burden and meaning of cultures and this makes the vision of hybridity so important. Bill Ashcroft thinks most of the postcolonial writings have focused on hybridity involved in the postcolonial culture more as strength than weakness. [post-structuralism]

Ref: Amar Acheraiou, *Questioning Hybridity, Postcolonialism and Globalization* (2011). Homi K Bhabha, *The Location of Culture* (1994). MM Kraidy, "Hybridity in Cultural Globalization", *Communication Theory,* 12 (3) 2002. Robert Young, *Colonial Desire: Hybridity in Theory, Culture and Race* (1995).

Hymn <Greek *hymnos*> A song of praise, mainly in honour of the ancient gods, although heroes also are often addressed. Strictly speaking, now it is a song used in Christian worship, usually sung by the congregation and characteristically having a metrical, strophic, non-biblical text. Similar songs, generally termed hymns, exist in all civilizations, including those of ancient Sumer, Greece and India. Christian hymnody derives from the singing of psalms in the Hebrew temple. Hymnody developed systematically only after Emperor Constantine had legalized Christianity (AD 313) and it flourished earliest in Syria. The Byzantine Church adopted the practice and developed complex types such as the *kanon* and *kontakion*. Saint Ephraem, a 4th-century Mesopotamian deacon, poet, and hymnist, has been called the father of Christian hymnody. By the late Middle Ages, trained choirs had supplanted the congregation in the singing of hymns. The pattern of secular lyrics also influenced the hymn texts of Martin Luther (1483-1546) and his contemporaries. Swiss, and later, French, English, and Scottish Calvinism promoted the singing of metrical translations of the Psalter austerely set for unaccompanied unison singing. English and Scottish Protestantism admitted only the singing of psalms. English metrical psalms were set to tunes adapted from the French and Genevan Psalters. The principal impetus to English hymnody came in the late 17th century from the independent hymn writer Isaac Watts. Finally, the evangelical revival of the mid-18th century under John and Charles Wesley, founders of Methodism, finally established hymnody in England and America.

Ref: Routley and Richardson, *A Panorama of Christian Hymnody* (1979). Ian Bradley, *Abide with Me: The World of Victorian Hymns* (1997).

Hyperbaton/Anastrophe/Inversion A Figure of Speech from Greek *hyper,* 'over' and *bainein* 'to step', i.e. transposition of words, which otherwise syntactically or grammatically belong together, often to emphasize the first of the separated words or to create a certain image, poetic or even rhetorical effect. A reversal of position taking place ahead is *anteposition*: "Much have I travelled in the realms of gold." An inversion of order, the cart before the horse position, is *hysterology*: "Out of the suffering comes the serious mind" (Ruskin). When the exchange is confined to two words only, it is *anastrophe*: "said he." And when the transposition is intricately done, it is *synchysis*: "Is piety thus and pure devotion paid?"—Milton.

Hyperbole <Greek *hyper,* beyond + *ballo,* I throw> A Figure of Speech, overstatement or exaggeration for the sake of prominence and emphasis: "Not in the legions/ Of horrid hell can come a devil more damn'd/ In evils to top Macbeth" (Shakespeare). Andrew Marvell's "To His Coy Mistress" too has brilliant examples of the figure: "My vegetable love should grow/ Vaster than Empires, and more slow/ An hundred years should go to praise/ Thine eyes, and on thy forehead gaze;/ Two hundred to adore each Breast:/ But thirty thousand for the rest." As literary devices, *hyperbole*, and its opposite *understatement*, *litotes*, are much used in comedy and satire in which something or some quality is reduced to the most possible lower rank.

Hyperfiction A Fiction (often poem) that is available on the internet, CD-ROMs and floppy disks and that often includes sound and graphic art. They are fragmented texts and readable in a non-sequential way. This type of texts is called *decentred,* since the readers are provided with hop-over texts and subtexts from the primary document through links. Whereas most conventional novels, in a linear fashion, run from beginning to end in an unbroken order, a hypertext fiction can split itself; the reader can take advantage of the fluidity of the electronic media and can move from one place and episode in the text to another non-sequential place and episode at his will to trace an idea or follow a character. Examples: Michael Joyce's *Afternoon* and Stuart Moulthrop's *Victory Garden*. [Cf. cyberfiction, cyberpunk, interactive novel]

Hypertext A document containing words or phrases that hooks up to other documents. Mostly used in the internet language, these connecting words are called *links* and are easily selectable by users. A single hypertext document may easily refer to thousands of documents available on the web. In the context of the web, words or graphics may serve as links to other documents, images, videos and sounds. Links may or may not follow a logical path; it depends on programs and accessibility determined by the creator of the source document. Overall, the web contains a complex virtual network of connections among a vast number of documents, graphics, videos and sounds. This complex networking of documents has given birth to a new form of fiction known as *hyperfiction* or *hypertext fiction*.

Ref: George P Landow, *Hypertext: The Convergence of Contemporary Critical Theory and Technology* (1992).

Hysteron Proteron A Figure of Speech in which *later-earlier* inversion of the natural sequence of events, often meant to stress the event which, though later in time, is considered the more important. In this device the speaker breaks the rule of chronological order of an action. It gives importance to an action itself and thus frames his sentence accordingly. "Put on your shoes and socks". Or, "Let's fight and take up weapons." [Cf. hyperbaton]

I

Iamb/Iambic/Iambus A common and quite popular metrical foot in English versification. An iambic foot consists of minimum two syllables, first one with a weak stress followed by a strong, i.e. an *unaccented syllable* followed by an *accented.* The example here from Wordsworth has iambic *tetrameter* alternated by an iambic *trimeter*:

Ă slúm | | bĕr díd | | mў spí | | rĭt séal;
  Ĭ hád | | nŏ hú | | măn féars.

However, *iambic pentameter* is more popular metrical scheme than other forms in English versification. Originally a tool of satire and abusive criticism, iambic meter has developed much over the centuries and has been used in a variety of poetic genres. Shakespeare and Marlowe are to a great extent responsible for popularizing iambs, making iambic pentameter the dominant metrical scheme of English dramatic poetry. Of all the iambic metres, iambic pentameter is the most admired poetic vehicle in the English language. [Cf. foot, scansion]

Ref: James McAuley, *Versification: A Short Introduction* (1996).

Icon <Greek 'eikōn', image> A type of sign that can signify what it represents by some inherent similarity to that object, person or place or whatsoever. Icon, in fact, is Charles Sanders Peirce's term for a sign that functions by means of sharing resemblance with what it signifies. Portraits or maps, for example, are natural resemblances rather than arbitrary and conventional signs. Icon is a graphic representative sign of something and *iconography*, thus, refers to the study of any subject, not necessarily religious, represented in the visual art form, including its conventions and symbolic significance. Often icon and symbol become inseparable. [Cf. symbol]

Ref: Mary Paloumpis Hallick, *The Story of Icons* (2001). WK Wimsatt, *The Verbal Icon: Studies in the Meaning of Poetry* (1954).

Image/Imagery A concrete representation of an object or sensory experience. Such representation helps evoke the feelings associated with the object or experience itself. There are two types of images: *literal image* and *figurative image.* Literal images are especially concrete and involve little or no extension of meaning of the words used; whereas figurative images are more flexible and do not follow the literal restriction of words. Images in literature are usually visual, but it can also refer to the representation of any sensory experience. In his poem, "The Shepherd's Hour," Paul Verlaine presents the following image: "The Moon is red through horizon's fog; / In a dancing mist the hazy meadow sleeps." The first line is broadly literal, while the second line involves figurative meaning associated with dancing and sleeping. Hence the mental picture that images create in totality is called imagery that may refers to a word or group of words in a literary work, which appeal to one or more of the senses: *Tactile Imagery* (touch/skin), *Kinesthetic Imagery* (movements/body), *Visual Imagery* (vision/eye), *Auditory Imagery* (sounds/ear), *Olfactory Imagery* (smell/nose), *Gustatory Imagery* (taste/ tongue), *Subjective Imagery* (personal experiences/emotions). Imagery may often be a figure of speech to describe an abstract idea vividly. The following example of imagery in TS Eliot's "The Love Song of J. Alfred Prufrock", in the form of a simile, uses picture of pain and sickness to describe the evening, which, as an image, itself represents society and the psychology of Prufrock himself: "When the evening is spread out against the sky/ Like a patient etherized upon a table."

Ref: AR White, *The Language of Imagination* (1990). PE Morris & PJ Hampson, *Imagery and Consciousness* (1983). Pierre Ouellet & Larry Marks, "The I's Eye: Perception and Mental Imagery in Literature", *Substance,* Vol. 22, No. 2/3, Issue 71/72: (1993).

Imagism A school of poetry, mainly an American literary stylistic movement. The imagist poetic agenda was formulated around 1912 by Ezra Pound in collaboration with fellow poets, such as Hilda Doolittle, Richard Aldington, and FS Flint. The movement was encouraged by the critical views of TE Hulme in revolt against the lackadaisical judgment, romantic buoyancy and utter sentimentalism he found most prevailing on the literary scene. The Imagists rejected the sentiment and discursiveness of many Romantic and Victorian poets. The Imagists tried terse and clear verses, and rigid outline in which a precise visual image made a total poetic statement. Imagism was a successor to the French symbolist movement, but, whereas symbolism had an affinity with music, Imagism sought analogy with sculpture. The imagist poets used very precise language for sharply defined solid objects, probably under the influence of Japanese Haiku tradition. In 1914, as Pound turned to Vorticism, an art tradition, led by painter-writer Wyndham Lewis and Amy Lowell, largely took over leadership of the group. Among other practitioners of Imagist poetry, major poets like John Gould Fletcher, Harriet Monroe, Conrad Aiken, Marianne Moore, Wallace Stevens, DH Lawrence and TS Eliot were much influenced by the trend. The important Imagist anthologies (*Des Imagistes,* 1914; *Some Imagists,* 1915, 1916, 1917), and the magazines *Poetry* (1912) and *The Egoist* (1914) in the US and England, respectively, published the work of a dozen Imagist poets. The influence of Imagism can be seen traced in the work of the *objectivist poets*, who came to prominence in the 1930s under the auspices of Pound and Williams.

Ref: Ezra, Pound, *ABC of Reading* (1934). Julian Symons, *Makers of the New: The*

Revolution in Literature, 1912–1939 (1987). SK Coffman, *Imagism* (1951). TE Hulme, *Speculations*, Ed. Herbert Read (1924). William Pratt, *The Imagist Poem, Modern Poetry in Miniature* (1963).

Impressionism A term probably derived from Claude Monet's painting "Impression: Soleil Levant," first exhibited in Paris, 1874. The impressionists were a school of painters who were particularly concerned with the transitory effects of light and they wished to depict the fleeting impression from a subjective point of view. They were not interested in a precise representation; the resulting impression depended much on the perception of the spectator. As a literary term it refers to writings that capture fleeting impressions of characters, setting and events as they appear to the subjective mood. William Hazlitt (1778-1830) puts it in his essay, 'On Genius and Common Sense'—"You decide from feeling, and not from reason; that is from the impression of a number of things on the mind." For the school the formlessness and the homogeneity of impression were its ultimate virtues. It, therefore, is less concerned with the particulars and details than with the text that will directly induce a state of mind or mood. The French symbolists, followers of aestheticism and stream of consciousness have almost all been either impressionists or impressionistic in their writings and criticism to a certain degree. It focuses on a particular character's fleeting perception of events. The edges of reality are blurred by choosing points of view that lie outside the norm. However, the link between impressionism and literature is quite obscure. The impressionist writers had quite a bit in common with those writers categorized as symbolists and such names as Baudelaire, Henry James, Mallarmé, Rimbaud, Verlaine and Laforgue come to one's mind easily. In English literature, Virginia Woolf and James Joyce link up for either one or both the movements. One aspect of this type of writing is the unconventional use of time and space; the reader absorbing the past, present and even future all mixed up together. *The Heart of Darkness* of Conrad is often cited as one of the preeminent examples of impressionistic literature. The USA novelist Kate Walbert's *The Sunken Cathedral* (2015) is a recent example of this type.

Ref: John Rewald, *The History of Impressionism* (1973). W Epsom, 'Virginia Woolf', *Argufying: Essays on Literature and Culture* (1988). A Parkes, *A Sense of Shock: The Impact of Impressionism on Modern British and Irish Writing* (2011).

Innuendo A rhetorical device that is employed to indirectly point out some unpleasant or derogatory aspect of a thing or person or an idea. As a device it is very subtle and it demands a great deal of language skill so that an unmistakable mark of accusation or indictment operates without making the charge explicit: "After half an hour of the enthusiasm of an army, one feels the need of a little sea-air"—GB Shaw. Another example from TS Eliot: "Shall I part my hair behind? Do I dare to eat a peach?"—Obviously, this remark comes from the speaker's sexual frustration. An innuendo is almost perceptible here—the reflection of impotence of the speaker. [Cf. euphemism]

Intentional Fallacy An idea that the assessment of a literary work based absolutely on the author's manifested or implied intentions is false and deceptive. Critics who believe in the concept of intentional fallacy argue that a literary work itself is an adequately complete matter for investigation, even though they may agree that an author's statement of purpose can be a useful aid. Wimsatt Jr. and Monroe Beardsley in *The Intentional Fallacy* (1940) countered assumption that the original creator's intention for a work was equal to the meaning and merit of the work. This raised serious questions in the critical realm about intentionality, autobiography, cultural context and the fixed or unfixed nature of meaning: "... the design or intention of the author is neither available nor desirable as a standard for judging the success of a work of literary art, and it seems to us that this is a principle which goes deep into some differences in the history of critical attitudes." Therefore, analysis of William Wordsworth's *Lyrical Ballads* or any of his poems based on the observations about poetry he makes in his *Preface* is an example of the intentional fallacy.

Interactive Novel A novel, normally a web fiction, with more than one possible series of events or dénouements. The reader is given the opportunity at various places to choose what will happen next. It is, therefore, possible for several readers to experience different novels by reading the same book, or for one reader to experience different novels by reading the same one twice and making different choices. An online interactive web novel of this kind is called '*wovel*.' On the internet a reader can read a novel like a player playing a video game. He can pick his character and direction and go with the storyline. Text adventure has become a popular computer game for the young generation especially in the western countries and it forms a subset of the adventure genre. The player uses text input to control the game and the game is relayed to the player via text output. During the 1980s some software companies introduced the genre for commercial purpose. *Adventureland* (1978), by Scott Adams, is a defining works of interactive fiction and *The Hobbit* (1982), by Philip Mitchell and Veronika Megler, is an example of transforming a popular fiction into an interactive novel/wovel. [Cf. cyberfiction, cyberpunk, hypertext fiction]

Ref: Nick Montfort, *Twisty Little Passages: An Approach to Interactive Fiction* (2005).

Interior Monologue A mode of narrative in which characters' subjective thoughts, emotions and sensations that appear to be uncontrolled by the author are revealed to the reader through a free indirect discourse. It portrays emotional experiences as they occur at both the conscious and unconscious levels. Images and the connotations they evoke lead the reader to the inside of a character's mind. Interior monologue functions much the same way as soliloquy does in drama. It can be either direct or indirect. One of the best-known interior monologues in English is the Molly Bloom section at the close of James Joyce's *Ulysses.* The interior monologue is also common in the works of Virginia Woolf. However, Laurence Sterne's *Tristram Shandy* (1760-67) can be cited as an early example of the type. [Cf. monologue, soliloquy, stream of consciousness]

Intertextuality A term coined by Julia Kristeva to explain the pre-existing body of discourse that makes a particular text reasonable and explicable. Every text, it is said, diverges from and converges to other versions of texts, and no text can be read independently without relocating it in terms of those texts. The meaning of a text is, therefore, conditioned by other texts that it absorbs from and responds to. As Roland Barthes puts it, "the text is not a line of words releasing a single *theological* meaning...but a multi-dimensional space in which a variety of writings, none of them original, blend and clash" in "one place where this multiplicity is focused is the reader, not, as was hitherto said, the author. The reader or his consciousness is the space on which all the quotations that make up a writing are inscribed." Jonathan Culler further interprets that "the text is a kind of formless space whose shape is imposed by structured modes of reading." Intertextual figures that make such construction possible are: allusion, quotation, plagiarism, translation, pastiche and parody, etc. The operative concept is intertextuality.

Ref: RS Miola, *Seven Types of Intertextuality* (2004). H Jacobmeyer, *Ever After: A Study in Intertextuality* (1998).

Invective <Latin *invectus*, abuse> A speech or piece of writing that abuses, denounces or attacks. In Aristotelian idiom an invective is a part of *epideictic rhetoric* which is ceremonial discourse: speech or writing that praises or blames. However, an invective never praises; it always blames or insults. It can be directed against a person, cause, idea, or system. It employs a fierce use of negative as well as emotive language: "I cannot but conclude the bulk of your natives to be the most pernicious race of little odious vermin that nature ever suffered to crawl upon the surface of the earth"—is an example of how Swift could hurl his invectives. Invectives are obvious form of discourteous verbal or textual missiles or discourse intended to inflict insult on somebody. In satires of Swift and Pope one may come across applications of powerful invectives frequently. It is more potent, direct and scathing diatribe than satire, irony, innuendo and sarcasm, etc. The opposite of invective is *encomium*, which is a tribute or eulogy in prose or verse. Here is another example of a long and biting invective composed of successive negative adjectives from Kent's speech to Oswald in *King Lear* (II. ii): "A knave, a rascal, an eater of broken meats; a base, proud, shallow, beggarly, three-suited, hundred-pound, filthy worsted-stocking knave; a lily-livered, action-taking, whoreson, glass-gazing, super-serviceable, finical rogue; one-trunk-inheriting slave; one that wouldst be a bawd in way of good service, and art nothing but the composition of a knave, beggar, coward, pander, and the son and heir to a mongrel bitch: one whom I will beat into clamorous whining if thou deni'st the least syllable of thy addition."

Invocation An introduction, a formal device for invoking powers before launching a grand subject. In ancient religious cultures the hymns begin with invocations of the names of the gods to whom they are addressed. The invocation was believed to have a magical value. The Greek poetic prayers contain three essential parts: an *invocation* of the god, a *justification for fulfilment* and a *conclusion* that formulates the request, such as in the prayer to the goddess Athena in *The Iliad.* Prayers of praise developed mainly out of experiences of religious elevation and were utilized in both public and private ceremonies. Classical literary convention typically required such an introductory address to the muses. In epic tradition the invocation was usually addressed to Calliope, muses of epic poetry, or to Clio, muse of history. It remained in vogue till the Neoclassical Period. John Milton in his *Paradise Lost* (1667) invokes Urania, the muse of astronomy in antiquity. His Urania, unlike the seven classical muses, does not reside on Olympus, but far above, being a heavenly entity. This practice of invoking some sort of super power is almost common in all classical literatures. The great Indian epics—*The Ramayana* and *The Mahabharata*—too open with prayers that are incidentally very similar to the convention of western invocation. [Cf. muse]

Irony An indirect mode or figurative presentation. The term irony has its root in the Greek comic character Eiron, a clever underdog, who by his wit repeatedly triumphs over the boastful character Alazon. The *Socratic irony* of the Platonic dialogues derives from this comic origin. Feigning ignorance and humility, Socrates goes about asking silly and obvious questions of all sorts of people on all sorts of subjects only to expose their ignorance as more profound than his own.

In its modern usage the old insinuation persists. It is the use of words in a sense or a context that implies the opposite meaning to what is actually said. It is a linguistic device either in the form of a [1] *verbal irony,* in spoken or written form, in which the real meaning is concealed or contradicted by the literal or contextual meanings of the words; or [2] *dramatic irony*, in a theatrical situation in which there is an incongruity between what is understood by the speaker and the actuality the audience knows. Verbal irony arises from a sophisticated or resigned awareness of contrast between what is and what ought to be and expresses a controlled pathos without sentimentality. It is a form of indirection that avoids overt praise or censure as in the casual irony of such statement as, "And Brutus is an honourable man," actually meaning diametrically opposite of what the word "honourable" may ordinarily convey. Irony can be traced in various interesting forms —from the tragedy of Sophocles to the novels of Jane Austen and Henry James; but is specially important in satire, as in Voltaire's and Swift's. In John Milton, a profoundly compassionate irony pervades the moving last lines which describe Adam and Eve as they depart from Eden, not now the majestic lords of creation, but two frail human beings beginning life anew in the world of sin and sorrow and death, though "with Providence their guide" and the hope of achieving a "paradise within." The nonliterary use of irony is usually considered as sarcasm.

However, irony of fate, often known as *cosmic irony*, involves Gods, universal process or situations that are beyond human capability, as found in some Greek plays and the novels of Thomas Hardy. Chekov's short stories (like "The Gift of the Magi") are classic example of powerful ironies common people encounter in ordinary life.

Ref: Claire Colebrook, *Irony* (2004). Douglas Colin Muecke, *The Compass of Irony* (1969). Wayne C Booth, *A Rhetoric of Irony* (1975). John Lippitt, *Humour and Irony in Kierkegaard's Thought* (2000).

J

Jargon A specialized word, originally chatter of birds. Technically speaking, any language or part thereof that is used for a special purpose and commonly understood by a select group of people can be treated as jargon. In this way it refers to terminology used in a profession, such as computer jargon, medical jargon, etc. For example some medical jargons are BP (Blood Pressure), FX (Bone Fracture) and JT (Joint), etc. It may also refer to anything apparently unintelligible to common people. Literary examples of jargon are François Villon's *Ballades en Jargon,* which is written in the secret language of the Coquillards, and Anthony Burgess's *A Clockwork Orange,* narrated in the fictional character's language of Nadsat. Other small items that are frequently used by literary critics, such as, allusion, foil, sestet, script, etc too often serve as jargons. Jargons are normally related to specialized professions whereas slang may not be profession specific. [Cf. Slang]

Jazz A form of music. The Jazz is the most characteristic contribution of America to the world of music just as the Musical Theatre is the contribution of America to the world. Before the First World War Jazz was primarily the music of the Southern Negro, specially of the Negro in and around New Orleans. During the 1920s there was in fact a plethora of this genre of music and it decidedly declared the supremacy of the Black over the White. After the War, along with the migration of the Black to the north, Jazz moved north and to Chicago and only after that the jazz really spread beyond the Black community. Among the artists a few like Louis Armstrong and Duck Ellington are still household names in the US. Many literary artists like Walt Whitman, Tennessee Williams and Scott Fitzgerald have been greatly influenced by the Jazz.

Jeu D'esprit A French term, meaning *play of spirit*, better rendered as flight of fun or fancy. Any light hearted, witty piece of work, epigrammatic expression or anything written in a gusto of fun and fancy is included in this category. Limerick, a short comic piece of drama or fiction, witticism of Oscar Wild or Bernard Shaw often expresses jeu d'esprit. Accordingly, a part of a long work, a small expression or even the whole work can have jeu d'esprit in operation. Thomas Carlyle's *Sartor Resartus* has recurring jokes and humours that exemplify proper exposition of jeu d'esprit at its best.

K

Kitchen-Sink Drama A derogatory definition applied to some realistic dramatic practices in England during the 1950s and 1960s. John Osborne, Arnold Wesker, Alun Owen and others created a kind of wave of a new realistic dramatic tradition depicting the lives of the working-class people instead of the middle-class drawing room scenario. The term comes from Arnold Wesker's play *Roots* (1959), which in fact begins with a character cleaning the dishes in a kitchens-sink. In 1958 Wesker announced he would write plays not simply for the refined people who acknowledge plays to be a legitimate form of expression, but also for the bus driver, the housewife, the miner and the Teddy boy. The sophisticated Londoners reacted to this agenda adversely and termed these plays as kitchen-sink drama. Though the tradition gained notoriety in 20th century British culture for their angry criticism directed towards the social-economic establishment, the plays were significant for they realistically depicted the most intimate aspects of domestic life. In 1956, British playwright John Osborne introduced a different type of drama—*Look Back in Anger* that was one of the first plays to use a working-class setting with working-class characters. [Cf. angry young men]

Knight A military aristocrat in medieval Europe and England who swore services to a liege lord in exchange for control over a piece of specified land. The term comes from the Old English word *cniht,* meaning young man or page. The process of becoming a knight was long, beginning as page at court, serving food and drink to the elders, running messages and errands and at the same time learning the niceties of polite society. The next rigorous phase of apprenticeship was again service as a *squire* under an able knight. After successful completion of the training and acquiring proper chivalry, the final stage of knighthood was a semi-religious ceremony. In the late medieval period, the position of knights often became hereditary and the titles—*Sir*, *Ser* or *Don*—were indicative of their ranks. In peacetime, knights often demonstrated their martial skills in tournaments, which were usually watched by ladies and lords. By the end of 15th century the tradition was weakening. In English literature, the reference to knight occurs passim, often referred to as Red-cross Knight. Geoffrey Chaucer (Knight's Tale), Edmund Spenser (*The Faerie Queene*), John Keats (La Belle Dame Sans Merci), Lord Tennyson (The Lady of Shalott), and even TS Eliot (*Murder in the Cathedral*) have their works peopled with knights. [Cf. romance]

Ref: Ewart Oakeshott, *A Knight and His Horse* (1998). G Duby, *The Chivalrous Society* (1977). William Arthur Shaw, *The Knights of England* (1966).

L

Lake Poets/Lake School A group of poets known by this name; a common factor among them being that all of them lived in the Lake District of England at the turn of the 19th century. As a definition, Lake Poets or Lake School did not refer to any deliberate literary or philosophical agenda, as they followed no single school of thought or literary practice. *The Edinburgh Review* rather consistently used the term to demean their works. The main poets of the Lake School were Robert Southey, William Wordsworth, Samuel Taylor Coleridge and John Wilson, etc. Among them, Wordsworth and Coleridge, of course, had a common platform of a literary movement known as Romanticism. Southey, on the other hand, was mostly a prose writer and he never subscribed to the poetic agenda of Wordsworth and Coleridge. Wilson too had a different set of ideas as against those of Wordsworth and Coleridge. Charles Lamb, Charles Lloyd and Thomas De Quincey too are associated with the ill-assorted group. For many, Lake Poet identity often became synonymous with the romantic group of poets although many romantic poets did not have anything to do with Lake District.

Ref: Thomas De Quincey, *Recollections of the Lakes and the Lake Poets*, Ed. David Wright (1970).

Legend <Medieval Latin *Legenda*, story, from Latin *Legere,* to read> A story or group of stories coming down through generations of popular oral culture. It deals with past stories of actual or fictitious monarchs and heroes. Legends can be distinguished from myth in that they concern human beings rather than gods and supernatural powers. Thus legends establish better historical basis than myth. A legend describes the effects of primitive events on history. Therefore it is a history revealed through imagination and one as fabulous as the prehistoric mysteries that brought that history into being. The repetitiveness and redundancy of legends emphasize the fact that many different legends spring from the same mythic sources. But variants of legend are reminders that myths and their outcomes are historically conditioned and questioned. Because of their local frame of reference, legends vary and widely different accounts emerge from diverse locales and periods. Favourite legendary themes are the struggles and miraculous adventures of fascinating heroes. In a nutshell the word legend usually characterizes a traditional tale thought to have a historical basis, as in the legends of King Arthur or Robin Hood. [Cf. folklore, myth]

Ref: DB Vitaliano, *Legends of the Earth: Their Geological Origins* (1973). JCJ Metford, *Dictionary of Christian Lore and Legend* (1983).

Leit Motif/Motiv/Leitmotiv <German for leading motif> In a literary work leit motif may refer to a theme, character type, image, metaphor or any other verbal element that recurs throughout a single work of literature or occurs in a number of different works over a period of time. For example, longing for the golden past, known as the *ubi sunt* motif, occurs passim in literary works, specially the romantic literature and also in modern diasporic writing in the form of looking back home. The term *Leit motif*, first applied to Wagnerian musical dramas to designate a motif, i.e. a particular character, mood or theme, is now a frequent phrase in literary criticism since the 19th century. For example, the frequent manifestation of the white colour in Herman Melville's *Moby Dick* is a specific motif, while the trials of star-crossed lovers are a conventional motif in literature of all periods. The older term, *topos* (plural = *topoi*), which may mean a stock device of rhetoric, comes very close to the idea of leit motif. [Cf. theme]

Limerick A light and humorous verse, usually anapaestic. Its usual form consists of five lines with the rhyme scheme: a-a / b-b / a. Conventionally, the first, second and fifth lines contain three feet, while the third and fourth usually contain two feet. Limericks range in subject matter from the silly to the obscene. Early examples, notably those of Edward Lear in his *Book of Nonsense* (1846), set the trend and style of its versification. The limerick is always a self-contained little poem, either celebrating humorous fun or jeu d'esprit. Many obscene limericks are written anonymously. Since the time had Edward Lear popularized them in the mid-19th century, children and adults have equally enjoyed this comic type. Here is an anonymous example of the genre:

There was a young lady of Clyde,
'T was of eating green apples she died.
The apples fermented
Inside the lamented,
And made cider inside her inside.

Ref: Carolyn Wells, *A Nonsense Anthology* (1903). Edward Lear, *More Nonsense, Pictures, Rhymes, Botany,* etc (1872). Gershon Legman, *More Limericks* (1988).

Liminality <Latin *limen*, margin or threshold> An anthropological term. In any structure of positions, liminal period refers to an in-between stage, a fluid condition that implies continuity. Anthropologist Arnold van Gennep (1873-1957), in his renowned book *Les rites de passage*; [Trans. *The Rites of Passage* (1960)] tried to see the rites as means by which individuals are eased, without social disruption, through the difficulties of transition from one social role to another. On the basis of an extensive survey of preliterate and literate societies, he held that the rites consist of three distinguishable, consecutive elements, called in French, *séparation, marge* and *agrégation* or separation, transition and reincorporation, or as pre-liminal, liminal, and post-liminal stages. The person (or persons) on whom the rites centre is first symbolically severed from his old status; then he undergoes adjustment to the new status during the period of transition, and is finally reincorporated in society in his new social status. The concept is now being employed to interpret specially cross-cultural experience in diasporic literature in which the process of cultural transformation of immigrant people is portrayed.

Litotes <Meiosis> A Figure of Speech, from Greek *litos,* meaning *small*, the rhetorical use of understatement to imply the opposite. The Bible abounds in litotes. An example, "A prophet is not without honour, except in his own country, and among his own kin, and in his own house"—shows how an *understatement*, for intensification, by denying the contrary of the thing is being affirmed. [Cf. hyperbole, innuendo]

Lost Generation An expression used in 1920 by Gertrude Stein at her residence, Flat No. 27, Rue de Fleurs, Paris, when she remarked that Hemingway and his contemporaries were "all a lost generation." However, Hemingway himself, in *The Sun Also Rises* (1926), used this phrase as an epigraph. During this time the young generation of American artists was disillusioned by the aftermath of the War. All traditional values were suddenly crushed down and a general vacuum in the American culture was strongly felt. This group, the 'Lost Generation', consisted of the great writers who appeared on the American literary scene during the decades following the First World War: Ernest Hemmingway, William Faulkner, Scott Fitzgerald, Ezra Pound, Hart Crane, John Dos Passos and the like. The term refers to the generation's own feeling that there was almost nothing in the contemporary American culture and tradition they inherited and hence the generation was described as 'lost.' They highlighted the defects of the conventional public life. Dissatisfied with America, many of them preferred the life of expatriates elsewhere in Europe, mainly in Paris. However, the group happens to be the first coherent group of writers in the history of American literature.

Ref: Frederick J Hoffman, *The Twenties: American Writing in the Post-war Decade* (1990).

Lyric A poetic genre, perhaps the most seminal form of poetry. The word *lyric* may cover many kinds of poem, but the basic lyrical quality brings all of them together under this head. The poems sung by individuals or chorus to the lyre, or sometimes to the flute, were called *melic* or *elegiac*, in which *hexameter*, or verse line of six metrical feet, alternated with a shorter line. But they were also used for personal poetry, spoken as well as sung. Two broad categories of the lyric are often mentioned: [1] *Dorian lyric*, which is associated with dance and song, and [2] *Ionian lyric*, which expresses the author's personal feeling.

Lyric poetry's personal elements—emotions, thoughts and feelings—are sometimes contrasted with narrative poetry and verse drama, which relate events in the form of a story. Elegies, odes, and sonnets are all different kinds of lyric poetry. In ancient Greece an early distinction was made between the choral lyrics and the song that expressed the sentiments of a single poet. The latter, the *melos,* or song proper, had reached the height of technical perfection in Greece as early as the 7th century BCE. Later, in great poets like Bacchylides and Pindar the tradition of the dithyrambic odes reached its highest development. Latin lyrics were written by Catullus and Horace in the 1st century BCE; and in medieval Europe the lyric form is found in the songs of the troubadours, in Christian hymns, and in various ballads. In the Renaissance, the most finished form of lyric, the sonnet, was developed by Petrarch, and in England, nourished by Shakespeare, Edmund Spenser and John Milton. Especially identified with the lyrical forms of poetry in the late 18th and 19th centuries were the Romantic poets, including such diverse figures as Robert Burns, William Blake, William Wordsworth, John Keats, PB Shelley; and in other European countries Alphonse de Lamartine, Victor Hugo, Wolfgang von Goethe, Heinrich Heine, etc. With the exception of some dramatic verse, most Western poetry in the late 19th and the 20th century may be classified as lyrical.

Lyric poetry is specially marked by personal emotions or feelings as its basic ingredient and is typically spoken in the first person. The verse lines are normally metered—iambic and trochaic being the most popular vehicle in English tradition. In the 20th century the English Georgian poets such as AE Housman, Walter de la Mare, Edmund Blunden and WB Yeats continued the lyric tradition of English poetry. During the modernist era, poets like Ezra Pound, TS Eliot and William Carlos Williams, etc almost rejected the English lyrical form because of its melodic quality and they found it unsuitable for modernist reality. However, despite resistance from some quarters the basic form of lyric poetry never lost all its ground in England and America.

Ref: Carrie Noland, *Poetry at Stake: Lyric Aesthetics and the Challenge of Technology.* CM Bowra, *Greek Lyric Poetry: From Alcman to Simonides* (1961). Ernest Rhys, *Lyric Poetry* (1913). Peter Childs, *The Twentieth Century in Poetry: A Critical Survey* (1999). RS Crane, *Critics and Criticism* (1952). ML Rosenthal, *The Modern Poets* (1960).

M

Magic/Magical Realism <German *magischer realismus*> A term first used by Franz Roh in 1925. Magic realism is a form of fiction or narrative characterized by a strongly fantastical element (often drawing on myth or fairytale) juxtaposed with everyday reality. Cuban writer Alejo Carpentier was the first author to use the term. The term is broadly descriptive rather than critically rigorous. Matthew Strecher defines magic realism as 'what happens when a highly detailed, realistic setting is invaded by something too strange to believe.' Such fiction often contains labyrinthine plots and multiple worlds. The term was applied to explain the quasi-surrealistic works of some painters. Only during the 1940s and after, the term was applied to fiction characterized by a mixture of realistic and fantastic elements. In magic-realistic works, plots often handle both the elements side by side to highlight a *third* position of the characters between these two extremes, the position that is valid for many diasporic authors and their literary characters. Carpentier's novel, *The Kingdom of This World* (1949), fused time making it fluid, synchronous and looping rather than linear. Magic realism is, he claimed, "exclusive to the Americas," arising from the singular history of the New World, the only sane response in the face of overwhelming insanity whirling off into the dream-sense of wild imaginings and make of it something profound and uplifting. Magic realism builds an alternative reality upon recognizable foundations—Moscow, London and New Delhi—but strangely moulds and bends them, affording the magical elements the same status as the mundane. Elements of this device turn up in writers from Dickens to Kafka. It thrives on chaos. For this reason it has lent itself readily as the voice of the colonized, the uprooted and the subaltern. Mainly applied to some Latin American works the term is extended to other works. The best-known magic-realistic works are Franz Kafka's *The Trial*, Mikhail Bulgakov's *The Master and Margarita*, Gabriel García Márquez's *One Hundred Years of Solitude*, Angela Carter's *The Magic Toyshop*, Milan Kundera's *The Unbearable Lightness of Being*, Salman Rushdie's *Midnight's Children*, and Italo Calvino's *If on a Winter's Night a Traveller*, etc.

Ref: Amaryll Beatrice Chanady, *Magical Realism and the Fantastic: Resolved Versus Unresolved Antinomy* (1995). Dr. Clark Zlotchew, *Varieties of Magic Realism* (2007).

Matthew C Strecher, "Magical Realism and the Search for Identity in the Fiction of Murakami Haruki", *Journal of Japanese Studies*, Vol. 25, No. 2 (1999).

Malapropism <French *mal,* bad + *à propos,* to the purpose, meaning *bad application*> A term comes from the name of a character, Mrs. Malaprop, in Richard Sheridan's play, *The Rivals* (1775). As a literary term it refers to misusing of words without mispronouncing on the part of a speaker who is apparently confident about his/her ability to use sophisticated words; while the audience knows what is what. This is a clever device on the part of the dramatist, who is interested in exposing the hollowness of a person or a social class. Malapropism involves the confusion of two polysyllabic words that sound somewhat similar but have different meanings. Examples abound in English literature, especially in the dramatic form. For instance, [1] In Richard Sheridan's (1751-1816) Mrs. Malaprop prides herself on "her nice derangement of epitaphs" (*epitaph* for *epithets*). [2] A black maid in Edgar Rice Burroughs's *Tarzan of the Apes* series cries out as she falls into a river, "I sho' nuff don't want to be eaten by no river allegories, no sir" (*allegories* for *alligators*)! [3] Dogberry, the Watchman, in Shakespeare's *Much Ado about Nothing* comments, "Comparisons are odorous" (*odorous* for *odious*). The best malapropisms are close enough in sound to the correct word so that the audience can both recognize the intended meaning and laugh at the incongruity produced from such inadvertent and spontaneous mistakes. *Spoonerism* is slightly different from Malapropism in that spoonerism comes from rather a slip of the tongue or shift of consonant or vowel sound accidentally; whereas Malapropism's origin is ignorance: "Go and shake a tower" instead of "Go and take a shower" is an example of spoonerism.

Mandala <Sanskrit, *circle*> A symbol of totality in Hindu and Buddhist spiritual philosophy. Mandala is a systematized illustration of the cosmos, chiefly characterized by a concentric organization of geometric shapes. Its protective circle is a pattern of order super-imposed on psychic chaos. Sometimes its geometric form is seen as a vision—it is a square with four gates containing a circle in the centre. Mandala has its topographical and religious variants. The circular designs symbolize the notion that life is never-ending and they have spiritual significance to an individual or an ethnic group. The Hindus were one of the first people to use a Mandala as a spiritual tool; but the term is more familiar to the Buddhists. In Hinduism, in Buddhism, in India, China and Tibet intricacies of the symbol and their meanings are different. In Hinduism it is a spiritual guiding tool and an aid to meditation and trance. In Buddhism it represents mind—the mind as a microcosm representing various divine and healing powers at work in the universe and an enlightened mind prepared for the *nirvana.* It is said that the Swiss psychoanalyst Carl Jung observed the motif of the circle and was influenced by the concept.

In fiction the Mandala motif has been used by English writers, mostly from outside England. For example American writer Pearl S Buck has a novel called

Mandala (1970) based on an Indo-US encounter. Australian novelist Patrick White has extensively used the Mandala motif in *The Solid Mandala* (1966), *The Tree of Man* (1955), *Voss* (1957) and *Riders in the Chariot* (1961). In his novels Mandala is the Eastern symbol of totality and he has artistically exploited the motif.

Ref: Giuseppe Tucci, *The Theory and Practice of the Mandala* (1973). M Brauen, *The Mandala: Sacred Circle in Tibetan Buddhism* (1997). Nitin Kumar, *Mandala: Sacred Geometry in Buddhist art/Exotic India* (2000).

Mannerism An exaggerated and artificial adherence to an artistic manner or style. It may also refer to a popular style of the visual art of late 16th century Europe that was marked by elongation of the human form and by intentional spatial distortion. Literary works that are self-consciously high-toned and artistic are often said to be *mannered.* Authors of such works include Henry James and Gertrude Stein. In English literature, mannerism is strongly identified with the qualities of the Metaphysical poets like John Donne, Andrew Marvell, George Herbert and others. The witty sortie of a Baroque writer, John Dryden, against the metaphysical mannerism in the previous generation, affords a concise contrast between Baroque and Mannerist aims.

Ref: Grossmann F, *Between Renaissance and Baroque: European Art: 1520-1600* (1965). Helen Louise Gardner, *The Metaphysical Poets* (1972). Wylie Sypher, *Four Stages of Renaissance Style: Transformations in Art and Literature, 1400-1700* (1955).

Marxist Aesthetics/Criticism An aesthetic school based on Marx's theory of history and class-consciousness. This school attempts to show the place of art in the theory and practice of revolution. William Morris (1834-1896) in England, and Georgy V Plekhanov (1856-1918) in Russia, attempted to unite Marx's social criticism with a conception of the nature of artistic labour. The aesthetic theories of the Russian Revolution owe something to Plekhanov, something to the school of Formalist criticism, typified by the proto-Structuralist Bakhtin and something to the anti-aesthetic propaganda of the Russian constructivists. Marxist critics use literature to describe the competing socio-economic interests that too often uphold capitalist interests, such as money and power, rather than socialist interests, such as morality and justice. They argue that literature and literary criticism are essentially political, because they either challenge or support economic oppression. Because of this strong emphasis on the political aspects of texts, Marxist criticism focuses more on the content and themes of literature than on its form. The official approach of the Soviet art, however, was typified by the adoption of Socialist Realism under Joseph Stalin (1879-1953) as the only basis for artistic practice. Subsequently, Walter Benjamin, Christopher Caudwell, György Lukács, Jean-Paul Sartre, Louis Althusser and many others have given a comprehensive and coherent shape to the theory.

Discussing on the complex relation between literature and ideology, Terry Eagleton, however, rejects the 'vulgar Marxist' notion that literary works, as an element in the 'superstructure' of society, are simply a passive reflection of the economic base. In his *Criticism and*

Ideology he argues that text is neither a slavish expression of a dominant ideology nor a wholly autonomous element. [Cf. socialist realism]

Ref: Christopher Caudwell, "English Poets: The Decline of Capitalism", *Illusion and Reality* (1973). George Lukács, "Critical Realism and Socialist Realism", *The Meaning of Contemporary Realism* (Trans. John & Necke Mander, 1963). Peter Demetz, *Marx, Engels, and the Poets: Origin of Marxist Criticism* (Trans. Jeffrey L Sammons, 1967). Terry Eagleton, *Marxism and Literary Criticism* (1976).

Mask/Masque A festival in which participants offer gifts to their host incognito, and then join together for a ceremonial dance. Later, the masque consisted of a group of costumed and masked persons of the same sex who, accompanied by torchbearers, arrived at a social gathering to dance and converse with the guests. The masque could be simply a procession of such persons introduced by a presenter or it could be an elaborately staged show in which a brief lyrical drama heralded the appearance of masquers, who having descended from their pageant to perform figured dances, revelled with the guests until summoned back into their pageant by farewell speeches and songs. The theme of the drama presented during a masque was usually mythological, allegorical or symbolic and was designed to be complimentary to the noble or royal host of the social gathering.

It has its probable origin in primitive religious rites and folk ceremonies. Later it evolved into a detailed court show that entertained royalty throughout Europe. The Italian *intermezzo* comes very close to this form. The *intermezzi* (plural form) included a dance or masked ball where the guests mingled with the actors. A non-dramatic variation, the *trionfo,* or triumph, evolved from these Italian court masques and, arriving in France, gave rise to the *ballet de cour.* During the 16th century the European continental masque travelled to Tudor England, where it became a court entertainment played before the king. Gorgeous costumes, spectacular scenery with elaborate machinery to move it on and off the stage and rich allegorical verse marked the English masque. During the reign of Elizabeth I the masque provided a vehicle for compliments paid to the queen. Under the Stuarts the masque reached its zenith when Ben Jonson became the court poet. He endowed the form with great literary as well as social force. Ben Jonson's *The Masque of Blackness* is an early Jacobean era masque, first performed at the Stuart Court in the Banqueting Hall of Whitehall Palace on 6 January 1605. Jonson invented the *antimasque* (also *antemasque, antic masque*), the false masque, and produced the first of its kind in 1609. It took place before the main masque and concentrated on grotesque elements, and provided a direct contrast to the elegance of the masque that followed. In later years the masque developed into opera, and the antimasque became primarily a farce or pantomime. After Jonson's retirement, masques lost their literary value and became mainly vehicles for spectacle. Masque entertainments in England ceased with the beginning of the English Civil Wars and later revivals never equalled the originals.

Ref: Allardyce Nicoll, *Stuart Masques and the Renaissance Stage* (1937). Barbara Ravelhofer, *The Early Stuart Masque: Dance, Costume, and Music* (2006). Enid Welsford, *The Court Masque* (1927).

Mediaevalism/Medievalism A system of belief and also literary and cultural interest in some aspects and practices of the medieval period or the Middle Ages—a long period of time spanning almost from the 8th century to the 15th century. From the fall of Rome to the pre-Renaissance period was an age of decline for many reasons; but this is the period that prepared the European mind for a kind of rebirth also. However, the concerns for European national folklore, emulation of the primitive literary forms and accentuation of medieval themes, such as, castle, fairies, fair ladies, archaic diction, chivalry, knights, etc are included in the concept widely known as medievalism. Other forms of medieval practices, such as, sacredotalism, dictatorship of 'man on horseback', craftsmanship and dialectics, etc are regarded as components of medievalism. One of the most striking manifestations of medievalism in English literature was the Gothic revival, which later merged with the Romantic Movement. Medievalism supplies considerable inspiration to the 19th century English literature, traces of which can be assembled in works from Walter Scott's *Ivanhoe* (1819) and Keats poems, "La Belle Dame Sans Merci," "The Eve of St Agnes," to romances of William Morris, Thomas Carlyle's *Past and Present* and even John Ruskin's *The Stones of Venice*, etc. A scholar and expert working on some aspects of the Middle Ages is a *medievalist*. The medieval period or as often said, the Dark Age, has all along remained a steady resource for artistic works.

Ref: A Chandler, *A Dream of Order: The Medieval Ideal in Nineteenth-Century English Literature* (1971). Kathleen Davis & Nadia Altschul, Eds. *Medievalisms in the Postcolonial World: The Idea of "the Middle Ages" outside Europe* (2009). M Alexander, *Medievalism: The Middle Ages in Modern England* (2007).

Melodrama <Greek *melos,* music, and French *drame,* drama> A form of play; in strict scholarly and historical contexts. A melodrama is a Victorian drama in which elaborate music or song was used to accompany the action. The term is now also applied to ordinary stage performances, novels, movies, and television and radio broadcasts with or without music. However, it is applied specially to drama and applicable to any literary work that relies much on unlikely events and sensational action for the pleasure of the reader and viewer. The Victorian melodramas typically restricted the conflict between good and evil in which plot rather than characterization was important. Usually, a melodramatic story ends happily, with the hero defeating the villain at the last possible moment. Many revenge tragedies too are melodramatic in some respects. Thus, melodrama entertains the reader or audience with exciting action while still conforming to the traditional sense of justice. Augustin Daly's *Under the Gaslight*, Dion Boucicault's *The Octoroon, The Colleen Bawn* and *The Poor of New York* are examples of melodramas. In fiction, Dickens too is often charged of catering melodramatic stuff. Melodrama debuted in England in 1802 with *A Tale of Mystery*, a play adapted from *Clina* by Thomas Holcroft. To ensure success of serious plays, melodramas were often offered as afterpiece. Even Shakespeare's plays were no exceptions in this regard. The most popular media for the 20th century melodramas are motion pictures and television serials. Nowadays the term melodrama is used rather in a pejorative sense. [Cf. drama, comedy, farce]

Ref: Peter Brooks, *The Melodramatic Imagination:* Balzac, Henry James, *Melodrama, and the Mode of Excess* (1995). James Redmond, Ed. *Melodrama* (1992).

Memoir A historical record composed from personal observation and experience. Writers of memoir are usually persons who have played roles in or have been close observers of historical events and whose main purpose is to interpret those from a personal viewpoint. This form is different from the autobiography since memoir may not centre round the author's own life and experience; and also from the biography since it focuses on matters known to the memoirist only. Julius Caesar is often given the credit of writing memoirs in ancient Roman era; but as a regular practice it came into being as a genre much later. The French have specially excelled at this genre. A great memoirist, for example, was the Duc de Saint-Simon, whose *Mémoires* (covering 1690 through 1723), famous for their penetrating character sketches, provide a precious source of information about the court of Louis XIV. Another notable French memoirist was François-René, who devoted the last years of his life to his *Mémoires d'outre-tombe* (1849-50). In the 20th century, many distinguished statesmen and military men have described their experience in memoirs. Notable reminiscences of the Second World War are the memoirs of England's Viscount Montgomery (1958) and Charles De Gaulle's *Mémoires de guerre* (1954-59); *War Memoirs* (1955-60). Some recent examples of this genre are Marian Wright Edelman *Lanterns: A Memoir of Mentors* (1999) and novelist John Bailey's *Iris and Her Friends* (2000). A kind of novel that pretends to be memoirs is called *memoir novel.* In the emergence of the modern novel during the 18th century some works have definite propensity either to gathering materials from memoirs or to becoming memoir-turned novels. Daniel Defoe's *Moll Flanders* (1722) and John Cleland's *Memoirs of a Lady of Pleasure* or better known as *Fanny Hill* (1748-49) are often included in this category. A wholly or partially fabricated memoir, journal or a diary presented as fact by a genuine or fake individual, is known as *fake memoir*. [Cf. dairy]

Ref: Jane Taylor McDonnell, *Living to Tell the Tale: A Guide to Writing Memoir* (1998). JC Major, *The Role of Personal Memoirs in English Biography and Novel* (1935). William Zinsser, Ed. *Inventing the Truth: Art and Craft of Memoir* (1998).

Metalanguage <Greek *meta*, above/ about + *language*> A language above *object language* (first order language, i.e. what usually makes the body of texts). Simply speaking, it is a language or technical vocabulary used to discuss, analyze another language or its syntax. First introduced by Danish linguist Louis Hjelmslev, the term is further elaborated by Roman Jakobson (1896-1982). The term basically refers to a system of notation, descriptive and/or technical terms and so on which we use to explain a text written in object language. Hence metalanguage becomes a specialized language to explain a common language. For example, word and phrases such as 'adverb', 'proper noun', 'present perfect continuous', 'phrasal verb' and 'zeugma' etc. are all examples of classroom meta-language. These are used only to explain a language to the student and an ordinary speaker may not understand these technicalities. Some structuralists have tried to give metalanguage a distinct status above the object language. In their view, thus, a critic's language is different from a poet's. Poststructutalists, however, differ on this issue. Their view is that criticism too shares the same common language; therefore, in principle there is no distinction between criticism and literature.

Metanarrative A postmodern discourse to refer to a narrative about narratives, or a story to justify stories and clarify which story is *central* and which are *marginal*. Metanarrative is thought to prevent narratives deemed marginal from upsetting or subverting the cultural order. According to Jean-François Lyotard (1924-1998) postmodernism is defined as "incredulity toward metanarratives" and thus represents openness to marginal narratives. A metanarrative is often equated to the broader concept of an ideology or worldview; however, this equation is not entirely accurate, as the Western concepts of ideology and worldview are themselves influenced by Western metanarratives. A metanarrative is more correctly a story about ideologies and worldviews. For example, while Marxism and atheism are ideologies, the story of human and scientific progress is a metanarrative supporting those ideologies. Similarly, the story of human liberation is a metanarrative supporting both libertarianism and humanitarianism. Lyotard proposed that metanarratives should give way to more modest and localized narratives i.e. *micronarratives,* which can throw off the grand narratives by bringing into focus the particular events and specific local contexts as well so that the diversity of human experience could multiply new theoretical premises as against metanarratives.

Ref: Jean-François Lyotard, *The Postmodern Condition* (1979). John Stephens & Robyn McCallum, *Retelling Stories, Framing Culture: Traditional Story and Metanarratives in Children's Literature* (1998). Geoffrey Bennington, *Lyotard: Writing the Event* (1988).

Metaphor A Figure of Speech, a statement of identity between two things expressed through an implied simile, e.g. "he is a donkey" or "she is a peach." The relationship must not use the comparative signifiers—*like, as, as if*, and *than,* etc.; for if these are present, the figure is simply a simile or analogy. In metaphor the image used to figure something else is the *vehicle* of the Figure of Speech and the thing represented is called the *tenor*. In the first example *he* is the tenor and *donkey* is the vehicle. The point of similarity is only implied in metaphor. When Shakespeare says, "All the world's a stage", he metaphorically invokes some salient features common between the real world and a dramatic stage and the reader has to dig up that hidden treasure. Viewed as an aspect of language in both its oral and written forms, metaphor qualifies as a style, in particular, style characterized by a type of analogy. Aristotle believed that the use of metaphor made learning a pleasing process. Jacque Lacan comments that the "creative spark of metaphor does not spring from the presentation of two images, that is, of two signifiers equally actualized, it flashes between two signifiers one of which has taken the place of the other in the signifying chain, the occulted signifier remaining present through its (metonymic) connexion with the rest of the chain." [Cf. Tenor/vehicle]

Ref: IA Richards, *The Philosophy of Rhetoric* (1936). Jacque Lacan, "The Instance of the Letter in the Unconscious or Reason since Freud" (1957). Max Black, *Models and Metaphors: Studies in Language and Philosophy* (1962). George Lakoff, *Metaphor We Live By* (2003).

Metaphysical Poetry A term applied to a style of some 17th century poetry. It was William Drummond of Hawthornden (1585-1649) who first used the term for poets who used "metaphysical ideas and Scholastic Quiddities." John Dryden in 1693, while commenting on Donne's poem, observed: "He affects the metaphysics not only in his satires, but in his amorous verses...and perplexes the minds of the fair sex with fair speculations of philosophy." Dr. Johnson's observation focuses on the highly intellectual and, often obscure, imagery in Donne's poems: "The most heterogeneous ideas are yoked by violence together, nature and art are ransacked for illustrations, comparisons and allusions; their learning instructs, and their subtlety surprises...." The use of conceit is a common factor among the metaphysical poets. In them the conceits reveal a play of intellect, often resulting in puns, paradoxes, and witty and unorthodox comparisons. Unlike other poetry where the metaphors usually remain in the background, here the metaphors sometimes take over the poem and control it. Chief among the metaphysical poets are John Donne, George Herbert, Richard Crashaw, Andrew Marvell and Henry Vaughan. While their poems are widely varied (the metaphysical are not a thematic or even a structural school), some common characteristics bring them together: [1] Argumentative structure, [2] Dramatic and colloquial mode of utterance, [3] Acute realism, and [4] Metaphysical wit. Metaphysical poetry represents a revolt against the conventions of Elizabethan love poetry and especially the typical Petrarchan conceits (like *rosy cheeks*, *eyes like stars*, etc.). Samuel Johnson has, however, severely criticized the use of metaphysical conceits and images, as many of them are very unconventional and often incompatible with the associated ideas highlighted in the poem. [Cf. discordia concours]

Ref: Boris Ford, Ed. *New Pelican Guide* (Vol. 3): *From Donne to Marvell* (1990). TS Eliot, "The Metaphysical Poets" (1921). Helen Gardner, *The Metaphysical Poets* (1957). HJC Grierson, *Cross Currents in English Literature in the Seventeenth Century* (1929).

Metadrama/Metatheatre A variety of theatre/drama, not to be grouped either as traditional tragedy or comedy. Lionel Abel suggested this term to refer to serious plays that are not tragic by nature. Considering the fact that the concept of Christianity precludes the idea of tragedy, Abel termed all serious plays like Shakespeare's *Hamlet*, Arthur Miller's *Death of a Salesman*, Tennessee Williams's *A Streetcar Named Desire*, etc. as metatheatres. It is, as a form, not something like a third theatre, but a new name instead of the popular ones. Since real tragedy is not possible, the existence of comedy too is threatened as comedy presupposes the existence of tragedy. Metatheatre is a convenient name for the quality or force in a play which challenges theatre's claim to be simply realistic—to be nothing but a mirror in which we view the actions and sufferings of characters like ourselves, suspending our disbelief in their reality. Metatheatre begins by sharpening our awareness of the *unlikeness* of life to dramatic art; it may end by making us aware of life's uncanny likeness to art or illusion of the life we live, it marks those frames and boundaries that conventional dramatic realism would hide. It may present action so alien, improbable, stylized or absurd that we are forced to acknowledge the estranging frame that encloses a whole play. It may, on the other hand, break the frame of the 'fourth wall' of conventional theatre, reaching out to assault the audience or to draw it into the realm of the play. Abel relates this type to the character of Don Quixote, whom he considers to be the prototypical, metatheatrical, self-referring character.

Ref: Lionel Abel, *Tragedy and Metatheatre: Essays on Dramatic Form* (2003). Richard Hornby, *Drama, Metadrama, and Perception* (1986). Andrés Pérez-Simón, *The Concept of Metatheatre: A Functional Approach* (2011).

Meter/Metre <Greek *metron*> A style of versification that gives a rhythmic pattern within a verse or verse lines. Meter, in other words, is the prosodic pattern of *accented* and *unaccented* syllables in a poem. Meter may either run with the content of the poem, or by its rhythm that challenges the sense. A good poet knows how to make the best use of this prosodic tool. A verse line is usually divided into a number of *feet* (e.g. *iambic, anapaestic, dactylic, pyrrhic, spondaic*, and *trochaic*, etc.), counted on the basis of systematic arrangement of numbers of *stressed* and *unstressed* syllables used and Meter is the sum total of those feet in a poetic line. For example, "Thĕ wáy || wăs lóng || thĕ wínd || wăs cóld"—has four feet or measures. Therefore, the name of the meter the line refers to is *tetrameter*. Ordinarily the names of meters used by the scholars are: *monometer* (1 foot), *dimeter* (2 feet), *trimeter* (3 feet), *tetrameter* (4 feet), *pentameter* (5 feet), *hexameter* (6 feet), *heptameter* (7 feet), *octameter* (8 feet), *novameter* (9 feet), decameter (10 feet), etc. Scansion of a poetic line depends on simple mathematical calculations taking into account the number of feet and accented and unaccented syllables. [Cf. accent, foot, scansion]

Ref: Bose & Sterling, *Elements of English Rhetoric and Prosody* (1908). James McAuley, *Versification: A Short Introduction* (1996). JB Mayor, *Chapters on English Metre* (1968). P Kiparsky & G Youmans, Ed. *Rhythm and Meter* (1989). Philip Hobsbaum, *Metre, Rhyme and Verse Form* (1996).

Metonymy A Figure of Speech based on association. Normally a metonymy replaces the name of one thing by something else somehow associated with it. For example, a *skirt* may mean a woman; *the crown* is used to signify the monarchy; and by the expression "he's taken to the bottle," one means—he's taken to drinking. Another example from Shakespeare: "Friends, Romans, countrymen, lend me your ears." The speaker refers to the 'ears' of his countrymen only to draw *attention*. Metonymy operates by the association between two concepts, whereas metaphor is based upon their analogous similarity. When people use metonymy, they do not typically wish to transfer qualities from one referent to another as they do with metaphor. "The pen is mightier than the sword" is a popular metonymic expression. Metonymy is regarded as a potential trope. [Cf. synecdoche]

Ref: Charles Gaines, "Reconsidering Metaphor/Metonymy: Art and the Suppression of Thought" (2003). www.art-lies.org

Mimesis/Imitation <Greek for *imitation*> A concept referring to the process of artistic creation. Since Plato and Aristotle mimesis has been appearing as a critical term. The term embraces many ideas including the act of imitation and act of representation; both are central issues in literary studies. By the time of Plato, dialogue and deliberation on the content of truth in myths acquired not only a currency, but the myth themselves came to be debated upon and scrutinized. The fundamental question was whether mimesis provided truth or falsehood in art. Plato suspected artistic inspiration and, therefore, thought mimesis was misleading; while Aristotle upheld the case and argued that imitation was natural and it could improve the world.

Aristotle opens with the statement that mimesis is a valuable method for artistic representation. He further explains how rhythm, language and harmony become the basic channels through which artistic imitation is made possible. After claiming that epic, tragedy, comedy, dithyramb, flute or lyre playing are all modes of mimesis and that the object and manner of mimesis is different in each case. These media—Language, Rhythm and Harmony—are manifested as the six elements of tragedy—myth (plot), ethos (character), dianoia (argument), lexis (diction), melopoiia (music) and opsis (spectacle). Like Plato, Aristotle believed that imitation was involved while making a copy of a model, but the Platonic denigration is reversed in his theory. When an artist makes a copy of an object, he incorporates certain universal elements in it; but he does fall short of any absolute model of universality. But whatever universality the art holds leads to knowledge. The pleasure that mimesis provides is on account of knowledge that is acquired through mimetic or imitative acts, even when this knowledge is of the particular. Therefore, an artist cannot be a liar. Aristotle was clear that the purpose of imitation was to provide proper pleasure by imitating action. Mimesis of men in action was mimesis of all human life. Through music the artist imitates anger, mildness and courage; dance imitates character, emotion and action, etc. However, Aristotle was speaking specially of drama and his argument is a controversial issue for centuries. The question is still unsettling if any form of art can represent reality truthfully and realistically. [Cf. representation]

Ref: Erich Auerbach, *Mimesis: The Representation of Reality in Western Literature* (1953). Karl F Morrison, *The Mimetic Tradition of Reform in the West* (1982). SH Butcher, *Aristotle's Theory of Poetry and Fine Arts* (1951). WB Stanford, *Greek Tragedy and the Emotions: An Introductory Study* (1983).

Mock Epic/Mock Heroic A form of satire that adjusts the grand heroic style of the classical epic to a trivial subject. The tradition, which originated in classical times with an anonymous burlesque of Homer, the *Batrachomyomachia (Battle of the Frogs and the Mice)*, was sharpened to a fine art in the late 17th and early 18th century Neoclassical period. A double-edged satirical weapon, the mock epic was sometimes used by the *moderns* of this period to ridicule contemporary *ancients*. More often, it was used by *ancients* to hold up the unheroic character of the age by subjecting thinly disguised contemporary events to a heroic treatment. The classic example of this is Nicolas Boileau's *Lutrin* (1674-83), which begins with a quarrel between two ecclesiastical dignitaries as to where to place a lectern in a chapel and ends with a battle in a bookstore in which champions of either side hurl their favourite *ancient* or *modern* authors at each other. Jonathan Swift's *Battle of the Books* (1704) is a variation of this theme in mock-heroic prose. The outstanding English mock epic is Alexander Pope's brilliant poem, *The Rape of the Lock* (1714), which concerns a society beau's cutting off of a lock of hair from a society belle. His *Dunciad* too belongs to this category. Byron's *Don Juan*, John Gay's *Trivia* and *Beggar's Opera* are mock-heroic in style and treatment and Samuel Johnson's *London* is very close to the mock-heroic subgenre.

Most mock epics begin with an invocation of the muse and use the familiar epic devices of set speeches, supernatural interventions and descents to the underworld as well as infinitely detailed descriptions of protagonist's activities. Thus, they provide much scope for display of the author's ingenuity and inventiveness. An American mock epic, Joel Barlow's *Hasty Pudding* (1793), celebrates in three 400 line cantos his favourite New England dish, cornmeal mush. Robertson disagrees with literary theories that stresses the autonomy of the literary work and that rejects intertextuality. In his opinion intertextuality is essential to mock epic. [Cf. burlesque, epic]

Ref: Ian Jack, *Augustan Satire: Intention and Idiom in English Poetry 1660-1750* (1978). Ritchie Robertson, *Mock-Epic Poetry from Pope to Heine* (2009).

Modernism/-ist A post-First World War reaction in the intellectual world, a turning away from the rigidity of the social and creative conventions predominant during the long pre-War era. After the war had physically devastated and psychologically disillusioned the West, a search for wide variety of new and experimental forms and techniques took place in literature and other art forms. All these put together give the image of a vacuum and desperate artistic attempt to respond to that. WB Yeats' line—"Things fall apart; the centre cannot hold;/ Mere anarchy is loosed upon the world" is perhaps the best expressed spirit of modernism. One the one hand, in the background, there is hope often invigorated from the past resources, and on the other, a bleak future ahead—together what makes a complete picture of modernism.

So far as literature is concerned, in Europe as well as in America the spirit of modernism—a radical and utopian spirit stimulated by new ideas in anthropology, psychology, philosophy, political theory and psychoanalysis—was in the air, expressed rather mutedly by the pastoral and often anti-modernist poets of the second Georgian period (1912-22) and more authentically by the English and American poets of the Imagist movement, to which Ezra Pound first drew attention and TE Hulme, FS Flint, Richard Aldington, Hilda Doolittle, Amy Lowell and others added further intellectual and artistic properties. Many modernists incorporated the new psychoanalytic theories of Sigmund Freud and Carl Jung into their works and paid particular attention to language. Their works reflected the pervasive sense of loss, disillusionment and even despair in the wake of the Great War; hence their emphasis was placed on historical continuity and the alienation of humanity. The gloom continued and it was a Kafkaesque nightmare resulted from the Wars, Hiroshima, Nagasaki, Hitler, etc. God left the world to Nietzsche and Hemingway to define it as a world of the *nada*, nothingness and wasteland. Although modernist authors tended to perceive the world as fragmented, many, such as TS Eliot and James Joyce, believed there could be some help somewhere, in art, religion, myth, etc to counter that disintegration. Such writers viewed art as a potentially integrating, restorative force, a remedy for the uncertainty of the modern world. To this end, even while depicting disorder in their works, modernists also injected order by creating patterns of allusion, symbol and myth. Thus modernism itself remains an incomprehensible definition—god, nada, despair, art, Albert Camus, Marcel Proust, destruction, construction, deconstruction, decolonization, neo-colonization, Ernest Hemingway, William Faulkner, WB Yeats, Thomas Mann, Tennessee Williams, Eugene O'Neill, James Joyce, belief, disbelief, rise of science and fall of human values—all in one. [Cf. post-modernism]

Ref: CJ Bryne, "Understanding Modernism and Post Modernism", www.writing.com (2017). Pericles Lewis, *The Cambridge Introduction to Modernism* (2007). Peter Childs, *Modernism* (2008). Malcolm Bradbury & James McFarlane, Eds., *Modernism: A Guide to European Literature 1890-1930* (1978). Stephen Kern, *The Culture of Time and Space* (1983).

Monologue <Greek *mono*, one + *logos*, speech> A speech or communiqué in poetry or drama uttered by a single individual. Actually, Greek drama initially began with a single character and his monologue; the question of dialogue did not exist there. Playwrights later expanded the convention to have two characters on stage, accompanied by the chorus, which again grew to three characters (protagonist, *deuteragonist*, and *tritagonist*). Monologue has no set length, although it is normally several lines long. A long monologue is called an *extended monologue,* that is, a monologue of great length and seriousness. An extended monologue usually occurs in the one-Act or one-character plays, such as *The Stronger* by August Strindberg. On the other hand, a dramatic monologue involves one character speaking to another character normally not to be seen by the spectator or reader. Characters generally present their monologues either to another character or to the audience in the understanding that other characters are able to hear. Monologue should be carefully differentiated from aside, soliloquy and apostrophe. [Cf. interior monologue]

Monorhyme A manner of rhyme scheme than a poem or its part in which all the lines have the same rhyming end. It is a common rhyme scheme in Latin, Italian, Arabic, Welsh and Slav poetry, especially in the Slav poetry of the oral tradition. In English, the pattern is not much popular except in doggerel. However, Shakespeare often made use of this scheme. For instance, in *The Merchant of Venice*, Arragon has the following mono-rhyme speech (II. ix. 62-67):

The fire seven times tried this;
Seven times tried that judgment is
That did never choose amiss.
Some there be that shadows kiss,
There be fools alive, iwis
Silver'd o'er–and so was this.

The rhyme scheme here is very simple: a-a-a-a-a-a. It does not add to the poetic quality, but its monotony may help depicting a drab character properly.

Multiculturalism A cultural and social worldview arising out of a context in which different cultures meet together. A multicultural society accommodates peoples from various cultures and multiculturalism encourages endorsement of a strong bond among people of assorted cultural groups there to achieve a common social and institutional goal. For the last two decades or so, the term has evoked much controversy and the social, political and ethnic situations in the US, England, India or other multicultural societies are yet to offer what multiculturalism theoretically aspires for. As a concept it directs attention away from "purely visible aspects of diversity to the deeper philosophical and political implications of the coexistence of different orientations to engagement with world, and the way in which those differences jostle for recognition within national and global boundaries, sometimes in relative harmony with each other, sometimes in real conflict."

Multicultural conditions, rather than multiculturalism, however, have given birth to a vast body of literature, mostly fiction, in the US, England and even in many third countries. These works are known as *multicultural fiction*. These works emerge from the participants' contact with and experience of different socio-cultural conditions. A multicultural novel is written by a member of or about a cultural minority group, giving insight into non-Western or non-dominant cultural experiences and values, either in the United States or other diasporic spaces. Examples are Chinua Achebe's *No Longer at Ease*, Amy Tan's *The Kitchen God's Wife*, Jhumpa Lahiri's *Interpreter of Maladies*, etc. Some of them are categorized under such heads as postcolonial and diasporic works also.

Ref: Brian Barry, *Culture and Equality: An Egalitarian Critique of Multiculturalism* (2002).

CW Watson, *Multiculturalism* (2005). David Theo Goldberg, *Multiculturalism: A Critical Reader* (1994). Neil Bissoondath, *Selling Illusions: The Myth of Multiculturalism* (2002). Tariq Modood, *The Politics of Multiculturalism in the New Europe: Racism, Identity, and Community* (1997). Will Kymlicka, *Multiculturalism in Asia* (2005).

Muses A group of nine Greek mythological goddesses, all daughters of Zeus and Mnemosyne (Memory). Each muse patronized a specific area of the liberal arts and sciences: [1] Calliope presided over epic poetry, [2] Clio over history, [3] Erato over love poetry, [4] Euterpe over music or lyric, [5] Melpomene over tragedy, [6] Polyhymnia over hymns to the gods, [7] Terpsichore over dance, [8] Thalia over comedy, and [9] Urania over astronomy. Poets and writers traditionally made appeals to the Muses for inspiration in their work. John Milton invokes the aid of Urania at the beginning of the first book of his *Paradise Lost*. Incidentally, Urania, the muse of astronomy in antiquity was remade by Christian writers of the Renaissance into a heavenly Christian muse. [Cf. invocation]

Mysticism A belief and spiritual quest for hidden truth or wisdom, the goal of which is union with the divine or sacred (the transcendent realm). Such knowledge is beyond the comprehension of the five senses and it can only be realized through intuition. Forms of mysticism are found in all major religions and other ecstatic practices of non-literate cultures and in secular experiences. Although mysticism is often set over against theology and is said to be more authentic or more subjective, the two forms of religious thought have in fact existed side by side, frequently in the same individual. The mystical theologians have been most explicit in their insistence that no theological systematization can capture or explain the unique experience of mystical purgation, illumination and union. Hindu religious texts, concept of yoga, Buddhist practice of meditation and Sufism of the Islamic order—all bear testimony to the presence of mystic elements in different forms and fashions.

Many literary works bear imprint of the mystic element. William Blake, William Wordsworth, ST Coleridge, Lord Tennyson have frequently tried to seize upon something incomprehensible intuitively and have recognized the limitation of rationality in explaining some mysterious elements in nature. Followers of American transcendentalism, specially RW Emerson, Herman Melville, Walt Whitman have cultivated the artistic cult of mysticism. [Cf. transcendentalism]

Ref: Colin Wilson, *Poetry and Mysticism* (1986). J Bright-Fey, *Mystique Poetica: Living Philosophy through Revealed Wisdom* (1998). Richard H Jones, *Philosophy of Mysticism* (2016). William James, *The Varieties of Religious Experience* (1902).

Myth An anonymous story emerging from the traditional beliefs of a cultural or social group. Myth often embodies the nearest approach to absolute truth that can be stated in terms of human language. However, myth is basically a narrative that expresses the basic valuation of a religious community. Myths often use supernatural explanations for natural phenomena. They may also explain cosmic issues like creation and death, the process through which the world is created and given a definite form within the universal scheme. They also serve as bases for the orientation of man, his place in the universe and his relationship with other humans, nature and the entire nonhuman world. The cosmogonist myth is the myth par excellence. In this sense, the myth is akin to philosophy, but, unlike philosophy, it is constituted by a system of symbols. There is an order and structure to the myth, but this is not to be confused with rational, philosophical order and structure; myth has its own distinctive order. Again, myth and history represent alternative ways of looking at the past. Where writing is absent, or literacy is restricted, traditions embedded in myths through oral transmission may constitute the principal sources of authority for the past. A collection of myths, *mythology*, is common to all cultures; but the best-known myths belong to the Norse, Roman, Greek and Indian origins. Myths make their presence in folktales, folklores, legends and almost all forms of literary genres.

Greek and Roman myths influenced English literature a great deal. English authors have deliberately exploited Greek and Roman mythology to dress their works. In Shakespeare's Juliet cries: "Gallop apace, you fiery-footed steeds,/ Towards Phoebus' lodging." Phoebus was the god of the sun, and Juliet urges him to hurry home and bring on night so she can be with Romeo. Later many poets, including Blake, Keats, Shelley and Yeats, etc have extensively used mythical elements from Greek, Roman and even Celtic sources in poetry. Wide-ranging English literature of our time too have its share of myth in authors such as Salman Rushdie, Sherman Alexie, Margaret Atwood, Donald Barthelme, Umberto Eco, Louise Erdrich, David Mitchell, Michael Ondaatje and dozens more. Postmodern literature often jumps back and forth in time and contains obscure references. However, nobody believes in myths anymore. After the World Wars, people have lost their faith in the overarching myths, or meta-narratives, as Lyotard calls them that had held people's identity and sense of belonging before. Now, each person has to find a personal truth. This new distrust is another name for postmodernism.

Ref: Charles Mills Gayley, *The Classic Myths in English Literature and in Art* (1911). Hellen Hull Law, *Bibliography of Greek Myth in English Poetry* (1932). James G Frazer, *The Golden Bough* (1890). Joseph Campbell, *The Hero with a Thousand Faces* (1949).

N

Narcissism <Greek *Narkissos*> An abnormal love, admiration and almost deification of the self. The term has its origin in the mythical figure of Narcissus, a young man who fell in love with his own reflection on the water body. Narcissism is a perception in psychoanalytic theory introduced by Sigmund Freud in one of his essays. To a certain degree, everybody is Narcissistic; but only the extreme form of the characteristic is considered a psychological disorder. Even in ancient Greece too much of egocentric love was regarded as a form of hubris. The mythical story of Narcissus goes like this: An attractive and swaggering Greek youth, Narcissus, who rejected the frantic advances of Echo, a nymph, eventually indulged in self-love or fell in love with his own shadow in a pool of water. However, finally the man was transformed into a flower that is named after him, Narcissus—a flower of the daffodil group. Modern clinical research studies have associated Narcissism with the problem of personality disorder and have focused on certain negative traits, such as shamelessness, arrogance, selfishness, puffed-up body language, egoistic awareness, etc as symptomatic features of the problem. Many psychoanalysts, however, try to diagnose the problem with sexual disorder and the term *Sexual Narcissism* is defined as an egocentric pattern of sexual attitude having a magnified notion of sexual virility and sexual authority. Narcissism is a fake way of feeling important in the world and a narcissist is a pretender, sort of a scarecrow, stuffed with duplicity, deception and self-delusion. Both men and women may become a victim of the disorder. Freud opines, "Women, especially if they grow up with good looks, develop a certain self-contentment which compensates them for the social restrictions that are imposed upon them in their choice of object. Strictly speaking, it is only themselves that such women love with an intensity comparable to that of the man's love for them."

The notion of Narcissism, either directly or indirectly, has often been treated in literary works of all ages. Truly speaking, any autobiographical writing too has its origin in self love. However, autobiography does not normally come within the definition of Narcissism; for a good autobiography has many other elements to demonstrate than the author alone. Some glaring examples of writings influenced by the Narcissistic drive are: Euripides' *Medea* (431 BCE); Ovid's *Metamorphoses* (8th c); Milton's *Paradise Lost* (1667) partly in its direct allusion to Narcissus in Eve's recounting of her first responses after creation; Jean-Jacques Rousseau's play *Narcissus, or The Self-Admirer* (1752); George Eliot's *Middlemarch* (1874); and Oscar Wilde's *The Picture of Dorian Gray* (1890) etc. Some famous works of André Gide, Henry Miller and Paul Valéry, among others, may illustrate some of the basic Narcissistic concerns. Shakespeare's megalomaniac hero, King Lear, too reflects some of the same neurotic obsessions. Modern social consumerist conditions look very productive for the narcissistic culture. Christopher Lasch locates the source of the disorder in a culture in which every action and relationship of a person is defined by the self-gratifying need to acquire the symbols of wealth. During the last few years or so too much opportunities of exposure on the electronic media, Facebook, Instagram, twitter, digital mobile and crazy 'selfies' have emerged as the latest trends of Narcissism as a 'routine culture' among many of the new generation people.

Ref: Andrew P Morrison, *Shame: The Underside of Narcissism* (1997). Elan Golomb, *Trapped in the Mirror: Adult Children of Narcissists in their Struggle for Self* (1995). Jeffrey Berman, *Narcissism and the Novel* (1990). Sigmund Freud, "On Narcissism: An Introduction" (1914).

Narrative A written or oral account of some events or situations, true or fictitious, either in verse or prose. In literary theoretic approach, narrative is narrowly defined as fiction-writing mode in which the narrator is communicating directly to the reader. A story has a narrative since somebody narrates something in it. However, a play presents events and actions, in fiction they are *told* or *narrated.* Narratives range from the shortest accounts of events, as in Julius Caesar's remark, "I came, I saw, I conquered," to the longest historical or biographical works, as Edward Gibbon's *The Decline and Fall of the Roman Empire,* as well as diaries, travelogues, novels, ballads, epics, short stories, and other fictional forms.

The word can be used adjectivally also. The method, or the way a narrative is presented is called *narrative technique*, and poetry in which a story is told is known as *narrative poetry*, such as ballad, epic and verse romance, etc. Even a dramatic work often may have a narrative speech. Broadly speaking, narratives are no longer restricted to fiction or literature only. It has recently emerged as very central to human culture. An important blanket term, narrative, incorporates in its fold newsreader's top story about, say, Iraq war, an advertisement clipping or even gestures of a mime. Roland Barthes says, "narrative is international, trans-historical, trans-cultural: it is simply there, like life itself." Narratives are now considered to be playing an important part in human life, not just in stories. Explaining the primacy of narrative Jonathan Culler says that it is narrative that gives sense to things "whether in thinking of our lives as a progression leading somewhere or in telling ourselves what is happening in the world." Since the 1980s narrative theories are proliferating and now it is believed that narrative voices may have their own distinctive language, in which they recount everything in the story or they may adopt and report the language of others. Bakhtin throws some new light on the narrative theory. He describes the novel as fundamentally polyphonic or dialogic rather than monological. Within the narrative, therefore, the possibility of many voices is not ruled out. [Cf. narratology]

Ref: Gérard Genette, *Narrative Discourse,* trans. Jane Lewin (1980). MM Bakhtin, *Dialogic Imagination: Four Essays* (1981). Robert Scholes & Robert Kellogg, *The Nature of Narrative* (1966). Roland Barthes, "Introduction to the Structural Analysis of Narrative," Ed. S Sontag, *A Barthes Reader* (1982). Franz Karl Stanzel, *A Theory of Narrative,* trans. Charlotte Goedsche (1984).

Narratology A study of the narrative structure. Like structuralism, from which it is derived, narratology is based on the idea of a common literary language or a universal pattern of codes that operates within the text of a work. The development of this body of theory accelerated in the mid-20th century.

Narratology focuses on the components of a narrative structure and tries to examine the organic relationship of events arranged in it. As early as in Aristotle's *Poetics,* the issue has been touched upon, but in modern times narratology has assumed new import. Narratologists see it not just as a simple method of representation; rather it has become an explicitly constructed system, i.e. how narratives give a meaning or discourse to actions and incidents. French structuralists have further problematized the issue. Narratology undoubtedly owes to criticism mostly committed to the formalist close reading of a text, which push aside socio-historical issues with a view to emphasizing the text itself, i.e. on the technical operations of a narrative. Structuralist narratology developed an impressive terminology for the description of technique, analyzing narrative in the way that a grammarian would scrutinize a sentence. However, it is difficult to say if the structuralist narratology could have advanced as it did if it had not been for its formalist progenitors in the European and Anglo-American traditions. Notably the study of narrative point of view in New Criticism, the critiques of realism in Russian Formalistic Criticism, or the analysis of speech and thought in British stylistics were all places in which the systematic analysis of narrative was advanced either before or alongside the structuralist approach.

Ref: David Pinault, *Story-telling Techniques in the Arabian Nights* (1992). Gerald Prince, "Narratology," *Johns Hopkins Guide to Literary Theory and Criticism*, Ed. Michael Groden and Martin Kreiswirth (1994). Mieke Bal, *Narratology: Introduction to the Theory of Narrative* (1985). Vladimir Propp, *Morphology of the Folk Tale* (1928). Wayne Booth, *Rhetoric of Fiction* (1961).

Narrator A speaker narrating a story or trying to relate meaning to action. Fiction is the art of the storyteller. Not only does the writer tell the story, normally within every story he/she presents a new storyteller, the narrator of the tale. It is the narrator's voice that readers hear while reading a story. He tells the story and finally dismisses the reader at the end. The narrator describes scenes and characters, relates events, sets the tone and supplies whatever meanings or explanations the author sees fit to provide. Thus, between the story and the author, it is the narrator who functions. Fiction mostly deals with a duality—duality of man as a human being and a social being. A narrator has the ability to look in two directions: he looks into his characters, revealing their minds and feeling to the reader and also he looks out at society to which his characters belong.

The *omniscient narrator* or *third person narrator*, as the name indicates, is a know-all person. He knows about the characters and events and all that there is to know. Somewhat detached by his greater knowledge from action and actor alike, omniscient narrator projects an air of authority over their materials. He stands somewhat apart from the story; having no role in the action himself he can interpret events and characters impartially. The *second person narrator* establishes a persuasive communication with reader as addressee. This mode is quite rare in fiction. The *first person narrator*, on the other hand, is a participant in his own story. He tells about something that happened to him from his own point of view. He cannot see into the minds of other characters. His knowledge, therefore, is limited than that of an omniscient narrator. The more is the first person narrator's knowledge limited, the more expanded is the role of the reader, and his own wisdom and judgment come into play. The reader weighs the narrator's perceptions against his own understanding. Often, therefore, the first person narrative is rich in irony with the narrator's describing what he thinks, he sees and the reader's interpretation of what really happens. This is why the first person narrator is often called *unreliable narrator*. Sometimes, of course, a fiction fluctuates in time and space, and in a single novel both the types of narrators operate on different planes. In RK Narayan's *Guide* (1958) and Ruth Jhabvala's *Heat and Dust* (1975) both the third person and the first person narrators are effectively employed. [Cf. narratology, unreliable narrator]

Ref: MW Smith, *Understanding Unreliable Narrators* (1991). Wayne Booth, *Rhetoric of Fiction* (1961). Gérard Genette, *Narrative Discourse: An Essay in Method*, trans. Jane Lewin (1980).

Nativism A tendency to be more interested in seeing certain essential traits typical of a particular society or a culture being enacted through ages. The tendency stresses on the philosophical generality over historical specificity. Basically, it is a cultural tendency or practice of preserving or reviving an indigenous culture. As defined by Edward said, nativism is a tendency to "leave the historical world for the metaphysics of essences…in a word, to abandon history." In other words nativism is a tendency to look back on the past heritage and negate many of the present developments for the sake of maintaining 'purity' and 'original' identity as a group or nation. This concept found expression in the idea of nationalism, counter discourse and resistance of the colonized people of Asia, Africa and many other parts. Now, however, the context is different. The movement called nativism gained its name from the Native American parties of the 1840s and 1850s. The issue is strongly related to immigration and nationalism as it aimed at the policy of protecting the interests of native inhabitants against those of immigrants. Nativism is an almost exclusively American concept of majority-ethnic nationalism which applies to people who consider themselves native to or first settlers of a country and want to protect their "demographic predominance in that territory." The opposition to immigration arises in many countries because of issues of national, cultural and religious identity. The phenomenon has been studied especially in Australia, Canada, New Zealand and the United States, as well as in some countries of Europe. Thus nativism has become a general term for "opposition to immigration" based on fears that the immigrants will distort or spoil cultural values.

In the American context and also in some diasporic perspectives, theory of nativism goes against the immigrant people who have been living overseas. It is believed that nativism was one of the first features of Donald Trump's 'core ideology' as a Presidential candidate, 2017.

Ref: Anthony Appiah, *Topologies of Nativism* (1992). John Higham, *Strangers in the Land: Patterns of American Nativism, 1860-1925* (1955). Tyler Anbinder, "Nativism and Prejudice against Immigrants, *A Companion to American Immigration,"* Ed. Reed Ueda (2006).

Naturalism A philosophy, a doctrine that believes only natural—neither supernatural nor spiritual—forces operate in the world. The term was coined in 1983 by philosopher Paul de Vries. A literary movement of the late 19th and early 20th centuries was based on this philosophy. Naturalistic writers were influenced by the evolution theory of Charles Darwin. Naturalism aspired to examine human life with the objectivity of scientific inquiry. It has been used to describe various writers ranging from Shakespeare and Rabelais to Byron and Shelley to specify various phenomena. In the 18th century naturalism signified a philosophical system that defined man in purely materialistic terms and denied any possibility of transcending human experience to any higher metaphysical plane. In the 19th century, the word 'naturalist' referred to a painter who produced an exact replica of natural objects on the canvas. From there it entered the world of literary criticism. The movement's major theorist, the French novelist Émile Zola, who first used the term in his *Therese Raquin* (1867), is considered to be the pioneer writer of naturalist fiction. His 1890 novel, *The Human Beast,* summed up the main idea behind the philosophy. In naturalism, humans are analyzed like any other beast. The naturalists typically viewed human beings as either the products of biological determinism, ruled by inherited instincts and engaged in an endless clash for survival, or as the products of socioeconomic determinism, ruled by social and economic forces beyond their power. In their works, they generally disregarded the social upliftment and focused on degradation associated with it, such as, poverty, alcoholism, prostitution, psychosis and various deranged syndromes. Naturalism received a momentum after the First World War, when many felt they had a responsibility to depict the filth, suffering and degradation of the soldier's life, without euphemism or circumlocution. Joyce's *Ulysses* (1922) was the first novel to illustrate a total physical candour in terms of its artistic, as opposed to moral, aim—which was to depict with almost scientific objectivity every aspect of an ordinary life. Whereas realism believed in some degree of human free will, naturalism surrendered to situations. The naturalists never comment on morality; they never raise optimism. Authors, who were influenced by naturalism, such as Émile Zola, Henrik Ibsen and Thomas Hardy, believed that human beings were higher animals and, therefore, were subject to forces of nature, heredity and surroundings and that life was an unavoidable trap. However, critics like Harry Levin and L Deffoux see naturalism as an intensified form of realism. In the United States, in particular, naturalism had a profound impact. Authors who followed the tradition are Theodore Dreiser, Eugene O'Neill, Stephen Crane, Jack London, Frank Norris and the like. [Cf. realism]

Ref: Mario De Caro and David Macarthur, eds., *Naturalism in Question* (2004). Paul Civello, *American Literary Naturalism and its Twentieth-Century Transformations* (1994).

Negative Capability A term used by John Keats. In a letter to his brothers (21 Dec 1817), Keats defines the term as the poet's capacity to be "in uncertainties, mysteries, doubts, without any irritable reaching after fact and reason." Keats believes that most people in their quest to rationalize and categorize uncertain things in fact distort them and thereby reduce reality without perceiving it. Therefore, what he recommends is the poet must be able to accept intuitive insights for what they really appear as, instead of trying to formulate them into rational categories. Thus negative capability is the poet's ability to negate his rational self and get outside himself with a view to seizing reality in its multiple complexities. That is, Keats was in favour of 'whatever comes naturally from inside' as true poetry. His concept of Negative Capability is precisely a rejection of set philosophies and preconceived ideas forced from outside. Keats' concept of negative capability and his notion of 'submission' are associated with the Zen philosophy. [Cf. objectivity]

Ref: Li Ou, *Keats and Negative Capability* (2009). Walter Jackson Bate, *Negative Capability: The Intuitive Approach in Keats* (2012).

Negritude A cultural and literary issue of the Black writers which sought to reclaim an African heritage and counteract the negative stereotyping of colonialism. The movement started in the 1930s and continued through the 1950s, mostly led by the French-speaking African and Caribbean writers living in Paris as a protest against French colonial rule and the policy of assimilation. First started by Aimé Césaire and Léopold Senghor, it sought to glorify, even idealise, traditional African culture and experience. The movement might have been influenced by the Harlem Renaissance, a literary and cultural movement of the black thinkers and artists in the US during the 1920s. Initially coined in France and used in terms of former French colonies, the term negritude has been influential throughout America, the Caribbean and African countries. Through the movement the black people asserted their 'black voice' and felt that though the policy of assimilation was theoretically based on the concept of universal equality, it still tilted towards the superiority of European culture as against its African counterpart. They were aware of the suffering of the African people colonized by the white and now they asserted that the mystic warmth of African life, gaining force from its closeness to nature and its constant contact with ancestors, should be continually placed in proper perspective against the rigid materialism of the West. So negritude was kind of celebration in support of the attitude of the Negro. However, though vital for rejoicing African culture, it is often criticized for its romanticizing and stereotyping Africans and their past. Some of the artists and their works in this group include Wole Soyinka (*A Dance of Forests*, 1963), Athol Fugard (*The Coat*, 1966), Nadine Gordimer (*Burger's Daughter*, 1979), JM Coetzee (*Life and Times of Michael K*, 1983), etc.

Ref: Aimé Césaire, *Return to My Native Land* (1997). Peter Thompson, "Negritude and Changing Africa: An Update", *Research in African Literatures* (2002).

Neoclassicism/Age of Reason A re-energized form of classicism during the post Miltonic and pre-Romantic era. In literature, the term suggests the revival of the classical literary conventions. It is generally used to describe a period in European history beginning in the late 17th century and lasting until about 1800. In its purest form, Neoclassicism marked a return to old Roman order, proportion, control, logic, precision and etiquette. In England, where neoclassicism perhaps was most admired, it reflected the influence of some 17th century French writers, especially dramatists. Neoclassical writers in general reacted against the intensity and gusto of the Renaissance period. They appealed to the intellect, using elevated language and classical literary forms, such as, satire and ode. Neoclassical works were often regulated by the classical goal of moral teaching. English neoclassicists include Alexander Pope, Jonathan Swift, Joseph Addison, Sir Richard Steele, John Gay, Matthew Prior and the French counterparts were Pierre Corneille and Jean-Baptiste Moliere. This period is often called the Augustan Era, for the writers of the period mostly copied the classical Roman traditions of the great masters like Horace, Ovid, Livy, etc. who worked during the reign of the Emperor Augustus. Politically the age was a conflicting time between the Whig and the Tory and a fertile period for the development of English prose writing. The Augustan era is considered a high point of English satiric writing, both prose and poetry and the masterpieces were Swift's *Gulliver's Travels, A Modest Proposal*, Dryden's *Absalom and Achitophel*, Pope's *Dunciad, Epistle to Dr Arbuthnot*, Samuel Johnson's *The Vanity of Human Wishes, London*, Henry Fielding's *Shamela, Jonathan Wild*, and John Gay's *The Beggar's Opera,* etc. To speak in a few words, the Neoclassical Era was marked with so many important and urgent components—poetry, prose, satire, wit, humour, wigs, the Whigs, the Tories, *the Rambler, the Tattler, the Idler*, the Enlightenment, and of course, Sir Isaac Newton. [Cf. classicism, romanticism, renaissance]

Ref: Ford Boris, Ed. *The New Pelican Guide to English Literature,* Vol. IV. (1984). Ian Jack, *Augustan Satire* (1978). James Sutherland, *Preface to Eighteenth Century Poetry* (1948). RS Crane, "Neoclassical Criticism" (1943).

New Criticism A movement in literary criticism dating from the late 1920s that stressed close textual analysis in the interpretation of a work of literature. The New Critics saw little merit in historical and biographical criticism or analysis. Rather, they aimed at examining the text alone, free from the question of how external events, biographical or otherwise that might have facilitated its shape. Primarily it was an American school named "New Criticism" by one of its practitioners, John Crowe Ransom. Other important critics of the school include Allen Tate, RP Blackmur, Robert Penn Warren and Cleanth Brooks. The new critics, like the flag bearers of aesthetic movement, believed that a piece of art has only *autotelic* purposes, i.e. an art work exists for itself alone without other support systems from outside the text. While the formalistic criticism was more concerned with illuminating the modes of operation of an entire genre, such as fiction, the new critics concentrated on individual literary works. *Close reading* of a text was their slogan, the purpose of which was not analysis of literary devices or motifs; it was instead the elucidation of the way literature embodies or concretely enacts universal truth—what they called "concrete universals." The New Criticism was, in fact, a reaction to the older philological and literary history schools of criticism that flourished in the US. It, however, may appear that new criticism was opposed to reader-response school of theory; but Cleanth Brooks argued that the new criticism was not diametrically opposed to the general principles of reader-response theory and that the two could complement one another. [Cf. aestheticism, genetic criticism, new historicism]

Ref: Cleanth Brooks, *The Well Wrought Urn: Studies in the Structure of Poetry* (1949). Kenneth Burke, *The Philosophy of Literary Form* (1974). John Crowe Ransom, *The New Criticism* (1941). René Wellek, *A History of Modern Criticism 1750-1950* (1986). WK Wimsatt, *The Verbal Icon: Studies in the Meaning of Poetry* (1954).

New Historicism An approach to literature that developed in the 1980s. It is often seen as a reaction to the text-only approach of the Formalistic Criticism. The school emphasizes the interaction between the historical context of a work and a modern reader's understanding and interpretation of it. The theory was initiated in the 1950s by Stephen Greenblatt who insisted on the study of history through the study of literature and the study of a literature through the study of the corresponding culture. New Historicists attempt to describe the culture of a period by reading varieties of texts and paying close attention to different dimensions of a culture, including political, economic, social and aesthetic concerns. The school believes that history, what we know of one text or event, is depending upon a number of texts. History is only that which is written and it is the manner in which it is recorded; maybe this is done by means of a Shakespearean drama or a merchant's diary that interests them. They regard texts not simply as a reflection of the culture that produced them but also as productive of that culture playing an active role in the social and political conflicts of an age. New Historicism acknowledges and then explores various versions of history, sensitizing us to the fact that the history on which we choose to focus is coloured by being reconstructed from our present circumstances. The basic drawback of the theory is that in it literature loses much of its significance; literature becomes kind of a footnote for the study of history. [Cf. historical criticism, new criticism, intertextuality]

Ref: H Aram Veeser, Ed. *The New Historicism* (1989). Harold Veeser, Ed. *The New Historicism* (1994). John Brannigan, *New Historicism and Cultural Materialism* (1998). Stephen Greenblatt, *Renaissance Self-Fashioning* (1980). William Dray, *Philosophy of History* (1964).

New Journalism A kind of writing in which a journalist presents factual information in a fictional form. Popularized during 1960s and 1970s, New Journalism emphasizes description, narration and character development to bring readers closer to the human element of the story and is often used in personality profiles and in-depth feature articles. It is not compatible with *straight* or hard news-items, which is generally composed in a brief, terse, and a fact-based style. The new style thus has narrowed down the traditional distinctions between journalism and fiction. New journalist authors such as Hunter S Thompson, Gay Talese, Thomas Wolfe, Joan Didion and John McPhee are well-known names in this field. Many journalists and critics have reservations about the newness of New Journalism as well as whether it qualifies as an independent literary genre.

Ref: Michael Johnson, *The New Journalism: The Underground Press, the Artists of Nonfiction, and Changes in the Established Media* (1971).

Novel (Latin *novellas>novus,* new) A genre of fiction and when any piece of fiction is long enough to constitute a whole book, then it may be said to have achieved distinction as the novel. When a very long novel steps out the limits of a single volume it becomes *roman-fleuve,* or river novel. Length is thus one of the very significant dimensions of this genre. It is to be noted that, despite examples of novelists of the most profound seriousness, such as Tolstoy, Henry James, Fyodor Dostoyevsky, Virginia Woolf and so on, the term novel still in some quarters carries overtones of lightness and frivolity, may be because of its connection with romance and novella. Novel, no doubt, can descend to shameful depths of sentimentality or pornography and it also can achieve the distinction of great art.

Such ancient Roman fiction as Petronius' *Satyricon* and Lucius Apuleius' *Golden Ass* contain many of the popular elements that distinguish the novel from its ancient counterpart, the epic. In the fictional works, the medium is prose, the events described are un-heroic and the settings can be streets or taverns. There is more flirting than princely combat; the gods do not move the action; the dialogue is homely rather than aristocratic. It was, in fact, out of the need to find a literary form that was anti-epic both in substance and language that the first prose fiction of Europe seems to have been conceived. The medieval chivalric romance restored a kind of epic view of man, not heroic pagan, but a Christian. At the same time, it bequeathed its name to the later genre of continental literature, the novel, which is known in French as *roman,* in Italian as *romanzo,* etc. But that later genre achieved its first great flowering in Spain in the beginning of the 17th century in an anti-chivalric comic masterpiece, Miguel de Cervantes' *Don Quixote* (1605), which contains many of the elements that have been expected from prose fiction ever since.

Poets like Milton, Spenser who told big stories were responsible for the new narrative art. However, the fiction that was produced before the development of the novel, were never based on actual people but on mythical figures whom everyone was familiar with, Hercules, Adam and Eve, Knights, etc. Thus, the success of an author was mainly based on whether or not he could re-invent an already popular story and model the traditional classics from the days. On the English soil Samuel Richardson's *Pamela* (1740) is unanimously taken for granted as the first novel. Since then by degrees the form has beaten all other literary forms. Growth in literacy and leisure, too, has lent to the speed at which the novel captured readers' imagination between 1740 and 1900. The new generation novelists experimented with forms and contents and gave it a standard and respectable position. From Richardson's epistolary novel, it was a lengthy tradition of novel writing—the picaresque, then Gothic, sentimental, romantic, realistic, sociological, historical, detective, psychological, modernist, and finally to postmodernist, diasporic, postcolonial, multicultural and cyberfiction, etc., etc.—it is a spectacular panorama of long history of the genre. And the craftsmen and craftswomen, who have dominated the imagination of the English readership are Henry Fielding, Daniel Defoe, Tobias Smollett, Laurence Sterne, Horace Walpole, Jane Austen, Emily Brontë, George Eliot, George Meredith, Charles Dickens, Thomas Hardy, Henry James, DH Lawrence, EM Forster, Joseph Conrad, Somerset Maugham, HE Bates, Graham Greene, Virginial Woolf, Agatha Christie, James Joyce, John Barth, William Gibson, William Golding, Kingsley Amis, so on and so forth.

Ref: Arnold Kettle, *An Introduction to the English Novel* (1951). Brean Hammond & Shaun Regan, *Making the Novel* (2006). EM Forster, *Aspects of the Novel* (1927). Ian Watt, *The Rise of the Novel: Studies in Defoe, Richardson and Fielding* (1957). Mikhail Bakhtin, "Discourse in the Novel" (1934-35). Ralph Fox, *The Novel and the People* (1937). Michael McKeon, *Theory of the Novel: A Historical Approach* (2000). Virginia Woolf, "Modern Fiction" (1919). Walter Allen, *The English Novel* (1954).

Novella/Novelette An Italian term for fictional prose narrative longer than a short story, but shorter than a novel. Structurally novella generally features fewer conflicts than a novel, yet more complicated than a short story. Originally novella was a kind of enlarged anecdote like those to be found in the 14th century Italian classic, Boccaccio's *Decameron*, each of which exemplifies the etymology well enough. The stories are little new things; but they are well-structured narrative, realistic and satiric in tone, often humorous, political or amorous in nature and they are lacking in weight and moral earnestness. There is no standard of length recommended; but since conventions are sometimes useful, it can be said that the short story ends within 20,000 words, while the novel begins at about 50,000. Thus, the novella is a fictional work of about words between 20,000 and 50,000. Notable examples are Henry James' *Daisy Miller,* Robert Louis Stevenson's *Dr. Jekyll and Mr. Hyde* and Joseph Conrad's *Heart of Darkness,* Leo Tolstoy's *The Death of Ivan Ilich,* Fyodor Dostoyevsky's *Notes from the Underground* and Henry James's *The Aspern Papers* and Ernest Hemingway's *The Old Man and the Sea,* etc.

O

Objective Correlative A critical term introduced by TS Eliot in his essay "Hamlet and His Problems" (*The Sacred Wood: Essays on Poetry and Criticism,* 1916) and defined as an outward set of objects, image, situation or chain of events corresponding to an inward experience and evoking this experience in the reader. He says that the "only way of expressing emotion in the form of art is by finding an 'objective correlative'." What Eliot means perhaps is to turn an object, event or character in the story into an inspiring agent that stimulates some greater emotional response from the reader that is not possible to be evoked otherwise. When an author fails to do that, he fails to convey the exact emotion intended in the work. According to Eliot's argument of this theory, Shakespeare's *Hamlet* was "an artistic failure" meaning that Hamlet's strong emotions "exceeded the facts" of the play and there was a kind of mismatch between Hamlet's emotion and the corresponding materials in the text used to sustain that amount of emotion. The term, supposedly coined by the American artist Washington Allston, got currency only after Eliot's essay had raised the issue. However, Eliot's explanation so far has evoked mixed responses.

Ref: Eliseo Vivas, "The Objective Correlative of TS Eliot" *Critiques and Essays in Criticism*, Ed. Robert W Stallman (1949).

Objectivity A quality in writing characterized by the absence of the author's personal opinion or feeling about his subject matter. This is often applied to writings in which personal emotions of the author remain uninvolved or at least unobtrusive. The novels of Henry James, Ernest Hemmingway and, to a certain extent, the poems of John Larkin demonstrate clear objectivity. Whereas John Keats's concept of negative capability discourages rational categorization of certain realisation, objectivity discourages the writer's emotional involvement into his art. Lyric poetry and poetry written under the ambience of romantic environment are basically subjective; but for that matter the works cannot be described as compromised. The theory of objectivity has its limitations. Only certain categories of literary work can be attempted objectively. Critical and journalistic writing usually attempt to be objective. The concept is often applied to criticism that is more descriptive than normative. In this sense objective criticism, in which the critic can apply his objectivity, consists of analysis of the more clearly identifiable and reportable components of literature, such as verse, meter and form, etc. *Objective criticism*, thus, categorically avoids both interpretations of meaning and judgments of value; analysis and assessment takes place only with reference to certain intrinsic criteria—form, coherence and organic unity, verbal quality, etc. Extrinsic criteria—poet, audience, socio-historical context and external reality, etc are rendered almost irrelevant. [Cf. formalistic criticism, realism, subjectivity]

Ref: Adrian Cussins, "The Connectionist Construction of Concepts", *Oxford Readings of Philosophy: The Philosophy of Artificial Intelligence,* Ed. Margaret Boden (1990).

Occasional Poem <French *vers d'occasion*, verse of the moment or occasion> A poem written to celebrate a specific private or public occasion. Occasional poem itself is not a genre. Such poems as Yeats' "Easter 1916," and possibly, Donne's "Nocturnal upon St. Lucy's Day," etc are poems of occasions. The term is a bit confusing, for composing a poem needs some sort of inspiration, may be from some event or some experience. Arthur Hallam's death occasioned many poems of Tennyson. Wordsworth's "Daffodils" too is a poems occasioned by the poet's visit to a particular place. There are examples of odes composed with a clear view to marking important events. In a very strict sense, thus, all poems are occasional poems, no matter the occasion is explicitly stated or not. However, the term refers to poems that mainly commemorate certain events; and the poems are written to mark those events. [Cf. ode]

Octosyllabic Couplet A couplet or two successive rhyming verse lines, in which each line contains eight syllables. French poems are more than often octosyllabic whereas English octosyllabic couplets are not that frequent. Octosyllabic couplets, according to English prosodic order, are tetrameter either iambic or trochaic:

Thou canst | | guard thy | | creatures | | sleeping,
Heal the | | heart long | | broke with | | weeping

Hoggs' lines are a trochaic couplet. Here is another example from Dorothy Parker's 'Symptom Recital' that is iambic: "I hate | | my legs, | | I hate | | my hands, / I do | | not yearn | | for love | | lier lands."

Ode A long serious and thoughtful lyric poem that treats a noble subject in a suitable language. By nature it can be a ceremonious poem on an event of public or private importance in which personal emotions and/or general meditations are synthesized. The Greek word *ode*, which has been accepted in most modern European languages, meant a choric song, usually accompanied by a dance. Alcman (7th c. BCE) composed the *strophic* (part/stanza) arrangement of the ode, which is a rhythmic system made of two or more lines repeated as a unit; and Stesichorus (7th-6th c. BCE) invented the *triadic*, or three-part, structure (strophic lines followed by antistrophic lines in the same meter, concluding with a summary line, called an *epode*, in a different meter) that characterizes the odes of Pindar. Choral odes were also an integral part of the Greek drama. In Latin the word was not used until about the time of Horace, in the 1st century

BCE. His *carmina* (songs), written in stanzas of two or four lines of polished Greek meters, are now universally called odes. The implication that they were to be sung to the accompaniment of a lyre was probably only a literary convention. Both *Pindaric ode* and *Horatian ode* forms were revived during the Renaissance and continued to influence lyric poetry into the 20th century. The first version of Allen Tate's widely acclaimed "Ode to the Confederate Dead," for example, was published in 1926.

With the publication of Pierre de Ronsard's four books of French *Odes* (1550), the Pindaric ode was adapted to the vernacular languages. Imitation of Pindaric odes was written in England by Thomas Gray in 1757—"The Progress of Poesy" and "The Bard." Abraham Cowley's *Pindarique Odes* (1656) introduced a looser version known as Pindarics. These are irregular rhymed odes in which the length of line and stanza is impulsively varied to suggest, not reproducing the style and manner of Pindar. These forged Pindarics are some of the greatest odes in the English language, including John Dryden's "Alexander's Feast" (1697), William Wordsworth's "Ode: Intimations of Immortality from Recollections of Early Childhood," PB Shelley's "Ode to the West Wind," Alfred Tennyson's "Ode on the Death of the Duke of Wellington," and John Keats' "Ode on a Grecian Urn," etc. Most modernist poems called odes, e.g. Robert Penn Warren's "Ode to Fear" and WH Auden's "Ode to Gaea" are odes only in the sense of formal Horatian odes, i.e. they contain stanzas of similar length, rhyme scheme and rhythmical patterns. The English odes follow the most common rhyme scheme: ab-ab cde-cde.

Ref: Helen Vendler, *The Odes of John Keats* (1983). George Naumann Shuster, *English Ode from Milton to Keats* (1964). John D Jump, *The Ode* (1974).

One-Act Play A dramatic work having just one act instead of the customary five acts. What the short story is to the novel, almost in the same way, the one-act play relates to the full-length play. The history of the one-act play dates back to the early *mystery* and *miracle plays*. Much later, in the late 18th and 19th centuries, any standard programme at a London theatre consisted of a full-length play preceded by a *curtain raiser*, a short play of dissimilar nature. Later the curtain raiser disappeared; but theatre groups began experimenting with shorter pieces, the result being self-contained one act plays. The one-act play is brief and complete in itself. Brevity is the soul of it; but it has to follow the classical conception of dramatic art—single main episode and is either a pure comedy or a pure tragedy. The adherence to the Neo-classical concept of time, place and action is almost a must for this type. Some best known one-act playwrights are JM Singe (*In the Shadow of the Glen* and *Riders to the Sea*), JO Francis (*Birds of a Feather*), Laurence Houseman (*Brother Wolf*), Hugh Stewart (*A Room in the Tower*), AA Milne (*The boy Comes Home*), Lady Gregory (*The Rising of the Moon*), Joe Corrie (*Hewers of Coal*), Harold Pinter (*Landscape* and *Silence*), Anton Chekhov (*The Bear*), Jean-Paul Sartre (*Huis-clos*), David Campton (*Four Minute Waning*), Allan Bennet (*An Englishman Abroad*, *A Question of Attribution*) and Eugène Ionesco (*The Bald Soprano*), etc.

Ref: RJ Rees, *English Literature: An Introduction for Foreign Readers* (1973). Michael Y Bennett & Benjamin D Carson, eds., *Eugene O'Neill's One-Act Plays: New Critical Perspectives* (2012).

Onomatopoeia A Figure of Speech, in Greek, *make,* i.e. sound makes the sense. In this figure the use of words are so made as to imitate non-verbal, natural sound or to accommodate sound to sense. For example 'hiss', 'bang', 'pop', etc signify the meanings through the sound effects they produce. Poets use onomatopoeia to address the reader's auditory sense and create rich soundscape. It is one of the many poetic devices dealing with sounds of poetry. In addition to creating some musical effect, onomatopoeia actually tries to seize upon the object or the sensation referred to by the words. Australian poet Lee Emmett has a beautiful example: "water plops into pond/ splish-splash downhill/ warbling magpies in tree/ trilling, melodic thrill."

Opera A type of stage performance, usually a drama, in which the dialogue is sung. Opera incorporates many of the elements of the theatre, such as acting, scenery, costumes and sometimes it includes dance. Vastly popular in different parts of Europe, specially Germany, France, England, Eastern European countries and also in Russia, opera carried the traces of the Greek tragedies. Classic examples of opera include Giuseppi Verdi's *La traviata,* Giacomo Puccini's *La Boheme* and Richard Wagner's *Tristan und Isolde.* Major 20th century contributors to the form include works of Richard Strauss and Alban Berg. Often a romantic comic opera is called *operetta*. John Gay's *The Beggar's Opera,* Richard Sheridan's *The Duenna* and numerous works by William Gilbert and Arthur Sullivan are examples of operettas. Musical opera is more of a melodic style, in which notes are sung in a sustained fashion and is dominated by music. Perhaps the most obvious stylistic manifestation of modernism in opera is the development of atonality, i.e. a move away from traditional tonality and less use of orchestration.

Ref: John Louis DiGaetani, *An Invitation to the Opera* (1986). Leslie Orrey & Rodney Milnes, *Opera: A Concise History* (1987).

Orientalism A discourse referring to the Eurocentric account of the Orient. The term can be traced first with the foundation of the Asiatic Society (1784) and William Jones attempts to interpret India's classical texts. As far as literature is concerned Orientalism now refers to the European/Western discourse about the East, which comprises a vast body of literary, sociological, historical, linguistic, philosophical, political, anthropological and even scientific texts accumulating since the Renaissance; particularly since the 18th century. And all the Western knowledge of the Orient aggregates to a "textual universe" to which there is no counterpart in the East about the West. It was perhaps Anouar Abdel-Malek, in his *Civilizations and Social Theory* (1963), who first uses the term in its political sense. Later Edward Said gives the term a crucial ideological dimension that defines the entire Western attitude to the East in terms of political and cultural relationship between the two hemispheres. "Orientalism," as Said puts it, is "a Western style for dominating, restructuring, and having authority over the Orient" and the "Orient is an integral part of European *material* civilization and culture. Orientalism expresses and represents that part culturally and even ideologically as a mode of discourse with supporting institutions, vocabulary, scholarship, imagery, doctrines, even colonial bureaucracies and colonial styles." It is not that the concept has thrown light on the Western imperial discourse only; rather, Said's stand has given some direction to postcolonial discourse as a form of counter discourse to the Occidental construct of the Orient as well. [Cf. discourse, other, postcolonialism]

Ref: Edward Said, *Orientalism* (1978). Evgeny Steiner, Ed. *Orientalism / Occidentalism: Languages of Cultures vs. Languages of Description* (2012). Rana Kabbani, *Imperial Fictions: Europe's Myths of Orient* (1994). Stephen Howe, *Empire: A Very Short Introduction* (2000).

Other A central construction in connection with the understanding of colonial and postcolonial relationship in terms of social or literary contexts. A phenomenological term 'Other' is dissimilar to and the opposite of the Self. For Edward Said, Orientalist discourse was characterized by a positioning of colonized peoples and places as Other, in the sense of alien, non-Western and connotatively, therefore, inferior: "The Orient is not only adjacent to Europe; it is also the place of Europe's greatest, richest and oldest colonies, the source of its civilizations and languages…and one of its deepest and most recurrent images of the Other." The term *Othering* thus describes the reductive action of labelling a person as someone who belongs to a subordinate or marginal social category defined as the Other. [Cf. discourse, orientalism]

Ottava Rima <*Ottava d'oro*, the golden octave> A stanza of eight lines of *iambic pentameter* of the rhyming scheme: a-b-a-b-a-b c-c. It appeared in the religious and minstrel poetry of the late 13th century. Used by Italian writers, such as Boccaccio and Ariosto, it was brought into English writing by Sir Thomas Wyatt in the 16th century and is used to great efficacy by Lord Byron in *Don Juan* (1819-24).

Oxford Movement A 19th-century religious protest centred at the University of Oxford that sought a renewal of the Roman Catholic doctrines within the Church of England in opposition to the Protestant deviations. It occasioned out of a conflict between the state and the Church of England in 1828 and the movement continued through 1832. Leaders of the movement were, among others, John Henry Newman (1801-90), a clergyman and subsequently a convert to Roman Catholicism, Richard Hurrell Froude (1803-36), a clergyman and John Keble (1792-1866), a clergyman and poet. This was fundamentally a religious movement and one of its aims was to rehabilitate the dignity of the Church and to deliver it from the grasp of secular control. Although it began to appropriate the doctrine and practice of the Anglican Church, the movement was criticized for its propensity toward 'Romanising' the Anglican Church. The Oxford Movement too was criticised for being secretive and collusive.

Between the Romantic Revival and the Oxford Movement, some critics locate something strangely common. The romantic interest in the Middle Ages for their mystery and splendour is one of such factors. As Moody and Lovett put it, the movement stood for "the restoration of the poetry, the mystic ritual and service which had characterised the Catholic Church in the Middle Ages." It was this medievalism which was probably responsible for the ultimate entry of Newman into the Roman Catholic fold. The romantic tendency of the protagonists of the Oxford Movement is also apparent in a different way through their poetry. As Eugene Fairweather, a Kemble professor of divinity, points out, "their poetic sensibility—which cannot be ignored, in view of the fact that Keble, Newman and Williams were all fluent, if 'minor', poets—was 'romantic' in tone." John Henry Newman's (1801-1890) most important literary work was *Apologia pro Vita Sua* (1864). He also has to his credit a book of verse. He wrote well, but the only memorable poem written by him is the famous prayer poem, *"Lead Kindly Light."* The other writers associated with the movement were William George Ward (1812-1882) and Richard William Church (1815-1890), etc. The Oxford Movement was more than a passing ripple on the surface of cultural life of England. Their conviction that literature could play an important part in directing minds to God liberated female followers, such as Charlotte Yonge and Christina Rossetti, who often could give complex expression to the notion of 'silent self-sacrifices' as the ideal mode of service for the Christian woman. Some of the Movement's features—distrust of contemporary reformers, contempt for liberalism, conviction of the primacy of faith over reason, desire to preserve the mystery and beauty of creation in the face of reductive rationalism, etc continued till the Victorian era.

Ref: Elisabeth Jay, *The Oxford Movement* (2011). RW Church, *The Oxford Movement: Twelve Years, 1833-1845* (1891). Samuel Hall, *A Short History of the Oxford Movement* (1906).

Oxymoron A popular Figure of Speech, an extreme form of epigram. In an oxymoronic construction two opposite ideas are juxtaposed. Its use may be intentional or unintentional, e.g.: *regularly irregular*. The following speech from William Shakespeare's *Romeo and Juliet* uses several oxymorons together in a series: "Why then, O brawling love! O loving hate!/ O anything, of nothing first create!/ O heavy lightness! serious vanity!/ Mis-shapen chaos of well-seeming forms!/ Feather of lead, bright smoke, cold fire, sick health!/ Still-waking sleep, that is not what it is!/ This love feel I, that feel no love in this. Dost thou not laugh?" [Cf. antithesis, epigram and paradox]

P

Pantheism <*Pan + Theo + ismo*> A philosophical school according to which God is an impersonal being or principle, not to be found outside nature, but identified very much with it. Pantheism, in fact, dissolves God in nature, rejecting the supernatural elements associated with Him. John Toland (1670-1722), an English advocate of free thinking, introduced the term in 1705. Earlier the concept included materialist ideas on nature, but now it has been transformed into a religious and idealist theory of the existence of God and is an attempt to reconcile religion with science. Similar Pantheistic ideas, however, were a common attitude in the early societies of Egypt, India and Greece also. The term derives from the Greek words *pan* meaning *all* and *theos* meaning *deity*. It later became a significant part of the Christian faith. William Wordsworth and Ralph Waldo Emerson and Spinoza are among those writers who have frequently expressed the pantheistic overtone in their works.

Parable A small story, either in prose or verse, intended basically to teach a moral lesson or answer an ethical question. In the West, the best examples of parables are those of Jesus Christ in the New Testament (Gospels), such as "The Parable of the Prodigal Son" or "The Parable of Good Samaritan." The parables were exemplary uses for explaining identical situations with appropriate analogies. It is difficult to differentiate between fables and parables; except that fables are beast stories, parables are not. However parables are also used in Hasidism, Sufism, Zen Buddhism and Rabbinic literature. Many of the stories in *The Jataka* are all parable in spirit. [Cf. fable]

Ref: J Alexander Findlay, *Jesus and His Parables* (1950).

Paradox A Figure of Speech. A statement that at first seems to be unsound or self-contradictory yet ultimately proves to embody a complex truth. In New Criticism, the term is extended to embrace any complexity of language that endorses multiple meanings and deviates from the norms of ordinary usage of language. Hence Cleanth Brooks's claim that "the language of poetry is the language of paradox," and again, "paradox is the language appropriate and inevitable to poetry." For an example of a common paradox here is a statement: "The most corrected copies are commonly the least correct" – Francis Bacon. And the famous Socratic paradox is: "I know one thing: that I know nothing." [Cf. antithesis, epigram, oxymoron]

Ref: Cleanth Brooks, "The Language of Paradox" (1956).

Paralepsis/Praeteritio A Figure of Speech, for pretended omission but intended assertion as a rhetorical device. It involves a speaker's assertion that he/ she will not discuss something that he/ she is in fact discussing. Marc Antony's famous speech in *Julius Caesar* begins with a paralepsis or praeteritio: "Friends, Romans, countrymen, lend me your ears;/ I come to bury Caesar, not to praise him." What follows is an unreserved praise of Julius Caesar. Anthony judged the sentiment of the audience tilting towards Brutus; therefore, in a roundabout way, by means of this device, he forced the audience to listen to what was perhaps unacceptable to them. Paralepsis often makes good advertisements for commercial purposes. [Cf. irony]

Parody A mocking imitation of something serious. Customarily a parody, in writing or utterance, exaggerates another person's style with a view to mocking its salient features. A parodist exploits the peculiarities of an author's expression, his mannerism or whatever that may mark the original. The parody may also be focused on an improbable plot with too many convenient events. Fielding's *Shamela* is, in large part, a parody of Richardson's *Pamela*. In music there are numerous examples of parody. [Cf. mock-heroic, pastiche, plagiarism]

Pastiche <French/Italian *pasticcio An* imitation> A literary or musical piece openly imitating the previous works of other artists, often with satirical intent. Or it may mean incongruous parts, a hodgepodge, such as: "In...a city of splendid Victorian architecture...there is a rather pointless pastiche of Dickensian London down on the waterfront" etc. In recent usage, it refers to a literary technique employing a generally light-hearted tongue-in-cheek imitation of a known style. For example, David Lodge's novel *The British Museum Is Falling Down* (1965) is a pastiche of works by James Joyce, Franz Kafka and Virginia Woolf. So is John Fowler's novel *The French Lieutenant's Woman* (1969) modelled on Victorian novels. Pastiche is frequently found in postmodernist and postcolonialist works. Rewriting the colonial cannon has often been a conscious effort on the part of a postcolonial writer. While doing so, some have deliberately used the known English models. The Caribbean author Jean Rhys's *Wide Sargassso Sea* (1966) thus remain a bit incomprehensible unless it is read side by side with Charlotte Brontë's *Jane Eyre* (1847). In this case it becomes part of an ideological agenda, i.e. projection of a counter discourse against the colonial one. Pastiche is also found in non-literary works, including art and music. For instance, Charles Rosen has characterized Mozart's various works in imitation of the baroque style as pastiche. Pastiche is more frequent in popular culture. Many genre writings, particularly in fantasy, are essentially pastiches. However, pastiche should not be confused with plagiarism in the sense that in the latter the author steals something and deceptively tries to pass it to his own credit, whereas the former never claims to be something original; the part imitated becomes an artistic tool there. [Cf. parody]

Ref: Ingeborg Hoesterey, *Pastiche: Cultural Memory in Art, Film, Literature* (2001). https://en.wikipedia.org/wiki/Pastiche (accessed 13 June 2017).

Pastoral An adjective referring to literary works of rural setting that generally highlights the glory of the rustic way of life. As a noun it is applied to the class of literature that presents the society of shepherds as free from the complexity and corruption of city life. Among the writers who have used the pastoral convention with striking success and vitality are the classical poets Theocritus, Virgil, and among the English poets Edmund Spenser, Robert Herrick, John Milton, PB Shelley and Matthew Arnold.

The popular themes in the pastoral convention include love and death. The tradition and theme were largely established by Theocritus, whose *Bucolics* are the first examples of pastoral poetry. The tradition was passed on, through Bion, Moschus and Longus, from Greece to Rome, where Virgil (who transferred the setting from Sicily to Arcadia, in the Greek Peloponnese, now the symbol of a pastoral paradise) used the device of alluding to contemporary problems—agrarian, political and personal—in the rustic society he portrayed. His *Eclogues* exerted a powerful effect on the Renaissance poets including Dante Alighieri, Francesco Petrarch and Giovanni Boccaccio in Italy; Pierre de Ronsard in France; and Garcilaso de la Vega in Spain. These were further influenced by medieval Christian commentators on Virgil and by the pastoral scenes of the Old and New Testaments (Cain and Abel, David, the Bethlehem shepherds and the figure of Christ the good shepherd).

In English poetry some examples of early pastoral poems of the 16th century were almost clouded by 1579 with the appearance of Edmund Spenser's *Shepheardes Calender*, which imitated not only classical models but also the Renaissance poets of France and Italy and brought about a genuine vogue for the pastoral. Sir Philip Sidney, Robert Greene, Thomas Nash, Christopher Marlowe, Michael Drayton, Thomas Dekker, John Donne, Sir Walter Raleigh, Thomas Heywood, Thomas Campion, William Browne, William Drummond and Phineas Fletcher all wrote pastoral poetry. The craze, however, was subjected to some mocking comment in Shakespeare's play *As You Like It,* though itself a pastoral play. Apart from Shakespeare, dramatists who attempted *pastoral drama* include John Lyly, George Peele, John Fletcher, Ben Jonson, John Day and James Shirley. The climax of this pastoral tradition was reached in the unique blend of freshness and learned imitation achieved in the poetry of Herrick and Andrew Marvell. A growing reaction against the artificialities of the genre, combined with new attitudes to the natural man and the natural scene, sometimes resulted in a bitter injection of reality into the rustic scenes of such poets and novelists as Robert Burns, George Crabbe, William Wordsworth, John Clare, George Eliot and Thomas Hardy. Other terms that often synonymously used to refer to the pastoral are *idyl, eclogue* and *bucolic poetry*. [Cf. Arcadia]

Ref: Frank Kermode, *English Pastoral Poetry: From the Beginnings to Marvell* (1952). Raymond Williams, *The Country and the City* (1973). William Empson, *Some Versions of Pastoral* (1935).

Pastoral Elegy A species of the elegy. As its name implies, the pastoral elegy combines the forms and traditions of the elegy with those of the pastoral. Basically a lyric poem, it is more formal than a dirge. Pastoral elegy is a popular poetic form for a poet to lament and grieve the loss of a friend or a poet. As the subject matter demands, it is composed in a lofty and dignified style. In this type of elegy what is important is that it represents both the mourner and the mourned equally prominently. The dead poet or friend is traditionally given a Greek name in an attempt to connect it with its ancient Greek pedigree. The Greek poet Theocritus is frequently credited with creating the form. An early example of which is Moschus's "Lament for Bion" (c. 150 BCE). The pastoral elegy became so popular in Europe during the 16th through 19th century that any type of elegy on another poet contained pastoral element.

The pastoral elegy is highly conventional, generally opening with an invocation of the muses and then follows a statement of the poet's great sorrow and a subsequent description of a procession of mourners. In addition to human mourners this procession often includes nature and supernatural beings—plants, animals and even things to which the dead poet gave imaginative existence. In *Adonais,* Shelley's elegy for Keats, the procession includes "All he had loved and moulded into thought." The pastoral elegy also discusses fate and its implications at length or some similar philosophical topic and, ultimately, the speaker comes to conclusion to the effect that all is well and has turned out as it should have been. In *Christian elegies*, such statements imply or explicitly involve affirmation of belief in an afterlife. Expressions of bewilderment, tirades against death, belief in immortality, arrangements of flower and the use of pathetic fallacy are also conventional elements of the pastoral elegy. In addition to Milton's *Lycidas* (1638) for Edward King, Matthew Arnold's *Thyrsis* (1866) for Arthur Hugh Clough exemplifies this category. Tennyson's *Morte d'Arthur* for his friend Arthur Hallam, although elegiac in tone, the poem is not a pastoral elegy proper since it lacks many of the conventional pastoral qualities. [Cf. elegy, pastoral]

Ref: Ellen Zetzel Lambert, *Placing Sorrow: A Study of the Pastoral Elegy Convention from Theocritus to Milton* (1977). Iain Twiddy, *Pastoral Elegy in Contemporary British and Irish Poetry* (2012).

Pathetic Fallacy A form of personification that involves the attribution of human emotions, sympathy or other human characteristics to inanimate, specially natural objects; or in other words, the reading of one's emotion into external nature in order to evoke a sympathy which is usually facile: "Earth felt the wound; and Nature from her seat,/ Sighing through all her works, gave signs of woe"—Milton. Whereas in personification animals, abstract ideas, inanimate objects, natural or extra-natural things are invested with human abilities and qualities, the application of the pathetic fallacy is restricted to natural objects only. The personification is a more powerful device and the pathetic fallacy has rather a narrowed down area of application. The term was first used by John Ruskin in the third volume of his *Modern Painters* (1856). He did not recommend frequent use of the figure. However, in Walt Whitman's "When Lilacs Last in the Dooryard Bloom'd" (1865-66) an almost unconventional treatment of the pathetic fallacy of attributing grief to nature is achieved. Some early imagist poets, however, have made use of it rather freely and effectively. The falsification involved in the use of the pathetic fallacy may be justified as part of the privilege, known as poetic licence that poets enjoy. [Cf. personification]

Pathos A quality in speech, writing, music or any form of artistic representation, in events, which excites a feeling of pity or sadness; power of stirring tender or melancholy emotion. In Greek it simply meant *passion* or *strong feeling*. Aristotle refers to this in his *Rhetoric* as "awakening emotion." As a modern critical tool it applies to a situation, a scene, a stanza or passage so framed as to evoke such human feelings as pity, sympathy from the reader or audience. It must be noted that tragic felling is a more dignified concept evoking a stronger "sense of loss of a gift so splendid" which pathos cannot achieve. In fact a genuine tragic feeling comes from a great man's human limitation against a greater adversity; whereas pathos may arise from simple situations that may not have the potency to acquire tragic grandeur. Charles Lamb, in his works, has extensively used pathos sliced with candid humour. A sense of true pathos as has been conceived of by Lamb can be found sparkling in his "Rosamond Gray," in his description of his dead brother in "Dream Children," the flight of Favel from the university in "Poor Relations," the story of the sick child in "The Old Margate Boy," and in many other essays.

Ref: Norman Gardiner, *Feeling and Emotion: A History of Theories* (1937). WW Fortenbaugh, *Aristotle's Rhetoric on Emotions* (1974).

Periods of English Literature

450-1066	Old English/Anglo-Saxon Period	
1066-1500	Middle English Period	
1500-1660	R E N A I S S A N C E	
	1558-1603	Elizabethan Age
	1603-1625	Jacobean Age
	1625-1649	Caroline
	1649-1660	Common Wealth Period / Puritan Interregnum
1660-1785	N E O-C L A S S I C A L P E R I O D	
	1660-1700	Restoration
	1700-1745	Augustan/Age of Pope
	1745-1785	Age of Sensibility/Age of Johnson
1785-1832	R E V I V A L O F R O M A N T I C I S M	
1832-1900	V I C T O R I A N P E R I O D	
	1848-1860	Pre-Raphaelite Age
	1880-1900	Aestheticism/Decadence
1900-1910	E D W A R D I A N P E R I O D	
1910-1936	G E O R G I A N/M O D E R N P E R I O D	
1914-1945	M O D E R N P E R I O D	
1945-onwards	POSTMODERN / POSTCOLONIAL PERIOD	

Peripety/Peripeteia <Greek for *reversal*> A critical moment in the development of a tragic drama. Peripety is the sudden turning point in a play after which the plot sharply turns toward its dénouement. Aristotle discussed it in his *Poetics* as the shift of the tragic protagonist's fortune from good to bad, which is essential to the concept of a tragic plot. It is often an ironic twist, as in Sophocles' *Oedipus Rex* when a messenger brings Oedipus news about his parents that he thought would cheer him, but the news, instead, slowly brought about the awful recognition that leads to Oedipus' catastrophe.

Aristotle considered the plot to be the soul of a tragedy and placed character in the second place. The goal of tragedy is not suffering but the knowledge that issues from it; as the play progresses towards the end—dénouement or catastrophe. The most powerful elements of emotional interest in tragedy, according to Aristotle, are peripeteia, reversal of situation and anagnorisis, recognition scenes; and each is most effective when one is coincidental with the other. In *Oedipus*, for example, the messenger who brings Oedipus the news of his real parentage, intending to allay his fears, brings about a sudden reversal of his fortune, from happiness to misery by compelling him to recognize that his wife is also his mother.

Coup de théâtre too implies suddenness of events. It usually involves the unveiling of a disguised character or the reappearance of one assumed to be dead. By nature it refers more to surprising elements, whereas peripeteia is more decisive in shaping the future of the protagonist. In comedy the term peripety may refer to the hero's shift from misfortune to prosperity. For example, in *Twelfth Night* (1623), when Cesario reveals to the Duke that he is really Viola, the circumstances abruptly take a turn in Viola's favour. Normally, however, the term peripeteia is associated more with tragedy than comedy. [Cf. anticlimax, deus ex machina, hubris, tragedy]

Ref: Aristotle, *Poetics.* FL Lucas, "The Reverse of Aristotle", *Classical Review*, Vol. XXXVII Nos. 5-6 (1923). MS Silk, *Tragedy and the Tragic: Greek Theatre and Beyond* (1998).

Periphrasis A rhetorical figure, a way of speaking in heightened language and unnecessarily making a roundabout statement of a topic rather than stating it directly. Periphrasis may be intended to heighten anticipation through delay, to enable ornament or to delay coming to pain as in euphemism. Alexander Pope's reference to fish as "the finny tribe" in *The Rape of the Lock* is periphrastic. Samuel Johnson's style, known as *Johnsonese,* often comes close to periphrasis. In *Hamlet*, Polonius' way of speaking is marked with this element of the figure and the roundabout features of his speech matches his character as well.

Persona <Latin for *mask*> An assumed identity or the fictional 'I'. Personae (plural form) are the characters or narrators in a fictional work of literature. It is often seen as a mask used to project the writer's personality through another character. Whether the story is told by an omniscient narrator or by a character in it, the actual author of the work often distances himself from what is said or told by adopting a persona, a personality. A persona, thus, is a character who, acts as a narrator or an *implied author*, a voice created by the author to act as the narrator for himself or herself. The speaker in a narrative poem or a dramatic monologue too is not the author himself—he is persona. Some examples of personae include the narrator of Geoffrey Chaucer's *Canterbury Tales* and Marlow in Joseph Conrad's *Heart of Darkness.*

Personification A Figure of Speech based on figurative use of language, which attributes human qualities to abstract ideas or inanimate objects. In other words, it is a kind of attribution of personality to an impersonal thing: "The Pyramids themselves, doting with age, have forgotten the names of their founders" (Fuller). By this figure, as Nesfield thinks, one can ascribe "intelligence and personality" to inanimate things too:

> By yonder comes the powerful *king* of day,
> *Rejoicing* in the east. The lessening cloud,
> The kindling azure, and the mountain's brow
> Illumed with fluid gold, *his near approach* Betoken glad.
>
> —Thomson.

The employment of the personification is as old as poetry itself and is found passim in allegorical poetry. Such works as *Everyman* (c. 1500), the medieval *morality play*, and John Bunyan's *The Pilgrim's Progress* (1678) have extensively personified Biblical vices and virtues such as Death, Knowledge, Sin, Sloth and Piety, etc. Playwrights like Marlowe and even TS Eliot have made use of the device; and such examples as Good Angel, Bad Angel, Pride, Envy, Wrath, Sloth, Tempters, etc are all personified abstract ideas. The personification became rather a fashion or almost an automatic mannerism in the 18th century Neo-classical poetry.

An extreme form of the personification, especially when the personified figure can speak is known as *Prosopopoeia*. A lower kind and lesser form of personification is seen in such phrases as *the smiling morn, the frowning rock, the blushing rose,* etc. These are often known as *personal metaphor*. The personification shares with the pathetic fallacy as both visualize human quality in nonhuman elements. However, the use of the pathetic fallacy is mainly restricted within its field of application—whereas personification bestows human characteristics upon anything inanimate or nonhuman, the pathetic fallacy bestows those especially only on nature: "...Nature might stand up/ And say to all the world, 'This was a man'!" (Shakespeare). Personification is sometimes known as *anthropomorphism*.

Phenomenological Criticism A method of literary criticism based on the philosophy of phenomenology that things have no existence outside human consciousness or awareness. Proponents of this theory believe that art is a process that takes place in the mind of the observer as he/she reflects on an object or event itself rather than a quality of the object. The German philosopher Edmund Husserl (1859-1938), who founded the phenomenological thought in the first part of the 20th century, gives importance to non-sensory data as valuable as long as they present themselves intuitively. Consequently, Phenomenology does not reject universals; and, in addition to analytic a priori statements it recognizes knowledge of the synthetic a priori, a proposition whose subject does not logically imply the predicate but one in which the truth is independent of experience, based on insight into essential relationships given within empirically. The Polish thinker Roman Ingarden is one of the first critics to incorporate this philosophy into literary theory. He argues that a literary work begins in the intentional act of its author's consciousness and that the reader receives it as an object and as his own consciousness. In this process of transfer of content from the author to the reader there are certain gaps that must be bridged by the reader. As a reader he must act as a 'co-creative' partner and resolve the ambiguities in the work. This form of criticism is often associated with the Geneva School. Other critics of the phenomenological school are George Poulet and Marcel Raymond. [Cf. consciousness criticism]

Ref: Pierre Thévenaz, *What is Phenomenology? And Other Essays,* Ed. James M Edie (1962). Robert Magliola, *Phenomenology and Literature: An Introduction* (1968). Wolfgang Iser, "The Reading Process: A Phenomenological Approach", *New Literary History* 3 (1972).

Picaresque Novel A variety of the novel form. In Spain, the novel about *pícaro*, rogue, was a recognized form and such English novels as Defoe's *The Fortunate Mistress* (1724) can be regarded as picaresque in the etymological sense. But the term has come to connote as much the episodic nature of the original species as the dynamic of roguery. Fielding's *Tom Jones,* whose hero is a bastard, amoral and nearly a gallows-meat, has been called picaresque, and *The Pickwick Papers* of Dickens, whose eponym is a respectable and even childishly ingenuous scholar, can be accommodated in the category.

The requirements for a picaresque novel are apparently length, loosely linked episodes almost complete in themselves, intrigue, fights, amorous adventures and such optional items as stories within the main narrative, songs, poems or moral homilies. Perhaps inevitably, with such a structure or lack of it, the driving force must come from a wild or roguish rejection of the settled bourgeois life, a desire for the open road, with adventures in inn bedrooms and meetings with questionable wanderers. In the modern period, Saul Bellow's *Adventures of Augie March* (1953) and Jack Kerouac's *Dharma Bums* (1959) have something of the right episodic, wandering, free, questing character. But in an age that lacks the unquestioning acceptance of traditional morality against which the old picaresque heroes played out their villainous lives, it is not easy to revive the *novela picaresca* as the anonymous author of *Lazarillo de Tormes* (1554) conceived it, or as such lesser Spanish writers of the beginning of the 17th century as Mateo Alemán, Vicente Espinel and Luis Vélez de Guevara developed it. Scholes and Kellogg think that the narrative in a picaresque could be turned outward to expose the weakness of society or it could be turned inward in a confessional mood to record the moral restoration of the narrator. *Huckleberry Finn* is remarkable in this respect; it blends both: it is a condemnation of corruption and moral decay of the society to which Huck is a witness and it is also a modest account of his moral growth in respect of his relation with Jim. In modern times, ever-decreasing social authority over individual, gradual liberalization of moral norms, availability of purchasable means of adventures, etc have almost closed and narrowed down the possibility of a traditional picaresque hero.

Ref: Alexander Augustine Parker, *Literature and the Delinquent: The Picaresque Novel in Spain and Europe* (1967). Robert Alter, *Rogue's Progress: Studies in the Picaresque Novel* (1965). Robert Scholes & Robert Kellogg, *The Nature of Narrative* (1966).

Plagiarism An unlawful practice of claiming someone else's written material as one's own. Plagiarism can take the form of direct word-for-word copying or the theft of the substance or idea from other's intellectual and/or artistic property. More prevalent in ancient times, plagiarism has been severely condemned in the distant past; and now the copyright laws have preventive measures against it. However, many great writers have often been allegedly charged for the offence; the persons being no less than such venerated artists as Herodotus, Aristophanes, Sophocles, Menander and the like. The borrowed materials, words and phrases, concepts and forms, once duly acknowledged, are not regarded as plagiarism. Milton believed that copying without improving was plagiarism. In our time, when on the one hand, electronic media have opened up vast resources for information and intellectual properties, and on the other, electronic measures have reduced the trouble of gathering them through just copy or cut-and-paste technique, the question of plagiarism has become a very threatening issue. Nowadays there are many paid and free software measures available that can be of some help in this regard. In spite of legal measures, the proliferation of information technology, however, has equally encouraged indiscriminate plagiarism.

Platonic Criticism A germinal form of literary criticism. Platonic criticism stresses an artistic work's extrinsic purpose or usefulness as an agent promoting and engineering social and moral upliftment rather than any intrinsic quality or value of the work itself. Platonic criticism takes as its starting point the ancient Greek philosopher Plato's (428/427-348/347 BCE) comments on art in his *Phaedrus, Ion* and *Republic.* In his dialogue he argued that imaginative literature leads people to believe in lies; shows both man and God in bad light, and is, therefore, useless. What we call *art*, in his view was a copy of a copy—an imitation of an imitation. This system of his metaphysics made poetry and fiction seem unimportant and inadequate. In an ideal state, therefore, the only imaginative literature permitted, according to Plato, would be that which served some good political purpose, such as inspiring soldiers with courage or honouring gods and great men. This concept of Plato has been one of the important influences on Western classical thought. Many, specially a group of puritans, have strictly followed Plato in thinking that imaginative literature must either be worthless or dangerous. However, Plato's student, Aristotle, did not agree with his master. His theory of catharsis in *Poetics* is an answer to Plato's charge against imaginative art. The controversy between the Platonic and the Aristotelian remains a living issue even today in many guises.

Ref: Jurgis Brakas, "Plato, Aristotle and the Third Man Argument", *Just the Arguments: 100 of the Most Important Arguments in*

Western Philosophy, Ed. Michael Bruce & S Barbone (2011).

Platonic Love A concept of love as envisaged by Greek Philosopher Plato. In his *Symposium* and *Phaedrus*, Plato has deliberated on the issue. Later Plotinus has further developed the idea and that continued for a long period until the medieval practice of courtly love displaced it. Although homosexual relationship has been referred to in some classical texts, it is the heterosexual love that was the main issue in Plato's discussions. Appreciation of purely physical beauty of a lover has been approved of, but a lover of beauty should strive for beauty of a more spiritual order. The worship of physical beauty is no more than the first step; then path is led to a higher kind of beauty and ultimately to the absolute beauty in and of God. The classical understanding of love, expressed in the Platonic concept of *eros*, was opposed by the biblical understanding of love, *agape*, in Christendom. Although erotic love has frequently been understood primarily as sexual desire and passion, its classical religious and philosophical meaning was the idealistic desire to acquire the highest spiritual and intellectual good. The word *Agape* was translated into Latin as *caritas* and thus appears in English as *charity*, and later *love*. Héroët Antoine, often known as La Maison-Neuve, Renaissance court poet whose works are representative of the amalgam of Platonism and Christian humanism produced the modern concept of Platonic love. Héroët imitated Plato's *Symposium* in explaining the mystery of the origin of love in his poem *L'Androgyne* (written 1536; published 1542). However, commonly mistaken notion about Platonic love is that it is a kind of asexual love, which is often termed as romantic love.

Ref: David Boloton, *Plato's Dialogue on Friendship* (1979). GRF Ferrari, "Platonic Love", *The Cambridge Companion to Plato,* Ed. Richard Kraut (1992). SJMC D'Arcy, *The Mind and the Heart of Love: Lion and Unicorn: A Study in Eros and Agape* (1956).

Plot An arrangement and interrelation of events in a story. In fiction and in drama, the structure of interrelated actions, consciously selected and arranged by the author, is called plot. It involves a considerably higher level of narrative organization than normally occurs in a story or fable. According to EM Forster a story is a "narrative of events arranged in their time-sequence," whereas a plot organizes the events according to a "sense of causality."

In the history of literary criticism, plot has undergone a variety of interpretations. In his seminal work, *Poetics*, Aristotle assigned primary importance to *mythos*, plot, and considered it the very soul of a tragedy. Later critics tended to reduce plot to a more mechanical function until in the Romantic era the term was theoretically degraded to an outline on which the content of fiction was held. Such outlines were popularly thought to exist apart from any particular work and to be reusable and interchangeable. They might be endowed with life by a particular author through his development of character, dialogue or some other elements.

In the 20th century there have been attempts to redefine it and some critics have even reverted to the position of Aristotle in giving it primary importance in fiction. These *Neo-Aristotelians* (known as Chicago School), following the leadership of the critic Ronald S Crane, have defined plot as the author's control of the reader's emotional responses—his arousal of the reader's interest and anxiety and the careful control of that anxiety over a period time. The Chicago School is frequently called Aristotelian, or *Neo-Aristotelian*, because of its debt to the critical writings of Aristotle, in particular to his method of analyzing the parts of a text in terms of their relative importance in producing the author's desired effect. This practical approach enabled the Chicago critics, as teachers, to emphasize the author's achievement in terms of his responses and solutions to specific artistic problems involved in the appreciation of a given text. The most complete expression of the group's critical approach is set forth in *Critics and Criticism,* edited by Ronald Crane and also in his study, *The Languages of Criticism and the Structure of Poetry* (1953). Wayne C Booth, a younger critic, made a brilliant application of the group's principles to fiction. This approach is only one of many attempts to restore plot to its former place of priority in fiction. In recent criticisms a plot or narrative structure has been seen as a tool for representing an ideology, or a discourse by which it either attempts at dominating the marginalized culture, or resisting the dominating one. [Cf. narrative]

Ref: EM Forster, *Aspects of the Novel* (1927). Foster-Harris, *The Basic Formulas of Fiction* (1960). Ronald Crane, Ed. *Critics and Criticism: Ancient and Modern* (1952). Wayne C Booth, *The Rhetoric of Fiction* (1961).

Poetic Drama A form of the dramatic art. A drama written fully or partly in verse necessarily may not be a poetic drama. This dramatic type, to be precise, is a merger of the poetic and the dramatic elements. The vehicle of poetry used in a poetic drama is not meant for any lyrical or decorative purpose. *Dr. Faustus* and *Hamlet,* for example, are perfect models of early English poetic drama. The vehicle, i.e. poetry and the subject matter, plot and character support one another to create a higher philosophical and artistic plane. In a poetic drama the elements should be poetically conceived and sustained. As Eliot says, poetic dramatist articulates the deeper passions of men. Besides, he emphasized, "...the craving for poetic drama is permanent in human nature."

In England, poetic drama had its glorious days during the Elizabethan period. The general environment of society and affluence of the English language inspired by a public craze for poetry, drama, amusement and proper patronizing of the dramatists together made the theatre almost a national enthusiasm. But the glory did not last for long and its decline was precipitated by the victory of the puritan fanaticism. The Neoclassical era was absolutely unfit for the genre; 19th century and part of the 20th were fully occupied with realistic plays. Ibsen, Bernard Shaw, Galsworthy took the stage with problem plays of real life drudgery. However, in the wilderness, JM Synge, WB Yeats and Sean O'Casey turned against the mainstream prosaic vogue. In tune with the aspiration of the Irish Renaissance, Synge successfully concentrated upon the unsophisticated Irish peasantry and their poetic folk language. Synge's *The*

Riders to the Sea and *The Play Boy of the Western World* enjoyed huge popularity and whose vitality and permanence of appeal remained unaffected by familiarity and decay of time. The attempt to find a contemporary idiom for verse drama did not really bear fruit until the 1930s, when such poets as TS Eliot and WH Auden began to use free verse. TS Eliot's arrival on the scene invigorated both the dramatic and the theoretical aspects of the art. He realized "no play should be written in verse for which prose is dramatically adequate." His verse-plays are concerned not with the outer, but with the inner emotional and psychic realities. Thus the core of his first play *Murder in the Cathedral* (1935) is the psychic struggle of the hero with the temptations offered to him, and that of *The Family Reunion* the psychological guilt-complex of Harry, the hero of the play; *The Cocktail Party* is a study in the awareness of personal inadequacies of married life in the modern context. In Britain there was a short-lived vogue for poetic drama in the years after World War II, when such plays as Christopher Fry's *The Lady's Not for Burning* (1949) almost in conventional setting created some ripple because the play was a delightful entertainment. Poetic drama, Eliot said, was possible in the 20th century, but, "it cannot be the work of one man or of one generation working together, but has to evolve by the small contributions of a number of people in succession, each contributing a little."

Ref: Glenda Leeming, *Poetic Drama* (1989). JC Trewin, *Verse Drama since 1800* (1956). Priscilla Thouless, *Modern Poetic Drama* (1934).

Poetic Justice An ideal righteousness distributed by the poet. The idea of poetic justice is as old as Aristotle. Although not dealt with discretely, his concepts of hamartia (fatal flaw) and *Nemesis* (personification of divine retribution) may indirectly refer to the idea of poetic justice. Thomas Rymer (1643-1713), English literary critic who introduced into England the principles of French formalist Neoclassism, coined the expression *poetic justice.* In the Neoclassical period Aristotle's *reasonableness* was replaced by *rationality* and his moral ambiguity by the mechanics of poetic justice. He demands that dramatic action be probable and reasonable and it instructs by moral precept and example and characters behave either as idealized types or as average representatives of their class. In terms of poetic justice Rymer's assumption is that a poem (tragedy also) is an autonomous world and it should be regulated by its own terms, principle and morality. The real world order cannot be applicable to poetry. Therefore the concept demands that allocation of reward or punishment at the end of a dramatic or narrative work must be proportionate with the virtue and vice attached to the characters. Miss Prism, in Oscar Wilde's play, *The Importance of Being Earnest* echoes almost a similar view: "The good ended happily, and the bad unhappily. That is what Fiction means."

Hegel's (1770-1831) emphasis on the correction of moral imbalances in tragedy is reminiscent of the poetic justice of the Neoclassicist theory. He sounds remarkably like Jean Racine (1639-1699) when he claims that, in the tragic dénouement, the necessity of all that is experienced by particular individuals is seen to be in complete accord with reason and is harmonized on a true ethical basis. For him, the final issue of tragedy is not the misfortune and suffering of the tragic antagonists but rather the satisfaction of spirit arising from reconciliation. In Schopenhauer (1788-1860), however, there is no question of a Hegelian struggle to achieve a more comprehensive good. There is rather the strife of will with itself, manifested by fate in the form of chance and error and by the tragic personages themselves. Schopenhauer rejects the idea of poetic justice since the demand for poetical justice, as he thinks, rests on entire misconception of the nature of tragedy, and, indeed, of the nature of the world itself. The true sense of tragedy is the deeper insight; it is not his individual sin that the hero atones for, but the original sin, i.e., the crime of existence itself.

Ref: Thomas Rymer, *The Tragedies of the Last Age* (1678). Richard Eldridge, "Poetic Justice", *Journal of Philosophy,* 94.8 (1997).

Poetic Licence/License A special privilege enjoyed by the poet. Shelley believed that poets were "the unacknowledged legislators of the world." As legislators, therefore, the poets, by convention, have been granted certain imaginative and linguistic prerogatives. This particular privilege the poets are entitled to enjoy and make use of in order to create a world far removed from the world of reality is called poetic licence. It is not that poets create a fantastic imaginative building for Kubla Khan in Xanadu ensuring "sunny pleasure dome with caves of ice" alone, Poetic licence also allows them to deviate from formal prose standards of factual accuracy, even syntax, grammar or pronunciation where these items may lend their hands to produce a more satisfying artefact, imaginative world or a particular metrical order. When Ben Jonson said, poetry "speaketh somewhat above a mortal mouth," he tried to legitimize the poet's freedom of deviation from the normal. However, poetry, too, attempts at a precision of its own with respect to what is not in the same sense measurable, nor even in the same sense accessible to scientific observation. That serves to distinguish one's sense that the artwork is always somewhat removed from what people are pleased to call the real world, operating instead, in Immanuel Kant's (1724-1804) shrewd formula, by exhibiting "purposefulness without purpose." To much the same point is what ST Coleridge remembers having learned from his schoolmaster: "I learnt from him, that Poetry, even that of the loftiest and, seemingly, that of the wildest odes, had a logic of its own, as severe as that of science; and more difficult, because more subtle, more complex, and dependent on more, and more fugitive causes."

Within his/her jurisdictions and conventions, the poet has the licence to use elision or syntactic inversion to regulate the meter of a line, *eye rhyme* or broken rhyme to fit a rhyme scheme, or unusual diction, illogical figures, or the imaginative liberties ranging from personification and pathetic fallacy to inaccuracies of chronology, geography, or natural sciences. And by virtue of all these, poetry become a separate class of object by its own right, recognizable as such. That poets have capacity to arouse futile and destructive emotions and create an illusion of reality by the use of poetic licence was a charge levelled by Plato and he proposed a ban on them. However, Aristotle rehabilitated the poets soon after.

Ref: PB Shelley, *A Defence of Poetry* (1840). Emily A Bernhard Jackson, *Liberty and Poetic Licence: New Essays on Byron*, Ed. Bernard Beatty, et al. (2008).

Poetry <Greek *poiesis*, making> A literary genre, perhaps the most ancient of all forms that evokes an imaginative understanding of experience through chosen words artistically arranged for its message, sound, rhyme and rhythm. In Edgar Allan Poe's words, "Poetry is the rhythmical creation of beauty in words." May be, poetry predates literacy since it has its origin in the ancient oral tradition. All forms of folk songs, epic poems, hymns of the Indian Vedas, Chinese Shijing, etc were all examples of well developed form of poetry. Poetry may be distinguished from prose in terms of form by its compactness, by its employment of meter, its sensitive vocabulary and its freedom of syntax. But this is certainly not all. Poetry can lift a sensitive reader to a higher plane of imaginative reality; an ordinary prose work does not strive for that. In poetry the use of language, by which this higher plane is achieved, is extraordinary and the problem of defining poetry is in fact the problem of defining its extraordinariness of language. The verse form does not guarantee poetic quality, as prose is not an obstacle for producing poetry. A great part of Milton's *Paradise Lost*, for example, although written in a grand verse form, has no poetry proper in it; whereas many good prose, for example the ending of Lawrence's *Sons and Lovers*, is more poetic than many poems. The characteristic emotional substance of poetry finds expression through a variety of techniques, from direct description to highly personalized symbolism. The use of figures of speech often modifies and expands the reader's imagination through implicit or explicit comparison. Broadly speaking, there are two types of poetry: lyric and narrative—they may exist separately or both the types may mingle together. Epic, lyric, ballad, sonnet, ode, Limerick, elegy, Armenian Poezia, Spanish Poezio, Chinese Shi, Japanese haiku, Tanka, Indian Ghazal, Persian Rubaiyat and Arabic Alshaer, etc are the most common forms of poetry in different languages. Homer, Horace, Virgil, Dante Alighieri, Petrarch, Friedrich Schiller, Charles Baudelaire, Rainer Maria Rilke, Geoffrey Chaucer, Shakespeare, John Milton, TS Eliot, Walt Whitman, Valmiki, Jalal ad-Din Rumi, Omar Khayyam, Rabindranath Tagore, Pablo Neruda, Alexander Pushkin, etc are all internationally recognized stalwarts in the field of poetry.

In the 19th and 20th centuries poetry has reacted more to the expressive possibilities of poetic idiom and convention in different traditions. Some have experimented with reviving or acclimatizing the subject matter and forms of other times and places while the avant-garde have experimented with informal manner, an approximation of the stress-free rhythms and colloquial words of common speech, and a self-consciously prosaic imagery. The classical form of poetry was strict about the form and its content. Gradually, with the change of social institutions, the poetic form began to be more flexible and finally during the modernist and post-modernist era any recognized form or structure apparently fell out of fashion. The free verse form replaced the well structured trends of versification almost all over the 'civilized' world. However, despite its apparent formlessness, modern poems continued to hold on to an invisible structure inherent in the poetic conception itself and in fact this is exactly where poetry can be distinguished from prose.

Poem and poetry, often used interchangeably, may not mean the same thing. The Oxford dictionary gives an idea of the difference between the two related items: A poem is "a piece of writing in which the expression of feelings and ideas is given intensity by particular attention to diction (sometimes involving rhyme), rhythm, and imagery." Poetry, on the other hand, is "literary work in which the expression of feelings and ideas is given intensity by the use of distinctive style and rhythm; poems collectively or as a genre of literature." However, what a reader can see as a text is a poem, not poetry. Poetry is the essential quality hidden within a poem one has to appreciate through careful reading. The Indian guru of poets, Nissim Ezekiel, tries to make a distinction between the two:

A poem is an episode, completed
In an hour or two, but poetry
Is something more. It is the why
The how, the what, the flow
From which a poem comes,
In which the savage and the singular,
The gentle, familiar,
Are all dissolved; the residue
Is what you read, as a poem, the rest
Flows and is poetry.

Ref: Cleanth Brooks, *The Well Wrought Urn: Studies in the Structure of Poetry* (1947). Ezra Pound, *ABC of Reading* (1951). FR Leavis, *New Bearings in English Poetry* (1932). James Longenbach, *Modern Poetry after Modernism* (1997). John Ciardi, *How Does a Poem Mean* (1959). John Strachan & Richard Terry, *Poetry: An Introduction* (2000). Matthew Arnold, "Preface" to *Poems* (1853).

Point of View A vantage point from where the story is told. Traditionally, the narrator of the epic and mock-epic alike acts as an intermediary between the characters and the reader; the method of Fielding is not very different from the method of Homer. In fiction the *third person* or *omniscient narrator* boldly imposes his own attitudes; he always assumes an all-know approach that tends to reduce the characters to puppets and the action to a predetermined course with an end implicit in the beginning. The *first person narrator's* point of view, on the other hand, is very involved and thereby lacks objectivity.

The problem of a satisfactory narrative point of view is, in fact, nearly insoluble. The careful exclusion of comment, the limitation of vocabulary, the paring of style to the bare minimum—these puritanical devices work well for an Ernest Hemingway, but not for a novelist who believes that, like poetry, his art should be able to draw on the richness of word play, allusion and symbol. For even the most experienced novelist, each new work represents a struggle with the unconquerable task of reconciling all-inclusion with self-exclusion. It is noteworthy that Miguel de Cervantes (1547-1616) in *Don Quixote* and Vladimir Nabokov (1899-1977) in *Lolita*, join hands across nearly four centuries in finding most satisfactory device of the fictitious editor who offers a story for which he disclaims responsibility. But this highly useful method presupposes in the true author, a scholarly or pedantic faculty not usually associated with novelists. [Cf. narratology, narrator]

Ref: Alicia Rasley, *The Power of Point of View: Make Your Story Come to Life* (2008). Leon Edel, *The Modern Psychological Novel* (1964), Orson Scott Card, *Characters and Viewpoint* (1988). Stuart Hall, "The Recovery of Ideology" (1982). WC Booth, *The Rhetoric of Fiction* (1961).

Polyphonic A vocal composition in music in which three or four voices follow each other around in a canon at the unison or octave. The idea is often used in literary discussions. The idea of the polyphonic is associated with Mikhail Bakhtin's theory of *heteroglossia*, (different tongues) which suggests that in most literary narrations multiple voices or dialogues interact and even compete with the principal voice. While discussing his dialogic texts, Bakhtin argues that all novels are to some degrees polyphonic in the sense multiplicity of voices, i.e. discourses, ideologies, etc, through such agencies as characters, narrators, disrupt the official or dominant or monologic voice. Polyphonic is also known as *polyvocalic*. However, Bakhtin's definition of the modern polyphonic, dialogic discourse is made up of the plurality of voices that negate the single perspective of knowledge. "Thus Bakhtin's major principles of the novel" as Guerin and others think, "include the freedom of the hero, special placement of the idea in the polyphonic design, and principles of linkage that shape the novel into a whole —including multiple voices, ambiguity, multiple genres, stylization, parody, the use of negatives, and the function of the double address of the word both to another word and to another speaker of words." [Cf. dialogic criticism]

Ref: MM Bakhtin, *Problems of Dostoevsky's Poetics* (1963).

Polysyndeton A Figure of Speech, the repetition of conjunctions in a series of coordinate words, phrases or clauses: I said, "Who killed him?" and he said, "I don't know who killed him but he's dead all right, and it was dark and there was water standing in the street and no lights and windows broke and boats all up in the town and trees blown down and everything all blown and I got a skiff and went out and found my boat where I had her inside Mango Bay and she was all right only she was full of water"—Hemingway. Common conjunctions that function in a lengthy sentence are often 'and', 'but', 'or', etc. The device often changes the rhythm or mood of the narrative employed and it may focus on some characteristic features of the speaker as well.

Pornography <Greek *porne*, prostitute + graphy, writing> A writing about prostitutes and treatment of any obscene subjects. An article or a book or some visual item available in video or CD form that describes or shows human nakedness or sexual acts in order to make consumers sexually excited, specially in a way that many others find offensive, come within the definition of pornography. However, the definition of pornography is always a controversial issue since it is strictly a culture and time based notion. This becomes clear when we look at the fact that many of the books and movies now the publishers and producers market, some fifty years ago would surely have been instantly banned. Again what pornography is in today's Bollywood film industry may not be treated as such in Hollywood. Incidentally many of Shakespeare's plays too were declared unfit for the student and *decent* family consumption. Reverend Thomas Bowdler pruned Shakespeare and published his *Family Shakespeare* (1815) for the youngsters and 'refined' people. His attempt since then is known as *Bowdlerization*. However, erotic writing or painting for that matter, which an orthodox person or a period in a culture may label pornographic, has always appeared in prose or verse of every age. In ancient time we have Ovid's *Ars Amatoria*. During the European Middle Ages pornography was widespread but held in low repute, finding expression mostly in riddles, common jokes, doggerels and satirical verses. A notable exception is *the Decameron* of Giovanni Boccaccio, whose stories are licentious without indirection. A principal theme of medieval pornography was the sexual license of monks and other clerics and their attendants. Then Shakespeare's *Venus and Adonis* and even later Vladimir Nabokov's *Lolita* and many more like Margaret of Angouleme's *Heptameron,* John Cleland's *Memoirs of a Woman of Pleasure; or, the Life of Fanny Hill,* the anonymous *My Secret Life,* DH Lawrence's *Lady Chatterley's Lover,* Nancy Friday's *Fantasies for Women*, etc have been bracketed as pornographies and now many of them are still being read, if not for the erotic elements, for some other reasons.

The development of photography and later motion picture contributed greatly to the proliferation of pornographic materials. Pornography in the 20th century is unprecedented in the variety of media used and the enormous volume of works produced. Since the Second World War, written pornography has been largely superseded by explicit visual representations of erotic behaviour that are considered lacking in redeeming artistic or social values. The Websites and the Internet in our time have given further momentum to pornography and the blue-film industry.

Ref: Nadine Strossen, *Defending Pornography: Free Speech, Sex, and the Fight for Women's Rights* (2000). Susan Griffin, *Pornography and Silence: Culture's Revenge against Nature* (1981).

Post-Aesthetic Movement An artistic response made by African-American writers to the Black Art/Aesthetic Movement of the late 1960s and early '70s. While the Black Arts movement failed to reach a specific end point except asserting Black identity, certain events and works decisively marked shifted directions. Alice Walker's *Meridian*, spoke critically and retrospectively of the movement. The major figures of the movement became less prominent in the late 1970s as new generation African-American voices began to emerge marking a clear modification of the former agenda. Writers since then have adopted a somewhat dissimilar tone in their work, with less emphasis placed on the difference between the Black and the White in America. In the opinions of Post-aesthetic authors, such as Toni Morrison, John Edgar Wideman and Kristin Hunter, African-Americans are portrayed as looking inward for answers to their own questions, rather than always looking to the outside world. Now the aim was to liberate contemporary interpretations of African-American experience from sensibilities that were formalized and institutionalized during earlier social paradigms and thus to inaugurate a new era in African-American art. As Tate puts it, the new Black movement of the 80s was "witnessing the maturation of a post-nationalist black arts movement, one more Afro centric and cosmopolitan than anything that's come before." The point is that the present generation of black artists depends mostly on cross-breeding aesthetic references and while they might be marginal to the black experience as it is expressed in rap, *Jet* and *The Cosby Show*, "they're not all mixed up over who they are and where they come from." Two well-known examples of works produced as part of the Post-aesthetic Movement are the Pulitzer Prize-winning novels *The Color Purple* by Alice Walker and *Beloved* by Toni Morrison. The new Black movements that began germinating in the 70s and blossomed in the 80s have been crucial in shaping the country over the next two decades. [Cf. black aesthetic movement]

Ref: George Tate, "Cult-Nats Meet Freaky-Deke", *Flyboy in the Buttermilk: Essays on Contemporary America* (1992). Lisa Gail Collins & Margo Natalie Crawford, Eds. *New Thoughts on the Black Arts Movement* (2006).

Postcolonialism/-ist A counter discourse as against the Eurocentric or colonial view of literary criticism. The postcolonial theory, popular since the last decade of the 20th century, offers an approach to literature that focuses on the study of cultural behaviour and expression in relation to the colonized world. Postcolonial criticism refers mainly to the analysis of literary works written in English by writers from the Third World cultures or erstwhile colonies then controlled by European powers—such as Indian writers during and after British colonial rule. It also refers to the analysis of literary works written about colonial cultures by writers from the colonizing country. Many of the analyses point out how writers from colonial powers sometimes misrepresent the colonized cultures by reflecting more their own values. Colonial writing, therefore, often acts as a backdrop highlighting the particular concerns of postcolonial writers. Leading critics who are mainly responsible for the development of the postcolonial theoretical concept are Edward Said, Gayatri Spivak and Homi Bhabha.

The idea of post-colonial literary theory, as Bill Ashcroft and others think, "...emerges from the inability of the European theory to deal adequately with the complexities and varied cultural provenances of post-colonial writing." Whatever it is, there is no doubt that "the concept of the post-colonial has been one of the most powerful means of re-examining the historical past and re-configuring our contemporary world-wide cultural concerns." In this sense postcolonialism has been theoretically operating on two important levels: [1] It is amassing the Third World counter discourses as against the huge intellectual material the West as a whole has manufactured to define the East for centuries; [2] It has prepared a mindset of the non-European to liberate themselves ideologically from foreign-made intellectual and cultural properties. As a literary critical tool, however, postcolonialism is often discussed, as Peter Barry thinks, under major four heads: [1] If the first step towards a postcolonial perspective is to reclaim one's own past, then the second is to begin to erode the colonialist ideology by which that past has been devalued. [2] Language, or appropriation of the English language, becomes the second major concern in post-colonial criticism. [3] The emphasis on identity as doubled, or hybrid, or unstable is the third characteristic of this approach. [4] The stress on cross-cultural interactions is something that too is included in this methodology.

Though certainly not all, some of the areas of discussion of postcolonial literature takes place within the context of postmodernism. The post-colonial movement is an international phenomenon and interesting aspect of this modern trend registers a clear shift in focus, away from British literature produced by the British authors to world literature in English. That is only half of the story; another half deals with how the British canonical literature is being discussed by the post-colonial and non-canonical standards all over the world. [Cf. hybridity, orientalism]

Ref: Bill Ashcroft, et al., *The Empire Writes Back: Theory and Practice in Post-Colonial Literature* (1990) & *The Post-Colonial Studies Reader* (1995). Edward Said, *Orientalism* (1978) & *Culture and Imperialism* (1994). Dennis Walder, *Literature and the Modern World* (1990). HK Bhabha *The Location of Culture* (1994). John McLeod, *Beginning Postcolonialism* (2010).

Postmodernism/-ist An artistic and cultural movement in recent times, specially the second half of the 20th century. A label generally given to cultural forms or any of the many trends detectable roughly since about the 1960s has both continued and contradicted the philosophy and practices of modern art and literature. Briefly stated, postmodernism seeks to describe the late 20th century art and culture. Postmodernists point to a world which is dominated by mass media, information technology and one which is driven by production and consumption on a global scale. The spectacular changes in the world of technology that has virtually reduced the area between the local and the global may be seen as the main drive behind this multi-faced movement. Although the fundamentals of modernism like existentialism and alienation continue, it replaces many of the modernistic key concepts—*form* by *antiform, design* by *chance, hierarchy* by *anarchy, text* by *intertext, root* by *rhizome* and *narrative* by *metanarrative*, etc. In its reaction against Modernist ideals such as *autotelic* art and the original masterpiece, postmodern writing and art emphasize devices such as pastiche and parody and the stylized technique of the antinovel and magic realism. Postmodernism has also led to a proliferation of critical theories, most notably deconstruction and its offshoots, and the breaking down of the distinction between *high* and *low* cultures. Jean-Francois Lyotard sees the movement as making the death of the grand master narratives that used to make sense of the world for us. Although the term first used to refer to architecture, it is now used to refer to all art forms and even philosophy and theology. Postmodernist writers include Alain Robbe-Grillet, Thomas Pynchon, Margaret Drabble, John Fowles, Adolfo Bioy-Casares, and Gabriel Garcia Marquez. The thinkers like Jean-Francois Lyotard and Fredric Jameson are responsible for preparing the basics of the philosophical school.

Frederic Jameson, a Marxist literary critic, argues that postmodernism is simply another myth. The idea that truth is relative to the person perceiving it is another belief system that people cling to. According to Jameson, postmodern literature is not myth-less at all; on the contrary, post-war English literature, and Western culture in general, is writhing with myths. Humans are still fascinated by the myths they believe in, just as much as their ancient Indian, Greek and Roman predecessors did. [Cf. potstructuralism]

Ref: Fredric Jameson, "Postmodernism or the Cultural Logic of Late Capitalism," *New Left Review* 146 (1984). Ihab Hassan, *The Postmodern Turn: Essays in Postmodern Theory and Culture* (1987). Jean Baudrillard, *Simulations* (1983). Jean-Francois Lyotard, *La Condition postmoderne: Rapport sur le savoir* (1979). Linda Hutcheon, *A Poetics of Postmodernism: History, Theory, Fiction* (1988).

Poststructuralism/-ist A philosophical focus on reading the written condition of texts. The concept can be extended to literary criticism as well. The theory raised heated arguments in France and many other countries in the late 1960s. Poststructuralism, although it stands apparently in opposition with structuralism, does not seem to have a unified philosophical theory of its own. Poststructuralism thus remains a blanket term and it draws on diverse writings such as the Deconstruction of Jacques Derrida (1930-2004), the late criticism of Roland Barthes, the New Historicism of Michel Foucault, the psychoanalytic revisionism of Jacques Lacan, the Feminist Criticism of Gayatri Spivak, and so on and so forth. The theory backs up postmodernism with its analysis of language and knowledge. Poststructuralism holds that language is not a transparent medium that connects one directly with a *truth* or *reality* outside it but rather a structure or code, whose parts derive their meaning from their contrast with one another and not from any connection with an outside world. In a way, whereas the structuralist was concerned with *structure*, the poststructuralist is concerned with *structuration*, or the way in which the text is constructed by criticism. This change goes hand in hand with idea that a critical work should not maintain any pretence to objectivity, but must become more honest about its own role in projecting structure on to the literary work so that the reading can be reflexive and self-conscious of its own textuality, its own values and motivations. They, in fact, "recognized the impossibility of describing a complete and coherent signifying system, since systems are always changing." Major scholars associated with the movement include Roland Barthes, Jacques Lacan, Julia Kristeva and Michel Foucault.

Ref: Jonathan Culler, *On Deconstruction: Theory and Criticism after Structuralism* (1983). Robert Young, Ed. *Untying the Text: A Post-structuralist Reader* (1981). Jacque Derrida, "Structure, Sign and Play in the Discourse of the Human Sciences" (1972). Ronald Barthes, "The Death of the Author" (1977).

Pre-Raphaelitism An artistic movement in the mid-19th century England highlighting the aesthetic traits and values existing before the time of Italian high Renaissance painter Raphael. Revitalizing the pre-Renaissance artistic qualities of religious symbolism, lavish pictorialism, natural sensuousness and drawing much on the love of beauty of the Romantics, the Pre-Raphaelites cultivated a sense of mystery, melancholy and beauty that influenced later writers associated with movements, such as Symbolism and Decadence. The novelties championed by the Pre-Raphaelites were soon condemned by the mainstream school. John Ruskin stood by the new school for support. Together with Ruskin the Pre-Raphaelites were influential in spreading a taste for medievalism to be found in several aspects of Victorian literature and arts. In the 1860s Pre-Raphaelitism underwent a second wave, associated mainly with the work of Edward Burne-Jones, which departed from the realism of early pre-Raphaelite works and moved instead toward myth and aestheticism. The major members of the group include Dante Gabriel Rossetti, Christina Rossetti, Algernon Swinburne and Walter Pater. Rossetti, although the least committed to the brotherhood, continued the name and changed its style. Robert Buchanan seems to be very critical about this movement. He rather pejoratively describes this group as *Fleshly School of Poetry* as these artists delighted in the sensuous aspects of art. [Cf. aestheticism]

Ref: A Staley & Newall, *Pre-Raphaelite Vision: Truth to Nature* (2004). David Latham, Ed. *Haunted Texts: Studies in Pre-Raphaelitism in Honour of William Fredeman* (2003). Graham Hough, *The Last Romantics* (1949). James Sambrook, Ed. *Pre-Raphaelitism: A Collection of Critical Essays* (1974).

Primitivism A trend in philosophy founded by Auguste Comte (1798-1857), who declares natural sciences to be the sole source of true knowledge and rejects the cognitive value of philosophical study. Many see the development as an inability to solve philosophical problems, which emerged from scientific developments and discoveries. Extension of this premise led to the belief that primitive peoples were nobler and less flawed than civilized peoples because they had not been subjected to the tainting influence of civilization. Accordingly, many of them borrowed from the non-Western and/or prehistoric sources. Literary works such as Aphra Behn's *Oroonoko: Or, The History of the Royal Slave,* Jean-Jacques Rousseau's *Julie ou la Nouvelle Heloise,* Oliver Goldsmith's *The Deserted Village,* the poems of Robert Burns, Herman Melville's stories *Typee, Omoo,* and *Mardi,* many poems of William Butler Yeats and Robert Frost and William Golding's novel *Lord of the Flies,* etc have unmistakable marks of this philosophical position. Many of the Romantics too may have sympathy toward the concept.

Ref: S Frances Connelly, *The Sleep of Reason: Primitivism in Modern European Art and Aesthetics, 1725-1907* (1999). Stanley Diamond, *In Search of the Primitive: A Critique of Civilization* (1974).

Problem Play A play dealing with a major contemporary social or specific political problem with a view to creating public opinion. The type of play is also referred to as *thesis play*. Henrik Ibsen's *A Doll's House* (1879) powerfully raises the issue of women's position in society and in the same way Bernard Shaw's *Mrs Warren's Profession* (1902) discusses prostitution, and Galsworthy's *Justice* (1910) is again another play that debates on the social and legal system of England. These plays indirectly advocate for the social role of literature. Social issues accordingly are the main ingredients of this type and, through debates among the characters with conflicting points of view on stage, the play aims at finding a realistic solution. While social debates in drama were as old as Aristotle, the problem play of the 19th century was notable for their clear objective to deal with the spectator facing the dilemmas experienced by the characters. These plays usually reject romantic plots in favour of holding up a mirror that reflects not simply what the audience wants to see but what the playwright sees in them. Often, a problem play will propose a solution to the problem that may not coincide with prevailing opinion. The term is also used to refer to certain Shakespeare plays, specially his dark comedies, like *Measure for Measure* and *All's Well that Ends Well.* The name 'problem play' is, however, controversial since every play has to deal with certain problems, either individual or social. Problem plays generally deal with contemporary social problems with a view to rectifying society and social practices. Hence, didactic element, without question, remains a major objective of the plays. [Cf. angry young men, kitchen-sink drama, sociological novel]

Ref: Chris Baldick, *The Modern Movement: 1910-1940* (2004). GB Shaw, "The Quintessence of Ibsenism" (1891).

Prolepsis A Figure of Speech, in which [1] an anticipation (generally predicative adjective or a participle) of the result of the action of a verb, and [2] the positioning of a relative clause before its antecedent are registered. In such a Miltonic expression as "Dash thee down,/ To the hazard of thy brain and shattered sides"—the word *shattered* is used proleptically since it is not until one is actually dashed down that his sides can be shattered. Another example—'If you tell the cops, you're a dead man'—the operation of an event is referred to a time that precedes the warning. It is also an evocation in a narrative of scenes or events that actually take place much later in the story. [Cf. flash-forward]

Promethean A mythical tale associated with the Titan, Prometheus. The adjective form, *Promethean*, is derived from *Prometheus*, meaning *like Prometheus* or *having qualities of Prometheus*. The Greek poet Hesiod had two legends: The first is that Zeus, the chief god, hid fire from man. Prometheus stole it and returned it to Earth. As punishment for mankind Zeus created the woman Pandora and she littered the human habitation with evils, hard work and disease, etc. In the second legend Zeus had Prometheus chained to a rock and sent an eagle to eat his liver, which constantly replenished itself. The second legend is incorporated into *Prometheus Bound* by Aeschylus, who made him not only the carrier of fire and civilization to the world but also man's preserver, giving him all the arts and sciences and the means of survival. Shelley again created his own myth in *Prometheus Unbound* (1820).

Prose <Latin for *straightforward*> A text written for literary purpose that attempts to copy the language of everyday speech. The word is first used in English in 1330 to mean ordinary language for writing. It is distinguished from poetry by its use of un-metered, un-rhymed schemes, but mostly depending on logically related sentences. Prose is usually grouped into *paragraphs* that form a cohesive whole, such as an essay or a novel. Three kinds of Literary Prose are: [1] Descriptive Prose, [2] Narrative Prose, [3] Expository Prose.

Literary prose started developing from the 9th century with the *Anglo-Saxon Chronicle* under King Alfred who attempted to revive learning in his kingdom and it later flourished under prolific Anglo-Saxon writers such as Aelfric and Wulfstan. However, the Norman Conquest was a big blow for further development of the language until writers like Langland (1332-1386) and Chaucer (1343-1400) came to the literary scene of England. Some developments, mostly religious writings, can be traced during the 15th century. Fisher and Cranmer popularized theological writings and historical prose was presented in *The Chronicle of England* by Capgrave (1393-1464). At this stage the invention of printing machine by Caxton (1422-1490) was a powerful push towards writing good English. Sir John Fisher (1459-1535) and Sir Thomas More's (1478-1535) contributions are indisputable. Sir More's major English prose works include *The Lyfe of John Picus, The Historie of Richard III.* Robert Burton (1577-1613) made notable contribution to prose writing in *The Anatomy of Melancholy*. It is an elaborate and discursive study of melancholy. A contemporary writer of some dignified, often euphuistic, prose style was John Lyly (1553-1606). Lyly's first prose work *Euphues, the Anatomy of Wit* (1579) made him a foremost figure of his day. Francis Bacon (1561-1626) is another stalwart prose writer of the time. Then comes John Milton (1608-74); he was not only a great poet but also a great writer of prose whose work is among the finest controversial writings in the language. John Bunyan (1628-1688) and John Dryden (1631-1700) are perhaps the next great prose writers who are still respectfully remembered in the literary circle. The 18th century was doubtlessly an age of prose and reason. Matthew Arnold calls it a century of prose and suggests that even the poetry of the period was prosaic or versified prose. English prose had its great time during the Neo-classical era and soon after. Regular periodicals and journals had a lot many controversial political and social subject matters to write. On both sides of the Thames, English prose found its prosperity in black and white. The proliferation of periodicals like *The Tatler* (1709), *The Spectator* (1711), *The Guardian* (1713), *The Englishman* (1713), *The Reader* (1714), and *The Plebeian* (1719), etc gave the English language real footing and respectability. Defoe, Steele, Addison, Samuel Johnson, Edward Gibbon, Edmund

Burke had for them almost ready made language to prove their worth in writing prose. During the Romantic period of English literature, poetry flourished enormously. But there was silent prose writers like Lamb and Jane Austen, Hazlitt, De Quincey who carried on the responsibility with dignity. Victorian era gave the final touch to the art of prose writing—Dickens, Hardy, George Eliot, Ruskin, Carlyle, Matthew Arnold, Walter Pater, Stevenson and a lot many writers made the language fit for the complexity of the 20th century. Recognized masters on the other side of the Atlantic include Mark Twain, Ernest Hemingway, William Faulkner, Washington Irving, Edgar Allan Poe and many more. Some nonfiction prose writers such as Walter Pater and novelists like DH Lawrence, Graham Swift and Toni Morrison have attempted *poetic prose*, i.e. prose with traditional poetic devices to such a great extent that the boundary between prose and poetry becomes less distinct. [Cf. poetry]

Ref: IA Gordon, *The Movement of English Prose* (1966). JAK Thomson, *Classical Influences on English Prose* (1956). JR Southerland, *On English Prose* (1957).

Prosody A technical study of versification, including meter, rhyme, accent and stanza patterns. To a lesser degree prosody deals with sound system in poetry also so far as functions of onomatopoeia, alliteration, rhythm and other poetic and technical issues contribute to the structure of sound in speech and verse. Whereas both rhetoric and prosody concentrate on stylistic structures of verbal or literary languages, prosody specializes mainly in the analysis of versification in terms of stress or accent pattern. [Cf. scansion]

Ref: Bose & Sterling, *Elements of English Rhetoric and Prosody* (1908). G Saintsbury, *A History of English Prosody* 3 Vols. (1906-10).

Prosopopeia <Greek for *making a face/ mask*> A device to dramatize putting on a mask. This term is sometimes used simply as another word for personification. More subtly it names the rhetorical representation of a dead or absent person, or even nonhuman being speaking or acting. In Spenser's *Prosopopia or Mother Hubberd's Tale* is presented the human disguising of the ape and the fox. [Cf. personification]

Pseudonym A false name or alias used by a writer. It is also called *nom de plume* or *pen name*. Several reasons may be responsible for assuming a pseudonym: [1] Socio-political realities may make it disadvantageous for the author to expose his/her identity. Many women writers had to write under pen names since there was a time when women writers were not taken seriously. Pornographers too take the advantage of this device. [2] An author might have a certain type of work associated with a certain name, so that different names are used for different kinds of works. [3] An author may choose a pen name that sounds more impressive or that garners more admiration than the real name. Taking a pseudonym is a universal practice and many famous authors are known by their pseudonyms and often not by their real names. Only some examples of those great authors who have permanently or temporarily adopted pseudonyms are: Lewis Carroll (Charles Lutwidge Dodgson), Currer Bell (Charlotte Bronte), Ellis Bell (Emily Bronte), George Eliot (Mary Ann Evans),

Q (Arthur Quiller Couch), Lemuel Gulliver (Jonathan Swift), Richard Saunders (Benjamin Franklin), Saki (HH Munro), George Orwell (Eric Blair), O Henry (William Sydney Porter), Linda Brent (Harriet Jacobs), AN Roquelaure (Ann Rice), Mark Twain (Samuel Clemens), John Sedges (Pearl S Buck), Victoria Lucas (Sylvia Plath), Voltaire (Francois-Marie Arouet), Novalis (Friedrich von Hardenberg), Javier Miranda & Martin Sacastru (Adolfo Bioy-Casares), Robert Rich (Dalton Trumbo), Richard Bachman (Stephen King), AE (George William Russel), Rolf Boldrewood (Thomas Alexander Browne), Nikolai Arzhak (Yuli Markovich Daniel), Pablo Neruda (Jose del Carmen Reys) and the like. Among the Indian writers who adopted such names, Bhanu Singha (Rabindranath Tagore), Chanakya (Jawaharlal Nehru), Ghalib (Mirza Asadulla Baig Khan) and Munshi Premchand (Dhanpat Rai) are quite well known to the world of literature.

Psychoanalytic Criticism A form of criticism based on Freud's theory of psychoanalysis. Freud divided the human psyche into three divisions: [1] *the id*, the unconscious reservoir of instinctual and libidinal forces; [2] *the superego*, the moral censor that internalizes the "thou shalt not's" of a given social order; and [3] *the ego*, the conscious self that tries to mediate between the conflicting demands of *id* and *superego* through accommodation, repression, or sublimation. Despite the defense mechanisms of repression and sublimation, the *ego* is always in a state of conflict.

From Freud's position, literature is seen as the wish fulfilment or fantasy indulgence of desires denied by reality or prohibited by moral codes. These unconscious libidinal desires find symbolic expression in art as in dreams. Art is sublimation, the translation of instinctual desires into higher aims. Thus the goal of psychoanalytic criticism is to expose the latent content of the work that underlies and determines its visible content. A fusion of unconscious desires and a substitution of the socially tolerable for the socially undesirable are the two major resources of symbolism. Freud's impact on the criticism and theory of literature has been enormous. Harold Bloom uses it as an analogy for the relationship between a strong poet and his literary predecessors. Jacques Lacan develops a linguistic model of Freud, arguing, the "unconscious is structured like a language." Norman N Holland applies this concept to reader-response criticism. The Feminists deconstruct Freud's patriarchal assumptions. Moreover, *psychobiography*, that uses data from the author's real life and the fictional events produced in his works, is a product of psychoanalytic theory. The study of literary symbolism is greatly influenced by Freudian principles.

Ref: Griselda Pollock, *Psychoanalysis and the Image* (2006). Harold Bloom, *A Map of Misreading* (1975). Elizabeth Wright, *Psychoanalytic Criticism: Theory in Practice* (1984). Joseph H Smith, Ed. *The Literary Freud: Mechanism of Defence and the Poetic Will* (1980).

Pulp Fiction A form of novel written for the mass market and intended to be 'a good read'—often exciting, titillating, thrilling. Historically they have always been very popular; but critically sneered at as being of sub-literary quality. The earliest ones were the *dime novels* of the 19th century, printed on newsprint (hence pulp fiction) and sold for ten cents. *Westerns*, stories of adventure, even Horatio Alger novels, etc are considered pulp fiction.

Pun/Paronomasia A Figure of Speech, which is, in fact, a linguistic play with similar sounding words. It can often be an etymological wordplay also: "Thou art Peter (Greek *petros*), and upon this rock (Greek *petra*) I shall build my church" (Matthew 16). It can also be a play with a word that has more than one meaning: "*Grave men*, near death, who see with blinding sight" (Dylan Thomas), or, "If a woman loses her husband, she pines *for a second*. Since Pun involves ambiguity invoking two or more meanings, the effect it produces is often comic. An example of a *homophonic pun* is—"He has no right to write about a rite". *Homographic pun,* on the other hand, are spelt and/ or pronounced almost similarly but they mean different ideas—"The light that lies/ In women's eyes… / And lies and lies and lies."

Q

Quantitative Verse A verse written on the Greek and Latin models of alteration of long and short syllables for a rhythmic structure, rather than stressed and unstressed syllables. It is a kind of verse whose meter is based on *quantity*, i.e. the relative time it takes to pronounce a syllable. As English tends to be an accentual language, i.e. one is prone to use stress rather than length of sounds to convey meaning, the writing of English quantitative verse has proved neither very easy nor very rewarding. However poets like Spenser, Coleridge and Tennyson have experimented with this form of verse pattern and abandoned it finally.

Quatrain <*Quatre*, four> A stanza containing four lines. Often it may refer to an entire poem consisting of only four lines. For example, many of William Blake's poems are in quatrains. The following quatrain of TE Hulme is itself a complete poem, "Above the Dock":

Above the quiet dock in midnight,
Tangled in the tall mast's corded height,
Hangs the moon. What seemed so far away
Is but a child's balloon forgotten after play.

So are Edward Fitzgerald's stanzas translated from the *Rubaiyat of Omar Khayyam*:

Ah, Love! Could thou and I with Fate conspire
To grasp this sorry Scheme of Things entire,
Would not we shatter it to bits—and then
Re-mould it nearer to the Heart's Desire!

Usually no particular rhyme scheme or meter is recommended for quatrains as the term refers more to the number of lines in a stanza than any content or genre. In the above stanza, Fitzgerald follows a-a-b-a rhyme scheme. It could be a-a-b-b, or say, a-b-a-b, etc. A Shakespearean sonnet normally has three quatrains followed by a couplet, the rhyme scheme being: a-b-a-b / c-d-c-d / e-f-e-f / g-g. A stanza of three verse lines connected by rhyme is called *tercet*.

R

Rasa A Sanskrit word, meaning 'taste,' 'flavour' and 'juice' etc. In Indian poetics it happens to be one of the most frequently used terms and it has a technical meaning that refers to artistic refinement of such well-known dominant emotions, as the amorous, the ludicrous, the pathetic, the fearful, etc. The explication of the *rasa* theory is invariably attributed to Bharata (c. 5th century), a sage, who was an authority on Indian dramatic theory. Later rhetorician and philosopher Abhinavagupta (c. 1000 CE) applied the theory to dramatic art and poetry. While discussing Bharata's *Natyasastra*, PV Kane gives his exposition of the rasa theory or rasa-*sutra* as: "The permanent or dominant moods that may be aroused by a dramatic representation and brought to a state of pleasurable relish." According to Sanskrit aesthetics the *bhavas* (emotions) are eight in number: Rati (love), Hasya (laughter), Soka (melancholy), Krodha (anger), Utsaha (energy), Bhaya (fear), Jugupsa (repugnance) and Vismaya (wonder). The artistic employment of these *sthayi-bhavas* (dominant emotions) by an artist and the resultant aesthetic satisfaction derived by the spectator is called rasa. These rasas comprise the components of aesthetic experience. Bharata has tried to explain this process aphoristically: Rasa or aesthetic pleasure manifests itself when the *sthayi-bhava* (dominant emotion) of reader or spectator is correlated with [1] excitant agent, [2] ensuant response, and [3] transitory feelings—as all the three accumulated as one. However, it was believed that the power to appreciate rasa was a reward for doing something meritorious in some previous existence.

It may be noted here that the theory of rasa, as conceived by the ancient Indian aestheticians had been associated with a medicinal discipline, *Ayurveda*, also. However, the term has direct association with preparation of food and eating. The way health needs good food, mind too needs emotional nourishment. This view is in perfect tune with the philosophical trends in ancient India that insisted on *suddhi*, i.e. purification of the body and heart, as essential to all mortal culture. Indian rasa theory, thus, comes close to art therapeutics and Aristotelian theory of catharsis as well. [Cf. alamkara]

Ref: PV Kane, *History of Sanskrit Poetics* (1951). RK Sen, *Aesthetic Enjoyment: Its Background in Philosophy and Medicine* (1966). Satya Dev Choudhury, *Glimpses of*

Indian Poetics (2002). SN Das Gupta, *History of Sanskrit Literature* (1947).

Rastafarianism A concept originated from *Ras* (meaning *chief*), the title of an Ethiopian lord or prince, and *Tafari,* family name of the emperor. The concept developed in Jamaica which believed Ethiopia to be the ultimate home of all black people and its emperor Haile Selassie to be divine. The coinage emerged during the 1930s as a counter discourse as against the prevailing cultural modes in the Caribbean, particularly Jamaican societies as revealed through the beliefs and languages used by the rastafarianists. Rastafari is not a highly organized philosophical school; it is at best a movement and a creed. The movement encompasses themes such as the spiritual use of 'cannabis' and the rejection of western values. It also proclaims Africa as the original birthplace of humankind, and it encompasses various Afro-centric social and political aspirations. In "Wings of a Dove" Brathwaite has used the counter language of the Rastas as an inextricable element of his poetic diction.

Reader-Response Criticism A form of literary criticism that shifts the focus to the reader from the author. It offers a methodical inspection of the aspects of a text that stimulate, shape and guide a reader's response. The reader becomes a producer rather than a consumer of meanings. Critics of this school are not after a *correct* reading of the text or what the author presumably intended; instead, they are interested in the reader's individual experience with the text. Thus, there is no single definitive reading of a work, because readers create rather than discover absolute meanings in a text. However, this approach is not a rationale for mistaken or bizarre readings, but an exploration of the possibilities for plurality of readings. Reader-response criticism, however, does not have any specific theoretical premise. It can range from the phenomenological theories of Wolfgang Iser and Roman Ingarden (who argue that though the author's intended acts impose restrictions, the reader fills in the gaps) to the relativistic analysis of Stanley Fish, who argues that the reader creates the text. The theory, in short has two-fold approaches: [1] determine author's intent, taking into account literary translation as well as the likely influences on author's viewpoint, such as time period, race and gender; and [2] determine how it has attuned the reader, taking into account the reader's own perspective, including biases revolving around his/her age, gender and socio-political viewpoints.

Ref: Jane Tompkins, Ed. *Reader Response Criticism; Essays on Audience and Interpretation* (1980). Steven Mailloux, "Reader-Response Criticism"? *Genre* 10 (1977). Stanley Fish, "Interpreting the *Variorum*" (1976). Wolfgang Iser, "Indeterminacy and the Reader Response" (1971).

Realism An artistic approach to literature and arts that aspires accurate, detailed, unembellished depiction of nature and contemporary life. Realism rejects imaginative excesses in favour of a close observation of outward reality. In the visual arts realism can be found in ancient Hellenistic Greek sculptures accurately giving shapes to competent athletes and decrepit old women.

Realism coincided with Victorianism, yet it was a distinct collection of aesthetic principles in its own right. The realist novel was heavily informed by journalistic techniques, such as objectivity and fidelity to the facts of the matter. In literature, a conscious program of literary realism did not appear until the French journalist Champfleury, who popularized Courbet's painting style, transferred the latter's theories to literature in *Le Réalisme* (1857). In this decisive manifesto he emphasized that the hero of a novel should be an ordinary man rather than an exceptional figure. In the same year Gustave Flaubert's novel *Madame Bovary*, which attempted an implacably objective portrait of the bourgeois mind, with its scrutiny of every psychological nuance of an unhappy middleclass woman was both the masterpiece of realism and the work that established the movement on the European scene. Flaubert's *L'Éducation sentimentale* (1870), with its presentation of a vast panorama of France under Louis-Philippe, furthered the same goal. The 19th century realism is closely connected to the development of modern drama also which is said to have begun in the 1860s onwards with the work of Henrik Ibsen. Ibsen's realistic drama in prose has been enormously influential and the creed entered the mainstream European literature during this time. Its emphasis on detachment, objectivity and accurate observation, its lucid but restrained criticism of social environment, mores and the humane understanding that underlay its moral judgments became an integral part of the modern drama and novel. The novel, however, witnessed its maximum height of development during this time. The works of the 18th century English novelists Daniel Defoe, Henry Fielding and Tobias Smollett, much before, had already paved the way. Later Charles Dickens, Anthony Trollope and George Eliot in England, Ivan Turgenev, Leo Tolstoy and Fyodor Dostoyevsky in Russia, William Dean Howells in the United States; Gottfried Keller and the early Thomas Mann in Germany—all incorporated realist elements in their novels. A significant offshoot of literary realism was naturalism, a late 19th and early 20th century movement that aimed at an even more faithful and unselective representation of reality. Many realists, such as Virginia Woolf, turned from detailing the external accuracy to depict the internal detail, the thorough process of human mind and consciousness, giving another term, an offshoot of realism, *psychological realism*. [Cf. magic realism, and socialist realism]

Ref: Christine Baron & M Engel, Eds. *Realism/Anti-Realism in 20th-Century Literature* (2010). CP Snow, *The Realists: Portraits of Eight Novelists* (1968). Jerome Meckier, *Hidden Rivalries in Victorian Fiction: Dickens, Realism, and Revaluation* (1987). John Heilpern, *John Osborne: The Many Lives of the Angry Young Man* (2007). Raymond Williams, *Keywords: A Vocabulary of Culture and Society* (1976).

Reformation A religious movement in the 16th century Europe. The crucial concern of the movement, led by Martin Luther (1483-1546), was the reformation of the theological doctrines and institutions of the Christian Church. The late medieval Catholic Church, specially the papal office had become deeply involved in the political life and led to the increasing power of the Church and also deviation from its former spiritual creed. Corruptions such as the sale of indulgence deteriorated the spiritual authority of the church. The process of reform within the medieval church had started even before Martin Luther openly posted his Ninety-five Theses on the door of the Castle Church, Wittenberg, on October 31, 1517—the eve of All Saints' Day—the date traditionally believed to be the beginning of the Reformation. Martin Luther attacked corruption in the church and went to the theological root of the problem. In his Ninety-five Theses, he attacked the indulgence system, insisting that the pope had no authority over purgatory and that the doctrine of the merits of the saints had no foundation in the gospel. In 1521, Luther was tried and was eventually excommunicated. This gave birth to internal reform movement leading to the birth of Protestantism.

The spirit of Reformation spread to other European countries soon. In England the roots of Reformation were more political than religious. Henry VIII rejected papal overlordship and established the Anglican Church with the king as the supreme head. Henry's reformation of the church was felt in the growing awareness of the English language and literature, which included the preparation of The Book of Common Prayer in the English language. Literature, in general, reflected the political and religious inclinations of the elite close to political power. Much of the rightfully approved culture of Renaissance England can now be seen as a calculated attempt to create an illusion of conformity and national unity as a means of discountenancing internal and external oppositions. During the Reformations of the 16th and 17th centuries, the Protestants generally followed the critical views expressed by Renaissance humanists, but for different reasons. They saw classical antiquity as a golden time, not only because of the Latin literature, but because it was the early beginnings of Christianity. From the literary point of view, "the most striking feature of the reformation is its connection with the English Bible, and that Bible itself is its greatest monument" as assessed in the *Cambridge History of English and American Literature*. In the process of conflict "the history of the English Bible itself becomes mingled, strangely and sadly, with the history of religious strife. Beyond and above all that, however, its literary influence shows itself as uniquely as its power in giving an inspiration for life."

Ref: Patrick Collinson, *The Reformation: A History* (2006). Owen Chadwick, *The Reformation* (1964). "Renascence and Reformation", *The Cambridge History of English and American Literature,* Vol. III (1907–21).

Refrain A phrase, line or group of lines, either exact or with variation, repeated at regular intervals throughout a poem, generally at the end of each stanza. Refrains appear in literatures as varied as ancient Egyptian, Hebrew, Greek and Latin verses, popular ballads, and Renaissance and Romantic lyrics. Three common refrains are: the [1] *choric song*, recited by more than one person; [2] the *burden*, in which a whole stanza is repeated; and [3] the *repetend*, in which the words are repeated erratically throughout the poem. Alfred Tennyson's poem, "The Charge for the Light Brigade" exploits two words "six hundred" as a repetend at the end of each stanza. His poem "The Lady of Shalott" too makes use of refrain of the title itself. In "Itylus," Algernon Swinburne too has refrain of two alliterative words in the beginning of each stanza—*sister* and *swallow*.

Renaissance A period in European history that marks the end of the Medieval Period or the Dark Ages and proclaims "rebirth" through an intellectual and cultural movement that has far-reaching consequence transcending national boundaries in Europe. The period often seen as a transitional period that bridges between the end of the Middle Ages and the beginning of the Modern. Although it began in Italy in the late 14th century, broadly seen, it is found as spanning the 14th, 15th and 16th centuries. The Renaissance spirit did not reach Great Britain, for example, until around the 1480s and flourished only during 1485-1603, to be precise. The Renaissance saw an awakening in almost every sphere of human activity, especially science, philosophy and the arts. The period is best defined by the emergence of a general philosophy that emphasized the importance of the intellect, the individual and secular affairs. It is often seen more as a distinct historical epoch and cultural category than are most other historical and literary periods. The marked shift of interest from God to man and faith to science gives the period and the movement a distinctive status in the field of intellectual history of the world. The movement, therefore, contrasts strongly with the medieval worldview characterized by the leading concerns of faith, the socio-religious and spiritual deliverance. Prominent writers and artists during the Renaissance include Petrarch, Raphael, Michelangelo, Niccolò Machiavelli and Baldassare Castiglione, Miguel de Cervantes and Lope de Vega, Jean Froissart and Francois Rabelais, Desiderius Erasmus and others.

Sir Thomas More, Sir Philip Sidney, Bacon and Shakespeare are the best known Renaissance scholars in England. The leading forms of English Renaissance writing were poetry and drama. The basic varieties of poems that one finds in the 16th century England were the lyric, the elegy, the tragedy and some pastoral form of lyric poetry. Poetry of the period was invariably musical and actually meant to be accompanied by musical instruments. In any case, English Renaissance poetry was able to encapsulate beauty and truth in words. However, English poetry of the period was pretentious, repetitious to some extent. One attribute that tended to set English letters apart from the continent was the willingness to intermix different genres into a sort of experimental hodgepodge. This pastiche style is exemplified in Edmund Spenser's *Faerie Queen*, a long poem which mingled elements of romance, tragedy, epic and pastoral into an entertaining and still cohesive hold-all. "In the area of drama, no one matched William Shakespeare in terms of variety, profundity and exquisite use of language. His subject matter ran the gamut, from classical Greco-Roman stories to contemporary tales of unrequited love. Shakespeare is known for his ability to shift between comedy and tragedy, from complex character study to light-hearted farce. He is likewise highly regarded for the exquisite formal structure which all of his plays demonstrate. This goes beyond just acts and scenes, but encompasses the emotional and psychological arc of the action in the drama. More than anyone else, he elevated the English language to a level of sumptuousness that previous generations would not have thought possible." Beside him those who played the second fiddle were Christopher Marlowe and Ben Jonson.

In short, the impacts of the Renaissance on English Literature, thus, could be easily felt in the shift of emphasis to humanism and secular outlook in the writings of the era. The church and the state seemed to have lost much of their hold on the intellectual community. Accordingly, the growth of individuality found its expression in love poems, blank verses and the revival of classical texts.

Ref: CS Lewis, *English Literature in the 16th Century* (1954). HO Taylor, *Thought and Expression in the 16th Century* (1920). Michael Hattaway, Ed. *A Companion to English Renaissance Literature and Culture* (2000). Siobhan Keenan, *Renaissance Literature* (2008). Stephen Greenblatt, Ed. *Representing the English Renaissance* (1988). Sukanta Chaudhury, Ed. "Introduction", *An Anthology of Elizabethan Poetry* (1992). WK Ferguson, *The Renaissance in Historical Thought* (1948).

Representation An act of copying an object, action or event. This means an act of representation refers to how an individual, his action or historical events are portrayed in artistic forms. It involves the depiction and also ethical concern in visual arts and literature. In most cases, representation is associated with aesthetics and semiotics. The problem of imitation and representation was first raised by Plato and Aristotle in terms of ethics and poetics and now the concept has permeated to political and cultural domains. To be precise, in postcolonial criticism the concept has acquired extra dimensions—it has been linked to issues of biasness as any form of representation is bound to be coloured by the observer's cultural position that determines his notion and prejudice, no matter the artist is conscious or not about them. In that case a subject is seen as a simplified type rather than a complex human being and the process inevitably produces stereotypes. Since it does not recognize individuality, it practically dehumanizes him and creates a sense of the other. From an advantageous position, the leading culture, thus, attempts to restrict and modify representation to promote a certain discourse, or a set of ideology, thought patterns and values. Ferdinand de Saussure's study of semiotics examines the signs and types of representation that human beings use to express feelings, ideas, thoughts and ideologies. Although semiotics is often used in the form of textual analysis, it also involves the study of representation and its process. According to Saussure, two things are fundamental in the study of signs involving representation: [1] *Signified*, a mental cultural construct, and [2] *Signifier*, the verbal manifestation—i.e. the sequence of letters, sounds and linguistic realization. In short, therefore, no form of representation or field of enquiry is ever completely neutral, but is shaped by the institution which supports it. In a colonial context this is particularly relevant because representation of the colonized was entwined with a sense of authority on the part of the writer and a sense of degradation on the part of the colonized. However, postcolonial discourse often attempts to reverse the process.

Ref: F Lentricchia & T McLaughlin, Eds. *Critical Terms for Literary Study* (1990). Peter Barry, *Beginning Theory: An Introduction to Literary and Cultural Theory* (2002). S Hall, Ed. *Cultural Representations and Signifying Practice* (1997).

Revenge Tragedy/Tragedy of Blood A dramatic variety popular during the Elizabethan Age, in which the protagonist, directed by the ghost of his murdered father or son, inflicts retaliation upon a powerful villain as a mission of his life. Notable features of the revenge tragedy include violence, weird criminal acts, intrigue, madness, a hesitant protagonist, and the use of soliloquy. Thomas Kyd's *Spanish Tragedy* (1594) is the first and the trendsetter example of revenge tragedy in English and William Shakespeare's *Hamlet* is perhaps still the best artistic production of this genre. Extreme examples of revenge tragedy, such as John Webster's *The Duchess of Malfi,* are labelled as tragedies of blood. Although modelled loosely on the *Senecan tragedy* tradition, insofar as they depict violence, ruthlessness, ghost scenes, etc, the revenge tragedies are more horrifying in the sense that actual murders and horrendous events are brought on the stage for the spectator to witness. In Seneca they are only reported. One of the big conflicts of the revenge tragedy that takes place is between private revenge versus divine or public revenge. In his essay, 'Of Revenge,' Bacon observes that "the first wrong, it doth but offend the law; but the revenge of that wrong, putteth the Law out of Office. Certainly, in taking revenge, a man is but even with his Enemy. But in passing it over, he is Superior: For it is a prince's part to Pardon."

Ref: Fredson Bowers, *Elizabethan Revenge Tragedy: 1587-1642* (1959). Linda Woodbridge, *English Revenge Drama* (2010).

Rhetoric <Greek *rhētorikós*, oratorical> A style of language and science of persuasion. In other words, it is the art of oratory. The most precise definition of rhetoric incidentally comes from Aristotle, who considers it a counterpart of both logic and politics and defines it as "the faculty of observing in any given case the available means of persuasion". In the middle ages, in Europe specially, rhetoric was one of the important liberal arts and was studied as a separate discipline along with grammar and logic. The ancient Greeks exceedingly valued public political participation. Rhetoric, therefore, emerged as a crucial tool to influence politics. Consequently, rhetoric remains associated with its political origins. Even today rhetoric comprises all the techniques used to sway an audience or reader, notably the figures of speech, rhythm, diction or idiolect, temporal and logical structure, etc. [Cf. prosody]

Ref: Bose & Sterling, *Elements of English Rhetoric and Prosody* (1908). IA Richards, *The Philosophy of Rhetoric* (1936). James Jasinski, *Sourcebook on Rhetoric* (2001).

Rhetorical Question A question that does not require a formal answer. In fact the answer is very much embedded in the question itself in a particular context in which the question is put. Such questions only add to the effectiveness of a speech. In *The Merchant of Venice*, for example, when Shylock utters, "What judgment shall I dread, doing no wrong?"—he emphatically drives home his courage employing a rhetorical question before the Duke. His meaning is more than clear—he is *not* afraid of any judgment. Public speakers frequently resort to this device. A rhetorical question is, therefore, asked to produce a dramatic effect on an obvious answer than getting the answer itself.

Rhyme/Rime An artistic game with sound in verse lines. It is a conventional trend in English versification to end the final syllable of a line with a sound that corresponds with that of another line within the stanza and thus the endings of the two lines echo each another: "Up from the meadows rich with corn, / Clear in the cool September morn." Here *corn* and *morn* rhyme together. It is an example of *perfect rhyme*. An *imperfect rhyme* is less identical in sound: "Fair as a garden of the Lord/ To the eyes of the famished rebel horde." Poets exploit rhyme to produce sounds appealing to the reader's senses and to form a particular rhyme scheme. *End rhyme* (used at the end of a line to echo the end of another line, as shown above) is the most common, but *internal, interior* or *leonine rhyme* is frequently used as occasional ornaments in a poem, e.g. Shakespeare's "Hark; hark! the lark at heaven's gate sings."

Three kinds of rhymes are recognized by purists as true rhymes: *masculine rhyme* (two words end with the same vowel-consonant combination: hand/ land), *feminine rhyme* or *double rhyme* (two syllables rhyme: profession/ confession) and *trisyllabic rhyme* (three syllables rhyme: patinate/latinate). There is again *eye rhyme*, in which syllables are identical in spelling but are pronounced differently (but/put), and *pararhyme* (two syllables have different vowel sounds but identical penultimate and final consonantal groupings (grand/grind). *Feminine pararhyme* has two forms, one in which both vowel sounds differ, and one in which only one does (ran in/run on; blindness/blandness). *Weakened, or unaccented rhyme* occurs when the relevant syllable of the rhyming word is unstressed (lend/brightened). In *half rhyme*, words contain similar sounds but do not rhyme exactly. Half rhyme typically results from consonance or assonance, similarities in consonant and vowel sounds, respectively. Assonance was regularly used in French poetry until the 13th century, when end rhyme replaced it. It continues to be important in the poetic technique of Romance languages but performs only a subsidiary function in English verse.

Rhyme seems to have developed in the Western poetry as a combination of earlier techniques of end consonance, end assonance, and alliteration. It is found only occasionally in classical Greek and Latin poetry; but more frequently in medieval religious Latin verse and in songs, especially those of the Roman Catholic liturgy. In England Shakespeare interspersed rhymed couplets into the blank verse of his dramas; Milton disapproved of rhyme, but Samuel Johnson favoured it. In the 20th century, although many advocates of free verse ignore rhyme, others have continued to experiment with various rhyme schemes.

Rhyme Royal A seven-line stanza of *iambic pentameter* with the rhyme scheme a-b-a-b-b / c-c. It was named after King James I of Scotland (1394-

1437) who used this form in his dream vision, *The Kingis Quair*. Geoffrey Chaucer is, however, the first major English poet to introduce the pattern in his *Troilus and Criseyde*. Rhyme Royal has other variations: it can be either as a *tercet* followed by two couplets—a-b-a / b-b / c-c or a quatrain and a *tercet*—a-b-a-b / b-c-c. In the Middle Ages this pattern had extensive use in narrative poems.

Rhyme Scheme A pattern made by placing words which end in similar sounds at the ends of lines. To mark out a rhyme scheme, letters, starting with A, are assigned to the first occurrence of a sound, that of the first line is always A, and the first occurrence of the next sound is always B, and so on. For example, the pattern of the Shakespearean sonnet is three quatrains rhyming a-b-a-b / c-d-c-d / e-f-e-f, followed by a closing couplet rhyming g-g. This way the rhyme scheme of a Swinburne stanza (in "Itylus") looks like a-b-c / a-b-c:

Swallow, my sister, O sister swallow,
How can thine heart be full of the spring?
A thousand summers are over and dead.
What hast thou found in the spring to follow?
What hast thou found I thine heart to sing?
What will thou do when the summer is shed?

Here the first line has the rhyming partnership with fourth line, the second line with the fifth, and the third with the sixth. [Cf. rhyme royal]

Ref: J Walker, *Walker's Rhyming Dictionary of the English Language* (1936). John Hollander, *Rhyme's Reason: A Guide to English Verse (1981).* Philip Hobsbaum, *Metre, Rhyme and Verse Form* (1996).

Rhythm A regular pattern of the time period occurring in writing, frequently and most detectably in Poetry. Regular, reliable rhythm is known to be comforting to ears, while interrupted, unpredictable or rapidly shifting rhythm is unsettling. The poet opts for a particular rhythmic scheme on the basis of the theme of the poem and the kind of effect he wants to produce out of it. Thus a meditative poem relies much on slow, prolonged rhythm, while Browning tries to imitate the rhythm of a horse's movement in "The Last Ride Together." An example of an irregular rhythm is sprung rhythm. Quantitative verse, on the other hand, is very regular in its rhythmic movement. The rhythmic pattern in English verse line depends mostly on the arrangement of meter, i.e. regularity of stressed and unstressed syllables employed. Rhythm and meter are two different items in poetry. Meter is the basic plan for versification in terms of prosodic norms. Rhythm arises out of metrical scheme, that is, how words flow with the meter and often varying from it.

Ref: JB Mayor, *Chapters on English Metre* (1968). P Kiparsky & G Youmans, Ed. *Rhythm and Meter* (1989).

Ridicule <Latin *ridiculus*> A group of words intended to vilify a person or idea and arouse contemptuous laughter. The goal is to make fun, condemn or criticize somebody or something silly. It is one of the most powerful methods of criticism, partly because it leaves one almost defenceless. Even the bravest of men fear being laughed at. The fear of being laughed at is one of the most inhibiting forces in Western civilization. Ridicule may often become a weapon of the satirist. Lord Byron and Alexander Pope's satires often verge on the ridicule, specially when attacks are targeted on personal level. The old Greek comedies developed out of ritualistic ridicule and invective, improvised and hurled at individuals by the leaders of the phallic songs. The function of these iambic utterances, it has been shown, was magical; they were thought to drive away evil influences so that the positive fertility magic of the phallus might be operative. Ridicule, *deride, mock, taunt*, etc are synonymous in the sense they all mean to make somebody or something an object of laughter. While ridicule implies a deliberate often malicious belittling, *deride* suggests contemptuous and often bitter ridicule, *mock* implies scorn often ironically expressed as by mimicry or sham deference, *taunt* suggests jeeringly provoking insult or challenge.

Rococo A style of European architecture that flourished in the 18th century, especially in France. The extensive use of ornamentation, its light pretty themes, unusual gaiety and intimacy of tone, etc are the most characteristic features associated with the style. The classical purists have often been very critical of the style and have termed it as effeminate. In literary criticism, the term is often used disparagingly to refer to a decadent or over-ornamented style. Alexander Pope's *The Rape of the Lock* (1712-14) and Laurence Sterne's *Tristram Shandy* (1759-67) are often considered the most citable literary examples of rococo. [Cf. baroque]

Roman-à-Clef A kind of fiction. The term comes from French, meaning *novel with a key.* The novel's account cleverly represents actual persons and events thinly disguised by pseudonyms. The reader who has the key can read the novel as real history. Contemporary readers usually do not find it difficult to identify the real individual under a fictional name. Examples of this type include Ernest Hemingway's *The Sun Also Rises* (about the members of the Lost Generation), Lady Caroline Lamb's *Glenarvon* (about Lord Byron disguised as Ruthven Glenarvon), Aldous Huxley's *Point Counter Point* (about DH Lawrence and Middleton Murray), etc.

Romance <Latin *Romanicus*, "of the Roman style"> A fictional narrative about love stories, improbable events involving idealized characters that are quite unlike ordinary people. Knights on a quest for a magic sword and aided by characters like fairies and trolls would be examples of things found in romance fiction. Many ballads too contain some basic qualities of romance. By the 17th century romance usually referred to any extraordinary story with certain elements of love, supernaturalism, heroism, a struggle between the good and the evil, etc whether in verse or prose regardless of its origin. Miguel de Cervantes' *Don Quixote* and Sir Philip Sidney's *The Arcadia* are direct and later descendent of this genre. Gothic novels and even modern science fiction very much resemble old romances.

Technically speaking, there are two types of romance stories: [1] *Medieval romance* refers to the French and German poetry dealing with the chivalric adventures of knights in warfare and tournaments.

They resembled the earlier *chansons de gestes* and epics. A large number survives manly due to their popularity. England produced its own romances in the 14th century, including the *Lay of Havelok the Dane* and *Sir Gawain and the Green Knight*. In 1485, Caxton printed the lengthy romance *Le Morte D'Arthur* and initiated the tradition of prose romance. [2] *Modern romance* offers a more restricted meaning in contrast with medieval and Renaissance meanings of romance. In popular use, the modern romance novel is a formulaic boy-meets-girl or a girl-meets-boy story or a film, with initial obstacles and interferences and finally getting everything resolved in favour of the love-pigeons. Computer software is available for constructing these stereotyped tales. The conventional plot involves a third-person or a first-person narrative.

Ref: Corinne Saunders, Ed. *A Companion to Romance: From Classical to Contemporary* (2004). John G Cawelti, *Adventure, Mystery and Romance: Formula Stories as Art and Popular Culture* (1976). Kristin Ramsdell, *Romance Fiction: A Guide to the Genre* (2012). WRJ Barron, *English Medieval Romance* (1987).

Romantic Comedy A sub-genre of comedy popularized in England during the 16th century. In his plays of the 1590s, the young Shakespeare concentrated to a remarkable extent on romantic comedies. Shakespeare and other playwrights like Robert Greene (*Friar Bacon and Friar Bungay*), John Lyly (*Compaspe, Mother Bombie* and *Endimion*) and George Peel (*The Arraignment of Paris*), etc were mainly responsible for the development of this comedy type. The Latin form, with five-act division, of plays written by Terence and Plautus structured English romantic comedy right from Nicholas Udall's (1505-56) *Ralph Roister Doister*. The plays abounded in classical themes like love, intrigue, friendship, and character types like the braggart lover, the scrounger servant and the conniving old man. Primarily meant for aristocratic entertainment, romantic comedy mainly pursued the theme of love. The basic features of a romantic comedy are: [1] Normally it has a beautiful idealized heroine in the centre and a romantic love story gradually matures through a hazardous course. [2] Side by side the main plot a subplot (often subplots) is almost a formula requirement for a romantic comedy. The purpose of the subplot is to parody the main plot, and, wittingly or otherwise, to sort out the crisis of the main plot. The crisis of the main plot usually centres round the love affair of the hero and the heroine and the problem is solved through an agency, a disclosure of a secret or a trick. Often the resolution part takes in a place far away from where it arises (e.g. Padua, Messina or a forest of Aden, etc). [3] The aristocrats dominate the main plot whereas the subplot is invariably given to people belonging to lower social strata—the plebeians, the artisans, the mechanicals or the supernatural elements (the mechanicals and the fairies in *A Midsummer Night's Dream*, Sir Toby Belch in *Twelfth Night*). In *A Midsummer Night's Dream*, there are, in fact, four pairs of lovers—Theseus-Hippolyta, Lysander-Hermia, Demetrius-Helena and Oberon-Titania, and three sets of characters—the Athenian aristocrats, the mechanicals and the fairies. All of them mingle together in the shady world of the forest and create an incredibly dreamy world of fantasy. [4] Romantic comedy celebrates life, love and fruitfulness and its chief function is to entertain, not instruct. With songs and imaginative idealism, romantic comedy provides an easy escape route into a world of fancy and imagination from the grim realities of life.

Shakespeare's plays that easily come within this category are *A Midsummer Night's Dream, The Merchant of Venice, Much Ado about Nothing, As You Like It* and the like. However, in these plays accepted social values are never challenged. Love ends in happy marriage; adultery is denounced. Although romantic comedies, in general, treated ideal love affairs and during its best period Queen Elizabeth was held in high esteem, Elizabethan romantic comedies smack of inequality so far as the status of women is the issue. In the dramatic works status quo has been strictly maintained and the roles of women are subordinated to men's. [Cf. comedy, comedy of manners and satiric comedy]

Ref: A Leggatt, *Shakespeare's Comedy of Love* (1974). AH Thorndike, *English Comedy* (1929). CL Barber, *Shakespeare's Festive Comedy: A Study of Dramatic Form and its Relation to Social Custom* (1959). HTE Perry, *Masters of Dramatic Comedy* (1939). Northrop Frye, *A Natural Perspective: The Development of Shakespearean Comedy and Romance.*

Romanticism/Romantic A grand literary, artistic and philosophical movement that began in Europe in the last part of the 18th century and continued roughly until the mid-19th century. In its passionate focus on the individual consciousness, it was both a continuation of and a reaction against the Enlightenment. Taken together the ideas and applications of all the forerunners of Romanticism, it is argued that it strongly emphasized the individual, the subjective, the irrational, the imaginative, the personal, the spontaneous, the emotional, the visionary and the transcendental. Among its attitudes were a deepened admiration of the beauties of nature; a general exaltation of emotion over reason, and the senses over intellect; a turning in upon the self and a heightened examination of human personality; a preoccupation with the genius, the hero, and the exceptional figure; a new view of the artist as a supremely individual creator; an emphasis on imagination as a gateway to transcendental experience and spiritual truth; a consuming interest in folk culture, national and ethnic cultural origins and the medieval era; and a fondness for the exotic, the distant, the strange, the weird, the occult, the grotesque, the diseased and even the satanic. Romanticism is also used as a general term to refer to a type of sensibility found in all periods of literary history and usually considered to be in opposition to the principles of classicism. Many see romanticism as the aftermath of three important social events: the American Revolution (1776), the French Revolution (1789) and the Industrial Revolution (1760-1820). The Romantics brought to a fuller consciousness of their own powers in fashioning new world of the mind and emphasis on the imagination was strengthened by considerations, which are both religious and metaphysical. In England, the Romantic approach to literary creativity and criticism officially started with the publication of *The Lyrical Ballads* (1798), a joint venture, worked out by William Wordsworth (1770-1850) and ST Coleridge (1772-1834). The leading literary English practitioners of the school were Coleridge, Wordsworth, John Keats (1795-1821), PB Shelley (1792-1822), Lord Byron (1788-1824), John Clare (1794-1864) and the like. [Cf. classicism, transcendentalism]

Ref: AO Lovejoy, *Essays in the History of Ideas* (1944). CM Bowra, *The Romantic Imagination* (1950). Harold Bloom, Ed. *Romanticism and Consciousness: Essays in Criticism* (1970). MH Abrams, *The Mirror and the Lamp* (1953). Northrop Frye, *Romanticism Reconsidered* (1963).

S

Saga <On *Saga* (epic tale) Proto-Germanic *Sago*> A Norse name for a story of the exploits of a hero, or the story of a family told through several generations. These stories were mostly composed during the medieval era in the Scandinavian and Norse oral folk traditions. Stories of the exploits of Daniel Boone or Davey Crockett are sagas in the first sense. Alex Haley's *Roots* would be considered a saga in the second sense. The prose style of the old sagas stands apart from all other vernacular styles of the Middle Ages in its freedom from Latin influence, in its terseness and simplicity. Three types of saga are found: [1] *Family saga*, in which an Old Icelandic family story is the theme; [2] *Historical saga*, in which story turns back to homeland of an exiled author; and [3] *Lying saga*, in which fiction had the main part. John Galsworthy's *Forsyte Saga* (1906-21), a fictional trilogy, a modern family saga only in the sense that the story of the Forsyte family is extended over a considerably long period.

Ref: Margaret Clunies Ross, *The Cambridge Introduction to the Old Norse-Icelandic Saga* (2010).

Sarcasm <Greek *sarkasmós*, to tear flesh> A popular Figure of Speech, a conversational tool, a verbal sneer or a cutting remark with a clear intention to hurt one's feelings. The basic purpose of it is that sarcasm is often used as a defensive mechanism when bitterness is really hard to express in a pleasant way, or the purpose is to say something damaging without making it a crude hit directly. Sarcasm is intelligent in the sense it tends to disguise the attack, where as satire or irony is relatively more unveiled and broad-based. The non-literary use of irony is often called sarcasm. In most cases sarcasm is an apparent praise for dispraise, or a strongly damaging remark. For example, here is a Shavian sarcasm: "You would pet him and spoil him, and mother him to perfection." One from Mark Twain is: "Honesty is the best policy—when there is money in it." Another sarcastic statement: "I never forget a face, but in your case I'll be glad to make an exception" (Groucho Marx). Some old grammarians do not make any difference between sarcasm and irony. Sarcasm can give some different hints about characters, depending on the way it is used; but most often sarcastic characters are cynical, slightly bitter, solitary, perhaps arrogant and, of course, intelligent. Some old and modern sarcastic writers include such names as Aesop, Horace, Jonathan Swift, Samuel Butler, Ambrose Bierce, Anatole France, Anton Chekhov, O Henry, Aldous Huxley, Günter Grass, Chris Morris and the like. [Cf. irony, satire]

Satire/Satiric <Latin *satira/satura*, 'medley', being elliptical for *lanx satura*, 'a full dish, a hotch-potch'> A literary mode applied to censure and rectify individual or social follies or vices through irony, wit, ridicule, exaggeration, metaphor, oxymoron, and even sarcasm. The goals of the satiric mode are two-fold: to expose the hypocrisy involved in a particular social or moral practice and to trim down it by derision and disparagement. The satirist most often works within the framework of a widely cherished value system and relies on the implicit moral code understood by his audience and reader. The investment of comic element in the satire does not make it a comedy, since laughter is not the preferred goal of a satire; it never intends to entertain and amuse, but to expose, deride a folly to evoke a corrective feedback. Since the satire is more of a technique, any literary form is appropriate for its employment: poetry (Alexander Pope's *Rape of the Lock*), drama (Ben Jonson's *Volpone*), fiction (Jonathan Swift's *Gulliver's Travels*) or even film (Chaplin's *Modern Times*).

Satire is divided into two major categories—*direct* and *indirect*. Direct satire includes *Horatian satire*, which usually pokes fun at humble foils with a witty, even indulgent tone, and *Juvenalian satire*, which denounces human vices and faults in dignified and serious tones. In indirect satire, of which *Menippean satire* is most common, the intended satiric effect is achieved not through direct condemnation; but through modes of presentation and representation. During the 17th and 18th centuries the satire flourished to a great height. The genre has a long past history—originally from *satura* to the present *satire*—it has had contributions from classical writer like Lucilius, Verro, Menippus, Juvenal, Horace to later writers like Molière (*Tartuffe*), Voltaire (*Candide*), Swift, Pope, Dryden (*Absalom and Achitophel*), Butler (*Erewhon*), Byron (*Don Juan*), Huxley (*Point Counter Point*), Shaw (*Arms and the Man*), George Orwell (*Animal Farm*) and Sir Kingsley Amis (*Lucky Jim*), etc. Today the mode persists particularly to deride political figures and institutions.

Ref: Gilbert Highet, *The Anatomy of Satire* (1962), Ian Jack, *Augustan Satire* (1952), James Sutherland, *English Satire* (1958). John R Clark, *The Modern Satiric Grotesque and its Traditions* (1991).

Satyr Play A burlesque kind of comedy staged as comic relief at the end of a classical Greek trilogy. Satyr plays are believed to have developed from the dithyramb, a hymn to Dionysus, who was an incarnation of a "fundamental paradox inherent to the world, life giving but potentially destructive" (Rehm). They were introduced at the great Dionysia celebration at Athens in the late 6th century BCE. They were written by the competing authors of three tragedies (trilogy) and frequently featured a legendary hero. This character was joined by a cowardly, lecherous and wine-loving chorus of eleven satyrs led by Silenus, the foster father of Dionysus, in a farcical plot or a parody of a myth. Euripides' *Cyclops* is the only complete Satyr play available now.

Ref: Eric Csapo & Margaret Miller, Eds. *The Origins of Theatre in Ancient Greece and Beyond: From Ritual to Drama* (2007). Rush Rehm, *Greek Tragic Theatre* (1992).

Scansion An analysis of *stressed* and *unstressed syllables* (or *accented* and *unaccented syllables*) in a verse line to examine its meter and often its rhyme scheme. The commonest method of scansion uses accent marks (*slanted lines above syllables*) to show stressed syllables, either no marks or breves (˘) above syllables to show unstressed syllables, and vertical lines to separate each foot. For example here is a line from Alexander Pope—"We think our fathers fool, so wise we grow,/ Our wiser sons no doubt will think us so" for scansion:

Wĕ thínk | | ŏur fá | | thĕrs foól | | sŏ wíse | | wĕ grów,

Oŭr wí | | sĕr sóns | | nŏ dóubt | | wĭll thínk | | ŭs só.

The lines have five feet and ten syllables each. The first syllable of each foot is unaccented (*marked with breves above vowels*) and all the second syllables are accented (*marked with a slanted line above syllables*). Now the scansion gives the lines a particular metrical scheme, which is known as *lambic Pentameter.* It is *lambic* because of the accent pattern —unaccented syllables are followed by accented syllables, and *Pentameter* because the verse lines have five feet. The names of stressed and unstressed syllable patterns are shown in a chart below:

Foot Names	**Style Names**	**Stress Patterns**	**Syllables**
lamb	lambic	Unstressed + Stressed	Two
Trochee	Trochaic	Stressed + Unstressed	Two
Spondee	Spondaic	Stressed + Stressed	Two
Anapest	Anapestic	Unstressed + Unstressed + Stressed	Three
Dactyl	Dactylic	Stressed + Unstressed + Unstressed	Three
Amphibrach	Amphibrachic	Unstressed + Stressed + Unstressed	Three
Pyrrhic	Pyrrhic	Unstressed + Unstressed	Two

[Cf. meter]

Ref: Bose & Sterling, *Elements of English Rhetoric and Prosody* (1908). JB Mayor, *Chapters on English Metre* (1968). J McAuley, *Versification: A Short Introduction* (1983). P Kiparsky & G Youmans, Eds. *Rhythm and Meter* (1989). WK Wimsatt, *Versification* (1972).

Science Fiction A relatively modern form of fiction, often shortened to *Sci-Fi.* This is so-called because it deals principally with the impact of actual or imagined science upon society and/or individuals. Science fiction may include a careful and informed manipulation of scientific facts and principles, or it may range into far-fetched areas and contradict science with either fact or fiction. In either case, plausibility based on science is a prerequisite, so that such precursors of the genre as Mary Shelley's Gothic novel *Frankenstein or the Modern Prometheus* and Robert Louis Stevenson's *Strange Case of Dr. Jekyll and Mr. Hyde* are science fiction, whereas Bram Stoker's *Dracula* (1897), based as it is purely on the supernatural, is not. Other notable precursors of this genre are imaginary voyages to the moon or to other planets in the 18th century and space travel in Voltaire's *Micromégas*, alien cultures in Jonathan Swift's *Gulliver's Travels* and also science-fiction elements in the 19th century stories of Edgar Allan Poe, Nathaniel Hawthorne and Fitz-James O'Brien.

However, Science fiction proper began toward the end of the 19th century with the scientific romances of Jules Verne, whose fiction was rather on the level of invention, and the science-oriented novels of social criticism by HG Wells. The development of science fiction as a self-conscious genre dates from 1926 when American electrical engineer Hugo Gernsback coined the portmanteau word *scientifiction*. Writers as Isaac Asimov, Arthur C Clarke, Robert A Heinlein, Aldous Huxley, CS Lewis and Kurt Vonnegut added respectability to the form. A great boom in the popularity of science fiction followed the World War II. In the US particularly, science fiction was studied as literature in colleges and universities. Some of the modern acknowledged masters of the genre are AE Van Vogt, JG Ballard, Ray Bradbury, Frank Herbert, Harlan Ellison, Poul Anderson, Samuel R Delany, Ursula K Le Guin, Arthur C Clarke, Octavia E Butler and Brian Aldiss, etc. Such literary works such as Amitav Ghosh's *The Calcutta Chromosome*, Salman Rushdie's *Grimus*, and Boman Desai's *The Memory of Elephants* are generally classified as magic realist works but they make essential use of *Sci-Fi* tropes and techniques wittily.

Ref: Brian Aldiss, *Billion Year Spree: The True History of Science Fiction* (1973). Darko Suvin, *Metamorphoses of Science Fiction: on the Poetics and History of a Literary Genre* (1979).

Sensibility An acute perception of the mind having at least four layers of meaning: [1] ability to receive sensations, sensitiveness, [2] peculiar susceptibility to a pleasurable or painful impression, [3] awareness of and responsiveness toward something emotional, and [4] refined or excessive sensitiveness in taste with especial responsiveness to the pathetic. Sensibility became an English-language literary movement, particularly in the genre of the novel. In the 18th century, the term was a cult as literature positively valued the ability to respond emotionally to the feelings of others, the beauties of natural landscape and the sentimental novel developed into the *novel of sensibility*, which presented characters possessing a pronounced susceptibility to delicate sensations. The romantic literature too adopted many elements of the novel of sensibility including those like responsiveness to nature, belief in the wisdom of the heart and in the power of sympathy. It did not, however, assimilate the novel of sensibility's characteristic optimism. In the 20th century, the term became a critical shibboleth for the ability to respond sensitively to the aesthetic.

Ref: Ann Jessie Van Sant, *Eighteenth-Century Sensibility and the Novel: The Senses in Social Context* (1993). Paul Goring,

The Rhetoric of Sensibility in Eighteenth-Century Culture (2005).

Sentimental Comedy A variety of the drama of the 18th century, in which middle-class heroes and heroines proudly triumph over a series of moral tests. In France *comédie larmoyante*, similar to this type, was written principally by Pierre-Claude Nivelle de La Chaussée, whose *Le Préjugé à la mode* (*Fashionable Prejudice*) is a good example of the genre. In English dramatic tradition this was a post-restoration development. Such comedy aimed at generating tears rather than laughter. Sentimental comedies reflected contemporary popular beliefs of human beings as inherently good but capable of being led astray through bad examples. Although the plays contained characters whose natures seemed virtuous, and who passed all the trials too easily; audiences nonetheless accepted them as truthful demonstration of the human predicament. Sentimental comedy had its roots in early 18th century tragedy, which had a vein of morality similar to that of sentimental comedy but had loftier characters and subject matter than those in sentimental comedies.

Writers of the genre include, among others, Colley Cibber (*Love's Last Shift*, 1696) and George Farquhar (*The Constant Couple*, 1699). The best-known example of the genre is Sir Richard Steele's *The Conscious Lovers* (1722), which deals with the trials and tribulations of its penniless heroine, Indiana. Steele wished the play to arouse "a pleasure too exquisite for laughter." Sentimental comedies continued to coexist with such conventional comedies as Oliver Goldsmith's *She Stoops to Conquer* (1773) and Richard Sheridan's *The Rivals* (1775) until the sentimental genre waned in the early 19th century. [Cf. sentimental novel]

Ref: Ellis Frank, *Sentimental Comedy: Theory and Practice* (1991). Ernest Bernbaum, *The Drama of Sensibility: A Sketch of the History of English Sentimental Comedy and Domestic Tragedy 1696-1780* (1915). Lillian Isidora Harber, *Sentimental Comedy: A Definition* (1912). Oliver Goldsmith, "A Comparison between Laughing and Sentimental Comedy" (1773).

Sentimental Novel A sub-genre of the novel that puts sentiments above other emotions and reason. Broadly speaking, any novel that exploits the reader's capacity for tenderness, compassion, or sympathy to an uneven degree is a sentimental novel. In a different sense, the emergence of this type and also of the Gothic novels can be seen as reaction to the austerity and rationalism of the Neoclassicism school. The sentimental novel glorified feeling above reason and raised the analysis of emotion to the level of fine art. The type usually featured an overly optimistic view of the goodness of human nature and often highlighted the trends of the time toward humanism and the heightened value of human life inviting sympathy for the disadvantaged. Such novels as Oliver Goldsmith's *The Vicar of Wakefield*, Henry Mackenzie's *The Man of Feeling*, Laurence Sterne's *A Sentimental Journey* and Thomas Day's *The History of Sandford and Merton*, etc can be grouped in this category. An early example in France is Antoine-François Prévost's *Manon Lescaut* (1731), the story of a courtesan for whom a young seminary student of noble birth forsakes his career, family and religion. His downward progress, if not actually excused, is portrayed as a sacrifice to love.

Jean-Jacques Rousseau's (1712-1778) doctrine of the natural goodness of man and his optimism in moral development perhaps were big boosters behind the development of this kind of literature. In England, Samuel Richardson's sentimental novel *Pamela* (1740) was highly acclaimed by many and even clergymen recommended it as a means of educating the heart. In the 1760s the sentimental novel developed into the *novel of sensibility*, which presented characters possessing marked inclination to delicate impression. Such characters were not only deeply moved by sympathy for their fellowmen; but also reacted emotionally to the beauty inherent in natural settings and works of art and music. The prototype was Laurence Sterne's *Tristram Shandy* (1759-67), which devotes several pages to describing Uncle Toby's horror of killing a fly. The romantic literature too approved of certain elements of the sensibility novel, including responsiveness to nature and belief in the wisdom of the heart and in the power of sympathy. It did not, however, assimilate the novel of sensibility's characteristic optimism. [Cf. sentimental comedy]

Ref: John Mullan, *Sentiment and Sociability: The Language of Feeling in the Eighteenth Century* (1988). Laurence Lerner, "A Note on Sentimentality", *The Truest Poetry* (1960). RF Brissenden, *Virtue in Distress: Studies in the Novel of Sentiment from Richardson to Sade* (1974). Shirley Samuels, Ed. *The Culture of Sentiment* (1992).

Sequel <Latin *sequi,* 'to follow'> A novel or drama, or even a film that can be regarded as a continuation of an earlier work. It incorporates the same characters and often the same setting of the previous story. Sometimes the events and situations involve a continuation of the previous work and sometimes only the characters are the same and the events are entirely unrelated to the former work. When sequels result from the popularity of an original, they are often hastily written and may not be of the same quality as the original. Some authors who have sequels to their credit are: Mark Twain (*Adventures of Tom Sawyer*), Margaret Mitchell (*Gone with the Wind*), John Galsworthy (*Forsyte Saga*), Alexandra Ripley (*Scarlett*), Henry Reymond Fitzwalter Keating (*Bats Fly Up for Inspector Ghote*), etc. Other authors who demand attention for their sequels are Agatha Christie, and the latest craze, JK Rowling (*Harry Potter* series). May be noted, three books that tell a continuous story constitute a *trilogy*; four books make the series a *tetralogy*. Scholars refer to Shakespeare's *Richard III* and *Henry VI*, part-I, part-II, and part-III as his first tetralogy; while *Richard II, Henry IV* part-I, *Henry IV* part-II, and *Henry V* his second tetralogy. The opposite of 'sequel' is *prequel*.

Setting An environment given to a literary work. A story must have a locale and the events in it must be taking place in a particular period or moment of time. The setting of an episode within a work, therefore, is the particular physical location in which events take place in a particular time. For example, the setting in James Joyce's *Ulysses* is Dublin in the year 1904. Without space and time a story does not exist. Finding these two elements, better known as setting, is very seldom a problem unless the author tries to play a kind of hide-and-seek game with his reader. A good reader must find them out and decide whether this setting is particularly important to the plot, or simply serve as the background for the action of the story. The physical setting, for writers like Thomas Hardy, Edgar Allan Poe, William Faulkner, Emily Brontë and JM Synge, is an inseparable and important element in generating the right environment of a work. If one reads just two novels—*The Return of the Native* and *Wuthering Heights*—the importance of this aspect will be easily understandable. In both the cases incidents and events taking place in the novels if taken away from their physical contexts will just significantly reduce the charm of the works. In these cases stories become locale specific; i.e. the setting adds to the meaning and message of the novels. We are conscious of England in *Tom Jones* and *Vanity Fair*; we are only aware of the Yorkshire moors and Egdon Heath in *Wuthering Heights* and *The Return of the Native.* Whereas the settings in the former novels are two-dimensional having a length and a breadth, those in the latter have an additional dimension having a predominant atmospheric or environmental overtone—the narratives derive much of the philosophic aspects from the respective settings. A salient feature of the cinema is its ability to reproduce natural scenery, whereas in literature it is all a pen portrait.

Ref: David Lodge, *The Art of Fiction* (1992). Ron Rozelle, *Write Great Fiction: Description & Setting* (2005).

Seven Cardinal Virtues A set of virtues that include: [1] charity/love, [2] faith, [3] hope, [4] fortitude, [5] justice, [6] prudence and [7] temperance. The New Testament is the source of the first three of them—charity/love, faith and hope; and they have often been referred to as the *theological virtues*. The second set of four virtues—fortitude, justice, prudence, and temperance, known as *natural virtues*, can be traced in ancient Greek teachings. Virtue has been defined as conformity of life and conduct with the principles of morality. The virtues are thus the practical attitudes and habits adopted in obedience to those principles. The second set of virtues is sometimes known as the *four cardinal virtues* because on them all lesser attitudes hinge. Late Roman and medieval Christian moralists such as Ambrose, Augustine and Thomas Aquinas took over the Greek list as a convenient summary of the wisdom of the ancient philosophers. To the four, Christianity added three virtues. This classification was taken over directly from the Apostle Paul, who not only distinguished these three as the specifically Christian virtues; but also singled out love as the chief of the three. They are imparted by God through Christ and are then practised by the believer. [Cf. seven deadly sins, Ten Commandments]

Seven Deadly Sins A set of sins that include: [1] pride, [2] wrath, [3] envy, [4] avarice, [5] lust, [6] gluttony, and [7] sloth. These sins have often been listed under three major head: The *sins of the Devil* (the first three—pride, wrath/anger and envy); the *sins of the world* (the fourth sin—avarice/greed); and the *sins of the flesh* (the last three—lust, gluttony and sloth). Each of the Seven Deadly Sins corresponds to one of the

Seven Holy Virtue. Of all the deadly sins it is pride that was responsible for the fall of Satan and it is considered to be the worst of all. Medieval Christian church believed that committing any of the sins could bring to nothing less than eternal damnation and way to salvation was a rigorous process of penitence. The origin of some of the sins goes back to the early history of Christian monasticism; they were grouped together as early as the 6th century by St. Gregory the Great. They were classified as deadly or *cardinal sin* not merely because they cause serious offense morally but because they give rise to others. The classical discussion of the subject is in the *Summa Theologica,* by the 13th century theologian St. Thomas Aquinas. The deadly sins were a popular theme in the morality plays and art of the European Middle Ages. Christopher Marlowe, in *Doctor Faustus* (1604), has personified all the sins to accentuate the deviation of Doctor Faustus. [Cf. seven cardinal virtues, Ten Commandments]

Ref: James Stalker, *The Seven Deadly Sins and the Seven Cardinal Virtues* (1998).

Short Story A fictional prose narrative, usually shorter and more focused than a novella. NTC *Dictionary of Literary Terms* quotes Edgar Allan Poe's definition of it as "a short prose narrative, requiring from a half-hour to one or two hours in its perusal." The short story usually deals with a single episode and often a single character. HE Bates too gives a definition of the genre: "The basis of almost every argument or conclusion I can make is the axiom that the short story can be anything that the author decides it shall be." It differs from the *anecdote*, a simple and unsophisticated narration of a simple event, in the sense that the short story is a better-organized narrative structure. The tone, the author's attitude toward his/her subject and audience, is uniform throughout a story. Unlike a novel it frequently lacks dénouement, ending instead at its climax. The written protocol regarding what comprises a short versus a long story is vague. In fact the short story has many of the same characteristics of a novel including characters, setting and plot.

The origin of the short story dates back to ancient times when story telling was a part of community life. However, the formal short story is often linked with histories of Herodotus (c 480-425 BCE), anecdotes, the parables of the Bible, Giovanni Boccaccio's (1313-1375) *Decameron*, etc. In England Chaucer's *Canterbury Tales* too have inspired the art to a great extent. Since the latter half of the 19th century the development of the art form is unmatched. The spread of education, stricture on time and the growth of print media together have pushed its popularity to the zenith.

However, due to its length constraints, the basic story elements remain slightly unfulfilling and devices generally may not be as fully developed or complex as those developed in a full-length novel. Here lies the beauty of the short story. Some oft-referred short stories are Ernest Hemingway's "Hills Like White Elephants," Katherine Mansfield's "The Fly," O Henry's "Gift of the Magi," Eudora Welty's "Death of a Travelling Salesman," Yukio Mishima's "Three Million Men," James Joyce's "Araby," and Milan Kundera's "The Hitchhiking Game," etc. Anton Chekhov is often regarded as the master of masters in modern style of short story writing. There are many authors well known for the short story including Edgar Allan Poe, Arthur Conan Doyle, Saki, DH Lawrence, Rudyard Kipling, Somerset Maugham, Sherwood Anderson and Ernest Hemingway. Many critics think that American writers since Poe, who first theorized on the structure and purpose of the short story, have paid considerable attention to the form.

Ref: Clare Hanson, *Short Stories and Short Fictions, 1880-1980* (1985). HS Canby, *The Short Story in English* (1909). Frank O'Connor, *The Lonely Voice: A Study of the Short Story* (1962). Viorica Patea, Ed. *Short Story Theories: A Twenty-First-Century Perspective* (2012).

Simile A Figure of Speech that expresses the resemblance of two different things usually introduced by *as* or *like*. For example, such sentences as "...we two alone will sing like birds in the cage" (Shakespeare) and "Let us go then, you and I,/ When the evening is spread out against the sky/ Like a patient etherised upon a table" (TS Eliot) clearly thrive on similarities. A series or long sequence of similes put together is called *epic simile*, frequently found mostly in epic poems. Milton, in his *Paradise Lost*, has extensively used epic similes. Shelley's "To a Skylark" too has a series of similes marking out the flight of the bird so wonderfully. The most important aspect of this figure is that the resemblance brought together for emphasis must not be of similar category of things, i.e. Madonna's face cannot be compared with Cleopatra's. In such a case rose can serve the purpose of a simile. If the simile is implied; it becomes metaphor. [Cf. metaphor]

Slang A word or phrase mostly popular with a group of people in informal verbal communication that is generally unacceptable for formal writing or conversation. Slang words and phrases are often colourful exaggerations used to emphasize the speaker's point; they may also be shortened versions of a long word or phrase. Examples of some modern slang words include *yuppie* (an acronym for Young Urban Professional), *cool* (for excellent), *wired* (nervous or excited), and *chill out* (relax). If a slang expression continues to exist and accepted by all, it is no longer regarded as slang. The use of slang actually refers to the creativity of human mind and this is one of the sources of coining words. Simeon Potter thinks slang words in general "seek three things in various degrees and proportions: novelty, vivacity, and intimacy. Slang proceeds from a new way of looking at things and it exercises every form of intellectual wit and verbal ingenuity." There is a misconception in certain quarters that slang means words of low and disreputable meaning. In fact anything that comes from disreputable people is looked down upon in a class conscious society. In this issue if there is any stigma attached to a 'slang' language, it is temporary; if the word continues to linger on in practice; silently it is included in the standard vocabulary. The word *scientist*, for example, initially was slang, often branded as 'ignoble Americanism' or 'cheap and vulgar product of trans-Atlantic slang.' An ingenious example of a recent slang word is "photo bomb"—referring to somebody or something unwelcome that has accidentally or otherwise come into view in a photograph and thus has ruined the image. The new coinages like *selfie* and *groufie* are perhaps the slang words that found respectable footing in the shortest possible time thanks to the proliferation of the smart phone. *Back slang* is a form of slang in which words are spoken and/or spelled backwards: e.g. *nottub* (= button) and even more complicated one is *top o' reeb* (= pot of beer), etc. It is said that this form of slang was popular with the street-vendors in Victorian London.

Ref: Elisa Mattiello, *An Introduction to English Slang: A Description of Its Morphology, Semantics and Sociology* (2008). Eric Partridge, *A Dictionary of Slang and Unconventional English* (1984). Simeon Potter, *Our Language* (1966).

Social/Socialist Realism A school of literary theory based on Marxist aesthetics. Maxim Gorky was mainly responsible for the development of this ideological approach to literature. Socialist Realism follows the great tradition of the 19th century Russian realism in that it offers to be faithful and objective in portraying life. However, it differs from earlier realism in several respects. The realism of Leo Tolstoy and Anton Chekhov inevitably conveyed a critical picture of the society it portrayed (hence the term *critical realism*). Socialist realism, in its turn, demanded adherence to a communist worldview in works of literature. Its doctrines required an objective viewpoint intelligible to the working classes and subject matter of social struggle featuring strong proletarian aspirations. The primary theme of Socialist Realism, however, is the building of socialism and a classless society. In portraying this struggle, the writer could admit imperfections but was expected to take a positive and optimistic view of society and ideological standpoint. Soviet novel *Kak zakalyalas stal* (*How the Steel Was Tempered*, 1932-34), written by Nikolay Ostrovsky, is a classic example of the novel of socialist ideology. The hero, Pavel Korchagin, wounded in the October Revolution, overcomes his health handicap to become a writer of communist ideology for the reconstruction of his country. It has, of course, been a long-standing issue as to how much of dedication to a particular ideology is congenial to artistic freedom. Two Russian rebel writers Pasternak and Solzheitsyn have been much highlighted in the Western media. Marxist critic George Lukács has investigated different aspects of socialist realism. Socialist Realism remained the official aesthetic school of the former Soviet Union and some other eastern European countries until the late 20th century when Mikhail Gorbachev led to abandonment of the aesthetic. In England Ernest Jones and other Chartist writers were much influenced by the working class ideology in literature. [Cf. Realism, Marxist criticism, and Sociological novel]

Ref: Christopher Caudwell, *Studies in a Dying Culture* (1938). George Lukács, *Studies in European Realism* (1950) & *The Meaning of Cotemporary Realism* (1963). C Vaughan James, *Soviet Socialist Realism: Origins and Theory* (1973).

Sociological Novel A novel that makes social issues its primary concern. Usually some contemporary issues are raised in this form of novel in the way problem plays, such as Bernard Shaw and John Galsworthy's, raise social issues. This type of novel is also known as *problem* *novel* or *social novel* or *thesis novel*. In many cases a problem novel is an artistic expression of a particular ideology. A novel of this kind raises an issue, social or political, with a clear view to creating public opinion on an issue and thus accelerating some changes. Charles Dickens' many novels, specially *Hard Times, Bleak House* and *Oliver Twist*, etc have clearly stated social issues in them. Elizabeth Gaskell began her career as one of the "Condition of England" novelists of the 1840s, responding like Frances Trollope, Benjamin Disraeli and Charles Kingsley to the economic crisis of that troubled decade. Both *Mary Barton* (1848) and *Ruth* (1853) are Gaskell's novels about social issues, as is *North and South* (1854-55), although, like her later work, this book also has a psychological complexity. Other novels of this type are Upton Sinclair's *The Jungle*, John Steinbeck's *The Grapes of Wrath*, T Coraghessan's *The Tortilla Curtain*, Martin Amis's *Money*, etc. [Cf. angry young men, problem plays, social realism]

Ref: Arnold Kettle, "The Early Victorian Social-Problem Novel", *New Pelican Guide to English Literature,* Vol. VI (1990). George Lukács, *Studies in European Realism* (1964). Raymond Williams, *Culture and Society, 1780–1950* (1958). Raymond Southall, *Literature, the Individual and Society* (1977).

Soliloquy <Latin *solo,* one + *loquor,* I speak> A dramatic convention, a one-man's speech. A soliloquy in a drama is an aid to give the audience some necessary information about the speaker's mind and develop the speaker's character. It is typically a projection of the speaker's innermost thoughts, or as Matthew Arnold puts it, "The dialogue of the mind with itself." Usually delivered while the speaker is alone on the stage, a soliloquy is intended to present an illusion of unspoken reflection or a loud thought. A celebrated Shakespearean soliloquy is Hamlet's "To be or not to be that is the question." In classical plays there are few soliloquies; only during the middle Ages the device became popular and during the English Renaissance it became an integral part of the dramatic art. With monologue it has both similar and dissimilar points. Nowadays the practice of soliloquy as a dramatic device has become almost outdated. [Cf. interior monologue]

Sonnet <Old Italian musical term *sonata*> A conformist verse form, usually of fourteen lines, first eight being the *octave*, and the next six, *sestet*. These two parts are distinctly marked by the caesura or pause. The English form is usually written in *iambic pentameter*. The original Italian, *Petrarchan sonnet* is divided into an octave which rhymes a-b-b-a, a-b-b-a, and a sestet which usually rhymes c-d-e, c-d-e, or c-d, c-d, c-d. Dante followed the Petrarchan pattern in his *La Vita Nuova.* In England sonnet was first introduced by Thomas Wyatt (1503–1542) in the early 16th century. A sonnet revolves round a single thought without diversion. Ordinarily the argument heightened in the octave is resolved in the sestet part. The Miltonic sonnet follows the Petrarchan, but without significant break in meaning between the octave and sestet. A *Shakespearean sonnet* has three quatrains and a final couplet, which usually provides an epigrammatic statement of the theme. The rhyme scheme is a-b-a-b, c-d-c-d, e-f-e-f, g-g, or a-b-b-a, c-d-d-c, e-f-f-e, g-g. The *Spenserian sonnet* rhymes a-b-a-b, b-c-b-c, c-d-c-d, e-e, and often has no break in meaning between the first and the second part. It was Philip Sidney's *Astrophel and Stella* (1591) that started the English vogue for *sonnet sequence,* meaning series of sonnets together upholding some thematic connection.

Ref: JW Liver, *The Elizabethan Sonnet Tradition* (1966). Michael RG Spiller, *The Development of the Sonnet: An Introduction* (1992) and *The Sonnet Sequence: A Study of its Strategies* (1997).

Spenserian Stanza A complex stanza pattern evolved by the 16th century poet Edmund Spenser (1552/53-1599) for his epic poem, *The Faerie Queene* (1590). It is made up of a nine-line stanza, with the first eight lines in iambic pentameter and the last line in iambic hexameter, called Alexandrine. The rhyme scheme is: a-b-a-b-b-c-b-c-c. Edmund Spenser's *Faerie Queene* is written in this stanza pattern. The Italian form of stanza *ottava rima*, which consists of eight lines of iambic pentameter with the rhyme scheme a-b-a-b-a-b-c-c", comes very close to the Spenserian style. Spenser added an extra line to ottava rima structure. Many later poets, especially the young Romantics like Keats (*The Eve of St. Agnes*), Byron (*Childe Harold's Pilgrimage*) and Shelley (*The Revolt of Islam*), have used the pattern with or without modification of the original model.

Sphota <Sanskrit *sphoṭavāda*, bursting forth or spurt> An ancient Indian theory of speech production or transformation of a thought into spoken words. According to the 5th century linguist Bhartrihari, the process that communicates the meaning of a word or sentence is technically known as *sphota.* In his treatise *Vakyapadiya*, the concept of sound occupies a central role and Bhartrihari equates it with *sphota* to show the metaphysical nature of language. However, there is no use of *sphoṭa* as a technical term prior to Patañjali. The theory is a very comprehensive discourse and it implies that there is no knowledge that can be expressed without its relation with words—"All kinds of meaning depend upon the power of words... [and] there is no cognition in the world in which language does not figure." However, *sphota* is conceived of as three kinds: [1] *Varnasphota*, the alphabet, [2] *Padasphota*, the word and [3] *Vakyasphota,* the sentence. The process is intricate—letters turning into word, words into sentence and sentences into meaning—a kind of a fluid process, like buds bursting and blooming into a flower gradually. Thus, it is through the language that an object or meaning is understood. The *sphota* theory, therefore, is all about the process of unfolding of a meaningful speech as conceived by the speaker and received by the listener. The thought first flashes and takes form within the speaker's mind and next the same comes out as audible speech "riding the vehicle of words and sentences" and the idea is transported to the listener. In the process of utterance the first letter is defined better and better till the word is complete; the words are defined and redefined as the sentences unfold themselves and so on. Thus, according to the theory, in the process of utterance the meaning is always unstable, i.e. utterances have possibilities of producing thousands of meaningful linguistic units—"The communication of a sentence and its meaning is not complete until its last word is uttered. Thus, though the word-sounds reach the listener in a sequence, eventually they all merge into one and are grasped by the listener as a single unit. The same *Sphota* which originated in speaker's mind re-manifests in listener's mind, conveying the intended meaning." Many scholars think that Ferdinand de Saussure's classification of the *sign* he has detailed as *the signifier* and *the signified* comes very close to the *sphota* theory of Bhartrihari; Saussure may only have redefined the old Indian theory in terms of different phraseology.

Ref: Bhartrihari, *Vakyapadiya,* trans. Asiatic Society (1998). Harold G Coward, *The Sphota Theory of Language: A Philosophical Analysis* (1980). K Raghavan Pilliai, *The Study of Vakyapadiya,* Vol. I (1971). RS Tiwari, *A Critical Approach to Classical Indian Poetics* (1984).

Spondee A rare metrical pattern in English poetry. In a poetic line, a foot consisting of two long or stressed syllables occurring together is known by this term. This form is quite uncommon in English verse and is usually composed of two monosyllabic words. The first foot in the following line from Robert Burns's "Green Grow the Rashes" is an example of a spondee: "Greén grów || the ráshes, || O...." Here is another example of the spondaic pattern in Shakespeare: "Cry, Cry! Troy burns, or else let Helen go." [Cf. scansion]

Sprung Rhythm A term used by Gerard Manley Hopkins (1844-1889) to describe the rhythm of language and music, which he observed to be patterned by a regular beat of stressed syllables, interspersed with a variable number of unstressed syllables. Hopkins designed this to approximate the natural rhythm of speech. Accordingly, a foot written in sprung rhythm may have from zero to three unstressed syllables. Four types of rhythmic unit (foot), therefore, are suitable for this metrical pattern: [1] *monosyllable*, only one accented syllable: (́); [2] *trochee*, one accented followed by one unaccented: (́ ˘); [3] *dactyl*, one accented followed by two unaccented: (́ ˘ ˘) and [4] *paean*, one accented followed by three unaccented syllables: (́ ˘ ˘ ˘). Hopkins' "Pied Beauty" is an illustration of the use of sprung rhythm— "Glory be to God for dappled things—." [meter, scansion]

Stanza A group of lines considered as a unit forming a division or unit of a poem, and recurring in the same pattern with or without slight variations. The recurring pattern may include rhyme, line length, and meter also. A similar unit in a prose piece is known as a paragraph. However, poetic stanzas may too serve as units of thought in a poem much like paragraphs in prose. Some names of poetic stanza include the quatrain, terza rima, ottava rima, Spenserian stanza, etc. A poem may contain just only one stanza or as many stanzas as required to make the respective poem a complete whole. For example, W Cowper's "To a Young Lady" is just a ten-line poem of one stanza; whereas Shelley's "To a Skylark" has twenty-one stanzas of five lines each.

Ref: RM Alden, *English Verse* (1903).

Stereotype A term originally meant to name a replication made during the printing process. Later this led to its modern definition as a person or thing that is, or is assumed to be, the same as all others of its type without individuality. Common stereotypical characters include the absent-minded professor, the nagging wife, the troublemaking teenager and the kind hearted grandmother, etc. Many European writers prior to the 20th century projected the Jewish characters rather misleadingly. In *The Merchant of Venice* Shakespeare includes Shylock as the Jewish money lender stereotype. Especially in the context of postcolonial studies the term assumes further connotations. It analyses how individuals, people or historical events are portrayed and served as a tool for hegemonic agenda. No depiction is ever neutral; writing is not a mirror which reflects the world, but a means through which it is constructed. Stereotyping of the ruled by the ruler is a common practice throughout the colonial period. The subject, say, the concept of the ruled is 'produced', and not reflected through colonial writings. On the one level, to analyse colonial discourse is to study how colonized people were constructed, represented, stereotyped, and even silenced within colonial texts. They were silenced in the sense that their 'voices' were either absent or presented in such a way as to make them worthless or simply a confirmation of negative stereotypes. For example, in Anglo-Indian fiction the portrayal the Indian *ayah* and Hindu servant becoming Christian by Mary Sherwood, or the Indian voluptuous *nauch girl* by FE Penny are examples of stereotypes although they may not always be all negative. [Cf. discourse, hegemony, representation]

Ref: Russell Spears, "Social, Cultural and Cognitive Factors in Stereotype Formation," *Stereotypes as Explanations: The Formation of Meaningful Beliefs about Social Groups* Ed. Craig McGarty; Vincent Yzerbyt; Russell Spears (2002).

Stream of Consciousness A phrase used by William James in 1890 to describe the unbroken flow of thought and awareness of the waking mind. It is a special mode of *narrative technique* that undertakes to capture the full spectrum and the continuous flow of a character's mental processes—visual, auditory, physical, associative and subliminal—that impinge on the consciousness of an individual and form part of his awareness along with the trend of his rational thoughts. In this method sense perceptions mingle with conscious and half-conscious thoughts and memories, experiences, feelings and random associations. The Stream of consciousness novels commonly use the narrative techniques of interior monologue. But the two terms cannot be used as synonyms. *The Oxford Dictionary of Literary Terms* suggests, that "they can also be distinguished psychologically and literarily. In a psychological sense, stream of consciousness is the subject-matter, while interior monologue is the technique for presenting it" and again, "while an interior monologue always presents a character's thoughts 'directly', without the apparent intervention of a summarizing and selecting narrator, it does not necessarily mingle them with impressions and perceptions, nor does it necessarily violate the norms of grammar, or logic—but the stream-of-consciousness technique also does one or both of these things." Édouard Dujardin's *Les lauriers sont coupés* is credited by Joyce as the first example of this technique. Probably the most famous example of the type is James Joyce's *Ulysses* (1922), a complex evocation of the inner states of the characters, Leopold and Molly Bloom and Stephen Daedalus. Other notable examples include *Leutnant Gustl* (1901) by Arthur Schnitzler, an early use of stream of consciousness to re-create the atmosphere of pre-World War I Vienna; and William Faulkner's *The Sound and the Fury* (1929), which records the fragmentary and impressionistic responses in the minds of three members of the Compson family to events that are immediately being experienced or events that are being remembered. Another notable novelist of this group is Virginia Woolf whose works *Mrs Dalloway* (1925) and *To the Lighthouse* (1927), without doubt, fit into this category. [Cf. interior monologue]

Ref: Dorrit Cohn, *Transparent Minds: Narrative Modes for Presenting Consciousness in Fiction* (1978). Melvin Friedman, *Stream of Consciousness: A Study in Literary Method* (1955). Robert Humphrey, *Stream of Consciousness in the Modern Novel* (1954).

Structuralism/-ist A literary theory mostly comes from linguistic principles of Ferdinand de Saussure—"the whole set of linguistic habits which allow an individual to understand and to be understood." It deliberately disregards the historical aspects of language, the external context of linguistic acts, the agents who use language, etc and sees language as a system of differences and embraces the conventionality of the sign, brackets any consideration of the referent and generates a vocabulary of oppositions, all of which are more or less synonymous: langue and parole, synchrony and diachrony, system and event, signifier and signified, code and message, metaphor and metonymy, selection and combination, substitution and context, etc. In each case the first term is privileged.

An interesting aspect of the theory is how structuralism analogically extends it into the analysis of literature. Roland Barthes explains this: "Literature" he writes, "is simply a language, a system of signs. Its 'being' [*être*] is not in its message, but in this 'system.' Similarly, it is not for criticism to reconstitute the message of a work, but only its system, exactly as the linguist does not decipher the meaning of a sentence, but establishes the formal structure which allows the meaning to be conveyed." Rather than interpreting the meaning or value of a work, the critic examines the structures that produce meaning. The intention of the author is thereby disregarded; language and structures, not the perception of an author or the willed verbal acts, generate meaning. As a result, the text becomes a series of systems, deprived of its role as a source of meaning and thereby decentred. The self is an inter-subjective construct, a place where codes and conventions interact. In addition, the reader is privileged at the expense of the author, for, as Jonathan Culler points out, "the text is a kind of formless space whose shape is imposed by structured modes of reading." The operative concept is intertextuality. [Cf. poststructuralism]

Ref: Jonathan Culler, *Structuralist Poetics: Structuralism, Linguistics and the Study of Literature* (1975). Ronald Barthes, *Critical Essays* (1972). Robert Scholes, *Structuralism in Literature: An Introduction* (1974).

Style A manner of expression of a particular writer, fashioned by choice of words, grammatical constructions, employment of literary devices and all the possible areas of language. Some general styles might include scientific, ornate, plain and emotive, etc. Most writers have their own particular styles that are determined by individual distinctive manners of arranging words to suit their ideas and purpose in writing. In other words, the unique imprint of an author's personality upon his or her writing is what makes a style. Technically speaking, a style comprises the use of diction, different sentence structures, rhythm, Figure of Speech, rhetorical principles and other elements of composition. Styles may be classified according to period (Metaphysical, Augustan, Georgian), individual authors (Chaucerian, Miltonic, Jamesian), standard or level (grand, middle, low, plain), or language (scientific, expository, poetic, journalistic), etc. However, literary style is traditionally believed to be suitable for the educated readers. Seen from the chronological order the grand flamboyant style of the epic tradition has now been reduced to simply common people's language. Much of the focus of modern literature is on technique and presentation of a theme or an issue.

Ref: Diana Hacker, *The Bedford Handbook for Writer* (1991). Herbert Read, *English Prose Style* (1928). Graeme Harper & Jeri Kroll, Eds. *Creative Writing Studies: Practice, Research and Pedagogy* (2007). JM Murray, *The Problem of Style* (1925).

Subjectivity A term opposite to objectivity. Subjectivity is to be found in writings in which personal ingredients of the author are present; he/she cannot stay outside his/her text. The author's personal feelings, which may not even include factual information, become a part of the major plot of the work. Thus it is, in some degree, autobiographical by nature. Philosophically speaking, it has its roots in Descartes and Kant and its articulation now has depended on the understanding of what constitutes an individual. Although it is an inherently social mode that comes about through interactions within society, the subjectivity inherent in each individual can be recognized as distinct from others. However, in literary text, subjectivity is demonstrated in confessional literature, almost all lyric poems, and in such works as James Joyce's *Portrait of the Artist as a Young Man,* Samuel Butler's *The Way of All Flesh*, Thomas Wolfe's *Look Homeward, Angel*, and in a very recent and unusual sketches of Bob Dylan, *Chronicles: Volume One* (2004), which deliberately eschews any chronological structure, etc. When applied to criticism, the *subjective criticism* generally refers to the impressionistic approach, an expression of an individual taste or the reader's personal rejoinder to a particular work. Objective poetry is, therefore, impersonal and subjective poetry is personal. In the former the focus of attention is something that is outward—a praiseworthy act, a thrilling occurrence, a beautiful sight; in the latter it is the poet himself: whatever the subject may be, his mind is centred on his own thoughts and feelings. The neoclassical literature attempts to be objective; whereas in literature of the romantic era subjectivity is one of the major notional premises. The terms subjective and objective are perhaps introduced in England from the post-Kantian German criticism. Although initially an admirer of Wordsworth, in his mature days Ruskin was very critical about subjectivity and preferred the objectivity of the scientist instead. [Cf. objectivity, reader-response criticism]

Ref: Adrian Cussins, "The Connectionist Construction of Concepts", *Oxford Readings of Philosophy: The Philosophy of Artificial Intelligence,* Ed. Margaret Boden (1990). Andrew Bowie, *Aesthetics and Subjectivity: From Kant to Nietzsche* (1990).

Sublime A quality in art and literature that transports the reader to a higher aesthetic plane. The concept is often referred to the ancient Greek writer and critic philosopher Longinus. His treatise *On the Sublime* written around 1st century is both a discourse on aesthetics and a work of literary criticism. It is written in an epistolary form and the final part seems to have been lost. Longinus simply means that the distinction of words and artistic ability are the most important features in the concept of sublimity. A literary text is not sublime unless it can transport the reader to a higher plane of thought. The treatment of the sublime is intimately connected with the question and style and, therefore, he deals in detail with various figures of thought and diction in his discourse on the sublime. As he believes, sublimity does not just transports or persuades; it is a quality which carries the reader by the force of the writer's genius and, like a lightening, reveals at a stroke some extraordinary power in the writing or speech. As an example of the sublime, he refers to Sappho's *Ode to Jealousy* as the poem's goal is not so much to express empty feelings, but to arouse higher form of emotion in his audience. This is the first known critical discourse in which greatness of literature is ascribed to qualities innate in the writer rather than his art. The author further suggests that greatness of thought, if not inborn, may be acquired through cultivation of classical literature. The literary concept of the sublime came to the front in the 18th century with the 1757 treatise by Edmund Burke. The idea of the sublime was taken up by Immanuel Kant and the Romantic poets, especially William Wordsworth. For the romantic, the sublime was a favourite quest. Sublimity in literature has usually been attempted through grand style, subject matter or nobility of emotions. The Greek treatise *Peri Hypsous* (by Longinus or somebody else) first refers to this concept and it was discussed in that "golden booklet" that sublimity could be achieved through the combined effect of great thoughts, noble sentiments, heightened Figures of Speech, elevated diction, etc. [Cf. grotesque]

Ref: Edmund Burke, *A Philosophical Inquiry into the Origin of our Ideas of the Sublime and Beautiful* (1856). Robert Doran, *The Theory of the Sublime from Longinus to Kant* (2015). Thomas Weiskel, *The Romantic Sublime: Studies in the Structure and Psychology of Transcendence* (1986). WR Roberts, *Longinus on the Sublime* (1899).

Subplot A subordinate, secondary or minor events in a novel or drama, which may be related to the main plot as a parallel or contrast or diversion. Aristotle has no comment on this except that a play must be complete in itself. The neoclassicists insisted that there should be only one plot line, which might be relieved by a subplot, usually comic. During the Elizabethan period specially, this kind of application of *double plots* came into vogue. Shakespeare has taken full liberty and he has incorporated subplots with skill. In *King Lear* the subplot concerns the Earl of Gloucester, who spurns his honest son, Edgar, and believes his conniving illegitimate son, Edmund. The rich heiress of Belmont in *The Merchant of Venice*, Portia's selection of husband from among several men, her relationship with Bassanio is one of the play's important subplots. Marlowe's *Doctor Faustus* too has a stimulating subplot fashioned by the minor characters. Subplots are outstanding from the main plot by taking up less of the action, having fewer significant events to take place with less impact on the main plot except that the subplots, by contrast, highlight the main plot and cater a good dose of real comic fun to the audience. [Cf. frame]

Subtext An invisible text under the visible one. An author conveys something through his text that the reader apparently reads and something remains still unsaid —an intentional or unintentional effort on author's part. That unpronounced part in a poem, story or any literary genre, which the reader *discovers* is the subtext of the main text. Even a pause, silence or even punctuation marks in a particular dramatic, poetic or narrative context may lead to the subtext. Marxist critics Pierre Macherey and Fredric Jameson have tried to dig out ideological and political contents from the subtexts. They believe that it is critics' responsibility to highlight the subtextual contents of a given text. David Baboulene, in *The Story Book*, defines subtext as "the result of any form of gap in knowledge between any of the participants in a story; for example, between the author and a character, between two characters or between the audience and at least one character." In Ibsen's *Ghosts* subtext has more space for scrutiny and understanding the characters as ghosts cannot communicate because of social conventions and constrictions. [Cf. discourse]

Ref: Alan Wolfe, *Marginalized in the Middle* (1996). David Daboulene, *The Story Book: Guidance for Writers on Story Creation, Optimisation and Problem Resolution* (2010).

Supernaturalism <Latin *supra*, above + *naturalis*> An unbelievable phenomena, demanding the reader's tacit consent, treated in a literary work. Thus any literary treatment of the major mysteries of existence, metaphysical, mystical and even religious subjects; gods, demons, ghosts, magic, goblins, fantasies, fairies, etc may come within this definition. ST Coleridge prefers the term *preternatural* than supernatural. The proportion of the supernatural in a text may be either isolated or integral part of the narrative; and the transportation may be either gradual or through a sudden form similar to that of a deus ex machina. Literary examples abound, more in the ancient, medieval and Renaissance literatures. Greek tragedies have many of them as support system to the ancient life; Shakespearean plays (*Hamlet, Macbeth, Julius Caesar, A Midsummer Night's Dream*) thrive on them artistically and commercially; Coleridge theorizes its use and refines the crudity of this foreign element in his ballad, *The Ancient Mariner*, and in "Cristabel." Other literary examples of the use of the supernatural are Goethe's *Faust, Divine Comedy*, Christopher Marlowe's *Doctor Faustus*, Herman Melville's *Moby Dick*, Edmund Spenser's *The Faerie Queene,* John Milton's *The Paradise Lost*, almost all

Gothic tales, Hawthorne's *The Scarlet Letter,* Ibsen's *Master Builder,* TS Eliot's *Murder in the Cathedral*, Edgar Allan Poe stories, etc only to mention a few. One of the very recent examples of the paranormal category, mixed with fantasy, is Vicki Pattersson's *The Taken* (2012). Children's literature mostly thrives on this property. The range of the genre's literary expression is to be found from primitive folklore to the tales of the 20th-century and even after.

However, more important factor is how an author makes use of the foreign agents in literary works. Making a proper atmosphere is one prerequisite for the purpose. Gothic tales have the proper physical backgrounds for that; so have the marsh and the castle in *Hamlet* and *Macbeth*. Shakespeare takes his stories to those ancient days when breeding grounds of ghosts were fertile. The supernatural elements become so inseparable from the very beginning with the story line that without them story must have a premature death. *Moby Dick* has the awe and terror without the ghostly phenomena. Coleridge makes it happen in broad daylight, but not in the drawing room. Milton has banked on the religious faith. It is finally a question of credibility of the artistic process, not the supernatural. It is the author's artistic responsibility to make his readers believe in the unbelievable; he has to make sure what Coleridge believes, "suspension of disbelieve" to operate on the reader or audience. If he can do it, readers will never complain while involved in the artistic work; if he cannot, the author fails.

Ref: Christopher Warnes, "Naturalizing the Supernatural: Faith, Irreverence and Magical Realism" *Literature Compass* 2 (2005). EJ Clery, *The Rise of Supernatural Fiction* (1995). EV Bleiler, *The Guide to Supernatural Fiction* (1983). HP Lovecraft, *Supernatural Horror in Literature* (1973).

Surrealism A movement in the visual arts and literature that flourished in Europe between the World Wars. It flourished mainly out of Dadaism, which produced works of anti-art that calculatingly defied reason. Surrealism reacted against the rationalism that had led to World War I. André Breton initiated the school in 1924 with a view to joining dream and fantasy to everyday reality and forming "an absolute reality, a surreality." Drawing on Sigmund Freud, he concluded that the unconscious was the fountain of the imagination. Breton was a poet, but major achievements of Surrealism were to be found in painting. Surrealist works often feature the components of surprise, unpredicted combinations. However, many Surrealist artists and writers regard their work as an expression of the philosophical movement first and foremost, with the works being an *objet d'art*. While some artists practiced organic, emblematic or absolute Surrealism expressing the unconscious through suggestive yet indefinite biomorphic images. Others created realistically painted images, removed from their contexts and reassembled within a paradoxical or appalling framework. With its emphasis on content and free form, Surrealism provided a major alternative to the contemporary highly formalistic Cubist movement. The surrealists aimed at transfiguring human experience in all its aspects—psychological, socio-cultural and political. They had their agenda to liberate people from artificial reasonableness and restrictive customs and structures. Breton proclaimed that the true aim of Surrealism was "long live the social revolution." Literary figures like Antonio Artaud, Eugène Ionesco, Samuel Beckett, Dylan Thomas, Henry Miller and William Burroughs are much indebted to the principles of surrealism. However, the visual art remained the central area of the movement. The works of such painters as Jean Arp, Max Ernst, André Masson, René Magritte, Yves Tanguy, Salvador Dalí, Pierre Roy, Paul Delvaux and Joan Miró, etc summarized in a rather flexible sense the Surrealist approach in the visual arts.

Ref: AE Balakian, *Literary Origin of Surrealism* (1947). André Breton, *Conversations: The Autobiography of Surrealism* (1952). David Gascoyne, *A Short Survey of Surrealism* (1935). Durozoi Gerard, *History of the Surrealist Movement* (2004). Yvan Goll, "Manifesto of Surrealism" (1924).

Symbol/Symbolism A sign or something that stands for or suggests something else by reason of relationship, association, convention or accidental resemblance, especially a visible sign standing for something invisible (*lion = courage*) is a symbol. A work of art or literature too very often goes beyond the primary *meaning* and can make the piece stand for something else not principally associated with it. This particular artistic investment of additional *meaning* makes an item or a word a symbol. Thus a simple whale in Herman Melville's *Moby Dick* (1851) becomes a symbol of evil. In Tolstoy's *Anna Karenina* (1875-77) there is a constantly recurring item in the representational content, namely, *the train*—so much so that before the novel ends, it becomes apparent that the train is a symbol of the iron forces of material progress toward which Tolstoy had great antipathy. Blake's *rose* (O Rose, thou art sick), for example, has nothing to do with a simile or a metaphor or even an allegory. It is a personal symbol and it derives its symbolic significance from other words around it in the text. Some of the symbols are conventional and some are natural. The *cross* is a symbol of Christianity, and it is a conventional symbol of suffering and sacrifice. People have accepted the cross as such. Other symbols are natural—the *sun* as the symbol of life and energy, a *river* as the symbol of flux and flow of life. In these cases there are no agreements as to what would stand for what, for the relations are too obvious and the symbolism is much the same in the traditions of all nations and civilizations.

The extensive use of symbols has given birth to the symbolist movement that originated with a group of French poets in the late 19th century, spread to painting and the theatre and that influenced the European and American literatures of the 20th century to varying degrees. Symbolist artists, such as Baudelaire, Mallarmé, Verlaine, Rimbaud and others, sought to express individual emotional experience through the subtle and suggestive use of highly symbolized language. Symbolist works had a strong and lasting influence on much of British and American literatures in the 20th century. The experimental techniques and Symbolist theories bore fruit both in the poetry of WB Yeats and TS Eliot and in modern novels as represented by James Joyce and Virginia Woolf, in which word harmonies and patterns of images often take pre-eminence over the narrative. [Cf. image, symbolism]

Symbolism as an artistic movement came to England in the late 19th century from France and sought to use newly created or pre-existing symbols to provide intense complexes of emotion and thought which had a transcendent and unifying effect on the reader. The term has two widely usual senses of meaning. In historical criticism, it denotes an early modernist literary movement initiated in France during the 19th century that reacted against the established standards of realism. Writers in this movement aimed at evoking, indirectly and symbolically, an order of being beyond the material world of the five senses. Secondly, poetic expression of personal emotion figured strongly in the movement, typically by means of a private set of symbols uniquely identifiable with the individual poet. The principal aim of the Symbolists was to express in words the highly complex feelings that grew out of everyday contact with the world. In a broader sense, the term symbolism refers to the use of one object to represent another. Early members of the Symbolist movement included the French authors Charles Baudelaire and Arthur Rimbaud. In England William Butler Yeats, James Joyce and TS Eliot were influenced as the movement moved to Ireland, England and the United States. The movement in poetry marked its zenith in the 1890s and began to mark a straight drop in popularity by the end of the century. The unfocused imagery of Symbolist poetry eventually came to be seen as over-refined and artificial; the term *decadent* became a sarcastic charge against them signifying mere *fin-de-siècle* refinement. [Cf. image]

Ref: AG Lehmann, *The Symbolist Aesthetic in France, 1885-1895* (1950). Harry Levin, *Contexts of Criticism* (1957). Murray McArthur, *British Theory and Criticism: Symbolism* (1997). WB Yeats, "Symbolism in Poetry" (1900). WY Tindall, *The Literary Symbol* (1955).

Synaesthesia/Synesthesia (Greek, *feeling together*) is a technique common in symbolist verse whereby the writer brings several kinds of sense impressions together into play, in which one type is referred to in terms of another. For example describing sounds as colours, or colours as tastes to rouse the emotions through simultaneous force, to overwork, upon several senses comes under this method: "Nor what soft incense hangs upon the boughs,/ But, in embalmed darkness, guess each sweet...." Keats' lines here amply exemplify the concept.

Synecdoche A figurative use of language for understanding one thing with another, more comprehensive for less comprehensive, or vice versa. It is a figure based on association in which [1] part is made to stand for the whole: A man bowed down with *seventy winters* (= years); [2] whole for a part: The lavish moisture of the *melting year* (= rainy season); [3] species for the genus: Man must earn his *bread* by the sweat of his brows (= food); [4] genus for a species: Drink, *pretty creature,* drink (= lamb); and [5] individual for the class: *A Daniel* come to judgment! Yea a *Daniel!* (= wise judge).

T

Ten Commandments/Decalogue <Greek *deka*, ten; and *logue*, word> A list of *do's and dont's* in the book of Exodus. It is said to have been recommended by God Himself for His followers to adhere to—"And God spoke all these words, saying: "I am the Lord your God, who brought you out of the land of Egypt, out of the house of bondage." The Ten Commandments are listed in Exodus 20:1-17 and Deuteronomy 5: 1-22: [1] "You shall have no Gods before me" (for that any carved image and its worship is strictly banned); [2] "You shall not take the name of the Lord your God in vain"; [3] "Remember the Sabbath day, to keep it holy" (seventh day of week); [4] "Six days you shall labour and do all your work"; [5] "Honour your father and your mother"; [6] "You shall not murder"; [7] "You shall not commit adultery"; [8] "You shall not steal"; [9] "You shall not bear false witness against your neighbour"; and [10] "You shall not covet your neighbour's wife; and you shall not desire your neighbour's house." All these codes for the Jews of ancient times contained in the *Pentateuch*, which allegedly were engraved by God on two stone tablets entrusted to Moses on Mount Sinai. Some of these moral codes, for example, [6] "You shall not murder," however, only extend to members of the Israelites' own tribe, for God permits murder and destruction of other tribes (Deuteronomy 12: 1-28 and Exodus 21: 23-24). It is therefore difficult to accept the Commandments as a collection of norms for absolute morality appropriate in all times for all peoples. A significant aspect of Christian tradition is that what is recommended in the Old Testament is often rejected in the New Testament. [Cf. seven cardinal virtues]

Tenor/Vehicle A twin terms associated with metaphorical representation. In a metaphor what is being represented is the *tenor*; the instrument used to represent the tenor is the *vehicle*. It is IA Richards who first introduced the terms in the book *The Philosophy of Rhetoric* (1936). Richards viewed *tenor* and *vehicle* as the two equivalent parts of a metaphor. In a metaphoric expression like—Monica is an ass—*Monica* is the *tenor*, the main subject of the Figure of Speech, or the thing being represented. And how is so? Obviously it is by a clear reference to an *ass*, the *vehicle*. Therefore, *vehicle* is the tool (image, activity or concept), which throws some extra light on the *tenor*. Each

Figure of Speech makes use of a tenor and a vehicle. [Cf. metaphor]

Terza Rima A verse composed of three-line stanzas with a complicated interlocking rhyme scheme. This verse form became particularly famous because Dante used it in *The Divine Comedy*. The English composers did not approve of the rhyme scheme much because of the difficulty of composing such prolonged interlocking rhyme scheme. It requires three-line stanzas (*tercets*) with the rhyme scheme: a-b-a, b-c-b, c-d-c and so on. Shelley's "Ode to the West Wind" is one of the few poems, which followed this difficult scheme. Among the English poets it was Shelley who tried this pattern several times. His unfinished poem, *The Triumph of Life* is written in terza rima, the interlocking verse pattern that Dante had used in his *Divina Comedia* and Petrarch in his *Trionfi*. Shelley tried this form for the first time in *Prince Athanase* and also in *The Woodman and the Nightingale.*

Textual Criticism A branch of literary criticism that tries to establish the most authoritative text of a work, often a lost or unavailable work. Textual critics typically compare all known manuscripts or printings of a single work in order to assess the meanings of differences and revisions. This procedure allows them to arrive at a definitive version that supposedly corresponds to the author's original intention. Textual criticism was applied during the Renaissance to recover the classical texts of Greece and Rome. Modern works have been studied, for instance, to undo deliberate correction or censorship, as in the case of novels by Stephen Crane and Theodore Dreiser. The methods of textual criticism are however not to be taken as absolute rules. Paul Mass clarifies the scope as the "business of textual criticism is to produce a text as close as possible to the original." The objective of the textual critic's work is, therefore, a better understanding of the creation and historical transmission of texts. This understanding may lead to the production of a scholarly and critical edition containing a 'curated' text. The editors' intention is only limited to guiding readers with some informed judgment and do not in themselves lead to any truth. It is a form of objective criticism and the scope of the criticism is limited to only the controversial texts, such as different versions of Greek and Latin manuscripts, ancient tragedies, epics, the Bible, Shakespeare's plays, etc. Some of the canon makers of textual criticism are Johann Albrecht Bengel, Johann Jakob Griesbach and Brooke Foss Westcott, Joseph Bédier, etc. Most of their works is concerned with different versions of the Bible and medieval texts. [Cf. Chicago school, new criticism]

Ref: DC Greetham, *Theories of the Text* (1999). Paul Maas, *Textual Criticism* (1958). Paul Wegner, *A Student's Guide to Textual Criticism of the Bible* (2006).

Theatre of the Absurd <French *théâtre de l'absurde*> A 20th century, specially the post-Second World War, dramatic trend in France characterized by radical theatrical innovations to highlight the absurdity of modern human condition. The writers in the group believe that the only way to represent absurdity is to write in a matching absurd manner. Literature of the Absurd, both fiction and drama, is bizarre in style as it is bewildered in subject matter. In the works associated with this tradition, non-traditional, sometimes grotesque characterization, plots and stage sets reveal a meaningless universe in which human values are irrelevant. The Existentialist themes of estrangement, absurdity and futility link many of the works of this movement. The leading artists are: Franz Kafka, Samuel Beckett, Albert Camus and Jean-Paul Sartre and Eugene Ionesco etc. Harold Pinter and James Joyce are primarily responsible for developing the British trend, and in America Edward Albee has the leading role. Although initially theatre happens to be the main field adopted for practice, several novels written during the 1950s and 1960s in England and America contain the Absurdist elements.

Critic and writer Martin Esslin coined the term in his essay "Theatre of the Absurd." He explained the aim of the Absurd Drama was "to shock its audience out of complacency, to bring it face to face with the harsh facts of the human situation as these writers see it. But the challenge behind this message is anything but one of despair. It is a challenge to accept the human condition as it is, in all its mystery and absurdity, and to bear it with dignity, nobly, responsibly; precisely *because* there are no easy solutions to the mysteries of existence, because ultimately man is alone in a meaningless world." Many of the Absurdist artists had direct connections with the Dadaist and Existentialist. Although the Absurdist were contemporaries with Jean-Paul Sartre, the philosophical spokesman for existentialism; few was actually committed to Sartre's own existentialist philosophy.

Ref: James Knowlson, *Damned to Fame: The Life of Samuel Beckett* (1996). Jean-Paul Sartre, "Beyond Bourgeois Theatre", *Tulane Drama Review* 5.3 (1961). Martin Esslin, *Absurd Drama* (1965). Michael Y Bennett, *Reassessing the Theatre of the Absurd: Camus, Beckett, Ionesco, Genet and Pinter* (2011).

Theme A major issue or topic for literary treatment or for other art forms. It is something not exactly equivalent to subject matter. It is a salient, abstract idea and it may recur in a number of literary works. Usually the subject matter is described elaborately in terms of action (e.g. adventure of a newcomer in the big city); its theme will be described in more abstract terms (e.g. love, fate, war, revenge, drug addiction, etc). The theme of a work may be announced explicitly, but more often it emerges indirectly through the recurrence of motifs. For example, the theme in Jane Austen's *Pride and Prejudice* is matrimony though associated ideas of love, friendship, jealousy and affection are there in exact proportion. The whole narrative revolves around the major theme, i.e. matrimony.

Incidentally love has remained an all-time popular theme in fiction. Any novel dealing with love details what the lovers do and how they overcome obstacles. All these incidents make the subject matter of the novel; but the theme of the novel is *love*. The theme of a knight who undertakes adventures to prove to his lady that he is worthy of her love is represented by a variety of romances including the *Ipomedon* (1174-90) of Hugh de Rotelande and the anonymous mid-13th-century Anglo-Norman story *Gui de Warewic*. Another popular theme that has often been treated is the *persecuted heroine* theme. Philippe de Beaumanoir's *La Manekine* (*c.* 1270), Jean Maillart's *La Contesse d'Anjou* (1361) and Chaucer's *Man of Law's Tale* (1387?) all treat the theme of the tribulations of wife falsely accused and banished; but after many adventures, reunited with her husband. Theme like *war* too has preoccupied great writers like Homer, Tolstoy and Hemingway and others.

Ref: Alison Booth & Kelly J Mays, Eds. "Theme and Tone", *The Norton Introduction to Literature* (2010). David Lodge, *The Art of Fiction* (1992). Raymond Obstfeld, *Fiction First Aid: Instant Remedies for Novels, Stories and Scripts* (2002).

Three Unities A set of principles governing *time*, *place* and *action* in a play. A rigid observation of the unities, as allegedly recommended by Aristotle, implies that a play should be confined to a single action occurring in a single place and occupying no more than a single day's time.

The three unities evolved and were redefined by the Italian humanist Lodovico Castelvetro (1505-1571) in his interpretation of Aristotle's *Poetics* and are usually referred to as "Aristotelian rules" for dramatic structure. Actually, Aristotle's observations on tragedy are descriptive rather than prescriptive and he emphasizes only one unity, that of plot or action. In French classical tragedy, the unities were adhered to literally and became the source of endless critical polemics. In England, where playwrights often had two or more plots in a play; they mixed comedy and tragedy and freely switched over time and place. The unities were esteemed in theory but ignored in practice. Ben Jonson, an adherent of classical approach, in his prologue to *Every Man in His Humour* (1598), makes fun of the violation of the principle of three unities:

To make a child, now swaddled to proceed
Man, and then shoot up, in one beard, and weed,
Past three score years; or, with three rusty swords.
And help of some few foot-and-half-foot words...

Shakespeare always gives importance to the unity of plot and action and consciously ignored the other two. Dr. Johnson, however, strongly defends Shakespeare against charges of failing to adhere to the Neo-classical doctrine of the dramatic unities. He alertly observes that time and place are subservient to the mind. Since the audience does not confuse stage action with reality, it has no trouble with a shift in scene from Rome to Alexandria. Modern dramatists, too, do not bother about maintaining the unities of time and place.

Ref: John Dryden, *An Essay of Dramatick Poesie,* Ed. Jack Lynch (1668). Johnson Samuel, *Preface to his Edition of Shakespeare's Plays* (1765). J Lear, "Katharsis", *Essays on Aristotle's Poetics,* Ed. O Rorty (1992). Raymond Williams, *Modern Tragedy* (1966).

Tone An attitude of the writer toward his reader and his subject. It may also refer to the mood or moral view as presented in a work of art and literature. A writer can be formal, informal, playful, ironic, and optimistic or pessimistic. While both Swift and Pope satirize much the same subjects, there is a profound difference in their tone. A formal tone may create distance or convey politeness, while an informal tone may encourage a friendly, intimate or intrusive feeling in the reader. The use of language and setting mostly determine the mood of a literary work. In Shakespeare's *A Midsummer Night's Dream*, Milton's *Paradise Lost,* Hardy's *Return of the Native* or Synge's *Riders to the Sea*, it is the setting that sets the tone of the works.

Ref: Alison Booth & Kelly J Mays, Eds. "Theme and Tone," *The Norton Introduction to Literature* (2010). David Lodge, *The Art of Fiction* (1992).

Tragedy <*Tragos,* he-goat + *aeidein,* to sing = goat song> An ancient form of the drama (comedy being another form), in prose or poetry, about a noble, courageous hero/heroine of excellent character, in Aristotle's words, 'a good but not too good man' who, because of some tragic flaw or hamartia, brings ruin upon himself/herself. It is Aristotle who, for the first time, discussed the art of Tragedy at length in his seminal work *Poetics* (335 BCE). From the theatre of ancient Greece, of which survive only a few works of Aeschylus, Sophocles and Euripides, through the works of Shakespeare, Jean Racine and Friedrich Schiller to the more recent naturalistic tragedy of August Strindberg; Samuel Beckett's modernist engagements on death, loss and suffering; Müller's postmodernist discourse of the tragic canon, tragedy has remained a constant source of literary practice and investigation.

Tragedy, as Aristotle envisaged it, treats its subjects in a dignified and serious manner, using poetic language to help evoke pity and fear and bring about catharsis, a purging of these emotions: A tragedy accordingly is "the imitation of an action that is serious and also, as having magnitude, complete in itself; in language with pleasurable accessories, each kind brought in separately in the parts of the work; in a dramatic, not in a narrative form; with incidents arousing pity and fear, wherewith to accomplish its catharsis of such emotions." The ancient Greeks extensively practised this tragic dramatic form. In the Middle Ages, when classical works were virtually unknown, tragedy came to denote any works about the fall of a person from exalted to inferior condition due to any reason: fate, vice, and weakness, etc. According to the classical definition of tragedy, such works present *the pathetic*—that which evokes ordinary compassion rather than the tragic pity of which Aristotle speaks. The pathetic derivation is exemplified in "The Monk's Tale" in Chaucer's *Canterbury Tales.* Notable works produced during the 16th century revival include Shakespeare's *Hamlet, Macbeth, Othello* and *King Lear* and Marlowe's *Doctor Faustus*, etc.

In modern times, dramatists have attempted to adapt the form to the needs of modern society by drawing their heroes from the ranks of ordinary men and women and defining the nobility of these heroes in terms of spirit rather than exalted social standing. Both thematically and structurally modern tragedies are very different, but somewhere the essence remains the same. Hegel, in his theory of tragedy, throws some light on the issue: "The heroes of ancient classical tragedy encounter situations in which, if they firmly decide in favour of the one ethical pathos that alone suits their finished character, they must necessarily come into conflict with the equally justified ethical power that confronts them. Modern characters, on the other hand, stand in a wealth of more accidental circumstances, within which one could act this way or that, so that the conflict is, though occasioned by external preconditions, still essentially grounded in the character." Sophocles' *Antigone*, according Hegel is a perfect example of tragedy; it highlights the dialectic between two goods instead of a good force and a bad one. There is no question of a negatively tragic fault; Hegel stresses on the correction of moral imbalances. However, the greatest example of tragedy is Sophocles' *Oedipus Rex* which remains a model for all ages, though every age has its own tragic work suitable for the respective society, time and space. Modern dramatists of the tragic tradition include Henrik Ibsen, Arthur Miller and Eugene O'Neill. Arthur Miller's essay "Tragedy and the Common Man" (1949) argues that tragedy may also depict ordinary people in domestic surroundings.

Ref: AC Bradley, *Shakespearean Tragedy* (1904). Elder Olson, *Tragedy and the Theory of Drama* (1961). GW Knight, *The Wheel of Fire* (1951). FL Lucas, *Tragedy: Serious Drama in Relation to Aristotle's Poetics* (1927). Friedrich Nietzsche, *The Birth of Tragedy, Or, Hellenism and Pessimism* (1886). H Baker, *Induction to Tragedy* (1939).

Tragi-Comedy A hybrid subgenre of the drama in which attempts are made to accommodate both tragic and comic elements. The term specially refers to one that has tragic potentiality in plot, seriousness in tone, but ends with a clear comic note, or often, essentially a comic play tinged with some gloomy elements. Tragicomedy is associated with the Italian dramatic tradition initiated with Battista Guarini's *Il Pastor Fido* (1583). Guarini mixed high and low characters in it and aimed for a middle style between the tragic and the comic. The English dramatists Francis Beaumont and John Fletcher experimented with the idea in *The Faithful Shepherdess* (1608) and *Philaster* (1609). Tragicomedy remained fairly popular up to the mid-17th century and Fletcher's works were popular till the Restoration period. Shakespeare's *The Merchant of Venice, The Winter's Tale* and *Cymbeline* are often considered to have been influenced by the tradition. Tragicomedy is a common genre in post-World War II theatre with authors like Samuel Beckett (*Waiting for Godot,* 1952) and Harold Pinter (*The Caretaker*). Other examples of the subgenre are John Dryden's *Marriage à la Mode* and the Russian playwright Anton Chekhov's *The Cherry Orchard.* The main feature of tragicomedy is that it can accommodate dual nature of reality—both seriousness and absurdity—together.

Ref: EM Waith, *The Pattern of Tragicomedy in Beaumont and Fletcher* (1952). MT Herrick, *Tragicomedy* (1955). Verna A Foster, *The Name and Nature of Tragicomedy* (2004). FH Ristine, *English Tragi-comedy: Its Origin and History* (1963).

Transcendentalism/-ist A partly intellectual and partly activist theory emanating out of the works of Ralph Waldo Emerson (1803-1882), America's poet and priest between 1830s and the Civil War (1861-65). His doctrines centred round the message of personal salvation in an age of commodification of humanity. He stressed on guiding values in human souls and believed that a healthy society could evolve out of the soulfulness of individual rather than the sustainability of institutions. Transcendentalism was a form of American romanticism that had its roots in Europe in the works of Thomas Carlyle, Samuel Coleridge and Johann Wolfgang von Goethe. The Transcendentalists stressed the importance of intuition and subjective experience in communication with God. They rejected religious dogma and texts in favour of mysticism and scientific naturalism. They pursued truths that lie beyond the realms perceived by reason and the senses and thus came very close to an Indian philosophical school. On the other hand, Ram Mohan Roy (1772-1833) too was influenced by the transcendentalist philosophy. He found that Unitarianism came closest to true Christianity and had a strong sympathy for the Unitarians. The transcendentalists were active social reformers in public education, women's rights and the abolition of slavery. The prominent members of the group, other than Emerson, were Henry David Thoreau (1817-1862), Margaret Fuller, Orestes Brownson, James Freeman Clarke, George Ripley, Bronson Alcott, and WH Channingand. It is often said that Indian classical philosophical school strongly influenced the transcendentalist. There was a continuous concern for Indian thought in the US since Emerson's time. However, Nathaniel Hawthorne and Edgar Allan Poe criticized the transcendental school.

Ref: Arthur Versluis, *American Transcendentalism and Asian Religions* (1993). Philip F Gura, *American Transcendentalism: A History* (2007). Dale Riepe, "The Indian Influence in American Philosophy: Emerson to Moore", *Philosophy of East and West,* Vol. 17 (1967).

Transferred Epithet/Hypallage A Figure of Speech based on association. The figure simply refers to verbal or written language where the epithet (adjective) applied to a person or an object is displaced from its legitimate position (i.e. *before* the person or object), and located elsewhere ungrammatically. Bose and Sterling observe that the adjective is "transferred or shifted from the object to which it belongs, to another with which it is associated in the mind of the writer or speaker." Usually the transfer of the *epithet* happens to be "from a person to a thing" (Nesfield). For example, in such a line as "The ploughman homewards plods his weary way"—the epithet, *weary*, grammatically speaking, should be suffixed by *the ploughman,* not *way*; for it is the *ploughman* who is weary, not the *way*. Other examples of the case are: "The prisoner was placed in the *condemned cell*," "We're coming close to those little creeks now, and we keep a *discreet silence*", and "He lay all night on his *sleepless pillow*," etc.

The figure is often slightly confusing. Many think that transferred epithet is a weaker form of personification. Again, when a metaphor speaks of an inanimate object as if it were a living person without attributing human quality to it, it is a case of personal metaphor: "That to the sleeping woods all night/ Singeth a quiet tune." A transferred epithet is that way simpler; it is a deliberate case of misplacing adjective without either personifying noun or attributing to it any human quality. The purpose of a transferred epithet is either improving the quality of versification or heightening emotive appeal. In Lamb's essay, "Dream Children: A Reverie," an excellent use of transferred epithet—"I found myself quietly seated in my bachelor arm-chair"—humourously heightens pathos involved in a human situation.

Travesty A work that treats a serious subject frivolously or gives undignified treatment of a dignified subject with a view to ridiculing the dignified. The portrayal of a character in a play, opera, or ballet by a performer of the opposite sex is also known as travesty. In literary studies a comparison with the mock-heroic makes it clear. A mock-heroic poem has a trivial subject matter and an inappropriately grand style; whereas a travesty has the opposite—trivial style and a grand subject. *Don Quixote* (1605) is a travesty, whereas *The Rape of the Lock* (1714) is a mock-heroic poem. [Cf. parody]

Trilogy <Greek *tri*, three + *logia*, discourse> A group of three plays (novels also) somehow bunched together. Ancient Greek plays were usually presented at the Athenian festivals in the form of a trilogy—three tragic plays were performed followed by a fourth satyr play. Aeschylus' *Oresteia* is the only classical trilogy available today. Later dramatic instances are: Shakespeare's *Henry VI*, Eugene O'Neill's *Mourning Becomes Electra*, Arnold Wesker's *Chicken Soup with Barley, Roots* and *I'm Talking about Jerusalem*, etc. In fiction, Samuel Beckett's (1906-1989) trilogy of novels, *Molloy, Malone Meurt* and *L'Innommable* exemplify the tradition. The term is applied to the film also: *The Apu Trilogy* of Satyajit Ray is an example. A similar set of four plays or novels is called *tetralogy*. [Cf. sequel]

Trinity <Latin: *Trinitas*, combination of three> A Christian belief that God is one being made up of three distinct persons existing as the Father, the Son and the Holy Spirit. The three identities are distinct, yet are one "substance, essence or nature." The term 'Trinity' is, however, not to be found in the Bible; but most scholars agree that its meaning is clearly expressed. He is not three different gods, but three persons in the one and only God. The key Biblical verses in the New Testament that refer to the concept are:

> [1] *Go therefore and make disciples of all nations, baptizing them in the name of the Father and of the Son and of the Holy Spirit* ... (Matthew 28:19, ESV). [2] *[Jesus said,] "But when the Helper comes, whom I will send to you from the Father, the Spirit of truth, who proceeds from the Father, he will bear witness about me"* (John 15:26, ESV). [3] *The grace of the Lord Jesus Christ and the love of God and the fellowship of the Holy Spirit be with you all* (2 Corinthians 13:14, ESV).

The nature of the Trinity, however, has remained a controversial issue for centuries. Almost all the major Christian sects may be called *Trinitarian*. The Father, Son and Holy Spirit together—the Father as the protector of Jews, the Son, Christ, as the savior of mankind and the Holy Spirit as the preserver of the church—is a common doctrine accepted everywhere in Christendom.

It is relevant to note that the Indian concept of the Trinity is slightly different yet many of the Christian aspects are covered in it. The Hindu trinity—Brahma,

Vishnu and Shiva (Maheshwar)—are distinctly plural identities and respectively the creator, preserver and destroyer of the universe though they are also aligned as the transcendent Godhead, Brahma. The Trinity represents the Divine in its threefold nature and function. Each aspect of the Trinity contains and includes the others.

Ref: Robert Letham, *The Holy Trinity: In Scripture, History, Theology, and Worship* (2004). Peter C Phan, Ed. *The Cambridge Companion to the Trinity* (2011).

U

Unitarianism A Christian theological doctrine closely linked to the 18th century post-Enlightenment enthusiasm for reason and science as well as growing humanitarianism. Humanitarians, although remained a minority among the Christian groups, Unitarianism nevertheless was a potent force in the educational, cultural, socio-economic and political life in some pockets, particularly in Great Britain and the United States. Some view this trend as a reaction to the excesses of Puritanism. The central issue came from the belief that the concept of the Trinity—God in three avatars: the Father, son and Holy Spirit—does not stand critical tests. God, to Unitarians, is a single person; Jesus Christ, while divinely inspired, was a human being entrusted with teaching humanity the message of love. Beyond that, God has left human beings entirely on their own and His spirit does not move about here on earth entering people's souls and doing benevolent things. Although Unitarianism began as a scripture related movement, by the mid-19th century the leadership of James Martineau in England and Ralph Waldo Emerson and Theodore Parker in the US redirected it into a religion of reason. Human being, as the school stresses, is subject to fundamental reformation. Once enlightened with science and reason, man can achieve both goodness and greatness. The spiritual guide, Preacher William Channing, has underscored in the Unitarian agenda such benevolent issues as social welfare of the unprivileged, attack on slavery system, spread of education and even peace among nations, etc. Other than RW Emerson, the literary doyens, who later joined the school, were Elizabeth Gaskell, Henry Wordsworth Longfellow and Oliver Wendell Holmes.

Ref: Charles A Howe, *For Faith and Freedom: A Short History of Unitarianism in Europe* (1997). John White Chadwick, *Old and New Unitarian Belief* (1894).

Unreliable Narrator A narrator who gives his or her own understanding of a story instead of the explanation and interpretation the author wishes the reader to acquire. The term was coined and discussed by Wayne Booth in *The Rhetoric of Fiction*. He remarks, "An unreliable narrator however, 'does not tell the truth' ... Rather ... tells lies, conceals information, misjudges with respect to the narrative audience...."

This type of interference is likely to alter the audience or reader's assessment of the plot and conclusion of a story. An author quite famous for using unreliable narrators is Henry James. James is said to have made an incoherent and distorting "centre of consciousness" in his work, because of his frequent usage of deluding or unbalanced narrators. They are very noticeable in his novella *The Turn of the Screw* and also in some of his short stories. *The Turn of the Screw* is a story based solely on the consistency of the Governess's description of the events. Clear awareness of the unreliable narrators is essential, especially when a reader has to describe the characters and their actions to others, since the narrator, unreliable as they are, abandons the reader without the essential assistance to make responsible estimation. Thackeray's novel *Vanity Fair* is an early example of an unreliable authorial narrator. Agatha Christie's *The Murder of Roger Ackroyd*, where the narrator hides essential truths in the text through possible evasion and omission, is an excellent occasion for applying the method since a detective novel has to work on a sustained suspense throughout. Among the classic works of fiction, Charles Marlow in Conrad's *Heart of Darkness* (1899) and Nick Carraway in Scott Fitzgerald's *The Great Gatsby* (1925) belong to this class.

Ref: MW Smith, *Understanding Unreliable Narrators* (1991). Wayne Booth, *The Rhetoric of Fiction* (1961).

V

Valorization An empowering of certain key aspects or phrases in criticism. Literary criticism is a living process and every now and then a new school or approach emerges with new ideas and concepts. Certain words, phrases or points of view, etc are used as special tools with which that particular school declares its manifesto. These words or phrases generate extra value with the connotative implication in the contexts they are used. The concept may have come from Karl Marx's explanation of surplus value. However, the promotion, enhancement or privileging of those key words, ideas or aspects of literary or theoretical analysis thus valorises a school's critical principles. For example, New Criticism valorises *autonomy of literature*, whereas the theory of deconstruction valorises the limitless free play of *system of signs*. Thus, simply speaking, valorisation means substantiation of a particular method or thrust area for criticism. Philosopher Anton Barak's valorisation of literature is based on the two tenets: [1] that literature has to be an expression of a man in his totality, as an individual and social being; and [2] that the great art is born only out of some great pain. In postcolonial and subaltern studies, on the other hand, valorised areas are colonial experience, resistance of the suppressed and marginalized, counter discourse, etc.

Verisimilitude A degree of similarity between artistic presentation and reality, a quality that makes an imaginative work look probable. Verisimilitude, in realistic tradition, excludes improbabilities, whereas in non-realistic traditions, it disguises them. To say that a work has a high degree of verisimilitude means that the work is very realistic and believable, it is *true to life*. The works of Honour de Balzac, Gustavo Flaubert and Henry James, among other late 19th-century realist writers, are distinguished for the quality of verisimilitude. First Aristotle and then scholars of Neo-classicism have recommended this quality as indispensable. The term verisimilitude was crucial to the philosophy of Karl Popper, who for the first time recognized that truth is the aim of scientific inquiry and that most of the greatest scientific theories in the history of science may not be all true. However, the question of scientific truth cannot be equated with the kind of truth an artistic work strives for.

Verse A line in a poem. A literary composition that may have at least three layers of meaning: [1] a line of a poem, usually metrically assessable; [2] a stanza in a poem or song, that being metrically alike; [3] poetry in general, as distinct from prose. Horace tried to make a distinction between verse and poetry. The qualities attached to verse were more of metrical and technical nature and verse was regarded necessary in poetry; but was never thought indispensable. That means verse is opposed to prose and vice versa; but prose is not opposed to poetry. In modern times a prose poem has no verse in its old sense. In non-metrical compositions, like free verse, the word *verse* simply means *poem* without *verse* quality, or rather, verse-free poem.

Ref: John Hollander, *Rhymes Reason: A Guide to English Verse* (1981).

Versification An art of composing verse and its form as can be explained by a proper scansion. Identification of verse structure includes such mechanical components as meter, rhyme, rhythm, stanza, etc. In English versification, the feet are usually iambs (an *unstressed* syllable followed by a *stressed* one: (bĕ | cáuse'), *trochees* (a *stressed syllable* followed by an *unstressed one*: (tí | gĕr), or a combination of the two. *Iambic tetrameter* is, only next to *iambic pentameter*, the most common metre in English poetry; it is used in the English and Scottish traditional ballads, which are usually composed of four-line stanzas of alternating *iambic tetrameter* and *trimeter*. Some other traditional forms of versification are: spondaic, anapaestic, dactylic, etc. [Cf. accent, free verse, meter, scansion]

Ref: Bose & Sterling, *Elements of English Rhetoric and Prosody* (1908). James McAuley, *Versification: A Short Introduction* (1983). JB Mayor, *Chapters on English Metre* (1968). P Kiparsky & G Youmans, Eds. *Rhythm and Meter* (1989). WK Wimsatt, *Versification* (1972).

Vorticism An art movement after the First World War initiated by painter and writer Wyndham Lewis. Grouped with some other artists, he, under the banner of vorticism, combined the abstract art of the Cubists with the example of the Italian Futurists who conveyed in their painting, sculpture and literature the new sensations of movement and scale associated with such modern developments as automobiles and airplanes. With the typographically arresting *Blast: Review of the Great English Vortex* (two editions, 1914 and 1915) vorticism found its polemical mouthpiece and in its editor, Wyndham Lewis, its most active propagandist and accomplished literary exponent. His experimental play *Enemy of the Stars,* published in *Blast* in 1914 and his experimental novel *Tarr* (1918) can still surprise with their violent exuberance. Ezra Pound thought of poetry as essentially a matter of images; the image as the unifying element, "a vortex from which, and through which, and into which, ideas are constantly rushing.... The Vorticist will use only the primary media of his art. The primary pigment of poetry is the mage." Thus with regard to poetry vorticism is no more than another name for poetry. Of the eleven signatories of the Vorticist manifesto some big names, among others, were Ezra Pound, Richard Aldington and Lawrence Atkins. [Cf. imagism]

Ref: Ezra Pound, "Vorticism", *Fortnightly Review* 96 (1914). Mark Antcliffe & Vivien Green, Eds. *The Vorticists* (2010).

W

Weltanschauung A German term often used by critics of English literature. It refers to a person's *worldview* or philosophy, his cognitive orientation and even that of a society. Examples of *weltanschauung* include Thomas Hardy's view of the human being as the victim of fate, destiny, or impersonal forces and circumstances and the disillusioned and laconic cynicism expressed by such poets of the 1930s and most modern and postmodern writers as WH Auden, DH Lawrence, Sir Stephen Spender, Sir William Empson, TS Eliot, Albert Camus, Jean Paul Sartre and many others. In our modern/postmodern times man is fractured in many senses; so he has only limited and only individual worldview and ideology despite vast resources for information in his hand. The ancient folk epics dealing with commonality give better manifestation of worldviews of a group and society as a whole.

Weltschmerz A German term meaning *world pain* often used by critics of English literature. It describes a sense of anguish about the nature of existence, usually associated with a melancholy, pessimistic attitude. It may also refer to pain arising out of the conflict between the aspiration of the mind and the limitation of the body. *Weltschmerz* was expressed in England by Lord Byron in his *Manfred* and *Childe Harold's Pilgrimage*; in France by Viscount de Chateaubriand, Alfred de Vigny and Alfred de Musset; in Russia by Aleksandr Pushkin and Mikhail Lermontov; in Poland by Juliusz Slowacki; and in America by Nathaniel Hawthorne. The main ideas associated with existentialism come almost very close to this definition. [Cf. thatre of the absurd]

Western A very popular form of the novel set in the western US featuring the experiences of cowboys and frontiersmen typically set from the late 18th to the late 19th century. Many are little more than adventure novels or even pulp fiction; but some have literary value. Owen Wister first combined the ingredients—appealing gunman, sullen villain, pert schoolmarm, high plain setting—into a mix that established this type as a popular genre with the regulation shoot-out as plot climax. Examples: Owen Wister's *The Virginian,* Stephen Crane's *The Bride Comes to Yellow Sky,* Alan LeMay's *The Searchers,* EL Doctorow's *Welcome to Hard Times*, Frank Bergon's *Shoshone*, and Walter Van Tilburg Clark's *The Ox-*

Bow Incident, etc. Andy Davison's *In the Valley of the Sun—a Novel* and Melissa Lenhardt's *Blood Oath* are relatively later titles in this category.

Wit <OE *witan*, to know> A verbal ability to say or write things that are clever, amusing and intelligent. The word, however, in course of a long period, has achieved the status of a critical term coinciding with the frequent subtle shift of meaning every now and then from Devenant and Hobbes to Pope and Addison and even later. During the Renaissance it meant *mental aptitude*, wisdom, even genus as opposed to learning; in the 17th century it came close to mean fancy or agility of thought; in the 18th century ability to judge correctly. Pope stressed much on propriety first—"True wit is Nature to advantage dressed,/ What oft was thought, but never so well expressed"—and then, added a sense of invention to it. Addison has frequently tried to distinguish between *true wit* and *false wit*. A true wit, he insists, comes not only from resemblance, but from opposition as well. In true 'wit' the association is of the ideas; in false wit, it is merely of words. During the revival of Romanticism, wit faced demotion as it failed to match with imaginative overflow. TS Eliot, while discussing Metaphysical poetry, tried to restore its lost status for the reasonableness associated with the word. Now 'wit' is a clever expression, often epigrammatic without a tinge of derogatory content. While humour is a broader category, wit derives mostly from verbal resources. Authors famous for employing wit include, among others, John Donne, Alexander Pope, Jane Austen, George Bernard Shaw, Dorothy Parker and James Joyce. [Cf. bon mot]

Ref: Benjamin Errett, *The Elements of Wit: Mastering the Art of Being Interesting* (2014). DW Jefferson, "Tristram Shandy and the Tradition of Learned Wit", *Essays in Criticism* (1951). George Williamson, *The Proper Wit of Poetry* (1961).

X

Xanaduism A reference to academic research that focuses on the sources behind imaginative works of literature and fantasy. John Livingstone Lowes, in his publication *The Road to Xanadu* (1927), coined the term, Xanadu, which Coleridge exploits in his visionary poem "Kubla Khan." The very first line of the poem refers to this imaginary world of Xanadu—"In Xanadu did Kubla Khan a stately pleasure dome decree..." More recently, the term has been used in a pejorative sense to describe scholarship involving dubious scrutiny of unformulated, difficult-to-prove sources, especially unsophisticated studies lacking in any authentic theoretical perspective.

Z

Zeitgeist A German term meaning *spirit of the time* often used by critics of English literature. It refers to the moral and intellectual trends of a given era. Examples of *zeitgeist* include the preoccupation with the more morbid aspects of dying and death in some Jacobean literature (1603-1625), especially in the works of dramatists Cyril Tourneur and John Webster, and also of the decadence of the French symbolists. It can be simply defined as a general cultural, intellectual ambiance, or socio-cultural direction, and mood of a society or nation of a particular time. Thirst for inquiry, knowledge and discovery was a Renaissance zeitgeist.

Zeugma/Syllepsis A Figure of Speech that promotes the yoking of a word to one or two other words, which have different standing, for example, *bibles* in Pope's line—"Puffs, powders, patches, bibles, billet-doux." Zeugma effect may also be achieved by a verb or a preposition with two objects: "Give them thy fingers, me thy lips to kiss" (Shakespeare). Three types of zeugma are mentioned: *protozeugma* (in the beginning), *mezzozeugma* (in the middle) and *hypozeugma* (at the end). Zugma is often employed to produce the comic or satiric effect that results from the relation of a particular word with other apparently incompatible words either in terms of meaning or syntax. Syllepsis is another name for zeugma. Syllepsis is often said to have a single word used in relation to two other parts of a sentence but the word grammatically or logically applies to only one—"He drinks his wine, I mine" (to mean 'He drinks his wine, and I drink my wine). Or, in other words, syllepsis is an application of a word or expression to perform two syntactic functions, specially to modify or govern two or more words of which at least one does not agree in number, case or gender—as in the use of *are* in—"Neither he nor we are willing."

Index

F

G

H

I

Q

R

S

T